Discourses of Weakness and Resource Regimes

Discourses of Weakness and Resource Regimes

Edited by Iwo Amelung, Moritz Epple, Hartmut Leppin, and Susanne Schröter

Volume 1

Iwo Amelung is Professor for Sinology at Goethe-University Frankfurt and Speaker of the the DFG Collaborative Research Center 1095 "Discourses of Weakness and Resource Regimes".

Hartmut Leppin is Professor for Ancient History at Goethe-University Frankfurt and director of the Leibniz project "Polyphony of Late Antique Christianity".

Christian A. Müller is research coordinator of the DFG Collaborative Research Center 1095 "Discourses of Weakness and Resource Regimes" at Goethe-University Frankfurt.

Iwo Amelung, Hartmut Leppin,
Christian A. Müller (eds.)

Discourses of Weakness and Resource Regimes

Trajectories of a New Research Programme

Campus Verlag
Frankfurt/New York

The Collaborative Research Center 1095 is funded by the German Research Foundation.

Deutsche Forschungsgemeinschaft

ISBN 978-3-593-50901-3 Print
ISBN 978-3-593-43894-8 E-Book (PDF)

All rights reserved. No part of this book may be reproduced or transmitted in any form or by any means, electronic or mechanical, including photocopying, recording, or by any information storage and retrieval system, without permission in writing from the publishers.
Despite careful control of the content Campus Verlag GmbH cannot be held liable for the content of external links. The content of the linked pages is the sole responsibility of their operators.
Copyright © 2018 Campus Verlag GmbH, Frankfurt-on-Main
Cover design: Campus Verlag GmbH, Frankfurt-on-Main
Printing office and bookbinder: CPI buchbücher.de, Birkach
Printed on acid free paper.
Printed in the United States of America

www.campus.de
www.press.uchicago.edu

Contents

Introduction 9
Iwo Amelung, Hartmut Leppin, and Christian A. Müller

Chapter 1: Weakness: Ranges of Disciplinary Approaches 29
Kathrin Knodel and Anselm Spindler

Chapter 2: Representations of Weakness:
Functions, Images, Effects 53
Klaus Seidl

Chapter 3: Visions of Decline in Transhistorical Perspective:
Narratives, Images, Effects 79
Nadine Eikelschulte, Philipp Höhn, Sebastian Riebold, Klaus Seidl, and David Weidgenannt

Chapter 4: Counting Weakness?
The Institutionalisation of Data Collection in the Nineteenth Century
German Chemical Industry and Meteorology 151
Linda Richter and Frederic Steinfeld

Chapter 5: Resources—A Historical and Conceptual Roadmap 179
Daniel Hausmann and Nicolas Perreaux

Chapter 6: Perspectives of a Resource History:
Actions—Practices—Regimes 209
Christian A. Müller

Chapter 7: Resources in a Social World..223
Otto Danwerth, Teresa Dittmer, Seto Hardjana, Daniel Hausmann, Nicolas Perreaux, Linda Richter, Christian Scheidler, Frederic Steinfeld, and David Weidgenannt

Chapter 8: Power and Resource Regimes: A Study of the Impact of Social Relationships on the Function of Resources 255
Anna Dorofeeva and Alexander Krey

Chapter 9: Agency and Asymmetries: Actors and their Access to Resources in Colonial and Developmental Setting....................................293
David Rex Galindo, Melina Kalfelis, and José Luis Paz Nomey

Authors 328

A Word from the Editors

The acquisition and distribution of resources is one of the central challenges of our times. Survival, as well as the seizing of development opportunities, compels actors—be they states, groups or individuals—to use resources to achieve their objectives. The continuous inequality (and what economists frequently refer to as scarcity) in the distribution of resources throughout history, is also the cause for numerous individual, social and international conflicts. This constitutes a challenge for academic research: how do actors refer to their situation in terms of their usage of resources? How do they talk about their deficiencies? This very connection is the starting point for the present series *Discourses of Weakness and Resource Regimes*. Discourses that deal with weakness are a phenomenon that can be observed in all societies at all times. Frequently, those discourses are directly connected to the question of agency and the required resources. Employing a humanities perspective, the series examines the problem of how discourses of weakness influence the deployment and usage of resources. It delves into the question of how actors' self-description and self-assessment impact on and shape the handling and usage of resources.

The English and German texts in this series combine contributions from historians, cultural studies specialists and philosophers on the multifaceted changes of resource processes encompassing the evaluation, acquisition and handling of resources. It seeks to avoid a narrow understanding of resources, and, for instance, a conceptual bifurcation between natural and immaterial resources, and hopes to find robust and resilient alternatives to such distinctions. It is expected that the research results will help to further develop existing concepts of transformation and thus contribute to expanding approaches of modelling substantial historical change. The series presents the research results of the Frankfurt Collaborative Research Center 1095 *Discourses of Weakness and Resource Regimes*, which sought to find and evaluate new approaches to the problem of resources.

Introduction

Iwo Amelung, Hartmut Leppin, and Christian A. Müller

I. Towards the Interdependence of Self-placements and Self-efficacy

The acquisition and distribution of resources is one of the central challenges of our times. Survival, as well as the seizing of development opportunities, compels actors—be they states, groups or individuals—both to use and to exploit resources in order to achieve their objectives. The continuous inequality (and, what economists prominently refer to as, scarcity) in the distribution of resources throughout history is also the cause for numerous individual, social and international conflicts. This constitutes a challenge for academic research: How do actors refer to the situation in which they find themselves in terms of their usage of resources? How do they talk about their deficiencies in resources? Beyond such phenomena of self-perception, the dimensions of practice and the conditions for action are also of interest: Which factors influence the agency of an actor, and how are these factors shaped? How—to sum up—can such a multi-layered phenomenon as the *configuration of capacity to act* be described?

Currently, different disciplines offer different answers: production factors (as in economics[1]), resilience (as in psychology[2]), or majorities (as in political science[3]). Historical science stresses the contingency of the capacity to act, meaning the dependency on historically, culturally and geographically variable factors. The ability to act is always "socio-culturally" mediated,[4] so it is not something that was available to the actors at all times, but was shaped differently at different times, and thus needs an explanation of its diverse occurrences. To register phenomena of this kind, analytical

---

1 Wöhe (2010), *Betriebswirtschaftslehre*, 28.
2 Karidi et al. (2018), *Resilienz*, 6.
3 Schubert et al. (2014), *Politikfeldanalyse*, 157.
4 Winiwarter et al. (2007), *Umweltgeschichte*, 131.

boundaries need to be set up: if we assume that the configuration of the capacity to act has always had a *practical* and *discursive* dimension, then this perspective will be unfolded at the Collaborative Research Center (CRC) 1095 via two concepts: on the practical side, we assume that resources are crucial. There is little doubt about the high relevance of resources in many disciplines. However, resources only indicate the *potential* of acting; they establish the possibility for actors to do or not do something. They are a necessary, but by no means satisfactory, explanation for the accomplishments of goals. For the question of the capacity to act, additional factors are of importance in which the self-placement and positioning of actors also come into play. These self-placements can vary greatly both in their general direction and in their intended direction of impact. Moreover, they are of special importance when they are about weakness because they then demand change. This opens up a wide field of research because weakness has been addressed in very different ways and in the light of several motives and agendas. Furthermore weakness always refers to their effects, which can be usefully illustrated through discourses about the downfall of Europe or the weakness of Chinese state at the turn of the twentieth century. In both cases, the problematisation of the situations in question changed the action of the actors, but in completely different, and sometimes unexpected, ways. The Europeans often described themselves as weak, despite their relatively strong position, whereas the Chinese, who perceived as deficient what was, in fact, to become the starting-point of an immense global power in the twenty-first century. We will model such complex self-placements, as well as their effects and consequences, as *discourses of weakness*. Clearly, they do not have to be directly about resources and can contain disparate diagnoses and inventories. But—and this is the crucial feature—they do have a general link to the dimension of activeness. While the realisation of strength is an invitation to continue on existing paths, diagnoses of weakness create—sometimes acute—pressure for change. This initial dynamic of change is important because it indicates situations in which actors examine and, if necessary, correct their positions, and—as a consequence—their concomitant use of resources. Yet, knowledge about the correlation between self-placements and the handling of resources is fairly scarce, which is why the CRC 1095 wants to explore this perspective.

Introduction

From a natural sciences[5] and economic perspective,[6] but also in architecture or city-planning,[7] it is both usual and obvious to think about resources. Practical problems of acquisition and processing prevail, while discursive examinations about weaknesses and strengths play a lesser role. In the face, for example, of a looming scarcity of water—one could pointedly say—that it is worthless to know what "opinions" exists about water. But many developments in history and in the world of today show that resources cannot be separated from positioning and deliberation. The close relationship between weakness and resource is even present on an encyclopedic level: The Oxford dictionary defines resources as "means of supplying some want or deficiency".[8] In economics and in the area of marketing and planning, the terms "resource analysis" and "strengths/ weakness analysis" have long been used synonymously.[9] For a perspective on resources, it is important not to identify them hastily with the weakness or strength categorisation. Resources cause no strength, just as a lack of resources causes no weakness *per se*. Instead of this, the aspect of enablement is crucial, and is also to be found in historical research: resources offer the *potential* for actions,[10] but are not a guarantee of the capacity to act, and thus the general conditions, frameworks and interests become important. From this perspective, the view of resources becomes more complex and multi-layered: the utility of resources is steadily ambivalent, because they can be immensely precious as a part of a concrete course of action, while, on their own, they can be completely worthless. Resources are also polyvalent. The availability of a given resource for *different* purposes is a specific feature. Thus, the affordance of a resource has multiple characteristics. Finally, the handling of resources has paradoxical effects because, at the moment in which they present an opportunity to act, they also create dependencies that threaten the preservation of the opportunity.[11] In this way, enabling and endangering are somewhat similar. Since nobody can provide all the necessary resources on their own, the handling of resources is strongly shaped by such dependencies and ambivalences. Because of this

---

5 Neugebauer (2017), *Ressourceneffizienz*.
6 Müller-Christ (2011), *Sustainable Management*.
7 Hebel et al. (2017), *Beyond Mining*.
8 Oxford English Dictionary (1989), *Resource*, 730.
9 Dichtl et al. (1993), *Wirtschaftslexikon*, 1816.
10 See, for the aspect of potentiality, Jancke et al. (2015), *Ökonomie sozialer Beziehungen*, 17 ff.
11 The access constrains the opportunities for further access, see Luhmann (1988), *Wirtschaft der Gesellschaft*, 179.

starting-point, the use of resources is a highly non-determined process that needs description and explanation. Thus, the historic view on resources calls for a re-calibration: the focus is no longer on resources alone, but on resources as an initial point for regimes, which emphasises the embeddedness of their handling. To obtain a more complete insight into this embeddedness, the CRC 1095 not only focuses on well-known resource-based factors, such as scarcity or materiality, but also on the dimensions of self-awareness and self-assessment, which stresses the role of actors. The *framing of resources with a discursive approach* enables a perspective on correlative phenomena: discourses of weakness and strength possess the potential to irritate and change the handling of resources, which, in turn, can influence the original discourse. This interdependence, which can, of course, appear diversely, is the central of the CRC's research programme.

II. In Deficit: Discourses about Weakness and Strength

Within societies, deficits can be perceived in very different ways. Whether something is perceived as a deficit or not also differs. Concepts not only about the origin and the extent, but also about the consequences and the elimination of a deficit are, both historically and culturally, highly diverse. Discourses of weakness offer—in contrast to such phenomena as crisis,[12] failure,[13] insecurity,[14] and threat[15]—a to-date untested perspective on this matter. Like every conceptual term, discourses of weakness also need containment in order to remain meaningful when applied. This form of containment is called for both methodically and factually: as a research cluster, the number of sources varies greatly both in terms of epochs and in that of disciplines, since the research stretches from Mesopotamian traditions to ethnographic documentations. The methodical layout of discourses of weakness must therefore allow for cross-epochal identifications which contain ancient-Egypt scribes as well as the rich records of European expectations of decline. Practical aspects such as these also meet conceptual questions that beg to be answered: Is the simple lack of money or the loss

---

12 Mergel (2012), *Krisen verstehen*.
13 Köhler et al. (2012), *Pleitiers und Bankrotteure*.
14 Conze (2018), *Geschichte der Sicherheit*.
15 Frie et al. (2014), *Bedrohte Ordnung*.

of a battle already a referral to weakness? Here, the danger of inflations looms, because a lot of negative phenomena could be categorised as discourses of weakness.

Thus, the CRC 1095 has a broad concept of discourse, one which is understood as a thematic and specified organised context of assertions, while discourse analysis is understood as the re-construction of the regularity that determines the origin of these assertions.[16] For the CRC 1095, the internal structure of the discourse is as relevant as its instrumental character to the question of to what purposes the discourses are subordinated. The starting-point for the discourse concept is thus not Foucault,[17] but an opening towards a more prominent focus on actors. The role of actors when initiating, articulating and disseminating discourses of weakness is to be brought into focus, while, at the same time, bearing the specific contribution to the regularity of a discourse by an actor in mind. In this sense, discourses of weakness describe, as a working definition, the thematisation of deficiency, which is characterised by, at least, five aspects: a) discourses of weakness are *referential*, meaning they are thematic in the broadest sense. It is always someone or something (China, the West, the Hansa, a body of knowledge) that is described as weak; b) discourses of weakness are *relational*. Actors, situations or circumstances are put in relation to one another, not excluding fictitious or contra-factual references; c) discourses of weakness are *comparative*. The relations are compared and thereby enable the attribution of weakness;[18] d) discourses of weakness are *positional*, they go hand in hand with processes of placing, which can happen for a variety of reasons, including strategic reasons, in particular; and e) discourses of weakness are eventually *temporal* and *spatial*, as they contain or draft time-structures ("everything was better in the old days") or spatiality ("*Ex oriente lux*").

The five characteristics of the thematisation of deficiency mentioned above allow for very different modes of expression:[19] they can not only report (the weak position of a business on the market, *etc.*) or estimate (the

---

16 Landwehr (2008), *Historische Diskursanalyse*; Sarasin (2003), *Geschichtswissenschaft und Diskursanalyse*.
17 Foucault (1981), *Archäologie des Wissens*, 74.
18 Here you can find productive overlaps to the 2017 granted CRC 1288 "Practices of Comparing". Such practices cause various results so the question arises under which conditions a discourse of weakness emerges, which itself could change the practices of comparing.
19 Austin (2014 [1961]), *How to Do Things with Words*.

position of the business now and in five years, *etc.*), but also predict (the foreseeable trajectory of an entrepreneur if he or she does not change course, *etc.*) or scandalise (a business that is paying such high wages will not be able to compete, *etc.*). Every case points to the fact that discourses of weakness can also be a particular strategy of an actor, which introduces the question of when exactly actors participate in a discourse of weakness (and not in a discourse of strength, proven knowledge, deceit or violence), and what momentum and pitfalls accompany it.

Two fundamental dimensions of discourses of weakness can be analytically differentiated: they refer to (thematic) findings, on the one hand, and (social) relations, on the other. The Hansa has sometimes been portrayed as weak. This picture would, however, be incomplete without the tactical dimension of the discourse of weakness, meaning the intentions of the participants of the discourse. Thus, manipulative intentions in the use of discourses of weakness become of interest. Discourses of weakness were not and are not held to be "uninterested", but mask completely different goals, such as the avoidance of legal liability (as was the case with the Hansa in the fifteenth century), or the encouragement of group cohesion (as with the debates about the demise of Europe). These brief examples clarify that public or respectively mass-media diffused materials need always to be confronted with the originators of the discourse of weakness in order to enable the identification of unformulated discourse strategies and hidden interests. This inseparable entanglement of the thematic and the social dimension needs to be re-constructed in every case of a discourse of weakness. Clearly, this analytically very neat distinction will be a lot more blurred in the concrete historical world: we know of discourses of weakness that cannot be understood as a reaction to an important event, but which are constitutive for a constellation, as in the history of Christianity, where discourses of weakness are always present in authorative texts, while there is always a salvation-related discourse of strength as well. How exactly the thematic and social dimensions of weakness were completed empirically and are completed to this day, meaning how the manifestation of weakness in different constellations has configured and manifested itself, will be documented in the works of the current CRC 1095. Discourses of weakness are a multi-layered and—in a systematically way—until now disregarded phenomena: they often occur comparatively and bundle in a singular manner the action conditions and self-placements of actors in difficult circumstances and situations.

III. In Practice: Resources within Resource Regimes

Frequently, resources are subject to culmination in public debates: oil, education, or, as of late, data, are respectively made out to be crucial for the future development of societies. Accordingly, the contention about resources is drastically conceptualised as a "fight" or "escalation".[20] In human and social sciences, however, resources have been the subject of research for a long time, as can be seen, for example, in the so-called Resource Mobilization Theory in the 1970s or in various projects in the history of science and in economic history about resources as an important factor in historical change.[21] A prominent usage of resources is introduced by the social scientist Anthony Giddens in his theory of structuration.[22] Structures—according to Giddens—consist of rules and resources, whereby the latter is the initial point of power. Giddens differentiated between allocative and authoritative resources, providing a distinction between the control over objects or goods in contrast to the control over people. However, within historical research, the problem of application emerges because the relevance of resources is accompanied by an abstract meaning of the concept. So, it is necessary to specify the different situations and ways in which resources shaped the conditions of action open to an actor. To avoid an overt fixation on individual resources, researchers have offered different attempts at contextualisation, including, for example, resource complexes, resource cultures,[23] and resource ensembles.[24] Resource regimes,[25] however, have rarely been used to date. What all these

---

20 Reder et al. (2012), *Kampf um Ressourcen*. See, recently, The Economist (2017), *The World's Most Valuable Resource*.
21 An early use of the concept of resources is Penrose (1959), *Growth of the Firm*. For a general overview: Klein (2010), *Ressourcenkonfigurationsmanagement*, 38 ff. Since the 1970s social sciences uses the so-called Resource Mobilization Theory, see: McCarthy et al. (1977), *Resource Mobilization* and also 25 years later as a stock taking: McCarthy et al. (2001), *Enduring Vitality of the Resource Mobilization Theory*. Historical science also picked up this: see Mittag et al. (2014), *Forschung über soziale Bewegungen*, 241 ff. In history of science, the concept of resource is well established: see Ash (2002), *Wissenschaft und Politik*, and recently, Flachowsky et al. (2017), *Ressourcenmobilisierung*. See, also, the instructive research on natural resources: Haller et al. (2014), *Rechnen mit der Natur*, 8–19.
22 Giddens (1984), *Constitution of Society*, 256 ff.
23 Hardenberg et al. (2017), *Resource Turn*, 15, 19.
24 Ash (2002), *Wissenschaft und Politik*.
25 The term resource regime has been used sporadically until now: see Young (1984), *Resource Regimes*, who understands regimes as institutions. Also in economics there is a sporadic usage: Liebscher (2013), *Betriebliche Ressourcensicherung*, 264 ff. For a vivid usage

attempts have in common is that they try to avoid a reductionism in the sense of taking a given resource out of the lifeworld and treating it as an isolated phenomenon. Research agrees that resources are to be understood (i) in relation to other resources, and (ii) in their socio-cultural embeddedness, in order to obtain new and accurate insights.[26] The high value of a framework is, however, too unspecific, and need concretisation. This is where the research interest of the CRC 1095 begins, by trying to register resources in their specific embedment. On the one hand, the focus is on the rules, practices and norms for the handling of resources, a complex which we define as a regime.[27] These resource regimes enable us not only to register the resources themselves, but also their handling in a wider sense. The set of rules and regulations which organises the handling of resources opens up a perspective that transforms the resources into a broader issue. An example from the CRC 1095 can illustrate this vividly: the usage of sacred objects as a military resource in the sixth century is not analysed with regard to their materiality, scarcity, value or religious origin. In contrast to this, questions of another sort emerge: Who was allowed to use the object? Who was responsible for the effects? Who, if anyone, was responsible for their absence? How did they explain the unpredictability of effects? Could every sacred object acquire military status or was there a kind of "testing" which determined a specific worth? How did they deal with the usage of these objects on the battlefield (in contrast to the earlier urban usage), and who managed their adaptation to new environments? A description of this concrete regime refers not to a history of single objects but also to a set of rules and regulations that shaped (but not completely determined) the handling of the resource in question. It also refers—and this is important—to a distinct discourse about the weakness of the military clout of the Romans. Only then does the emergence of new military opportunities become understandable. In the light of these thoughts, it will be generally proven whether using heavily resource-related characteristics such as scarcity, materiality, distribution and substitution is constructive, and what alternatives could be used.

---

in the history of Early Modern Age, see Hübner (2015), *Soziale Ungleichheit*, 150–162. Hübner uses the term regime to characterise common properties.

26 See, for example, research about water as an issue of knowledge, engineering, infrastructure and power, von Reden (2015), *Wasser*, 9–25.

27 We have a non-pejorative understanding of regimes: see, referring to political sciences, Krassner (1983), *Regime as Intervening Variables*.

It has become clear that, on their own, resource regimes are not sufficient to provide a fully-faceted description of resources. The high importance of the actors that act within regimes leads us to believe that we should broaden the perspective on resources by the aforementioned process of self-placement and positioning. Such discursive factors, vividly manifested in discourses of weakness, have a relevant impact on the handling of resources: thinking about the state of affairs, about requirements, or about the re-direction of an involvement creates criteria for the use of resources, and we are interested in the relationship between both spheres: one instructive example refers to mobilising effects of discourses of weakness on the use of resources, whereas a clear and indicative effect of such discourses seems to be a special case. Discourses, in general, can develop their own dynamic(s), and they can also be inconsistent and without any consequences. So an important aim of the CRC 1095 is to develop conceptual tools to analyse both resources and the impact of discursive elements such as weakness and strength. How exactly the terms "resource regime" and "discourses of weakness" unfold and show their application in actual research is the subject of this volume, which inaugurates the CRC 1095 book series. It is the result of the cross-epochal and interdisciplinary work of young scholars in the first research phase. Our colleagues pay a lot of attention to the CRC-concepts, on the one hand, and to their particular doctoral and post-doctoral research projects, on the other. Going into detail and being general at the same time was a big adventure for everyone, and one which mirrors the typical situation of a research cluster of different disciplines.

The article entitled "Weakness: Ranges of Disciplinary Approaches" by Kathrin Knodel and Anselm Spindler portrays the wide range of weakness attributions, from reflections about unchangeable human nature (philosophy) to the investigation of highly changeable social positions (ethnology). The article puts a spotlight on an important conceptual feature of the CRC 1095, namely, that weakness does not exist *"per se"*, but in the discursive mode of various attributions. How this mode was shaped is an open question from a historic and cultural sciences standpoint. What the actual attribution looked like, what motives were behind it, and what "topic" (the weakness of the state, the downfall of Europe, for example) it dealt with, are all questions that characterise the analysis of discourses of weakness.

The article entitled "Representation of Weakness: Functions, Images, Effects" by Klaus Seidl then shows the unfolding of discourses of weakness: as an analytical concept, it contains a variety of structural aspects, which, for example, includes the connection between diagnosis and treatment. Diagnoses themselves contain many variations that need to be historically re-constructed. Besides these structural characteristics, representations of weakness need to be considered with a special focus on metaphors and images. Representations like this are not a mere effigy of a discourse of weakness, but have a performative character. Since the communicative exposure cannot be controlled by the actors, they are prone to develop their own dynamics, which can result in non-intended, but simultaneously potent, consequences.

Discourses of weakness are not bound to a certain form, but are highly polymorph. The article entitled "Visions of Decline in Transhistorical Perspective: Narratives, Images, Effects" by Nadine Eikelschulte, Philipp Höhn, Sebastian Riebold, Klaus Seidl, and David Weidgenannt demonstrates a comparatively illustrious kind of discourse of weakness. Decline is conceptualised as an analytical category that is based upon the existence of a change for the worse, which underlines a temporal dimension. The analysis of the origin of weakness and its future (negative) development is very telling because of two aspects: Decline is a category that historical actors resort to in order to comprehend and respond to challenges of their times and also to advance particular political agendas. Decline also informs us, and sometimes implicitly, about contemporary perceptions of inevitability or the accompanying possibilities of influence on an ongoing development.

Discourses of weakness occur at various levels and places in society and offer attractive opportunities for comparison. Two, at first sight, disparate phenomena are analysed in the article entitled "Counting Weakness? The Institutionalisation of Data Collection in the Nineteenth Century German Chemical Industry and Meteorology" by Linda Richter and Frederic Steinfeld. The problem of an uncertain future and being dependent on projections was a challenge to both enterprises (market success) and meteorologists (reputation). Both actors work this into discourses of weakness, thereby thematising their own situation. Despite different starting-points, both reacted to the weakness in, what is from today's view, an obvious, but, from a past view, a novel way: the systematic collection of data that differentiated into an institutionalised form of information acquisition. Both the case studies inspire reflection on to what extent societies develop typical and recurring patterns of problematisation, and solutions that can be identified upon the basis of discourses of weakness.

The article entitled "Recources: A Historical and Conceptual Roadmap" by Daniel Hausmann and Nicolas Perreaux delivers the first results on what has, to date, been a missing conceptual history of resources. Resources in today's understanding are founded on semantic changes in the eighteenth century, from which the expansion of the term took its course. Especially in the second half of the twentieth century, economic patterns of interpretation caused an increase in the usage of the term "resource", which is currently also used in social and cultural studies. The connection between conceptual and general history (particularly the relation between the term "resource" and the emergence of capitalism) offers attractive questions for future research at the CRC 1095.

The article entitled "Perspectives of a Resource History: Actions—Practices—Regimes" by Christian A. Müller asks what theoretical vocabulary can be used to describe the emergence of regimes. Here, the simple reference to means is not sufficient; instead, the registration of means in their "situatedness" is productive. The accompanying question is what action context is the base of a given means. It is proposed to embed means into actions, practices and regimes. Practices are an important indicator for the spread of means, while regimes signal their generalisation. Only under the circumstances of a regime should one talk about resources, because it indicates a rule-based and widespread phenomenon.

With empirical examples across various epochs, the motive of social embeddedness is demonstrated in the article entitled "Resources in a Social World" by Otto Danwerth, Theresa Dittmer, Seto Hardjana, Daniel Hausmann, Nicolas Perreaux, Linda Richter, Christian Scheidler, Frederic Steinfeld, and David Weidgenannt. Here, too, a perspective solely focused on resources is deemed insufficient. Rather, resources always point to regimes that distinguish themselves via processes of extraction, refining, circulation, transfer, as well as vanishing. Only the context of a regime creates the resources (and not simply the means). The formerly dominating economic understanding of resources is expanded with a socio-cultural view on resources.

The penultimate article entitled "Power and Resource Regimes: Processes in the Use of Resources Grounded on Norms and Practices" by Anna Dorofeeva and Alexander Krey, in collaboration with Nadine Eikelschulte, Lukas Jäger, Melina Kalfelis, Sebastian Riebold, Carla Thiel, and Marco Toste, presents another essential aspect of the CRC-approach: resources and their embedment in regimes cannot be understood without the dimension of power. In social sciences, the conceptual relation between resources and power is already known, but it is difficult to implement this into concrete research. Accordingly, the article illustrates resource regimes as a rule-based context of dealing with resources that can be used as a framework for the analysis of processes of power.

The concluding article entitled "Agency and Asymmetries: Actors and their Access to Resources in Colonial and Developmental Setting" by David Rex Galindo, Melina Kalfelis, and José Luis Paz Nomey asks how research into the mobilisation of resources at the concrete level of actors can be realised. The, in theoretical debates, long discussed term of agency has proved to be a pertinent concept. The starting-points of the three case studies are seemingly asymmetrical situations: foreign aid in Africa or, for a historical view, colonial rule in Mexico and Peru in the early modern age. In all situations, a highly uneven distribution of opportunities to act is to be expected. But a view on the concrete level of action then shows regularly unnoticed dynamics: agency in African and colonial regimes opens up perspectives on phenomena of action that can only be understood at local level which cannot be satisfyingly recognised from a macro-perspective.

IV. In Future: Perspectives and Prospects

From the explanations given above, it should have become clear that discourses of weakness and resource regimes can become powerful tools of historical research, and that they can help us a great deal to approach questions which are broadly linked to the larger problem of historical change or transformation. While weakness may, at the first glance, seem to be a rather fuzzy concept which appears to have much less explanatory power than more rigid approaches, such as "vulnerability",[28] we suggest that it is precisely the "relativeness" of the concept which makes the ascription of weakness to a historical formation so enlightening. Discourses of weakness constitute a "reflexive layer", which, in many cases, underlies decisions and attempts to change or adapt resource regimes.

To put it in more abstract terms, discourses of weakness are of importance for historical actors since they are extremely useful in order to

---

28 Hilhorst et al. (2004), *Mapping Vulnerability*.

determine the possibilities of action and to assess one's own capacity to act. Giddens,[29] and later Sewell[30] pointed out that the capacity to act—or agency—pre-supposes that actors have sufficient access to resources, which, in our scheme, are always to be considered within their resource regimes. At this stage, it is thus possible to claim that the methodological framework developed in this volume does not simply postulate agency or capacity to act from an *ex-post* perspective, but considers it as a socio-culturally imparted capacity. But how could an approach which takes actors seriously when dealing with discourses of weakness and resource regimes be refined further? Or to put it differently, how can other categories of historical and cultural research be applied fruitfully to the framework outlined above?

Due to their inherent comparative nature, discourses of weakness have, in many instances, a *spatial* aspect. Spaces, however, need to be considered as "representations of space", as Lefebvre has called it,[31] or, in our conception, as "projections of space". As such, their function is to provide a point of reference for comparison, in order to determine one's own strengths and weaknesses. Such spaces are commonly perceived as container-spaces, which are discrete and for which membership is determined by processes of inclusion and exclusion. These kinds of projection may become very powerful, especially when they are presented in a dichotomised form, as, for example, in the case of "China" *versus* "the West", *etc.*

Resource-spaces, in contrast, are to be perceived as a relational network consisting of resources, locations, and actors. They emerge when resources are tapped, appropriated and distributed in regimes—quite often grouped around a set of resources.[32] They are also contested and subjected to constant change. For these reasons, projections of space and resource-spaces may exist in a state of tension, and it is precisely this tension which enables a better understanding of phenomena of historical change. Projections of space are simultaneously related to processes of the negotiation of power.[33] Resource-spaces, on the other hand, may imply territorial appropriation or at least territorial control. A special case of space projections can be found in geo- or environmental-deterministic approaches, which argue that space

---

29 Giddens (1984), *Constitution of Society*.
30 Sewell (2005), *Logics of History*, 143 ff.
31 Lefebvre (1974), *La production de l'espace*.
32 Hauman (2016), *Konkurrenz um Kalkstein*, 29–58.
33 Bourdieu (1998), *Praktische Vernunft*.

itself is part of the resource-regime, so that the adaptation of the resource-regime requires the transformation of space itself. This is suggested, for example, in slogans such as "*Volk ohne Raum*" (people without space) during the Weimar and Nazi-period.[34] Another example of space projection is embodied in the Three Gorges Dam project on the Yangzi River in China, which, since the Republican era, has been legitimised by environmental constraints with regard to energy production, flood prevention, and inland shipping. This could only have been overcome by the massive transformation brought about by the erection of the Three Gorges Dam.[35] Clearly, space projections, which represent environmental deterministic reasoning, were also used historically to justify the "civilising mission" of colonialising empires in areas projected as geographically disadvantaged. These are ideas that were, in many cases, accepted with differing levels of resistance on the part of the élites in areas under colonial or semi-colonial control.[36]

Due to their inherently comparative nature, discourses of weakness also regularly employ *temporal* structures. Again, it is the actors who deploy narratives in their discourses of weakness, of success, and of crisis and historical change, which necessarily operate in time-structures and, in analogy with the above-mentioned space-projections, might be conceptualised as "time projections". Such time-projections are, when applied to the past, highly influenced by conceptions of time. Cyclical conceptions of history promised the periodic restoration of life to normality, crisis and change for the worse are thus perceived as much less threatening[37] than when a linear perspective of time and history is adopted that hints at irreversible decline.[38] Almost by definition, such narratives acquire an alarming and adhortative tone—the fate to be expected does not seem attractive at all and should be avoided for one's own historical formation. In this way, a discourse of weakness in some sense constitutes an exercise in risk assessment: past experiences are employed in order to make projections for a better (or worse) future, even if this is not spelled out in detail in all cases. Nevertheless, it is clear that past experiences constitute a layer of expectations, which may contribute to a better grasp of the future which may be

---

34 Köster (2002), *Die Rede über den ‚Raum'*.
35 Seeger (2014), *Zähmung der Flüsse*, 125 ff.
36 Chen Xiaomei has called this "Occidentalism"; cf. Chen (2002), *Occidentalism*.
37 Eliade (1954), *Cosmos and History*.
38 Kwong (2001), *Rise of the Linear Perspective*, 157–190.

seen as a necessary contingent.[39] While expectations of the future will remain fictional,[40] so that the assumption of future weakness can never be ruled out, discourses of weakness may directly hint at resources which might help to address the problem. These are, on the one hand, predictions and techniques of divination that suggest the possibility of "coping with the future",[41] and thus enable people to prepare for it by adjusting their own resource regimes. On the other hand, there are risk-assessments[42] that are based upon a large amount of more or less scientific data. Eventually, they are only able to reduce insecurity about future developments at the most, but they are not able to solve the fundamental problem of the unpredictability of the future. Nevertheless, discourses of weakness may bundle these different layers of time perception and experience in order to construct what are, at times, almost normative trajectories of demise or decline. This, however, may have a soothing effect. By carrying out the necessary adaptations of the resource regimes, the process is not as inevitable as is suggested, and, while there is need of much more research on these forms of time projection in discourses of weakness, it is nevertheless quite clear that historical actors gain importance greatly at this stage. They, too, are aware of the temporal structures that underlie resource regimes, such as the gradual depletion of natural resources such as coal and oil, as well as the question of the sustainability of resources, forests or wood, for example, already addressed by Mencius (Mengzi) (372–289 BC or 385–303 or 302 BC) in the pre-Christian era.[43] The temporality of resource regimes may also play a role with regard to the dynamics of knowledge, such as the pace of invention and the ideas of progress by which historical actors may spark dynamic developments. This may result in a complete change of resource regimes.

The articles collected in this volume should show that, by relating discourses of weakness and resource regimes to each other, historical research will be better equipped to understand the dynamics generated by human reflexivity on the acquisition, use, and distribution of resources. At first sight, both concepts, discourses of weakness and resource regimes, seem to aim at analysing structures, rather than events or development. This calls

---

39 Koselleck (1989), *Erfahrungsraum und Erwartungshorizont*.
40 Beckert (2016), *Imagined Futures*.
41 Lackner (2017), *Coping with the Future*.
42 Beck (1986), *Risikogesellschaft*.
43 Hughes (2009), *Environmental History of the World*, 70.

for the question of whether we, to paraphrase E.P. Thompson, are dealing with an orrery as the perfect model of planetary movement, without, however, knowing what makes it move.[44] We suggest that it is a systematic look into the spatial and temporal aspects which will help us to understand how historical actors exert their agency, and it will be additional and more detailed studies of these aspects that we hope will allow us to gain a better understanding of historical change and transformation.

This book is the result of the interdisciplinary discussions and collaboration of the doctoral and postdoctoral fellows of the CRC 1095 during the years from 2015 to 2018. For unwavering support in preparing the manuscript, we would like to thank Valentin Dieckmann and Carl Rumpeltes, who helped with the corrections, formatting and processing of the volume. Special thanks also go to Chris Engert for his efficient help in the language revision and copy-editing of the contributions. All administrative and planning issues relating to the research management were efficiently handled by Mi Anh Duong, and we are particular grateful for her help.

Literature

Ash, Mitchell G. (2002). Wissenschaft und Politik als Ressource füreinander. Programmatische Überlegungen am Beispiel Deutschlands. In Rüdiger vom Bruch and Brigitte Kaderas (eds.). *Wissenschaften und Wissenschaftspolitik. Bestandsaufnahmen zu Formationen, Brüchen und Kontinuitäten im Deutschland des 20. Jahrhunderts*, 32-51. Stuttgart: Franz Steiner.

Austin, John L. (2014 [1961]). *Zur Theorie der Sprechakte (How to Do Things with Words)*. Stuttgart: Reclam.

Beck, Ulrich (1986). *Risikogesellschaft. Auf dem Weg in eine andere Moderne*. Frankfurt/M.: Suhrkamp.

Beckert, Jens (2016). *Imagined Futures. Fictional Expectations and Capitalist Dynamics*. Cambridge MA: Harvard University Press.

Bourdieu, Pierre (1998). *Praktische Vernunft. Zur Theorie des Handelns*. Frankfurt/M.: Suhrkamp.

Chen, Xiaomei (2002). *Occidentalism: A Theory of Counter-Discourse in Post-Mao China*. Lanham: Rowman & Littlefield.

---

44 See Thompson (1978), *Poverty of Theory*, 1–210.

Conze, Eckart (2018). *Geschichte der Sicherheit. Entwicklungen, Themen, Perspektiven.* Göttingen: Vandenhoeck & Ruprecht.

Dichtl, Erwin, and Otmar Issing (eds.). (1993). *Vahlens Großes Wirtschaftslexikon.* Volume 3. Munich: C.H. Beck.

Foucault, Michel (1981). *Archäologie des Wissens.* Frankfurt/M.: Suhrkamp.

Eliade, Mirce (1954). *Cosmos and History: The Myth of the Eternal Return.* New York: Harper.

Flachowsky, Sören, and Rüdiger Hachtmann, Florian Schmaltz (eds.). (2017). *Ressourcenmobilisierung. Wissenschaftspolitik und Forschungspraxis im NS-Herrschaftssystem.* Göttingen: Wallstein.

Frie, Ewald, and Mischa Meier (2014). *Aufruhr – Katastrophen – Konkurrenz – Zerfall.* Tübingen: Mohr Siebeck.

Giddens, Anthony (1984). *The Constitution of Society.* Berkeley CA: University of California Press.

Haller, Lea, and Sabine Höhler, Andrea Westermann (2014). Rechnen mit der Natur: Ökonomische Kalküle um Ressourcen. *Berichte zur Wissenschaftsgeschichte,* 37, 8–19.

Hardenberg, Roland, and Martin Bartelheim, Jörn Staecker (2017). The 'Resource Turn': A Sociocultural Perspective on Resources. In Anke K. Scholz, Martin Bartelheim, Roland Hardenberg, Jörn Staecker (eds.). *Developments—Movements—Valuations: Sociocultural Dynamics and the Use of Resources: Theories, Methods, Perspectives,* 13–23. Tübingen: Universität Tübingen

Hauman, Sebastian (2016). Konkurrenz um Kalkstein. Rohstoffsicherung der Montanindustrie und die Dynamik räumlicher Relationen um 1900. *Jahrbuch für Wirtschaftsgeschichte,* 57, 29–58.

Hebel, Dirk E., and Philippe Block, Felix Heisel, Tomas Mendez Echenagucia (2017). Beyond Mining—Urban Growth: The Architectural Innovation of Cultivated Resources through Appropriate Engineering. In Alejandro Zaera-Polo, Jeffrey S. Anderson (eds.). *Imminent Commons: The Expanded City,* 116–127. Seoul: Actar Publishers

Hilhorst, Dorothea, and Greg Bankoff (2004). Introduction: Mapping Vulnerability. In Greg Bankoff, Georg Frerks, Dorothea Hilhorst (eds.). *Mapping Vulnerability: Disasters, Development, and People,* 1–9. London: Earthscan.

Hughes, Johnson Donald (2009). *An Environmental History of the World: Humankind's Changing Role in the Community of Life.* Routledge Studies in Physical Geography and Environment. London: Routledge.

Hübner, Jonas (2015). Soziale Ungleichheit in einem ländlichen Ressourcenregime der Frühen Neuzeit. *Jahrbuch für Geschichte des ländlichen Raumes,* 12, 150–62.

Jancke, Gabriele, and Daniel Schläppi (eds.). (2015). *Die Ökonomie sozialer Beziehungen: Ressourcenbewirtschaftung als Geben, Nehmen, Investieren, Verschwenden, Haushalten, Horten, Vererben, Schulden.* Stuttgart: Franz Steiner.

Josephson, Paul R. (2004). *Resources under Regimes.* Cambridge MA: Harvard University Press.

Karidi, Maria, and Martin Schneider, Rebecca Gutwald (eds.). (2018). *Resilienz. Interdisziplinäre Perspektivern zu Wandel und Transformation.* Wiesbaden: Springer.

Klein, Torsten (2010). *Dynamisches Ressourcenkonfigurationsmanagement.* Bern: Peter Lang.

Koselleck, Reinhart (1989). "Erfahrungsraum" und "Erwartungshorizont" – zwei historische Kategorien. In Reinhart Kosseleck (ed.). *Vergangene Zukunft. Zur Semantik geschichtlicher Zeiten,* 349–75. Frankfurt/M.: Suhrkamp.

Köhler, Ingo, and Roman Rossfeld (eds.). (2012). *Pleitiers und Bankrotteure: Geschichte des ökonomischen Scheiterns vom 18. bis 20. Jahrhundert.* Frankfurt/M.: Campus.

Köster, Werner (2002). *Die Rede über den "Raum". Zur semantischen Karriere eines deutschen Konzepts.* Heidelberg: Synchron.

Krasner, Stephen D. (1983). Structural causes and regime consequences. Regime as intervening Variables. In Stephen D. Krasner (eds.). *International Regimes* (Cornell Studies in Political Economy), 1-23. Ithaca: Cornell University Press.

Kwong, Luke S. (2001). The Rise of the Linear Perspective on History and Time in Late Qing China, c. 1860- 1911. *Past and Present,* 173, 157–90.

Lackner, Michael (ed.). (2017). *Coping with the Future. Theories and Practices of Divination in East Asia.* Leiden: Brill.

Landwehr, Achim (2008). *Historische Diskursanalyse.* Frankfurt/M.: Campus.

Lefebvre, Henri (1974). *La production de l'espace.* Paris: Anthropos.

Liebscher, Anna Katharina (2013). *Betriebliche Ressourcensicherung durch Nachhaltigkeitskooperationen.* Münster: Lit.

Luhmann, Niklas (1988). *Die Wirtschaft der Gesellschaft.* Frankfurt/M.: Suhrkamp.

McCarthy, John D., and Mayer N. Zald (1977). Resource Mobilization and Social Movements: A Partial Theory. *American Journal of Sociology,* 82, 1212–41.

McCarthy, John D., and Mayer N. Zald (2001). The Enduring Vitality of the Resource Mobilization Theory of Social Movements. In Jonathan Turner (ed.) *Handbook of Sociological Theory,* 533–65. Berlin, Heidelberg, New York: Springer.

Mergel, Thomas (2012). *Krisen verstehen. Historische und kulturwissenschaftliche Annäherungen.* Frankfurt/M.: Campus.

Mittag, Jürgen, and Helke Stadtland (2014). *Theoretische Ansätze und Konzepte der Forschung über soziale Bewegungen in der Geschichtswissenschaft.* Essen: Klartext.

Müller-Christ, Georg (2011). *Sustainable Management.* Berlin, Heidelberg, New York: Springer.

Neugebauer, Reimund (ed.). (2017). *Ressourceneffizienz. Schlüsseltechnologien für Wirtschaft & Gesellschaft.* Berlin, Heidelberg, New York: Springer.

Penrose, Edith (1957). *The Theory of the Growth of the Firm.* Oxford: Oxford University Press.

Reder, Michael, and Hanna Pfeifer (eds.). (2012). *Kampf um Ressourcen.* Stuttgart: Kohlhammer.

Sarasin, Philipp (2003). *Geschichtswissenschaft und Diskursanalyse.* Frankfurt/M.: Suhrkamp.

Schubert, Klaus, and Nils C. Bandelow (eds.). (2014). *Lehrbuch der Politikfeldanalyse*. Berlin/Boston MA: De Gruyter.
Seeger, Miriam (2014). *Zähmung der Flüsse. Staudämme und das Streben nach produktiven Landschaften in China*. Münster: LIT.
Sewell, William H. (2005). *Logics of History. Social Theory and Social Transformation*. Chicago IL: University of Chicago Press.
The Economist (2017). The World's most Valuable Resource. Data and the New Rules of Competition. 6–12 May.
The Oxford English Dictionary (1989). Volume XIII. Second Edition. Prepared by J. A. Simpson and E. S. C. Weiner. Oxford: Clarendon Press.
Thompson, E.P. (1978). The Poverty of Theory or an Orrery of Errors. In E.P. Thompson. *The Poverty of Theory and Other Essays*, 1–210. London: Merlin Press.
Winiwarter, Verena, and Martin Knoll (2007). *Umweltgeschichte. Eine Einführung*. Stuttgart: UTB.
Wöhe, Günter, and Ulrich Döring (2010). *Einführung in die Allgemeine Betriebswirtschaftslehre*. Munich: Franz Vahlen.
Young, Oran R. (1982). *Resource Regimes, Natural Resources and Social Institutions*. Berkeley: University of California Press.

Chapter 1
Weakness: Ranges of Disciplinary Approaches

Kathrin Knodel and Anselm Spindler

I. Introduction

One of the central concepts of the Collaborative Research Centre is the concept of weakness. In this chapter, we approach it from the perspectives of philosophy and anthropology. By introducing an exemplary case for each field—the political thought of Thomas Aquinas, and local non-governmental organisations (NGOs) in West Africa—we aim to explore what a typically philosophical and anthropological perspective on weakness might look like. Contrasting these two perspectives will turn out to be a fruitful exercise because they represent two extremes of a spectrum of possible views concerning the "ontological" dimension of weakness: in one case, weakness is considered to be an essential part of the human condition, one that imposes important constraints on individual and collective human agency. In the other case, weakness is considered to be not a natural fact about humans, but rather to emerge through social attribution to agents. However, we will argue that, despite the seemingly different "ontological" views of weakness that can be found in philosophy and anthropology, something akin to a common structure appears to emerge: whenever a certain kind of weakness is identified, the question of how to address this weakness adequately is raised. Thus, both ways of framing the issue suggest the idea that the identification of weakness in a certain context comes with a discourse that is meant to portray weakness as a problem that needs to be addressed through the mobilisation or re-organisation of suitable resources.

II. The Human Condition: The Concept of Weakness in Philosophy

By most standards, the concept of weakness is not considered to be a classical philosophical concept or one that has acquired the status of a technical term in philosophy. While concepts such as knowledge and justice have received an enormous amount of attention, weakness, as such, does not seem to be of much interest to philosophers.[1]

The term "weakness", however, does appear frequently in the philosophical literature. For one thing, there is the pervasive talk of "weak", as opposed to "strong", concepts (of knowledge, justice, *etc.*). In this case, "weakness" seems to be a metaphor for a concept having relatively few conceptual implications. A concept of knowledge, say, may be considered "weak" if it requires relatively few conditions to be fulfilled for a person to count as knowing something. That a concept is "weak", in this sense, may be a desirable or an undesirable feature of the concept, depending on the precise theoretical context in which it is put to use.[2] Another example can be found in the phenomenon called "weakness of the will", which has received a lot of attention in moral philosophy and philosophy of action.[3] In this context, the term "weakness" is used to describe an agent's psychological or moral inability to do what he or she judges to be the thing he or she should do. While most philosophers consider weakness of the will to be a problematical trait of an agent, some have suggested that, in certain respects, it might also be of value for our moral self-understanding.[4]

More importantly, however, philosophers do not just use the term "weakness" on a regular basis. There are also, as Michael O'Sullivan has shown in his study entitled *Weakness: A Literary and Philosophical History*, several substantial treatments of weakness that can be found in a variety of contexts, for example, in classical virtue ethics, Christian moral philosophy,

---

[1] An indication for this hypothesis may be the absence of an entry on weakness in philosophical dictionaries such as the *Historisches Wörterbuch der Philosophie* or the *Stanford Encyclopedia of Philosophy*.

[2] For examples of this widespread metaphorical use of the term weakness with regard to philosophical concepts, see, for example, Jäger (2009), *Why to believe weakly in weak knowledge*, or Wilfred Beckerman (1995), *How would you Like your 'Sustainability', Sir?*. Similar examples can be found in practically all branches of philosophy.

[3] See, for example, Davidson (2001), *How is Weakness of the Will Possible?*, and Hoffmann (2015), *Willensschwäche*.

[4] See, for example, Seel (2001), *Ein Lob der Willensschwäche*.

existentialism, feminist philosophy, and in the traditions of so-called "Eastern" philosophy such as Daoism.[5] O'Sullivan argues that exploring these rather dispersed treatments of weakness is a valuable philosophical undertaking that is of ethical importance, as it helps to reveal certain "core elements of a shared humanity",[6] and to "incite a humane regard for shared human endeavour".[7] It does so by promoting our "mindfulness [of] and insight"[8] into fallibility, precariousness, neediness, vulnerability, and fragility, which are all essential aspects of the human condition.

In what follows, we would like to introduce another example of a philosophical treatment of weakness, one that can be found in the political thought of Thomas Aquinas: it is the argument for the indispensability of government in human society that is at the heart of Aquinas' treatise *On Kingship (De regno)*. We would like to argue that this argument, though not relying explicitly on the language of "weakness",[9] allows for a compelling interpretation in terms of weakness. This interpretation shows Aquinas' theory of government in *On Kingship* to be a comparatively early example of a tradition in western political thought that makes a certain description of human nature and the human condition the starting-point of political theorising, a tradition whose most widely-known expression is probably Thomas Hobbes' theory of government.[10] In what follows, we will characterise the various kinds of weakness of individual and collective human agents that Aquinas relies upon in the different stages of this argument. Also, we will argue that, while Aquinas, too, is aiming to uncover certain "core elements of a shared humanity", he does not represent weakness as something to be valued, but rather as a defect or deficiency that needs to be compensated for or overcome. Thus, his main concern is to identify specific resources—for example, social co-operation or public authority—the mobilisation of which provides for a compensation for what he considers to be essential human weaknesses.

---

5 O'Sullivan (2012), *Weakness*, 1–6.
6 O'Sullivan (2012), *Weakness*, 2.
7 O'Sullivan (2012), *Weakness*, 5.
8 O'Sullivan (2012), *Weakness*, 6.
9 In this text, Aquinas does not use any Latin term that could be translated as "weakness", such as *infirmitas*.
10 Hobbes (1996), *Leviathan*. See, for example, Pettit (2008), *Made with Words*.

1. Weakness and the Human Condition in Thomas Aquinas' Treatise "On Kingship"

a) Background: Some Remarks on Thomas Aquinas' political thought

In the late 1260s and the early 1270s, Thomas Aquinas (c. 1225–1274) wrote the small (and unfinished) treatise entitled *"On Kingship"*.[11] This text, although modelled on the traditional genre of the *"Mirrors for Princes"*,[12] offers a general theory of government that relies heavily on Aristotle's practical philosophy and, in particular, on the *Politics*, a text which had only recently been translated into Latin for the first time by William of Moerbeke.[13] The most important document of Aquinas' close study of the *Politics* is the equally unfinished commentary *Sententia libri Politicorum*, which he composed roughly at the same time as the treatise *"On Kingship"*. Thus, the treatise *"On Kingship"* is an important example of how central themes of Aristotelian political thought found their way into medieval political philosophy.[14]

The argumentation that forms the basis of the theory of government in *"On Kingship"* establishes four fundamental claims: first, that it is natural for human beings to live in society; second, that some sort of government is indispensable in human society; third, that a distinction can be drawn between a just and an unjust form of government; and fourth, that monarchy—being one particular type of a just government—is the best type of government. Each step of this argument can be interpreted as pointing to a certain kind of weakness that can be found in individual or collective human agents. We will now have a closer look at each step of the argument in turn.

---

11 Thomas Aquinas, *De regno ad regem Cypri*. In what follows, We rely on the online-edition that is available as part of *Corpus Thomisticum* (http://www.corpusthomisticum.org/orp.html, last retrieved 19 December 2017).
12 See Miethke (2008), *Politiktheorie im Mittelalter*.
13 See Flüeler (1992), *Rezeption und Interpretation der aristotelischen 'Politica' im späten Mittelalter*. See, also, Söder (2007), *Die Wiedergewinnung des Politischen*.
14 See Spindler (2015), *Thomas von Aquin: Kommentar zur Politik*, esp. 29–41.

b) *The Weakness of the Loner: Society as a Compensation for Natural Human Imperfection*

According to Aquinas, the indispensability of government in human affairs results from socialisation. If human beings led solitary lives like many other animals, they would not need other human beings to govern them. Instead, everyone would be "his own king".[15] The necessity of socialisation, on the other hand, results from the specific natural set-up of human beings, as Aquinas explains:

> "[I]t is natural for man, more than for any other animal, that he is a social and political animal that lives in a multitude, which is shown by [his] natural exigency. For nature gave the other animals food, a covering of hair, and means of defence, such as teeth, horns, claws, or at least swiftness for fleeing. Man, however, is set up without having any of these things prepared for him by nature, but instead of these, he has been given reason by which he can produce these things for himself though the work of his hands, for which one man does not suffice. For one man, by himself, cannot sufficiently provide for his life. Therefore, it is natural that man lives in the society of many."[16]

So, for Aquinas, the driving force of socialisation is the fact that human beings—even though they were created in the image of God—are, in important respects, deficient beings, too weak to survive on their own. Their weakness consists not so much in the fact that they have a number of natural needs, but rather in the fact that, as individuals, they are not able to provide for those needs in a sustainable manner. In contrast to other animals, individual human beings are not equipped with the natural means to do so. All they have is reason and a pair of hands, but even reason and a pair of hands will not suffice if you live on your own. Therefore, Aquinas argues, human beings have to join forces and cooperate to provide for a sustainable livelihood.

---

15 Thomas Aquinas, *De regno I*, c. 1: "... ipse sibi unusquisque esset rex..."

16 Thomas Aquinas, *De regno I*, c. 1: "Naturale [...] est homini ut sit animal sociale et politicum, in multitudine vivens, magis etiam quam omnia alia animalia, quod quidem naturalis necessitas declarat. Aliis enim animalibus natura praeparavit cibum, tegumenta pilorum, defensionem, ut dentes, cornua, ungues, vel saltem velocitatem ad fugam. Homo autem institutus est nullo horum sibi a natura praeparato, sed loco omnium data est ei ratio, per quam sibi haec omnia officio manuum posset praeparare, ad quae omnia praeparanda unus homo non sufficit. Nam unus homo per se sufficienter vitam transigere non posset. Est igitur homini naturale quod in societate multorum vivat."

c) *The Weakness of Disunited Groups I: An Argument for the Indispensability of Government*

Thus, all individuals have an interest in living in social groups, rather than by themselves. However, in Aquinas' view, social groups, as such, are not automatically stable. For, while there is an overlap of interests (everyone profits from co-operation), there are also diverse personal interests that result from the individual's different conceptions of happiness. These diverse interests point in different directions and therefore tend to have disintegrating effects on a group, thus threatening the benefits of co-operation. For this reason, Aquinas argues, every group requires some sort of government, *i.e.*, a person or group of persons that acts on behalf of the common interest of all, and that acts as an integrating force in society:

"But while it is natural for man that he lives in a society of many, there has to be something among men through which the multitude is governed. For since there are many men and each of them provides for his own good, the multitude will scatter in diverse parts, unless there is something, which has the task of taking care of the good of the multitude [...]".[17]

Thus, Aquinas' idea seems to be that, while there is a common good in every social group since everyone profits from living in a social group, no individual member of the group *as such* has this common good as the goal of his or her intentional action, for every individual strives for his or her own happiness or good life. Therefore, Aquinas argues, every social group requires the institution of some sort of government, which represents the common good of all. A group without government, on the other hand, may be too weak to be stable because there is no institution to counter the centrifugal forces that result from the potentially diverging private interests of the individuals. And if the group should disintegrate, the benefit of co-operation, for the sake of which human beings live in society in the first place, is lost.

---

17 Thomas Aquinas, *De regno I*, c. 1: "Si ergo naturale est homini quod in societate multorum vivat, necesse est in hominibus esse per quod multitudo regatur. Multis enim existentibus hominibus et unoquoque id, quod est sibi congruum, providente, multitudo in diversa dispergeretur, nisi etiam esset aliquis de eo quod ad bonum multitudinis pertinet curam habens [...]."

*d)	The Weakness of the Slave: Political Government as a Stronghold against Tyranny*

With this general idea of the purpose of government in mind, Aquinas introduces a distinction between different forms of government and different types of government. The two fundamental forms of government differ according to the legal status of the subjects of government. The three types of government, in turn, differ according to the number of people in government:

> "But it is a different goal that is appropriate for a multitude of free men and a multitude of slaves. For a free man is one who is the cause of himself; but a slave is someone who belongs to someone else. If, therefore, a multitude of free men is oriented by its government to the common good of the multitude, it will be a right and just form of government, which is appropriate for free men. If, however, it is not oriented to the common good of the multitude, but to the private interest of those in government, it will be an unjust and perverse form of government [...]."[18]

In this passage, Aquinas adopts a number of Aristotelian ideas: first, inspired by Aristotle, he introduces a distinction between a free person and a slave, inspired by Aristotle.[19] A slave is characterised by a weak legal status in society: He lacks the kind of self-ownership or legal independence of a free person. Instead, he is the property of someone else.

Secondly, Aquinas adopts Aristotle's idea that the form of government differs depending on the legal status of its subjects.[20] A slave owner governs his slaves with his own personal interest in mind; he makes them work for him just as he uses other instruments in his possession to promote his own happiness. This form of government is called "despotic". In contrast, in the government of free persons, for example, in the political community (*civitas*), the normative constellation is reversed: the citizen has a strong legal status, for he is a free person who does not belong to anyone else

---

18 Thomas Aquinas, *De regno I*, c. 2: "Alius autem est finis conveniens multitudini liberorum, et servorum. Nam liber est, qui sui causa est; servus autem est, qui id quod est, alterius est. Si igitur liberorum multitudo a regente ad bonum commune multitudinis ordinetur, erit regimen rectum et iustum, quale convenit liberis. Si vero non ad bonum commune multitudinis, sed ad bonum privatum regentis regimen ordinetur, erit regimen iniustum atque perversum [...]."
19 See Aristotle, *Politics I*, 1253b1–1254a17. For Aquinas' reading of this passage, see his *Sententia libri politicorum I*, Chapters 2–4.
20 See Aristotle, *Politics I*, 1255b16–1255b40. For Aquinas' reading of this passage, see his *Sententia libri politicorum I*, Chapter 5.

other than himself. As a consequence, government works for the free people and the common good of the community—not for the private interest of the person in office. Thus, government is the servant of the citizens, and is meant to promote their well-being. This form of government is called "political".

Thirdly, and against this background, Aquinas introduces the Aristotelian distinction of three types of government, according to the number of people in office. Each of these types of government may be just or unjust, depending on the basic form of government:[21]

	Government of one	Government of several	Government of many
Political or just government	Monarchy (*monarchia*)	Aristocracy (*aristocratia*)	Polity (*politia*)
Despotic or un-just government	Tyranny (*tyrannis*)	Oligarchy (*oligarchia*)	Democracy (*democratia*)

The idea of this scheme seems to be that combining the two distinctions yields six regime types that differ according to the basic form of government and the number of people in office. Thus, monarchy, aristocracy, and polity are all versions of the "political" form of government. That is to say, those in office work in the service of the free citizens in order to promote the citizens' happiness and the common good. They differ only in quantity, *i.e.*, with regard to the number of people in office (one, a few, or many). Tyranny, oligarchy, and democracy, in turn, are all unjust regime types because the rulers force a despotic form of government on their free subjects. They treat them *as if they were slaves*, *i.e.*, as if they were mere instruments for the pursuit of the ruler or rulers' private happiness. Therefore, these are unjust forms of government that violate the strong legal status of the citizen.

e) *The Weakness of Disunited Groups II: An Argument for Monarchy*

In the final step of the argumentation, Aquinas investigates which one, of the different types of just government, is preferable. His central claim is that monarchy is the best type of just government (and therefore the best

---

21 See Aristotle, *Politics III*. For Aquinas' reading of these passages, see his *Sententia libri politicorum III*, Chapters 1–6.

overall?). His argumentation for this claim again relies on an important aspect of the invocation of weakness:

"So that is the goal for which the ruler of the multitude must strive, that the unity of peace persists. [...] Thus, in so far as a government is more efficient to serve the unity of peace, it is more useful. [...] But it is clear that unity can be produced more effectively by something that is itself one, than by many. [...] Also, it is clear that many cannot conserve the multitude in any way, if they completely disagree. For, in many, some sort of unity is required for them to be able to govern [...]. But many unite by way of an approximation to one. Therefore, it is better that one governs than many by an approximation to one."[22]

In this passage, Aquinas recalls his earlier point that the central function of government is to promote the integration or unity of the group, which he now specifies as a state of peace that allows for fruitful co-operation. The argument for monarchy as the best form of government is then simply that something that is itself already one (i.e., a monarch) is more effective and more reliable in promoting the unity of the group. A group of persons in government (as in an aristocracy or polity), on the other hand, must first turn into one agent, i.e., emulate a monarch, in order to be able to govern effectively. This unification, however, is threatened by disagreement among the individuals: a group of rulers in disagreement is unable to govern and is, therefore, an ineffective cause of political integration.

2. Weakness and Strength in Aquinas' Political Thought

As we saw, Michael O'Sullivan argues that there is a philosophical interest in weakness because exploring weakness brings to light important features of our common humanity. Therefore, knowing about our weakness is an essential part of knowing who we, as human beings, essentially are.[23] This idea is clearly present in Aquinas' argument for the indispensability of

---

[22] Thomas Aquinas, *De regno I*, c. 3: "Hoc igitur est ad quod maxime rector multitudinis intendere debet, ut pacis unitatem procuret. [...] Quanto igitur regimen efficacius fuerit ad unitatem pacis servandam, tanto erit utilius. [...] Manifestum est autem quod unitatem magis efficere potest quod est per se unum, quam plures. [...] Amplius, manifestum est quod plures multitudinem nullo modo conservant, si omnino dissentirent. Requiritur enim in pluribus quaedam unio ad hoc, quod quoquo modo regere possint [...]. Uniri autem dicuntur plura per appropinquationem ad unum. Melius igitur regit unus quam plures ex eo quod appropinquant ad unum."
[23] O'Sullivan (2012), *Weakness*.

government in the treatise *On Kingship*. At all stages of the argument, Aquinas refers to certain features of individual and collective human agents that can plausibly be described as weaknesses and that are, on Aquinas' account, rooted in certain essential characteristics of the human condition. And these weaknesses differ according to their subject, their kind, and their source: first of all, Aquinas seems to consider both individual human beings and social groups as potential subjects of weakness. Thus, an individual person may be considered as weak, or an entire group of persons may be considered as weak. Secondly, Aquinas claims that individuals and groups can have weaknesses of different kinds: an individual person may be weak in the sense that he or she lacks the capacity to care for himself or herself. Or she may be weak in the sense that she is not a free citizen. A social group, in turn, may be weak in the sense that it has only insufficient or precarious forces of cohesion. Or a group may be weak in the sense that it is ineffective as an intentional agent. Thirdly, it seems that Aquinas points to different sources of weakness in these cases: the source of an individual person's inability to provide sustenance for himself or herself is his or her insufficient natural power to do so on his or her own. The source of an individual person's lack of freedom is that he or she does not have an independent legal status. And the major source of a group's having insufficient forces of cohesion and of a group's ineffectiveness as an intentional agent is the disagreement amongst its individual members.

On the other hand, however, it seems that Aquinas' focus on weakness in this context is profoundly different from what O'Sullivan has in mind. Aquinas would not have rejected O'Sullivan's idea that the exploration of human weakness "can speak for both the recognition of limits and a pragmatic sense of possibility".[24] But it seems that, in the text that we have investigated, Aquinas is not contributing to the "more affirmative readings of weakness"[25] that can be found in the history of philosophy; his point is not that "weakness can be a strength".[26] Rather, his point is that natural human weaknesses is, first and foremost, a problem, and that it can be compensated for or overcome by what is the genuine strength of human beings, namely, their capacity for individual and collective intentional action: the response to the individual person's inability to provide sustenance for himself or herself on his or her own is socialisation. The response to

---

[24] O'Sullivan (2012), *Weakness*, 190.
[25] O'Sullivan (2012), *Weakness*, 1f.
[26] O'Sullivan (2012), *Weakness*, 1.

the threat of social disintegration is government. The response to tyranny and despotic rule is citizenship or political freedom. And the response to the threat of ineffective government is monarchy. This style of political theorising in the treatise *On Kingship* makes Aquinas a comparatively early exponent of a tradition of western political thought that makes a specific characterisation of human nature and the natural human condition the starting-point of political theory. According to this tradition of political thought, which is mostly known through the works of Thomas Hobbes,[27] the relevance of political institutions is due to the way in which they compensate for certain problematical features of human nature.

III. On Attributions: The Concept of Weakness in Social and Cultural Anthropology

What has been said about weakness in philosophy in the first part of this chapter is also true for anthropology: there is no specific or universal concept of weakness, at least not in an explicit sense. This does not mean that weak groups or individuals are not important or present within research, on the contrary. Interestingly enough, one could say that, in a very general way, anthropologists tend to carry out research on those individuals and groups that are often regarded as weak, under-privileged and marginalised in a given society (indigenous people, migrants, *etc*.). Research on the middle class and the élites[28] seems to be an obvious exception here, but it is still mainly situated in the Global South, which is composed of what were formerly called developing countries. A sub-discipline is even dedicated to those anthropologists who regard themselves as the advocates of the under-privileged group upon whom they are doing research. Action Anthropology includes a strong involvement of the researcher. In this case, he or she has a clear position and the intention to help the studied group. The person in question has decided to intervene in order to change the living conditions of this group for the better.[29]

---

27 Hobbes (1996), *Leviathan*. See, for example, Pettit (2008), *Made with Words*.
28 See, for example, Melber (2016), *The Rise of Africa's Middle Class*, and Abbink et al. (2013), *The Anthropology of Elites*.
29 See, for example, Hedican (2016), *Public Anthropology*.

But when we look for papers or monographs that discuss the idea of weakness in an explicit way, it is often in the context of weak states, institutions, organisations, connections or civil society.[30] As such, it refers to a structure on an abstract level, but not to individuals or groups. One rare but important exception is the book by political scientist James C. Scott entitled "*Weapons of the Weak: Everyday Forms of Peasant Resistance*",[31] which had a profound influence in the discipline of anthropology. Here, Scott describes the opposition of peasants who do not simply succumb to the dominance of the local élites. He sheds light on apparently less organised forms of resistance that exist permanently, whereas academics tend to focus on remarkable major historic events, such as rebellions. But, although the "Weak" are in his title, Scott does not give a clear-cut definition of the concept. Instead, he uses several synonyms such as "the subordinate class", "relatively powerless groups", or simply "the poor".[32]

Classical anthropological topics that treat weakness in an implicit way include, for example, studies relating to magic.[33] Here, an individual perceives himself or herself to be weak, exposed to danger, and is therefore looking for a solution in order to stop the source of this evil. Another example can be found in studies on clientelism, which are mainly located in the Mediterranean area,[34] but which can also be retraced in the context of international development co-operation.[35] Here, the uneven distribution of power is arranged in a complex system of giving and taking. Two more recent fields that treat weakness from their very unique points of view include medical anthropology,[36] where empirical data can be found on drug addicts[37] and HIV patients,[38] and moral anthropology,[39] where studies focus on moral duty, ethical freedom, and responsibilities in a global context. But is it possible to construct ex post from these studies a shared

---

30 See, for example, Little (2013), *Unofficial Trade when States are Weak*. Molutsi et al. (1997), *Developing Democracy when Civil Society is Weak*. Rynkiewich (2000), *Big-man Politics. Strong Leadership in a Weak State*.
31 Scott (1985), *Weapons of the Weak*.
32 A similar topic is treated in the book of equal value by Spittler (1978), *Herrschaft über Bauern*.
33 See, for example, Greenwood (2009), *The Anthropology of Magic*.
34 See, for example, Roniger et al. (1994), *Democracy, Clientelism and Civil Society*.
35 See, for example, Eisenstadt (1981), *Political Clientelism, Patronage and Development*.
36 See, for example, Nichter et al. (2002), *New Horizons in Medical Anthropology*.
37 See, for example, Page (2011), *Anthropology and the Study of Illicit Drug Use*.
38 See, for example, Fassin (2007), *When Bodies Remember*.
39 See, for example, Fassin (2015), *A Companion to Moral Anthropology*.

definition of weakness? The following discussion will negate this option and come up with a perspective that allows us to regard weakness as a category which is, instead, made and fulfilled by actors themselves.

We should step back for a moment and ask whether there is any possibility of describing these life situations which might be called weak in a more neutral way. Asymmetrical power relations do, of course, exist, and they do so in many different forms and on many micro- and macro-levels worldwide. This is a fact that cannot be neglected. But we are arguing here against weakness as an analytical tool. It is an attribution in a specific setting used by one group or another to make their point. So, we have to ask the following questions, instead: Is there a method, a lexis or a semantic field that can capture such constellations? We can assume that the researcher tries to describe the living conditions in the way in which they are or seem to be. The advantage of this phenomenological access is the absence of pre-conceived judgements or categorisations. But related concepts that could be employed are not more neutral or objective at all. These given life situations might be paraphrased as being affected by poverty, uncertainty, as people being vulnerable, fragile, under-privileged, disadvantaged, deprived, inferior, and groups that are said to be subaltern.[40] In particular, the two concepts of poverty and vulnerability have been largely employed in different disciplines. The latter gave relevant input to the sub-discipline of the sociology of disasters, for example. Often enough, both concepts come together and aim to create measurable categories in order to establish when, precisely, people are poor, and to what extent they are vulnerable.[41] It is very obvious that most of these descriptions suggest that there exists an underlying counterpart, consisting of individuals or groups of individuals who are superior and privileged. Most descriptions only make sense in contrast to the other(s) who are—in whatever way—in a better situation. Thus, the methodological challenges cannot be ignored. The idea of vulnerability might be one outstanding exception here. We have to differentiate between layers and actors in order to be clear about who is describing whom—or is described by whom—as weak, and what further implications this has for all the parties involved.

From an anthropological point of view that aims to include different perspectives in a given societal setting, it makes perfect sense to neglect the

---

[40] See Spivak (1988), *Can the Subaltern Speak?*. She states that as soon as the subaltern do speak, they are no longer subaltern.
[41] See, for example, Klasen (2013), *Vulnerability to Poverty*.

existence of weakness as an objective fact. There is nobody or no group that is simply essentially weak. Weakness must be understood as an attribution, one which is always embedded in a discourse and is related to claims that can be made from a certain position within this discursive field.[42] As such, it is related to strategical considerations and politics of identity. But, at this point, we have to differentiate between self-attributions and attributions by others.

1. Weakness as Self-Attribution and Attribution by Others

Thus, to attribute weakness means to categorise, to label and to mark.[43] The starting-point is always a subjective perception of a difference in particular life situations. This difference may refer to physical, psychological, moral aspects or to aspects of resources. What is of importance here is the question of who is the first to perceive and articulate this difference? What are the implications of this? How is it articulated? And in what way are the different roles distributed? How are they negotiated and what do the internal structures of these negotiations look like? When weakness comes as an attribution by others, it may take on the characteristics of a stigma[44] that is accompanied by humiliation, insults and affront. It mainly leads to a social exclusion and may put an end to the communication of the groups involved. Only a third group (an advocacy group) may intervene and support the stigmatised group. In other contexts, again, the labelling of a group as being weak has a clearer aspect of hinting at the need to help and support the others. This can come as a moral duty, which is often the case in humanitarian action and international development.[45]

If a group itself claims to be weak, it might refer to structural and long-lasting perceived differences. But often this perception is rather situational and spontaneous. Furthermore, it is experienced as a contemporaneous loss of control. This is often the case when the environment suddenly changes, for example, because of the arrival of migrants or refugees in a

---

42 See Schütz (1960), *Der sinnhafte Aufbau der sozialen Welt*, and Berger et al. (1966), *The Social Construction of Reality*.
43 For different forms of attributions, its shifting implications and consequences over time in given social settings see Holbig et al. (2016), *Negative Classifications and Symbolic Order of Social Inequality*.
44 Goffman (1963), *Stigma*.
45 See, for example, Van Arsdale et al. (2008), *A Theory of Obligation*.

given society. Homoeostasis is in danger as it is sensitive to weakness through externally induced changes. The perception of weakness is accompanied by the claim for the restoration of the former societal order that conveyed security and safety.[46] Here, as well, it is accompanied by more or less clear and explicit moral implications that demand help, support or compensation. It is not an inner monologue, but always addressed to others.

2. Hidden and Overlooked Weakness: Stigma and Marginalisation

There are two other possible cases that should not be ignored, although they do cause a veritable empirical and methodological problem. One case concerns individuals who try to hide or conceal a condition that could be interpreted as weakness by others. This is a situation that is related to shame,[47] or worse, to disadvantages.[48] For the other case, it is even difficult to describe it in an adequate way. It is a situation in which people are unable to articulate weakness or in which nobody is willing to perceive their under-privileged living conditions. For them, the label of weakness would be a chance to claim support and to improve their situation. But, very often, they and their situation are not perceived at all, and they are no object of research.

The act of labelling oneself or others as weak is always connected to some kind of implication for future action. People who are declared to be weak are under a certain form of protection, and receive special treatment. This may be provided by the labelling group or by a third advocacy group. Human rights, for example, refer in a very sensible way to children, the elderly, women, and refugees—groups that they mark as weak and vulnerable. And even if others do not feel responsible to take action, this position as a weak person or group enables the actors to empower themselves and

---

46 See, for example, Biolsi (2004), *A Companion to the Anthropology of American Indians*. Peters (1995), *Cambodia—Restoration and Revival*.

47 For an ethnography of shame, see, for example, Abu-Lughod (1996), *Honour and Shame*, Buggenhagen (2011), *Muslim Families in Global Senegal*, Fotta (2016), *Exchange, Shame and Strength among Calon of Bahia*, and Peristiany (1974), *Honour and Shame*. For a differentiated perspective on shame as something potentially negative as well as productive, see Milevska (2016), *On Productive Shame*.

48 See, for example, Bewes (2010), *The Event of Postcolonial Shame*.

to exercise what is very often described as agency.[49] This, however, is impossible for people affected by hidden or overlooked or non-perceived weakness, or, more precisely, by the eventuality of an expressed weakness.

3. Weakness and Non-Governmental Organisations (NGOs) in the Global South

In the following explanations, we will focus on examples from Burkina Faso, where we can find a very vivid and dynamic scene of NGOs and smaller versions of them, the so-called Associations. A reliable total number of these structures is difficult to obtain and many that have been registered once are not active at the moment. But, from everything that we hear in the field, there must be several thousands of them. We are trying to understand better the working and living conditions of these actors who are said to be essential partners in development processes of all kinds. The domain of development and NGOs is, of course, not new. Since participation is one of the most important principles in development, NGOs became relevant partners for co-operation and implementation, especially for donors from the Global North.

On a more general note, we can say that the whole business sector of international development co-operation is based upon the pronouncement that the Global South is weak, and it is said to be weak in many different respects. Again, we encounter the diagnosis that states and other governmental structures, as well as various forms of infrastructure, are weak. Thus, the population, as such, is also weak: many suffer from poverty, and here it is very important to be able to measure this poverty again in order to adapt measurable actions. But they are also weak in the sense that they are not able to play out their potential as their surrounding environment is not supportive. This is the underlying analysis that creates space for different actors to operate. Local NGOs form part of these actors. Many of their founders are local people who have created initiatives with their own means and with those of their supporters, initiatives which respond to the needs in their surroundings, neighbourhoods and communities. They campaign for different and specific needs, such as education, the empowerment of women, and better access to water and sanitation. As locals, they

---

[49] See Emirbayer et al. (1998), *What is Agency?*, and Ortner (2006), *Anthropology and Social Theory*.

know best the deficiencies of supply and the societal problems at large. In order to gain support beyond the local scale, which is often limited in its financial capacities, they can join in the globally effective discourse of a weak Global South which, by now, after all the decades of development co-operation, has reached the status of shared common knowledge. It is an arena, a room for manoeuvre, and a platform.

What is creative in their work? They regard themselves as part of civil society and interpret their responsibility as having to spot societal deficits that the state is not able to remove or even to notice because of the sheer scale of what needs to be done. In order to point to them and to ask for financial and/or infrastructural support, one has to be somewhat creative. As an NGO-worker, you might ask yourself: How do I talk about state deficits? Who exactly will I approach for support? This depends heavily on the target group of your project, which might concern women, orphans, the elderly, or even prisoners. The target group of an NGO might change from one project to the other, although they are under pressure to focus on one or two topics in order to be more efficient and credible. But the ever-changing donor programmes and guidelines create different frameworks and opportunities. In addition, it is very difficult to earn a living within an NGO, as the donors often do not pay for labour costs, projects are time–limited, and the future of these structures is often unpredictable. So, some workers just keep on dedicating their time and energy to the NGO, hoping for payment and a permanent position at some point in the future. This means that, at any particular moment, they have to manage other jobs in order to make a living. The co-ordination of these different obligations demands creativity as well. But to call these conditions "free working conditions" would be quite cynical.

Something interesting can be said about these NGO actors, especially the founders. They are often responsible for many different—or even all—domains of the NGO: project planning and execution, budget-related tasks, such as accountancy, financial planning, and the acquisition of funding at diverse levels, such as private persons, enterprises, ministries, embassies or international sponsors of different kinds. They have to choose a good name for the NGO, one that suggests trust and potentiality. They are responsible for an assured documentation in forms and on paper as well as pictures, because, as one chairwoman of an NGO explained while watching the huge amount of pictures on her laptop: "What hasn't been photographed, didn't happen."

This field—although not new—is becoming more and more professionalised and competitive, and this has also been remarked by most potential donors. This is why training takes place in order to help actors to make their NGO more trustworthy, reliable, viable, efficient, professional and credible. Thus, they themselves have to be creative, flexible, adjustable and versatile. They always try to learn more and gain ever-more qualifications. These professionals are impressive examples of lifelong learning, and, in doing so, they are constantly expanding their pool of capacities and experiences, which may range from nursery-school teaching and cooking competitions to hydraulic engineering and the maintenance of wells. But, very often, this means paying for the training without knowing if this investment will ever pay off at all. The same is true for the pre-payment of activities. Actors have to be willing and financially able to pay out of their own pocket for the first projects in order to build their network and to organise the promotion of upcoming project proposals.

Some of the big players, those with many years' experience and with a track record of successful projects, are impressive personalities who are outstanding in what they do, how they act, and sometimes even how they dress. They have a huge network, are internationally connected, and have travelled outside Africa. They have a vision and can easily recall a key moment in their lives that serves as the starting-point of their commitment. They are entrepreneurs whose reputation and networking abilities are more than decisive for their ability to secure their own jobs and those of the employees for whom they are responsible. Their ability to build up personal trust on both sides—that of the donors and the local communities—determines their success in the long run.

Furthermore, their semi-professional dedication in the social sphere sometimes leads to a remarkable re-interpretation of their social role within the private context. They do not feel the same social obligations that are binding for many. For example, instead of following the crowd and greeting a wedding party of a distant colleague, they prefer to go home and recover before leading an awareness campaign for youths on sexual education and unwanted pregnancy. They sometimes just feel that they are meant for greater things.

Remarkably, these brokers[50] between local needs and global donors have to be and prove to be the mere opposite of what the underlying nar-

---

50 See Bierschenk et al. (2002), *Local Development Brokers in Africa*.

rative is stating: they are active, dynamic, creative and strong, anything but weak.

This case study also shows—in extension of the above cited literature by, for example, Scott—that a close look within a group called weak is worthwhile. Differentiations can be made here. Individual actors oppose the label of the weak brought from outside—not only in their self-description, but also in their strategic necessity and even in the expectation of individuals. This is an invitation to a differentiated view with awareness of the internal structure within a group, which has a unifying label and is initially perceived as homogenous or wants to be perceived as such.

IV. Conclusion

In this chapter, we have approached the concept of weakness from the perspectives of philosophy and anthropology. In the first part, we examined the political thought of Thomas Aquinas, in particular, the argument for the indispensability of government in the treatise *On Kingship*. It turned out that this argument relies, in a number of ways, on the identification of certain kinds of weaknesses of individual and collective human agents—weaknesses that, Aquinas argues, need to be compensated for or overcome through political incorporation and the institution of government. This makes Aquinas an early exponent of a tradition of political thought, according to which the starting-point of political theorising is a certain characterisation of human nature and the human condition as deficient, precarious and essentially in need of compensation through the creation of political institutions. In the second part of the chapter, we argued that this philosophical perspective on weakness contrasts sharply with an anthropological one: anthropology does not expect to find people in their field that *are* weak, as their given human condition. But it does expect to encounter people who are *said* to be weak and who *claim* to be weak. Three aspects always accompany this weakness. It is relational: one can only be weak in comparison to others who are strong, superior, privileged, *etc.*, and, as such, it is an expression of disposing or not disposing of power. It is an attribution: either by oneself or by others. It is intentional: weakness is attributed and expressed because action is expected, claimed, or wants to be prepared. Weakness has always a specific potential to open up a certain arena of action.

With these two cases, we have highlighted two extremes of a spectrum of weakness. This is not the right place to discuss the general differences between the two disciplines of philosophy and anthropology that derive mainly from their pre-suppositions and methodologies. What makes this comparison such a fruitful exercise are the similarities, not the differences. So some common insights can be noted. Who is said to be weak? Individuals and social entities. But, in both cases, weakness is not the feature of a single individual mentioned by name. Other thinkable options that we have briefly mentioned include states or structures. How is their weakness to be characterised? As an unchangeable feature of human beings, on the one hand, or mediated through communication in a specific social setting, on the other? From where does it result? From a specific idea of man, or from interaction? Although biology has, at several points in history, been used to explain differences between humans and groups, no biologistic reasons are given here for the respective weakness. Other options would indeed include genes, a certain (cultural) origin, or even a divine order. What measures have to be taken? What is the result of this diagnosis of weakness? In both cases, a specific form of rule and power is legitimised by weakness. Other possible options include demand or claims.

And this might be the most notable insight. While the two approaches do not have the same underlying assumptions, they nonetheless come to the same conclusion. Whenever weakness is perceived and articulated, the question for the adequate answer and future action becomes relevant. Although there is no universal answer or reaction to weakness, it has the tendency to urge that a given situation be changed. In contrast, the perception of strength has a more affirming and re-assuring affect. In this sense, the mentioning of weakness is, at the same time, the legitimation upon which this very action will be based. This connection is mediated by a certain perception of justice, morality and temporality. Furthermore, this discursive effort hints at a specific handling of resources that is essential in order to overcome this weakness and to improve a given situation for at least one group of actors.

We can summarise that each discipline highlights and accentuates an important aspect of articulated weakness. The strength of anthropology and its method, for example, is the insight into the perspective of those involved, the emic perspective. We can say something about their emotions, their shame, as well as their strategical considerations. Philosophy, in contrast, is more oriented towards the revelation of normative issues.

Weakness might be represented as an anthropological determination or a communicative emergence. In either case, it opens up or shifts an arena of action. From this position, weakness itself is not an analytical tool. It is a flexible feature in the hands of actors. Instead, our CRC 1095 introduces the corresponding underlying discourse of weakness as an appropriate analytical instrument. Actors in our fields may use weakness as their way to construe reality. But, in order to describe this act of construing accurately, we use the idea of discursive practices. So whenever we used the words "weak" or "weakness" as a description in the examples above, we want them to be understood as quotations from our fields. What we present as an analytical concept of additional value is the discourse of weakness and its structure. Although there is no essence of weakness, it is highly inspiring for a sensitive discourse analysis. By focusing on this aspect, instead of the emic diagnosis, we are able to understand and depict the strategies and the logics of actors as well as their actions better.

Literature

Abbink, Jonand, and Tijo Salverda (eds.). (2013). *The Anthropology of Elites: Power, Culture, and the Complexities of Distinction*. New York: Palgrave Macmillan.

Abu-Lughod, Lila (1996). Honor and Shame. In Michael Jackson (ed.). *Things as they are. New Directions in Phenomenological Anthropology*, 51–69. Bloomington IN: Indiana University Press.

Aristotle (2013). *Politics*. ed. by Carnes Lord. Chicago IL: University of Chicago Press.

Beckerman, Wilfred (1995). How would you Like your 'Sustainability', Sir? Weak or Strong? A Reply to Critics, *Environmental Values* 4 (2), 167–79.

Berger, Peter L., and Thomas Luckmann (1966). *The Social Construction of Reality: A Treatise in the Sociology of Knowledge*. Garden City NY: Doubleday.

Bewes, Timothy (2010). *The Event of Postcolonial Shame*. Princeton NJ: Princeton University Press.

Bierschenk, Thomas, and Jean-Pierre Chauveau, Jean-Pierre Olivier de Sardan (2002): Local Development Brokers in Africa. The Rise of a New Social Category. *Working Papers of the Department of Anthropology and African Studies*, no.13.

Biolsi, Thomas (ed.). (2004). A Companion to the Anthropology of American Indians. Oxford: Blackwell.

Buggenhagen, Beth (2011). *Muslim Families in Global Senegal: Money Takes Care of Shame.* Bloomington IN: Indiana University Press.
Davidson, Donald (2001). How is Weakness of the Will Possible?. In Donald Davidson. *Essays on Actions and Events*, 21–42. Oxford: Oxford University Press.
Eisenstadt S.N. (ed.). (1981). *Political Clientelism, Patronage and Development.* Beverly Hills CA: Sage.
Emirbayer, Mustafa, and Ann Mische (1998). What is Agency?. *American Journal of Sociology*, 103 (4): 962–1023.
Fassin, Didier (2007). *When Bodies Remember. Experiences and Politics of AIDS in South Africa.* Berkeley CA: University of California Press.
Fassin, Didier (ed.). (2015). *A Companion to Moral Anthropology.* Malden MA: Wiley-Blackwell.
Flüeler, Christoph (1992). *Rezeption und Interpretation der aristotelischen 'Politica' im späten Mittelalter.* Amsterdam: Grüner.
Fotta, Martin (2016). Exchange, Shame and Strength among Calon of Bahia. A Value-based Analysis. In Micol Brazzabeni, Manuela Ivone Cunha and Martin Fotta (eds.). *Gypsy Economy. Romani Livelihoods and Notions of Worth in the 21st Century*, 201–20. New York: Berghahn Books.
Goffman, Erving (1963). *Stigma: Notes on the Management of Spoiled Identity.* Englewood Cliffs NJ: Prentice Hall.
Greenwood, Susann (2009). *The Anthropology of Magic.* Oxford: Berg Publishers.
Hedican, Edward J. (ed.). (2016). *Public Anthropology: Engaging Social Issues in the Modern World.* Toronto: University of Toronto Press.
Hobbes, Thomas (1996). *Leviathan.* edited by Richard Tuck. Cambridge: Cambridge University Press.
Hoffmann, Richard (2015). *Willensschwäche: Eine handlungstheoretische und moralphilosophische Untersuchung.* Berlin: Walter de Gruyter.
Holbig, Heike, and Sighard Neckel (2016). Negative Classifications and the Symbolic Order of Social Inequality: Evidence from East Asia. *Critical Asian Studies* 48 (3), 400–421.
Jäger, Christoph (2009). Why to Believe Weakly in Weak Knowledge: Goldman on Knowledge as mere True Belief. *Grazer Philosophische Studien* 29 (1), 19–40.
Klasen, Stephan (ed.). (2013). *Vulnerability to Poverty: Theory, Measurement and Determinants, with Case Studies from Thailand and Vietnam.* Basingstoke: Palgrave Macmillan.
Little, Peter D. (2013). Unofficial Trade when States are Weak. The Case of Crossborder Livestock Trade in the Horn of Africa. In Michael Bollig, Michael Schnegg, Hans-Peter Wotzka (eds.). *Pastoralism in Africa. Past, Present, and Future*, 389–411. New York: Berghahn Books.
Melber, Henning (ed.). (2016). *The Rise of Africa's Middle Class: Myths, Realities and Critical Engagements.* London: Zed Books.

Miethke, Jürgen (2008). *Politiktheorie im Mittelalter. Von Thomas von Aquin bis Wilhelm von Ockham.* Tübingen: Mohr Siebeck.

Milevska, Suzana (2016). On Productive Shame: Triangulations of Shame, Reconciliation, and Agency. In Suzana Milevska (ed.). *On Productive Shame, Reconciliation, and Agency*, 10–41. Berlin: Sternberg Press.

Molutsi, Patrick P., and John D. Holm (1997). Developing Democracy when Civil Society is Weak. The Case of Botswana. In Roberto O. Collins, James McDonald Burns, Erik Kristofer Ching; Kathleen S. Hasselblad (eds.). *Problems in the History of Modern Africa*, 147–51. Princeton NJ: Wiener.

Nichter, Mark, and Margaret Lock (2002). *New Horizons in Medical Anthropology. Essays in Honour of Charles Leslie.* London: Routledge.

Ortner, S.B. (2006). *Anthropology and Social Theory: Culture, Power, and the Acting Subject.* Durham NC: Duke University Press.

O'Sullivan, Michael (2012). *Weakness: A Literary and Philosophical History.* London: Continuum Literary Studies.

Page, J.B. (2011). Anthropology and the Study of Illicit Drug Use. In M. Singer, P. I. Erickson (eds.). *A Companion to Medical Anthropology*, 357–78. Oxford: Wiley-Blackwell.

Peristiany, John Georg (1974). *Honour and Shame: The Values of Mediterranean Society.* Chicago IL: University of Chicago Press.

Peters, Heather A. (1995). Cambodia—Restoration and Revival. *Expedition*, 37.

Pettit, Philip (2008). *Made with Words: Hobbes on Language, Mind, and Politics.* Princeton NJ: Princeton University Press.

Roninger, Luis, and Ayşe Güneş-Ayata (eds.). (1994). *Democracy, Clientelism and Civil Society.* London: Lynne Rienner Publishers.

Rynkiewich, Michael A. (2000). Big-man Politics. Strong Leadership in a Weak State. In Michael A. Rynkiewich, Roland Seib (eds.). *Politics in Papua New Guinea: Continuities, Changes and Challenges*, 17–43. Goroka: Melanesian Institute for Pastoral and Socio-Economic Services.

Schütz, Alfred (1960). *Der sinnhafte Aufbau der sozialen Welt: eine Einleitung in die verstehende Soziologie.* Vienna: Springer.

Scott, James C. (1985). *Weapons of the Weak: Everyday Forms of Peasant Resistance.* New Haven CT: Yale University Press.

Seel, Martin (2001). Ein Lob der Willensschwäche. *Merkur*, 55 (627), 614–19.

Söder, Joachim R. (2007). Hochmittelalter: Die Wiedergewinnung des Politischen. In Christoph Horn, Ada Neschke-Hentschke (eds.). *Politischer Aristotelismus. Die Rezeption der aristotelischen Politik von der Antike bis ins 19. Jahrhundert*, 53–76. Stuttgart: Metzler.

Spindler, Anselm (2015). *Thomas von Aquin: Kommentar zur Politik des Aristoteles, Buch I.* Freiburg: Herder.

Spittler, Gerd (1978). *Herrschaft über Bauern. Die Ausbreitung staatlicher Herrschaft und einer islamisch-urbanen Kultur in Gobir (Niger).* Frankfurt/M.: Campus.

Spivak, Gayatri Chakravorty (1988). Can the Subaltern Speak?. In Cary Nelson, Lawrence Grossberg (eds.). *Marxism and the Interpretation of Culture*, 66–111. Chicago IL: University of Illinois Press.

Van Arsdale, Peter W., and Regina A. Nockerts (2008). A Theory of Obligation. *The Journal of Humanitarian Assistance. Field Experience and Current Research on Humanitarian Action and Policy.* (available at: https://sites.tufts.edu/jha/archives/138, last accessed 29 December 2017).

Chapter 2
Representations of Weakness: Functions, Images, Effects

Klaus Seidl

I. Introduction

Figure 1: "Völker Europas, wahret eure heiligsten Güter" (1895), painted by Hermann Knackfuß based on a sketch by Wilhelm II. (Source: Kunstbeilage zur Illustrirten Zeitung Nr. 2733, 16 November 1895)

In 1895, at the end of April, Kaiser Wilhelm II paid a visit to his old school friend Emil Count Görtz at Schloß Schlitz. Here in Hesse, the German emperor found the leisure time to do some sketching. It took only a few hours to produce a remarkable, but gloomy, picture, a European horror scenario, which gained worldwide notoriety after Wilhelm commissioned Hermann Knackfuß to paint it.[1] In the foreground, it depicts the Archangel Michael with a flaming sword. He directs the gaze of the allegorical figures of the European nations to prosperous scenery that is threatened by a conflagration. The smoke emanating in the form of a dragon is presided over by a statue of a sitting Buddha. Under a radiating cross, Germania has already drawn her sword while some of the other heroines remain hesitant.[2] Wilhelm captioned the image with the urgent appeal:

"Peoples of Europe, Guard Your Most Sacred Possessions!" (*Völker Europas, wahret eure heiligsten Güter!*).[3]

Thus, the emperor depicted an alarming image of a looming danger even before the events of the Boxer Rebellion (1899–1901) and the Russo-Japanese War (1904–1905) had given rise to the spread of the so-called "Yellow Peril" slogan throughout Europe.[4] Looking back, it remains difficult to determine whether the painting served as "artistic treatment of imperial nightmares" or not.[5] It is certain, however, that the emperor himself used it—albeit with little success—for propagandistic purposes at a later point in time in order to persuade the other European empires to coordinate a common political strategy for Asia. In this context, Philipp Gassert recognises a deeply rooted European "superiority complex" and considers the emperor's painting (*Kaiserbild*) to be a "document of self-perceived strength, not weakness".[6] At first sight, this interpretation may seem surprising. Indeed, historians are inclined to de-construct the fear of the "Yellow Peril" by exposing its conscious or unconscious expectations,

---

1 See Röhl (2018), *Wilhelm II.*, 840; on the "Yellow Peril", see Gollwitzer (1962), *Gefahr*, a classic account from a European perspective; Mehnert, (1997), *Gefahr*; see, also, among others Hashimoto, (2008), *Peril*; Schmidt-Glintzer (2014), *Gefahr*; Klein (2015), *Peril*.
2 The description follows along the lines of the convincing interpretation offered by Gassert (2007), *Völker Europas*, 283.
3 This was only but one possible translation at that time. Wilhelm himself preferred: "Nations of Europe! Join in the Defence of your Faith and your Home."
4 About the context of its creation see Gollwitzer (1962), *Gefahr*; Röhl (2018), *Wilhelm II.*, 840–842.
5 Mehnert (1995), *Gelbe Gefahr*, 111.
6 Gassert (2007), *Völker Europas*, 280.

assumptions, and stylisations, and by identifying the narratives employed. In this case, however, Gassert switches the rhetorical devices at work with the effect intended by its creators. In countless speeches and images concerning the supposed "Yellow Peril", politicians, authors, and scholars not only diagnosed an Asian threat, but also discussed the current state of Europe—a state which they wished to change. This demonstrates that addressing one's own weakness can also serve as a strategy to enforce particular interests. However, the discourses of weakness which stand at the core of our research programme do not fully immerse themselves in such a strategy. In fact, a mere (or predominantly) functional analysis underestimates the complex dynamics that emerge from them.

We proceed on the assumption that ascertaining strengths often serves to maintain or conform to a certain state of affairs. Discourses of weakness, on the other hand, designate diagnoses of deficits that push for changes and corrections. As an analytical concept, a discourse of weakness proves helpful to examine situations in which contemporaries perceived forms of weakness, deficit, inferiority, or exclusion as serious problems which they deemed it necessary to resolve. This contribution first presents several criteria and characteristics of discourses of weakness. Further elaboration is dedicated to the particular meaning conveyed by images, metaphors, and representations in this setting. In evoking expectations and fears and altering attitudes, they open up a narrative dimension. Finally, the above-mentioned emperor's painting serves to illustrate some typical examples of how representations of weakness can be discursively transformed and thus unfold an unexpected momentum.

II. Discourse of Weakness—A Conceptional Approach

As Hartmut Leppin and Christian A. Müller note, applying discourses of weakness as an analytical concept is not restricted to phenomena in which historical formations denote themselves with the term "weak". Instead, the approach directs attention to a semantic field that describes a deficient state in many ways: "shortage, downfall, crisis, insignificance, ineffectiveness, disintegration, fleetingness, insecurity, vulnerability and so forth."[7]

---

[7] Leppin et al. (2015), *Discourse of Weakness*, 46; see, for example, the contribution dedicated to the concept of "decline".

This broad thematic scope has the considerable advantage of taking the special significance of these descriptions seriously, while, at the same time, being flexible enough to do justice to the trans-epochal and interdisciplinary range covered by the individual research projects. Certainly, these cases may also be well described, contextualised, and de-constructed from differing perspectives. But an analysis of discourses of weakness takes particular note of how attributions of weakness can further lead to historical change. For this purpose, it offers a particular set of tools that lays open the situational mechanisms, functions, and effects at work.

Discourses of weakness are characterised by a distinct order that combines: a) triggers, b) diagnoses of weakness, c) remedies, and d) results and effects.

a) The beginning of a discourse of weakness is marked by a *trigger*, which challenges certitudes, reveals difficulties, and produces uncertainty. To put it more pointedly, it is an event that is followed by a societal process of reflection. An analysis of discourses of weakness, therefore, does not look for a decisive moment or "key event", but an ensuing "follow-up communication" (*Anschlusskommunikation*).[8] To this effect, one can refer to the political scientist John Kingdon, according to whom a "focusing event" enables political élites to set agendas precisely because it directs attention in spatial and temporal terms and serves as a "powerful symbol" for a considerable problem.[9] The intention is not to identify an event as the actual trigger, but rather to discover the discursive practices that interpret and constitute it afterwards:

"Events unfold changing effects […], without being themselves intrinsically loaded with significance."[10]

b) At the very centre of a discourse of weakness, therefore, lies a communication about weakness, or, to put it more precisely, *diagnoses of weakness*. They recognise uncertainty, inferiority, and deficiencies (of the resource regime) and declare them to be a—generally solvable—problem. They are particularly productive since they connect events, experiences, and expectations within a context, thereby alarming people and institutions in order to mobilise resources or to re-organise resource regimes. According to Michel

---

8 Lenger et al. (2009), *Einleitung*, 8.
9 Kingdon (2003), *Agendas*, 94–100.
10 According to Klöppel (2010), *Konzept der Problematisierung*, with reference to Deleuze: 259.

Foucault, this might be described as a process of "problematisation".[11] However, this "doesn't mean representation of a pre-existing object, nor the creation by discourse of an object that doesn't exist".[12] It would be insufficient, therefore, to restrict the historical analysis to establish that the diagnosed weakness was "real", rather than examine the inherent attribution process. Nonetheless, we speak of a "diagnosis" for two reasons: first, the cognitive process of an individual stakeholder is quite similar to that of a medical diagnosis. It is based upon previous knowledge about the patterns of a disease and its symptoms, and it accords with related assumptions and expectations about the course and healing of a disease.[13] On the other hand, it is conspicuous that attributions of weakness often appear in the rhetorical guise of allegedly objective diagnoses. The diagnoses of weakness aim to be more convincing by pretending to draw scientific conclusions upon the basis of the existing data. Numbers, maps, tables or statistics are common means to objectify deficits in this context.[14]

c) From a structural perspective, the diagnoses are followed by *remedies* or, in reference to the conceptual reflections of the Tübingen-based CRC 923 "Threatened Order—Societies under Stress" (*Bedrohte Ordnungen*), by "crisis management" (*Bewältigungspraxis*), which intends to resolve the diagnosed weakness. In this context, it is possible to discern different individual or collective activities that pursue their respective special interests and are bound to existing routines.[15] With regard to the "communication about weakness", it is furthermore essential to underline the inseparable connection of diagnosis and procedure: the diagnosis of weakness is always accompanied by prescriptions, possibilities of treatment, and therapies. Here, action by no means follows speech, but the problematisation of weakness itself already delineates a broad range of possible remedies that are justified by—be it intended or not—the previously made diagnoses. This is because

---

11 See Foucault (2005), *Polemik*; for conceptual considerations for application, see, among others, Klöppel (2010), *Konzept der Problematisierung*; from the perspective of a political scientist, see Bacchi (2009), *Analysing Policy*; Bacchi (2012), *Problematizations*.
12 Foucault (1988), *Concern for Truth*, 257.
13 See Demandt (1979), *Metaphern*, 22–27.
14 See Chapter 3 "Decline".
15 See, for this, the persuasive approach to diagnosis of threat and crisis management (Bedrohungsdiagnose und Bewältigungspraxis) of the CRC 923 "Threatened Order—Societies under Stress ("Bedrohte Ordnungen") in Tübingen, which focuses on threat scenarios. The point of departure of our research is, however, the perception of one's own weakness that is made responsible for this situation. For further elaboration see http://bit.ly/sfb923fp [2018-03-26].

problematisation does not, according to Foucault, "assume a unique form that is the direct result or the necessary expression of these difficulties; it is an original or specific response—often taking many forms, sometimes even contradictory in its different aspects, to these difficulties".[16]

d) To put it more precisely, the *results* of a discourse of weakness must be separated from its *effects*, while both indicate a distinct form of transformation. Results essentially indicate the instrumental use of speaking about weakness by concerning the approach to, the appropriation, and the usage of resources. Simply put, stakeholders identify a weakness that is related to the deficiencies present in a resource regime. At the same time, remedies are devised that are applied in a successful case; weakness is then resolved through the re-organisation of the resource regime. Historical change would thus proceed as planned; it would occur according to the intentions of stakeholders capable of action in the sense of Arnold Toynbee's "challenge and response" or, under different circumstances, that of Jared Diamond's "collapse". Effects, on the other hand, emphasise the creative dimension of communicating about weakness, which constantly initiates a multitude of different possibilities of change by discussing— willingly or unwillingly—solutions, or because "unintended consequences"[17] exceed or fully replace the desired consequences of action. In other words, reflection and mobilisation can unfold a momentum that itself leads to transformation. Our concept of discourses of weakness keeps both forms of transformation in mind.

This structure can be found in different types of discourses of weakness which are examined by the research projects of the CRC 1095. Furthermore, four central elements characterise the discourses of weakness. Firstly, the underlying diagnosis of weakness identifies uncertainty, inferiority, deficiencies (of the resource regime), *etc.*, but, at the same time, refers to the possibility of changing this situation in an essentially autonomous fashion: the *agency* of historical stakeholders remains not only intact, it even figures as a central element of the discourse of weakness. Hence, the discourse of weakness functions so efficiently because it designates passivity and stagnation as a problem. There have existed, for instance, more or less effective measures even against seemingly inevitable natural catastrophes at all times: today, anyone who recognises man-made "cultural catastrophes" behind natural disasters will therefore, as a matter of fact, call for action.

---

16 Foucault (1984), *Polemics*, 381-390, 388 f.
17 Steiner (2015), *Nebenfolgen*.

But even those people who considered earthquakes, fires, and floods to be the punishment of God often believed that they would escape such catastrophes in the future by resorting to prayer, sacrifice or a pious life.[18] Secondly, and immediately connected with this are attributions of weakness that have an *appellative* effect, since they call for, often in an alarming fashion, a correction of the diagnosed weakness. Inevitably, they bring questions of range, of addressees, and of media circulation to mind. Attributions of weakness are furthermore essentially *functionalistic*, since they aim to acquire, mobilise, or substitute certain resources, or, rather, generally reorganise a resource regime. Thirdly, weakness is not only *relational* (in terms of a comparison with competitors or rivals), but also *referential* by evoking historical role models or future horror scenarios. It is, indeed, obvious that, in many cases, the procedure of comparing tends to produce a "narrative of deficiency" that revolves around the theme of "what the pear lacks to be an apple"—and not just in historiography.[19] More importantly, it seems that the resulting discrepancy can function as a means to form collectives and identities. Also significant is the *historicity* of discourses of weakness. These not only re-visit and draw from earlier discourses of weakness as traditions, but also establish a special connection between the past, the present, and the future. In relation to the above-mentioned "Yellow Peril", Gassert rightly points out that accounts such as *Die gelbe Gefahr in der Geschichte Europas* ("The Yellow Peril in the History of Europe") by Alexander von Peez possessed not merely an alarmist function, but also "always conveyed a reliable notion that Europe had but narrowly escaped catastrophe several times, while also being able to find ways and means to avert and even to repel the Eastern threats".[20] Therefore, the notion that history could repeat itself in any possible way—be it good or bad—is, in this context, a common and basic guiding principle.

One needs only to think of the comparisons frequently drawn about the glory and, even more so, the decline of the Roman Empire.[21] Even someone who portrays his own situation as unprecedented and accordingly objects to historical comparisons, since this would mean trivialising the present situation, will argue, nonetheless, from a historical perspective,

---

[18] See, for the management of natural catastrophes in modernity, Hannig (2018), *Kalkulierte Gefahren*.
[19] Pernau (2011), *Transnationale Geschichte*, 34.
[20] Gassert (2007), *Völker Europas*, 280.
[21] Demandt (2015), *Fall Roms*.

because it is through this rhetorical device that he can amplify both the threat scenario and the related appeal.[22]

III. Representations: Images, Concepts, Narrativity

Representations of weakness play a pivotal role in the context of the above-mentioned characteristics and elements. They pose as a recurrent and conjunctive feature that shapes the discourse of weakness in a considerable manner. Since weakness can only be experienced and analysed through statements about weakness, it seems adequate to examine images, representations, and strategies of staging that lend specific expressions to weakness.[23] Accounts of a present weakness may be of a descriptive character at first. They are, however, necessarily embedded in narrative structures since they are connected to the historical question of cause: Where does the deficit originate? And who is responsible for it? The identification of weakness, on the other hand, demarks a line of expectation (*Erwartungshorizont*) that denotes possible future ramifications; it takes all options into account, ranging from the total or partial elimination of the perceived weakness, to a solution that is not yet found. Here, narratives of rise and decline often not only stand together, but also refer to each other. Representations thus function in two regards as motives: first, as an image and embodiment of a discourse of weakness; and second, as an impulse and a driving force. They acquire a special significance because these manifold representations not only mirror the discourse or visualise the otherwise invisible underlying conditions. Rather, representations produce weakness through a performative action.[24] From a narratological perspective, one could also say that they are produced in the process of their "linguistical respective medial fixation".[25] In this context, Ansgar Nünning remarks that the "constitutive process" is "verbalisation" in the case of texts, just as "painting" is in the case of images.[26]

---

22 For example, the theologian Albert Schweitzer used to argue in this manner after World War I; see Gutsche (2015), *Niedergang*, 225 f.
23 See the detailed definition of the concept of representation by Bublitz (2010), *Beichtstuhl*, 35.
24 Fischer-Lichte (2004), *Ästhetik des Performativen*.
25 Nünning (2007), *Grundzüge*, 61.
26 Nünning (2007), *Grundzüge*, 61.

Representations of weakness can figure as actual images or paintings, as is the case with the *Kaiserbild*. However, they can usually be found in concepts or in metaphors that originate from a wider semantic field: from danger and threat, *via* decline and crisis, to rise (of the competitor), narratives indicate the state or the possible consequences of weakness.[27] Without continuing older somewhat philosophical debates which are situated between a conceptual history and a metaphorology, it should be emphasised that concepts and figures of speech (*Sprachbilder*) are inherently metaphorical, and, in both cases, "the meaning [...] is not once and for all but [they] are being shaped while shaping their times and surroundings".[28] It would be going too far to take "the image at its word and the word at its image".[29] In contrast to an abstract concept, metaphors can be "false" or "absurd", but are nonetheless persuasive or at least able to function.[30] In his *Weltgeschichte* ("History of the World"), the German historian Veit Valentin had already criticised the fatalistic and "naïve scheme" evoked by the ubiquitous metaphors of life and seasons. He nonetheless continued using such images whilst arguing that: "Great nations have not only *one* youth, not only *one* age. Their autumn may be followed by a summer."[31] In this context, Beck Lassen tried to combine some considerations by Reinhart Koselleck and Hans Blumenberg. He notes:

"Metaphors circumscribe a troublesome reality by indicating an '*Erwartungshorizont*' within which one can begin to imagine ways of thinking and acting."[32]

Moreover, "they make the world seem coherent", and also have "the ability [...] to establish likenesses where these might not exist [...] [and] to postulate connections in the world".[33]

But one can hardly overestimate the meaning of metaphors since they invoke "conventionalised schemes" and "fulfil far-reaching structuring,

---

27 Representations of weaknesses are not only expressed by images and concepts. They can also possess a corporeal or spatial dimension that a comprehensive analysis has to consider.
28 Beck Lassen (2010), *Metaphorically Speaking*, 64.
29 Demandt (1979), *Metaphern*, 449.
30 A classic account on the creative function of metaphors, see Ricœur (1975), *Métaphore*; see, also, Lakoff et al. (1980), *Metaphors*.
31 Valentin (1939), *Weltgeschichte*, 16.
32 Beck Lassen (2010), *Metaphorically Speaking*, 65.
33 Beck Lassen (2010), *Metaphorically Speaking*, 65.

narrative, and constructive functions".[34] Thus, as Nünning exemplifies, the metaphor of "crisis" not only connects notions of the course of disease and roles, such as physicians and patients, within a context of beginning, development, and a coherent end, but "also past, present, and future are merged within an overarching plot".[35] Here, prior aberrations, a present exigency for decision-making, and a thus specified future development process are inextricably interconnected. However, it needs to be stressed that the chosen metaphor has a structuring but not a determining function:

> "The spectrum of possibilities ranges from the extreme of recovery or even improvement to versions of sitting it out and twiddling one's thumbs in the middle (which usually leads to an aggravation and worsening of the crisis) right to the other extreme of death and destruction, which can befall both individuals and the Roman Empire as the result of a crisis."[36]

This relationship elucidates that metaphors are neither interchangeable nor fixed in their meaning. For one, it matters hugely whether one imagines the Ottoman Empire as a "sick man", China as a melon—to be divided amongst the colonial powers—or Europe as an abducted Phoenician princess, because these expressions evoke certain plot structures and a specific framing. For another, established representations present the opportunity—in fact, they downright provoke it—to reject, to change, or to refer to these representations themselves. This can be best illustrated with the example of the *Kaiserbild*.

IV. Re-Fixations and Transformation: The Emperor's Painting "Peoples of Europe" as an Icon and Slogan

As already mentioned above, the painting entitled "Peoples of Europe, Guard Your Most Sacred Possessions!" had been sketched by Wilhelm II in 1895 during the time of the Sino-Japanese War. It is likely that horror stories by the former envoy Max von Brandt may have upset the emperor and inspired him to draw the sketch.[37] In a letter to Tsar Nicholas II, to

---

34 Nünning (2007), *Grundzüge*, 65; see, also, Hoffmann-Rehnitz (2016), *Unwahrscheinlichkeit*, 179–185.
35 Nünning (2007), *Grundzüge*, 66; see, essentially, White (1973), *Metahistory*.
36 Nünning (2009), *Steps*, 246.
37 See Gollwitzer (1962), *Gefahr*, 204–206; Mehnert (1995), *Gefahr*, 113.

whom he immediately sent a copy, Wilhelm explained that the Archangel Michael would convoke the European powers:

"in order to call for resistance against the invasion of Buddhism, heathenism and barbarism to unite for the defence of the holy cross. Particular emphasis is put on the united resistance of *all* European powers that is as righteous as necessary even against our inner enemies: anarchism, republicanism, nihilism."[38]

The weaknesses described here are the disunity amongst the Europeans and the under-estimation of the thus enabled threat. The corrective is a united Europe under German or, more precisely, Prussian, leadership.[39] In this regard, Gassert explains how the invoked enemy image "telescopically" reduces the spatial distance of the threat and thus justifies the European intervention in Asia as a "pre-emptive defence" (*Vornewegverteidigung*).[40] From a narratological perspective, this holds true in relation to the temporal distance, too, since the feared "invasion" of Europe by the East had neither already taken place nor was to be immediately expected; it was, therefore, a mobilising and emotionalising projection of future expectations. This applies to the slogan as well as to the painting. Because of the apparent "intellectual simplicity"[41] and the symbolic overload of the representation even contemporaries had difficulties in taking the image seriously. Several members of the German Foreign Office were not happy about the emperor's artistic and political ambitions, nor did they like the prospect of having to present lithographs or paintings of the "Peoples of Europe" as gifts to foreign governments.[42] Historians, too, are interested in how the emperor managed to instrumentalise the "Yellow Peril" for devising his personal *Weltpolitik*.[43] Heinz Gollwitzer already emphasised that Wilhelm II could claim only "indirect authorship",[44] at best, of the phrase of the "Yellow Peril", despite allegedly having claimed in front of his dentist of being

---

38 Wilhelm II to Nicholas II, 6.9.1895, printed in: von Gerlach (1920), *Briefe*, 8 f.
39 Galle (2002), *Erzengel*, 143, thinks it possible that the emperor has represented himself "to a certain degree" in the figure. Furthermore, Archangel Michael is a classical element of Prussian-Hohenzollern memory culture in the nineteenth century, for example as dragon slayer of the revolution in 1848/49.
40 Gassert (2007), *Völker Europas*, 281f.
41 Gassert (2007), *Völker Europas*, 282; Gollwitzer (1962), *Gefahr* 206.
42 For example, Mehnert (1995), *Gefahr*.
43 See Gollwitzer (1962), *Gefahr*, 206, who entitles the corresponding chapter "Geopolitical Manipulation through a Catch Phrase" ("Weltpolitische Manipulation mit dem Schlagwort").
44 Gollwitzer (1962), *Gefahr*, 42f.

the original inventor of the slogan.[45] It is more probable that, on this occasion, the emperor was referring to his painting. With regard to representations of weakness, a passage of the Hale interview of 1908 is particularly revealing, since it deals with the relationship of the concept and image as well as the special disposition and the "*Erwartungshorizont*" of the cartoon:

"How long was it that I painted my picture of the yellow peril? [...] Mark you, nobody else painted a prophesy, nobody ever put a prophesy down, not merely in black and white, but in unmistakable colours. I do not speak in oracular verse. There was nothing sibylline, nor enigmatic, nor ambiguous in my prophecy [!]. There could be only one interpretation. I painted it on canvas. Words may be misunderstood but the eye makes no mistake about what it sees boldly represented. So I painted the yellow peril. That was fifteen years ago. I dare say the world smiled."

Convinced that history had proven him right, he added:

"The world does not smile now."[46]

First, it is noteworthy that Wilhelm II praises himself for his particular prophetic insight, but denies its characteristic openness to interpretation and declares it to be an unambiguous prognosis. Also, considering words to be misleading, he implies that he highlights the primordial character of his own picture *vis-à-vis* the "Yellow Peril" slogan.[47] Moreover, he emphasises that the reception of "Peoples of Europe" was not euphoric at all, and, accordingly, stylises himself as an unrecognised prophet. The history of the diffusion and reception of the image illustrates, in fact, how the picture and slogan changed in many ways.[48] Numerous caricatures reveal that ever more interpretations, appropriations, and reactions were possible. As already mentioned, the Foreign Office was quite aware that the public

---

45 Davis (1918), *Kaiser*, 102.
46 Notes by William Bayard Hales on his interview with Emperor William II, 19.7.1908, see: Winzen (2002), *Kaiserreich*, 344–348, 344.
47 Without a reference to the concept of "yellow peril", he maintained in a speech in front of the troops in the year 1900 to have drawn a sketch, but not to have written a treatise: "Ich beabsichtigte vor vier Jahren der Welt durch meine Zeichnung 'Völker Europas wahret eure heiligsten Güter', da sich die Worte zu leicht verwischen, einen Fingerzeigzugeben, aber meine Warnungen blieben unbeachtet." Klaußmann (1902), *Kaiserreden*, 360.
48 The following remarks reconstruct this process with selected European examples to illustrate the transformation of representations. They are restricted, therefore, to the reception and diffusion in Europe. For a brief insight to the Japanese reception, see Ilkura (2006), *Yellow Peril*, 86 f.

comments by the "media monarch" were politically hazardous. It therefore tried to prevent their diffusion or to control their reception, an undertaking that could barely succeed in the incipient age of the mass media.[49] In what follows, I will restrict myself to outlining the possible scope of the discursive transformation of representations of weakness by providing some examples; to elucidate this further, I present four (ideal-) typical modes of medial re-fixation which are distinct with regard to the intentions of their authors: 1. Reproduction; 2. de-contextualisation and montage; 3. caricature and persiflage; and 4. fragmentation.

1. Reproduction

Reproduction does not simply mean to copy but is necessarily accompanied by an interpretation process and thus always possesses a creative dimension. This holds true all the more so as the temporal and spatial context confers specific new meanings to the reproduction itself, which does not, at least not knowingly, contradict the—more or less assumed—intention of the author. Just a few examples should suffice to illustrate this.

At the end of the year 1898, the founder of the British "Japan Society", Arthur Diósy, printed the image of the emperor with his consent as a frontispiece in his book entitled *The New Far East*.[50] Although the personal signature of the emperor was missing, the caption identifies the image—arguably, for the first time—as "The Yellow Peril (The German Version)".

---

49 Regarding foreign politics, see Geppert (2007), *Pressekriege*; with a focus on the emperor's films, see Petzold (2012), *Kaiser und das Kino*.
50 Diósy (1898), *New Far East*, 331.

THE YELLOW PERIL.
(THE GERMAN VERSION.)

Figure 2: Yellow Peril. The German version (Source: Diósy, The New Far East, 1898)

At this point, this might have been in accordance with the original purpose of its creator, but it explicitly emphasised the reference to Asia.[51] In contrast, the drift of the original was defined by its appeal to the European nations *vis-à-vis* a rather vague threat. Neither the emperor nor Hermann Knackfuß had only the East in mind, but also explicitly referred to the "inner enemies" of Wilhelminism.[52] Soon, this original intention faded in Germany, too. Instead, Asia became more important. The sketch, for instance, was distributed among the German troops on the occasion of the

---

51 Wilhelm expressed his joy, for instance, in a letter to the tsar in 1907 about the fact that English newspapers had "used for the first time the expression yellow peril *from my picture* that will become true" ("zum ersten mal den Ausdruck gelbe Gefahr *von meinem Bild* gebraucht, das wahr werden wird." Highlighted in the original, Gollwitzer (1962), *Gefahr*, 212.

52 See the letter to Nicholas II mentioned above and a clarification by Hermann Knackfuß in *The Times*, 11 December 1895, 4: Aside from the "power of destructive force (as symbolised by the dragon)", the Buddha stands for "the danger for European civilisations arising from tendencies hostile or indifferent to Christianity, [...] not only in its Asiatic essential form, but also, and more especially, in the widespread transference of its ideas to European thought".

so-called "Hun Speech". In his address, the emperor appealed to his soldiers in a warlike manner to revenge the murder of the German minister in Beijing in the wake of the Boxer Rebellion. The infamous call of "No Pardon will be given" (*Pardon wird nicht gegeben*) thus found its way into the sketch.[53] Notwithstanding this, pacifists who campaigned for a "United States of Europe" continued to interpret the image in a Eurocentric fashion. For the influential journalist William Thomas Stead, it symbolised not an Asian threat scenario, but the desired "Federation of Europe". He printed it several times in his journal *Review of Reviews* and even hung the painting on the walls of his editorial office.[54] In addition, Nobel Peace Prize laureate Alfred Hermann Fried stylised Wilhelm II as a "peace-emperor" (*Friedens-Kaiser*), prior to the First World War. Thus, it is only with historical hindsight that Stead's eulogy seems absurd.[55] He believed it possible that Wilhelm II, "who more than any other ruler is saturated with the spirit and genius of our time", would also devise an allegory of a united Europe:

"It may be that as the artist whose pencil first portrays the symbolic figure of the Federated Continent, William the Second may render better service to the United States of Europe than by anything which he may do as German Emperor."[56]

2. De-Contextualisation and Montage

In the case of the title, it is apparent that it evolved to become a slogan. It soon symbolised not only the European fear of the "Yellow Peril", but also resulted in many other contexts of meaning.[57] This applied, for instance, to Bertha von Suttner, who had gladly picked up on the emperor's word (*Kaiserwort*) and re-interpreted the appeal into a pacifist call to arms: "Unite to guard the most sacred possessions!" (*Vereinigt Euch zum Schutz heiligster Güter!*)—from the perspective of the Nobel Peace Prize laureate, this common struggle was to be re-directed against the "Dragon of War"

---

53 See Röhl (2009), *Wilhelm II. vol. II*, 111.
54 See Stead (1904), *Asia*, 551. The former prime minister of Japan, Itō Hirobumi, may have seen it in Mowbray House, see Ilkura (2006), *Yellow Peril*, 86.
55 Fried (1910), *Kaiser*, II.
56 Stead (1897), *United States of Europe*, 18.
57 On its function, see Gollwitzer (1962), *Gefahr*, 5–10.

(*dem Drachen Krieg*).[58] Furthermore, publishers and writers, in particular around the turn of the century, used this appeal as a patriotic slogan to distribute propagandistic colportage literature, for example, in the context of the Boxer Rebellion.[59] The futuristic war fantasy "Peoples of Europe…—the War of the Future" (*Völker Europas…—Der Krieg der Zukunft*) is also indicative of the slogan's wide distribution since it contents itself only to hint at the *Kaiserwort* in the title. Similar to a considerable number of like-minded publications, the book concludes that the foundation of the "United States of Europe" "brings the yellow as well as the transatlantic world threat to an abrupt end".[60] In order to bid for public attention, the appeal "Peoples of Europe, Guard Your Most Sacred Possessions!" could be used in very different contexts that had nothing to do with the "Yellow Peril" or with Asia in general or even war itself. In the year 1900, for example, the "Monthly Journal of the German Youth Welfare" (*Monatsjournal der deutschen Jugendfürsorge*) chose it as its motto. Further varieties of applying the slogan were demonstrated during the monarch's journey to Palestine in 1898: it was easy to declare the "holy city" of Jerusalem as the actual object of the "most sacred possessions".

A corresponding postcard illustrates not only a view of the city and the portrait of the emperor, it also cites parts of the iconography of the archetype in putting a rocky prong in the foreground. In addition, Wilhelm's handwritten signature, this time set into the picture, clearly refers to the *Kaiserbild* and stylises the Hohenzollern as the patron saint of Christendom.

---

58 Suttner (1917), *Kampf*, 263.
59 The Berlin based publisher Weichert, for example, used it to advertise, among others, the novel "Die düsteren Geheimnisse des chinesischen Kaiserhauses oder die Totenmauern von Peking"; see Liu (2007), *Exklusion*, 126.
60 Bleibtreu (1906), *Völker Europas*, 657.

Figure 3: Postcard from Jerusalem 1898 (Source: Claude W. Sui: Die Reise ins Heilige Land und die Photographie im 19. Jahrhundert. In: Alfried Wieczorek (ed.) Ins Heilige Land. Pilgerstätten von Jerusalem bis Mekka und Medina, Mannheim 2006, p. 19)

3. Caricature and Persiflage

In hindsight, many of the examples mentioned may seem irritating, even comical. They should, however, be distinguished from those works that genuinely intended to mock the Kaiser's work of art. Generally, this mode can be targeted to criticise a concrete representation, to reveal its narrative and weak points, or to move the theme into a different light. Otherwise, it can also be about removing the object of the caricature from the realm of what is sayable and suppressing a discourse about a certain topic. As the career of the emperor's painting impressively shows, this rarely proved to be a particularly successful strategy, since the medial diffusion massively increased attention. With regard to the numerous caricatures, one can assert that "the painting and its concomitant rhetoric became enduring symbols of the Yellow Peril"—probably not *despite*, but *because of* "being almost immediately adapted by satirical magazines".[61] The inversion of the threat scenario, for instance, was widely diffused in this context as well as an expression of a more or less explicit critique of European imperialism.

Figure 4: Confucius: "Volkeren van Azie, verdedigt uwe heilige goederen!" (Source: Amsterdammer Weekblad 24.6.1900, p. 10A)

Against the background of the Boxer Rebellion, a Dutch caricature focuses on a group of Asians that observe a gunboat, with Uncle Sam and his European counterparts aboard, approaching the coast under the sign of a Christian cross.[62] Remarkably, this interpretation, although of European origin, might have corresponded to the Japanese self-image since it found its way into the Japanese daily *Yomiuri Shimbun*.[63] One could easily vary the motive of the peoples threatened by European imperialism in directing the appeal to the "Peoples of Africa".[64] It was furthermore consistent when caricaturists devoted their attention to the "most sacred possessions", a phrase that remained open to interpretation: for the satirical magazine "*Simplicissimus*", for example, these were being returned to the European

---

61 Klein (2015), *Yellow Peril*, 8.
62 See, also, Lehner (2013), *Bild vom Anderen*.
63 See Weber (2015), *Same Race*, 163–164.
64 See "Völker Afrikas, wahrt eure heiligsten Güter", Der Wahre Jacob 13 (1896) 265, 2278.

powers in the form of cannonballs.[65] The author of a contribution in the magazine *"Jugend"* appealed to East Asian people to protect their original way of life against the "blessings" of European "culture": alcohol and shares; insurance salesmen and vegetarians.[66] Even when their intentions contradicted the emperor's mentality, the satirical critique nonetheless reproduced the original plot structure as well as the threat scenario in which Asians and Europeans saw themselves confronting each other as distinct groups. Notably, it was caricatures and literary parodies in the first instance, not the originals, which retained the image and the slogan within the public sphere for so many decades.

4. Fragmentation

Over the years and with the growing distance from the debates at the turn of the century, the reference to the "Peoples of Europe" lost its focus; its image and appeal became fragments of a failed discourse of weakness. The superficial references and quotations no longer drew direct connections to the "Yellow Peril" threat of the turn of the century or to Wilhelm's prediction. Instead, they became separated from the initial problematisation. Particularly during World War I, Wilhelm's "Peoples of Europe" experienced a somewhat strange revival. Even if well-informed contemporaries might have known about its original context and its creator, the authors did not reveal it. Such circumstances failed to become a relevant subject of public debate. Like many advocates of European collaboration from the turn of the century, Dutch pacifists in 1915 marked a federation of European states as "a last resort" against the looming downfall of Europe.[67] Near the end of the pamphlet, published in multiple languages, appears the emancipatory appeal:

"Peoples of Europe! Do you want to protect your holiest possessions? Protect them together. […] If you want to live as free, noble human beings, then do not tolerate that diplomats commanding you like slaves, do not tolerate militarism agitating you against each other like wild animals. It is in your power […]."[68]

---

65 Printed in Gassert (2007), *Gefahr*, 287.
66 "Völker Ostasiens, wahret eure heiligsten Güter", Die Jugend 1 (1896) 5, 76.
67 See Seidl (2018), *Kassandra*.
68 Suchtelen (1915), *Rettung*, 7: "Völker von Europa! Wollt Ihr eure heiligsten Güter schützen? Schützt sie gemeinschaftlich. […] Wollt ihr leben als freie, edle Menschen, so dul-

Even more impressive is the illustration on a poster of the *"Verein Osthilfe"* that shows how the *Kaiserbild* is adopted as a fragment to instrumentalise single elements without context.

At the turn of the year 1918/19, after the abdication of the emperor, the poster presents, "loosely based upon the popular painting", a seemingly charred section in which Archangel Michael points to a skull amidst the plumes of smoke. The German, English, and French appeal, which had already appeared in this form in printed lithographs around the year 1900, was now directed against Bolshevism and warns of a "slaves' peace" (*Sklavenfrieden*). "It will further break down the dam in the East and plunge the whole of Europe into chaos!" Those who remembered that the cited artist was hardly innocent of the continent's current state may have held the poster to be the "genuinely grotesque act of a political fool".[69]

---

det nicht, dass Diplomaten über Euch verfügen wie über Sklaven, duldet nicht, dass der Militarismus Euch gegeneinander hetzt wie wilde Tiere. Es steht in Eurer Macht […]."
69 Meyer (1919), *Wettbewerbs-Hochflut*, 200.

Figure 5. Poster 1918/19: Osthilfe e.V. "Völker Europas, wahrt eure heiligsten Güter" (Source: Deutsches Historisches Museum / I. Desnica)

V. Conclusion

When Wilhelm II created the "Peoples of Europe", he had perhaps intended to project his genuinely felt concerns onto the canvas. By distributing the painting to the Western courts and governments and diffusing it in the public sphere, it became apparent that his desire was to pursue his own *Weltpolitik*. Bearing the contradictory history of its reception and diffusion in mind, one comes to the conclusion that the emperor failed in his undertaking to instrumentalise the Western fear of the "Yellow Peril" for his own purposes. The strategy showed its limitations not only with other actors, such as critics of imperialism and pacifists, using the image and slogan to promote their own interests. Like all representations of weakness, *Kaiserbild* and *Kaiserwort* opened up a wide spectrum of possibilities. In contrast to what was originally intended, this spectrum made other remedies seem sensible and appropriate with regard to the problem presented. Thus, the advocates of a democratic variant of the "United States of Europe" could invoke the emperor even though they were viewed prior to this as quixotic idealists. Since the function of diagnoses of weakness is to incite, to emotionalise, and to mobilise, they develop a momentum which often runs counter to the original intentions of their authors. In this regard, the applied metaphors possess a key function, since they evoke a whole spectrum of possible interpretations and basically do not rule out misunderstandings or contradictory usages. Against this background, Oswald Spengler had already bemoaned "people that confused the decline of the ancient world with the sinking of an ocean liner".[70] It was this kind of confusion that promoted historical change induced by diagnoses of weakness and not just when the initially proposed therapy was successfully implemented. Instead, they prove effective when they are understood differently, caricaturized, or taken out of context:

> "A philosophy reappears as an ideology; a party slogan as a heuristic device of high scientific value."[71]

While John Pocock referred to political ideas, this could also be a call to question allegedly incontestable facts. Even though authors complain about being misunderstood or wrongly quoted, a 'misinterpretation' is not

---

[70] Spengler (1924), *Pessimismus?*, 3–4: "Menschen, die den Untergang der Antike mit dem Untergang eines Ozeandampfers verwechseln."
[71] Pocock (2009), *History*, 5–6.

simply a false statement, but rather part of a discursive transformation. This is even more true for an attribution of weakness whose figurative dimension not only allows for, but often causes, an ambivalent interpretation. Thus, representations of weakness significantly contribute to the creative dimension of discourses of weakness which therefore seldomly lead to an intended or expected outcome. Hence, analysing them allows a look behind the scenes of historical change.

Literature

Bacchi, Carol (2009). *Analysing Policy: What's the Problem Represented to Be?*. Frenchs Forest: Pearson Education Australia.
Bacchi, Carol (2012). Why Study Problematizations? Making Politics Visible. *Open Journal of Political Science*, 2 (1), 1–8.
Beck Lassen, Frank (2010). "Metaphorically Speaking" – Begriffsgeschichte and Hans Blumenberg's Metaphorologie. In Riccardo Pozzo et al. (eds.). *Eine Typologie der Formen der Begriffsgeschichte*, 53-70. Hamburg: Meiner.
Bleibtreu, Karl [pseudonym] (1906). *Völker Europas… – Der Krieg der Zukunft*. Berlin: R. Bong.
Bublitz, Hannelore (2010). *Im Beichtstuhl der Medien: Die Produktion des Selbst im öffentlichen Bekenntnis*. Bielefeld: transcript.
Davis, Arthur N. (1918). *The Kaiser as I Know Him*. New York: Harper & Brothers.
Demandt, Alexander (1979). *Metaphern für Geschichte: Sprachbilder und Gleichnisse im historisch-politischen Denken*. Munich: C.H. Beck.
— (2015). *Der Fall Roms. Die Auflösung des römischen Reiches im Urteil der Nachwelt*. Munich: C.H. Beck.
Diósy, Arthur (1898). *The New Far East*. London: The British Library.
Fischer-Lichte, Erika (2004). *Ästhetik des Performativen*. Frankfurt/M.: Suhrkamp.
Foucault, Michel (1984). Polemics, Politics, and Problematization: An Interview. In Paul Rabinow (ed.). *The Foucault Reader*, 381-90. New York: Pantheon Books.
— (1988). The Concern for Truth. In Michel Foucault. *Politics, Philosophy, Culture. Interviews and Other Writings 1977–1984* (transl. Alan Sheridan and others, ed. Lawrence D. Kritzman), 255-70. New York: Routledge.
— (2005). Die Sorge um die Wahrheit. In Daniel Defert and François Ewald (eds.). *Schriften in vier Bänden. Dits et Écrits*, vol. 4, 823-36. Frankfurt/M.: Suhrkamp.
Fried, Alfred H. (1910). *Der Kaiser und der Weltfrieden*. Berlin: Maritima.
Galle, Maja (2002). *Der Erzengel Michael in der deutschen Kunst des 19. Jahrhunderts*. Munich: Utz.

Gassert, Philipp (2007). "Völker Europas, wahrt Eure heiligsten Güter": Die Alte Welt und die Japanische Herausforderung. In Maik Hendrik Sprotte, Wolfgang Seifert and Heinz-Dietrich Löwe (eds.). *Der Russisch-Japanische Krieg 1904/05: Anbruch einer neuen Zeit?*, 277-93. Wiesbaden: Harrassowitz.

Gerlach, Hellmuth von (1920). *Briefe und Telegramme Wilhelms II an Nikolaus II. (1894-1914)*. Vienna: Meyer & Jessen.

Geppert, Dominik (2007). *Pressekriege. Öffentlichkeit und Diplomatie in den deutschbritischen Beziehungen 1896–1912*. Munich: De Gruyter Oldenbourg.

Gollwitzer, Heinz (1962). *Die Gelbe Gefahr. Geschichte eines Schlagworts*. Munich: Vandenhoeck & Ruprecht.

Gutsche, Verena (2015). *"Niedergang". Variationen und Funktionen eines kulturkritischen Diskurselements zwischen 1900 und 1930. Großbritannien und Deutschland im Vergleich*. Würzburg: Königshausen & Neumann.

Hannig, Nicolai (2018). Kalkulierte Gefahren. Naturkatastrophen und Prävention seit 1800. Unpublished habilitation treatise. Munich.

Hashimoto, Yorimitsu (2008). *The 'Yellow Peril'. Anglo-Japanese Perspective 1893–1913*. Dissertation University of Lancaster.

Hoffmann-Rehnitz, Philip (2016). Zur Unwahrscheinlichkeit der Krise in der Frühen Neuzeit. Niedergang, Krise und gesellschaftliche Selbstbeschreibung in innerstädtischen Auseinandersetzungen nach dem Dreißigjährigen Krieg am Beispiel Lübecks. In Rudolf Schlögl et al. (eds.). *Die Krise in der Frühen Neuzeit*. Göttingen: Vandenhoeck & Ruprecht. 169–208.

Kingdon, John. W. (2003). *Agendas, Alternatives, and Public Policies*. Harlow: Pearson Education Limited.

Klaußmann, A. Oskar (ed.). (1902). *Kaiserreden. Reden und Erlasse, Briefe und Telegramme Kaiser Wilhelms II*. Leipzig: J.J. Weber.

Klein, Thoralf (2015). The "Yellow Peril". In European History Online (EGO), published by the Leibniz Institute of European History (IEG), Mainz 2015-10-15. URL: http://www.ieg-ego.eu/kleint-2015-en URN: urn:nbn:de:0159-2015100627 [2018-03-26].

Klöppel, Ulrike (2010). Foucaults Konzept der Problematisierungsweise und die Analyse diskursiver Transformationen. In Achim Landwehr (ed.). *Diskursiver Wandel*, 255-63. Wiesbaden: VS Verlag.

Lakoff, George, and Mark Johnson (1980). *Metaphors We Live By*. Chicago: University of Chicago Press.

Lehner, Monika (2013). Das Bild vom Anderen: "Gelbe Gefahr" – "Weiße Gefahr". In Mind the Gap(s), China-Bilder im Wandel der Zeit URL: https://www.mindthegaps.hypotheses.org/873 [2018-03-26]

Lenger, Friedrich, and Ansgar Nünning (2009). Einleitung. Medienereignisse der Moderne. In: Friedrich Lenger and Ansgar Nünning (eds.). *Medienereignisse der Moderne*, 7-13. Darmstadt: WBG.

Leppin, Hartmut, and Christian A. Müller (2017). Discourses of Weakness and Resource Regimes: Preliminary Remarks on a New Research Design. In Anke

K. Scholz and Martin Bartelheim, Roland Hardenberg, Jörn Staecker (eds.). *ResourceCultures. Sociocultural Dynamics and the Use of Resources—Theories, Methods, Perspectives* (Ressourcen Kulturen, vol. 5), 45–55. Tübingen: Universität Tübingen.

Likura, Akira (2006). The "Yellow Peril" and its influence on Japanese-German Relations. In: Christian W. Spang, Rolf-Harald Wippich (eds.). *Japanese-German Relations 1895–1945. War, Diplomacy and Public Opinion*, 80-98. New York: Routledge.

Liu, Weijian (2007). *Kulturelle Exklusion und Identitätsentgrenzung: zur Darstellung Chinas in der deutschen Literatur 1870–1930*. Bern: Peter Lang.

Mehnert, Ute (1995). *Deutschland, Amerika und die "gelbe Gefahr". Zur Karriere eines Schlagworts in der Großen Politik 1905–1917*. Stuttgart: Franz Steiner.

Meyer, Hans (1919). Wettbewerbs-Hochflut. *Das Plakat*, 10, 1.

Nünning, Ansgar (2009). Steps Towards a Metaphorology (and Narratology) of Crises: On the Functions of Metaphors as Figurative Knowledge and Mininarrations. In Herbert Grabes et al. (eds.). *Metaphors: Shaping Culture and Theory*, 229-62. Tübingen: Narr.

— (2007). Grundzüge einer Narratologie der Krise. Wie aus einer Situation ein Plot und eine Krise (konstruiert) werden. In Henning Grundwald, Manfred Pfister (eds.). *Krisis! Krisenszenarien, Diagnosen und Diskursstrategien*, 48–71. Munich: Wilhelm Fink.

Pernau, Margit (2012). *Transnationale Geschichte*, Göttingen: Vandenhoeck & Ruprecht.

Pocock, John G.A. (2009 [1962]). The History of Political Thought. A Methodological Enquiry. In John G.A. Pocock (ed.). *Political Thought and History: Essays on Theory and Method*. Cambridge: Cambridge University Press.

Ricœur, Paul (1975). *La Métaphore vive*. Paris: Le Seuil.

Röhl, John. C. (2009). *Wilhelm II. – Der Aufbau der Persönlichen Monarchie 1888–1900*. 2nd edition. Munich: C.H. Beck.

— (2009). *Wilhelm II. – Der Weg in den Abgrund 1900–1941*. 2nd edition. Munich: C.H. Beck.

Schmidt-Glintzer, Helwig (2014). Die gelbe Gefahr. *Zeitschrift für Ideengeschichte*, 8, 1, 43–58.

Seidl, Klaus (2018). Kassandra und Europa. Niedergangsdiskurse und Europäisierung im 20. Jahrhundert. In Fanny Platelle and Hélène Roth (eds.). *Le déclin dans le monde germanique. Mots, discours et représentations (1914-2014)*, 267–293. Reims: Presses universitaires de Reims.

Spengler, Oswald (1924). *Pessimismus?*. Berlin: Georg Stilke.

Stead, William Thomas (1904). Asia as a Conqueror, *Review of Reviews*, June 1904, 550–559.

Stead, William Thomas (1897). The United States of Europe, *Review of Reviews*, July 1897, 16–29.

Steiner, Benjamin (2015). *Nebenfolgen in der Geschichte. Eine historische Soziologie reflexiver Modernisierung*. Berlin: De Gruyter Oldenbourg.

Suchtelen, Nico van (1915). *Die einzige Rettung. Ein europäischer Staatenbund.* Amsterdam.

Suttner, Bertha von (1917). *Der Kampf um die Vermeidung des Weltkriegs. Randglossen aus zwei Jahrzehnten zu den Zeitereignissen vor der Katastrophe* (ed. by Alfred H. Fried), Vol I. Zurich: Art. Institut Orell Füßli.

Weber, Torsten (2015). Same Race, Same Fate? Theories of Asian Commonality and the Shift of Regional Hegemony. In Volker Barth and Roland Cvetkovski (eds.): *Imperial Co-operation and Transfer 1870–1930: Empires and Encounters*, 153-70. London: Bloomsbury Academic.

White, Hayden (1973). *Metahistory. The Historical Imagination in Nineteenth-Century Europe.* Baltimore MD: John Hopkins University Press.

Winzen, Peter (2002). *Das Kaiserreich am Abgrund. Die Daily-Telegraph-Affäre und das Hale-Interview von 1908.* Stuttgart: Franz Steiner.

Chapter 3
Visions of Decline in Transhistorical Perspective: Narratives, Images, Effects

Nadine Eikelschulte, Philipp Höhn, Sebastian Riebold, Klaus Seidl, and David Weidgenannt

I. Introduction

"So what can you do to persuade people who believe that the end of the world is nigh that people from every past generation have seen it coming before they did? Do you say that it's a sort of recurrent dream, like the dream that our teeth are falling out or that we suddenly find ourselves naked in the middle of the street? No, they'd reply, this time it's more important than all the other times."[1]

The seemingly eternal laments over the imminent demise of all that we hold true and dear are a constant companion to history, and not just in the eyes of Umberto Eco. Quite to the contrary, visions concerning the end of the world, the decline of a once glorious empire, or the downfall of cities, states or families are (and always have been) so ubiquitous in history that it is all too easy for historians to brush them off, often not without ridiculing them in the process.

It ought to be more promising to approach these "Visions of Decline" (as the authors of this chapter have chosen to call them)[2] instead as mean-

---

[1] Eco et al. (1999), *Conversations*, 181. Eco's scepticism towards apocalyptic visions is well established. In one of his earliest works on cultural criticism (Apocalittici e integrati, 1964), he differentiates (overly simplified, as he himself concedes) between "apocalyptic" and "integrated" intellectuals and analyses their respective attitudes toward "mass culture". The former "ostentatiously rejects" whereas the latter "accepts and builds on" the new world of mass culture (Eco (1994), *Apocalyptic and Integrated Intellectuals*, 17–19). Most illuminating for the present discussion is Eco's characterisation of apocalyptic intellectuals as figures attempting to "obstruct argument" and "straitjacketing discussion in emotional reaction" (Eco (1994), *Apocalyptic and Integrated Intellectuals*, 20). As we will argue in the conclusion, a similar observation can be made with regard to Visions of Decline. Note on translation: All translations are our own, unless noted otherwise.

[2] "Vision of Decline" is treated as a technical term in this chapter and conventionally capitalised.

ingful historical phenomena precisely because they may be found in virtually any historical context, albeit with different modifications. With "vision" (from the German *Vorstellung*), we have opted for a term which is largely devoid of theoretical "baggage" (as opposed to "semantics" or "discourses", to name but a few).[3] This has enabled us to cast our net wide and to first establish, within the scope of feasibility, a broad empirical basis. At the same time, "vision" highlights the constructed, even imaginary nature of the discursive structures under investigation here, and already hints at the fact that they constitute more than mere lamentations; they point to ways out of the perceived predicament—they offer *visions*. Since our respective sources are rather diverse and generally not strictly "narrative" in nature, "vision" offers the additional benefit of including "decline-talk" that is not embedded in a story.

It is the aim of this chapter to offer a panoramic sketch of a variety of specific ways in which "decline" was conceptualised and instrumentalised in different places at different times. In this fashion, we hope to demonstrate that inquiries into Visions of Decline are worthwhile endeavours, as they hint at the answers to different historical challenges and thus constitute useful points of comparison in transhistorical research.

It is not our intention to delineate an evolutionary trajectory of Visions of Decline from ancient Egypt until the modern period (and indeed, the case studies do not follow a strict chronological order). In other words, this chapter is not primarily concerned with the "history of decline" but with "decline in history". The authors make an attempt to shine a spotlight onto certain transhistorically observable recurring elements and characteristics that commonly emerge when decline (still looming or already come to pass) becomes a topic of discussion.

Against this backdrop, it is serviceable first to outline briefly the ways in which historians have, up to now, endeavoured to come to grips with the complex issue of decline. Even such a rudimentary overview will be sufficient to show that dismissive evaluations of the kind that Umberto Eco offered in the introductory quotation do not do justice to the phe-

---

3 "Semantics" is commonly associated with Luhmannian systems theory. In addition, "discourse" is reserved for the overall theoretical framework of CRC 1095. As not all the projects represented in this chapter employ "discourse" as a central working concept, we chose to coin a new term through which to approach our respective case studies, rather than imposing a pre-existing concept on the diverse source material assembled in the present chapter.

nomenon. It does not suffice to locate Visions of Decline among bizarre dreams and unsurmountable traumata.[4]

Studies from the field of intellectual history tend to stress continuities in narratives of decline, disregard shifts and ruptures, and overall fail to contextualise such narratives properly.[5] Conceptual history (*Begriffsgeschichte*), on the other hand, emphasises the multifaceted genealogy of the notion of decline. The eminent exponent of conceptual history, the Bielefeld historian Reinhart Koselleck (1923–2006), for instance, analysed the historical development of the relationship between "progress" (*Fortschritt*) and "decline" (*Niedergang*). He argued that these had been "successive concepts" (*Sukzessionsbegriffe*) and "counter concepts" (*Gegenbegriffe*) in antiquity, and were transformed into "concepts of correlation" (*Korrelationsbegriffe*) within the framework of the medieval recension of Plato's two-worlds ontology. During the course of the Enlightenment, a marked asymmetry developed between the two (to the detriment of "decline", not surprisingly).[6] "Progress" has, according to Koselleck, since advanced to become a modern "processual concept of reflexion" (*prozessualer Reflexionsbegriff*), whereas "decline" has shed neither its natural nor its biological implications. Nor does it offer a comparable "open future horizon" (*offenen Zukunftshorizont*). In the modern period, "decline" features solely as the "aporia of progress or the reproduction of decline by progress itself". More specifically, in the twentieth century, "decline", as Koselleck understands it, appears to us in the guise of acute disaster risk.[7]

If we were to follow Koselleck, the concept of Visions of Decline could not hope to inspire a historical formation to shape its future constructively and purposefully. Biological processes of decline (such as decay, withering, or aging) are, after all, irreversible. However, we will argue that this assessment falls short of providing a full picture of Visions of Decline, and "decay" will emerge as but one of their possible modes.

The philosophy of history, along with historical theory, in contrast, describes "decline" as a "world-historical category", which is, incidentally,

---

[4] See, also, Seidl (2018), *Kassandra und Europa*.
[5] See Herman (1998), *Propheten* (in original "The Idea of Decline in Western History"); Henschel (2010), *Menetekel*; Gutsche (2015), *Niedergang*; Pross (2013), *Dekadenz*.
[6] Koselleck (2006), *Fortschritt und Niedergang*, 163.
[7] Koselleck (2006), *Fortschritt und Niedergang*, 175.

precisely what Koselleck asserted that "decline" was not.[8] The *Annales*-historian Pierre Chaunu (1923–2009) thus emphasises:

"Decadence does not belong to anyone. It is enough to open one's eyes and take a look around. It is everywhere."[9]

Chaunu does not base his claims on an analysis of mentalities alone. Instead, he strives to award credence to his view by referring to ironclad physical laws. According to his understanding, Einstein's insights at the beginning of the twentieth century had conclusively proven the finite nature of the universe. This conviction enables him to interpret—as Oswald Spengler had done before him—the Second Law of Thermodynamics as a virtual "cosmic principle of decadence" (*principe de la decadence cosmique*).[10] Jeremy Rifkin, in his 1980s book entitled *Entropy*, conceives a similar "*New World View*" (as the subtitle has it).[11]

Such essentialist conceptions of decline are not only espoused by alarmist watchdogs that belong to the cultural-pessimist wing in social theory. Jürgen Kuczynski (1904–1997), for example, one of the most prominent scholars of the German Democratic Republic, followed an explicitly Marxist approach to history in his outline of a "comparative history of decline" (*vergleichende Niedergangsgeschichte*).[12] Similarly, biologist and geographer Jared Diamond took it upon himself to explain, using a broad range of historical cases, "why societies survive or perish (*warum Gesellschaften überleben oder untergehen*)".[13] Although he has a less dialectical take on the decline-phenomenon than Kuczynski, and approaches the topic with somewhat more optimism, to decline or not to decline ("collapse", in his terminology) is, for Diamond, ultimately a matter of "choice". It is not a pre-ordained destiny that decides a society's future.[14]

---

8 Koselleck (2006), *Fortschritt und Niedergang*, 171.
9 "La décadence n'est à personne. Il suffit d'ouvrir les yeux et de regarder autour de soi. Elle est partout." Chaunu (1981), *Histoire et Decadence*, 25–26.
10 Chaunu (1981), *Histoire et Decadence*. For the impact of thermodynamics, see Brush (1987), *Die Temperatur der Geschichte*.
11 Rifkin (1982), *Entropie*.
12 Kuczynski (1984), *Gesellschaften im Untergang*; see Demandt (2015), *Der Fall Roms*, 113–117.
13 Note the subtle but significant difference between the English and German subtitles. The original reads: "how societies choose to fail or succeed".
14 Diamond (2006), *Kollaps*. The issue of "determinism" versus "human determination" in turn-of-the-century Chinese political discourse is discussed by Pusey (1983), *China and Charles Darwin*, 50–58.

This chapter is far removed from the historical research based upon numerical data and statistics in which Diamond and his peers engage. In the context of this essay, Diamond's research is of interest—first of all—as a *recent instance* of a Vision of Decline, not a guideline as to how to approach the cultural phenomenon "decline".

The ruminations of theorists and historians such as those mentioned above are revealing even if one does not accept the premise of the "inevitable (eventual) downward trend" as a guiding principle of world history. The last two works which we have mentioned, in particular, already suggest that the analysis of processes of decline has to rely heavily on historical comparison. Indeed, we will show that Visions of Decline are inherently referential in nature.[15]

Conceptual history as well as the philosophy of history accentuate specific elements of narratives of decline and thus provide starting-points for our own investigations. In order to avoid the pitfalls of an all too narrow developmental history, on the one hand, as well as an essentialist bias, on the other, this chapter makes the case in favour of a more strongly cultural historical perspective. In this fashion, we hope to draw attention to the narrative, figurative, and performative dimensions of Visons of Decline.[16]

"Decline", and "Vision(s) of Decline", in the context of this chapter, serve as labels for a broad spectrum of semantically-related concepts and ideas that may be brought together under the umbrella of what Peter Burke termed a "change for the worse".[17] This "fuzziness" is already necessitated by the variety of (unrelated) languages in our source material. To mention just a few English-language examples, decline-terms include, but are certainly not limited to, demise, downfall, decline, decay, decadence, degeneration, autumn, dissolution, catastrophe, sickness, tragedy, collapse, and ruin. We do not *a priori* ascribe any special significance to the appearance of particular lexical items. When a turn-of-the-century Chinese author opts for *mieguo* ("destroy a state") rather than *wangguo* ("destroy a state", "lost state", among others),[18] the context will decide whether this may be treated as a stylistic choice or whether it must be seen as distinct encodings of distinct Visions of Decline—the former, if taken literally, implies utter

---

15 We discuss general characteristics of Visions of Decline in the conclusion.
16 For premodern history, see Jung (2012), *Zeichen des Verfalls*.
17 Burke (1976), *Tradition and Experience*, 138.
18 See Section V for a more detailed discussion of these terms and their possible translations.

"extinction", after all. We are therefore especially interested in the broader context in which the given decline-denoting linguistic items, the words, phrases, idioms, metaphors—collectively referred to here as "images"—appear, and the stories that they are used to tell. In this respect, our approach to the topic differs significantly from previous studies, as we will argue below.

Considering the semantic breadth of decline, which encompasses images of movement, biologistic (especially Darwinian) and medical imagery, as well as floral, theatrical, and architectural descriptions, it should be noted that all terms and phrases used to frame decline have to be treated as metaphors. A "decline diagnosis" does more than merely depict (in a descriptive fashion) the "change for the worse" in specific ways unique to the given context. It also strives to explain the mechanisms of change and points to possible remedies and corrective measures.

To ascribe and describe "decline" (that is, to offer a "decline diagnosis") is therefore never a sober, impersonal act guided by objectivity. In this respect, "decline" does not *per se* differ from "decadence", an ascription which has, at times, been characterised as inherently biased and laden with subjectivity.[19] Indeed, the key difference between the two terms seems to be that, in much of the existing literature, the former tends to reserve a higher degree of objectivity for itself in comparison to the latter. Neville Morley, professor for ancient history at the University of Exeter, for example, has underlined that, in both cases, the "diagnostician" has to make selections in order to deduce a general trend from individual, more or less measurable, aspects. Such a diagnosis always consists of a series of interpretative steps, each of which may be scrutinised and subjected to debate. Measurements, tables, charts, and statistics give the illusion of unassailability and are supposed to give an impression of the scientific, objective nature of the diagnosis, but do, in fact, have to be regarded as "rhetorical moves"[20] in critical analysis. In other words, to speak of "decline" is to make selections, to judge which factors are significant, and to present allegedly objective and generally applicable results based upon fragmentary data. Consider, for example, the "Failed States Index (FSI)" (now: Fragile States Index) published since 2005 by the think tank "Fund for Peace", a true masterpiece of number-based, objectivised decline ascription.[21] A

---

19 See, however, Section II of this chapter for a more nuanced view.
20 Morley (2004), *Decadence*, 576.
21 Messner et al. (2017), *Fragile States Index*.

critical (historical) analysis would be less interested in the feasibility of its methodology and would also have to do more than just reveal the sociocultural biases that underlie the report. It would, for instance, inquire into the diverse reception of the FSI in the "failed states" themselves and find out whether and, if so, how it features in internal narratives of decline. Is the tag "failed state" necessarily a bad thing? Or might it not be used for one's own political and propagandistic ends?

One might interject that some Visions of Decline have turned out to have been more accurate than others. For example, the demise of the Chinese Communist Party (CCP) has infamously been predicted (incorrectly, to the dismay of many observers) many times, ever since the end of Maoism in 1976.[22] The question of whether a prognosis is correct (rather than merely believable) is, however, irrelevant in the historical context in which it is originally conceived. This is because the accuracy of a prediction can only be made in retrospect and thus cannot inform past actions or decisions. In other words, it cannot *mobilise* resources in the past. "Decline", as it is understood here, is never essentialist decline. In this regard, our conception is certainly informed by the notion of "weakness" within CRC 1095.[23]

Furthermore, if we concede that Visions of Decline attempt to turn the "change for the worse" around, they are successful only to the degree to which they are, in the final analysis, incorrect.[24] Nevertheless, it is still worthwhile and necessary to expose the decidedly constructive nature of all decline diagnoses and to call into question all-too-common abstract categorisations such as subjective/objective or scientific/fictional.

In addition, the performative dimension of attributions of this nature needs to be emphasised. The choice of terminology, at least to a certain extent, pre-structures the manner in which the present is described or the future prognosticated. "Decline" has been conventionally reserved for gradual, slow working processes and structural causes, whereas the invocation of "decadence" tends to accentuate the proximate, socio-moralistic

---

22 Shambaugh (2016), *China's Future*, to name only the most recent publication.
23 The conviction that (possible) "changes for the worse" have to be treated as non-essentialist concepts is also shared by the increasing literature on the sociology of risk (Risikosoziologie) and related fields. See Fechner et al. (2014), *Bedrohungskommunikation*; Kasperson et al. (2005), *The Social Amplification of Risk*.
24 In the example above, this would imply that "doom-seers" may—to put it cynically—ironically have aided the CCP to stay in power.

reasons underlying a perceived "downward trend".[25] The key point is that such a clear-cut systematic distinction—and we have only discussed two of the more prominent ones (see the list above)—is hardly ever found in the relevant sources; at the very least, it cannot simply be pre-assumed to exist.

As a matter of fact, Edward Gibbon (1737–1794), in his magnum opus *The History of the Decline and Fall of the Roman Empire*, as well as Oswald Spengler (*The Decline of the West/Der Untergang des Abendlandes*, 1918)—who must be counted among the most prominent "prophets of decline" in the European context up to now—made it very clear that they understood *decline/Untergang* as metaphors, and thus did not fixate on their lexical meanings.[26] A superficial etymological approach that overly focuses on dictionary definitions thus has clear limitations as it, essentially, simultaneously both *overstates* and *underrates* the author's intention:[27] it "overstates" because it is imputed that a certain conceptual distinction is always rigorously made. And it "underrates" in the sense that one runs the danger of ignoring moments of self-reflexion on the author's part; for example, when a specific definition actually *is* provided (via annotation or footnote). Most crucially, exercises in *Wortklauberei* ("quibbleism") under-estimate that the images and metaphors of decline narratives develop dynamics of their own and are adapted, appropriated, and (mis-) used in contradictory ways. Furthermore, the semantics and connotations of "decadence" and "decline" (to keep to the semantic pair above) may differ significantly from language to language. A transhistorical perspective thus needs to address the issue of translation seriously, rather than constructing ways around it.

In summary, the performative dimension of Visions of Decline merit close scholarly attention.[28] "Decline" needs to be, in the confines of a specific research question, investigated in its entire semantic depth and variability. In particular, we must take into consideration that later recensions of a given Vision of Decline may very well not conform to the meaning intended by its originator.[29] For the authors of the present chapter, "decline" refers, beyond the narrow confines of any single concept, to a broad semantic field that may be analysed productively by focusing on the diverse narratives, images, and effects with which it is intertwined. These

---

25 On these "conventional" usages, see Hausteiner (2015), *Greater than Rome*, 106.
26 See Le Goff (1978), *Decadenza*, 416.
27 This charge could, for example, be levelled at Gutsche, note 5 above.
28 See Fischer-Lichte (2004), *Ästhetik des Performativen*.
29 See, for instance, the translation of Huxley's *Evolution and Ethics* discussed in Section V.

interconnections are, in our view, a fundamental and general characteristic of Visions of Decline. The present chapter brings together five case studies which draw on the study of Graeco-Roman antiquity, Egyptology, modern European history, Sinology, and the reception of medieval (Hanseatic) history in the early twentieth century. Each section (to varying degrees, depending on the specific setting of the Vision of Decline) deals with the stories explaining decline (narratives), the rhetorical devices used to construct them (images), and the relevant processes of reception and perception, which entails paying equal attention to non-intentional and potentially counteracting dynamics, misconceptions and the like (effects). In the conclusion, we will synthesise the findings into a first draft for a typology of Visions of Decline. We are aware, however, that the following five studies cannot hope to cover the entire breadth and depth of the decline-phenomenon. The reader is advised to treat them as part of a panorama that could be expanded virtually indefinitely, as Umberto Eco has cautioned us. This, however, is a key motivation behind this essay: to demonstrate that societies—past and present—were just as "obsessed" with their fall from grace as they were with their rise to glory.

We begin our empirical part with a study by David Weidgenannt on Roman occupied Greece, in which the author offers a brief introduction to "decadence" as an analytical concept (Section II). This provides the reader with a useful theoretical background for the subsequent sections, particularly Nadine Eikelschulte's inquiry into notions of "perversion" in Egyptian "pessimistic literature" (Section III). The fourth section, by Klaus Seidl, deals with the Pan-European Congress of 1926, and elaborates on the conviction that failing to unite is to perish. That this is, indeed, a recurrent *motif* in Visions of Decline is shown in the subsequent fifth study, in which Sebastian Riebold argues that *"s'unir ou mourir"* was a key concern for many political thinkers in China around the year 1900, as the country saw itself faced with major challenges both internal and external (Section IV). Finally, Philipp Höhn (Section VI), in his analysis of the correspondence between Thomas Mann and Fritz Rörig, not only brings together many of the aspects encountered in the preceding sections, but also makes a final addition to the emerging "panorama" in his treatment of decline as the dissolution of "organic" entities. In the conclusion (Section VII), we will comprehensively discuss the various modes of decline and reflect on possible ways forward for critical decline analysis.

II. Decadence and Discourse: The Honour of the Hellenes

The history of the Roman Empire is inextricably entangled with Visions of Decline. It is not only the ancient sources that mourn moral decay, modern historiography also framed Roman history in the terms of "decline and fall".[30] The transition from the Roman Republic to the Roman Imperial Period and the history of the later Roman Empire became the most prominent exponents of what has been described as periods of decadence. Less prominent in modern scholarship are the transformations that the Greek *poleis* underwent in the Hellenistic period[31] and under the Roman Empire. Nevertheless, ancient authors provide evidence for this question as well. Remarkably, it is not the transformation of the Roman Empire itself that some of these authors are interested in, but rather the history of the "Greek *poleis*" under Roman authority. Consequently, a single, grand narrative of decline does not exist. Instead, Visions of Decline in the period under consideration appear shaped in several forms. While individual discourses cover very different issues, they are characterised by relatively stable textual features. Kurt Lenk subsumed these features under the heading "*Dekadenztheorem*", which, in recent research, has been used for the description of discourses of decadence in the Late Roman Republic.[32] In this theorem:

---

30 Discourses, criticising the degenerate condition of contemporary affairs, can be found throughout Roman history: see, e.g., Cato, Sallust, Livy, Velleius Paterculus, Tacitus (see Biesinger (2016), *Römische Dekadenzdiskurse*). Gibbon's seminal work "The History of the Decline and Fall of the Roman Empire" (published in six volumes between 1776 and 1789) fostered the link between Roman History and decline and has made this relationship a widely discussed issue to this very day. The focus on the Roman Empire overshadowed the numerous other discourses about decline, fall or decadence that existed in antiquity: Widmer (1983), *Niedergangsthematik*.

31 See, e.g., Finley (1977 [1963]), *The Ancient Greeks*, 90–91: "[T]here is no escaping the evidence: the fourth century was the time when the Greek polis declined, unevenly, with bursts of recovery and heraldic moments of struggle to save itself, to become, after Alexander, a sham *polis* in which the preservation of the many external forms of *polis* life could not conceal that henceforth the Greeks lived, in Clemenceau's words, 'in a sweet peace of decadence, accepting all sorts of servitudes as they came'." See Harland (2006), *The Declining Polis?*, 22–28, for different models explaining the decline of the polis. For the fourth century, see especially, Eder (1995), *Die athenische Demokratie*, and Tiersch (2016), *Die athenische Demokratie*.

32 Biesinger (2016), *Römische Dekadenzdiskurse*.

"there exists a positively valued *status quo ante*: a culture or social order imagined actually to have existed in the past and where conservative values still held sway over society. All that is deemed indispensable for the existence of a morally sound culture (such as fixed social relations, values, obedience, and willingness to sacrifice) is projected therein. Thereupon follows a historical caesura, akin to the Biblical Fall of Man, which signifies the end of the "ancient order" (*i.e.*, the *status quo ante*). This dramatic watershed in the course of history is imagined as an infraction against the natural order of creation (= 'sin'): human hybris, deterioration of traditional authority, revolutionary subversive forces, cultural-revolutionary movements, and the like. The past is the field in which positive forces engage in battle against degradation, egoism, and libertinage. To resist general decay and decadence running rampant becomes the sworn task of conservative politics with the final aim of restoring the destroyed or threatened ancient order (estates of the realm, monarchy, meritocracy)."[33]

At the same time, the identification of decadence by a historical actor reveals his or her consciousness of living in a *Spätzeit* (waning period) and this knowledge, in turn, links discourses of decadence with historical awareness. But, as will be shown, decadence is not tied to historiography alone,[34] it can also be found in non-historical genres.

An example of this can be found in the 31st Rhodian oration, written in the first century AD by the orator and philosopher Dio Chrysostom.[35] The author, who came from a wealthy family, produced a vast amount of speeches on very different topics. We know that he was a student of the famous stoic philosopher Musonius Rufus, but his writings reveal that he was familiar with other philosophical traditions as well, and that he had a particular liking for Greek history and culture. Although researchers believe the oration to have been held in the people's assembly in Rhodes, both the length of the speech—an oral presentation which would have taken more than two hours—and its structure show that the oration has been heavily altered before publication.[36] Several intellectual innuendos have been added to meet the taste of sophisticated readers.

To date, the oration has mostly been treated as lengthy evidence of the re-use of statues and its implications for the Greek *poleis* under Roman

---

33 Translated from Lenk (1989), *Konservatismus*, 255–256.
34 Biesinger (2016), *Römische Dekadenzdiskurse*, 21.
35 The oration has been dated to the Flavian period (e.g., Arnim (1898), *Leben und Werke*; Jones (1978), *Dio Chrysostom*) or to the reign of Trajan (Sidebottom (1992), *The Date of Dio*, 409–414; Swain (1996), *Hellenism and Empire*, 428–429). For a recent re-evaluation, see Amato (2014), *Traiani Praeceptor*, 35–56, arguing extensively for a Vespasian date.
36 See Jones (1978), *Dio Chrysostom*, 28.

rule.[37] While this is certainly a major aspect of the speech, this narrative is embedded in a larger discourse unfolding around the great past of the Greeks and their situation under the new Roman rulers. This partly explains why the "main topic", the re-use of statues, is not addressed until Paragraph 8:

"It is in regard to these matters, men of Rhodes, that I ask you to believe that the situation here among you is very bad and unworthy of your state, your treatment, I mean, of your benefactors and of the honours given to your good men, although originally you did not handle the matter thus—most assuredly not! [...] but it is only that a habit in another way bad has prevailed here for some time, and that nobody any longer receives honour among you, if you care to know the truth, and that the noble man of former times who were zealous for your state, not alone those in private station, but also kings and, in certain cases, peoples, are being insulted and robbed of the honours which they had received. [...] But what occurs is quite absurd: your chief magistrate, namely, merely points his finger at the first statue that meets his eye of those which have already been dedicated, and then, after the inscription which was previously on it has been removed and another name engraved, the business of honouring is finished; and there you are!"[38]

It becomes clear that Dio's criticism of this behaviour in Rhodes is based upon the way in which they had dealt with honorary statues before. He explicitly states that the Rhodians did "originally [...] not handle the matter thus—οὐκ ἀρχῆθεν ὑμῶν οὕτω τῷ πράγματι χρωμένων" and that their current behaviour even brings "the noble man of former times—τῶν τε πρότερον γενναίων ἀνδρῶν" into disrepute. But, Dio's analysis of amoral conduct in Rhodes is not restricted to the re-use of statues. Before explicitly mentioning the central topic of his speech, he makes it clear that this is only a symptom of a more general condition:

"And I myself would venture to say that it is especially fitting that the majority should scrupulously observe the noblest and most sacred obligations; for in the state where such considerations are neglected, such neglect even reveals a sort of vice (κακίαν τινὰ) in the body politic and no other matter can be properly administered."[39]

---

37 Blanck (1969), *Wiederverwendung*; Platt (2007), *Honour Takes Wing*; Gangloff (2013), *Le langage des statues*; Harter-Uibopuu (2013), *Auf dass Ehren ewig währen*; Harter-Uibopuu (2014) *Rechtshistorische Überlegungen*; Bailey (2015), *'Honor' in Rhodes*.
38 Dio. 31.8–9 (trans.: Cohoon/Loeb, occasionally modified by author).
39 Dio 31.6. Cf. Fuhrer (2014), *Interesse am menschlichen Scheitern*, 25. Fuhrer points out that ancient historiography does not distinguish between different forms of failure: "Wer in einem Bereich versagt, tut es auch in den anderen." For a similar argument see 31.23–24.

The language deployed by Dio reveals that he is concerned with the degenerate situation of the island. He alludes to this throughout his speech. At a later point, Dio admonishes his listeners to look at the older statues that surround them.[40] This rhetorical device gives Dio's argument a deictic quality: his listeners are forced to perform an autopsy on their own situation in comparison to the *status quo ante*.[41] These statues were not so valuable because of their perceptible material quality; instead, they served as evidence of the ancestors who had guarded "the national honour of the Hellenes by their unaided efforts up to the present time".[42] Here again, Dio employs a vocabulary (τὸ κοινὸν ἀξίωμα) that is tightly connected to moral concepts.[43] Interestingly, Dio increases the obligation of the Rhodians to act according to an ancient set of principles by making them the last defenders of Greek moral values:

"For this reason, I think that you [sc. Rhodians] are justified in feeling greater pride than all the rest of them [sc. Greeks] taken together."[44]

While the rest of Hellas deteriorated by succumbing to envy (φθόνος), folly (ἄνοια) and rivalry (φιλονικία), abandoned excellence (ἀρετή), and "although no foreign power was troubling them [...] finally invited anyone who wished to be their master", the noble men of Rhodes kept striving for eternal fame.[45]

While Dio sets the noble man of former times as the yardstick against which the men of his time have to be measured, it becomes clear that they will never be surpassed:

"for we know that the exceedingly ancient men were demi-gods and that those who followed them were not much inferior to them; secondly, we understand that

---

40 Dio 31.8.
41 See, e.g., Dio 31.16 and esp. 160: "Nay, it is rather the stones which reveal the grandeur and the greatness of Hellas, and the ruins of her buildings; her inhabitants themseves [sic!] and those who conduct her governments would not be called descendants of even the Mysians."
42 Dio 31.18. For the exceptional role of Rhodes as a defender of crucial Greek values, see 31.117, 157–159, 161. The semantic value of the statues as a trace and proof of manly virtue is clearly expressed in Dio 31.14, 16, 20, 22, 146–147.
43 For the use of τὸ κοινὸν ἀξίωμα, see Dio 31.157–160.
44 Dio 31.18.
45 Dio 31.19. A similar list can be found in 31.25, 141.

their successors steadily deteriorated in the course of time, and finally, we know that the men of to-day are no better than ourselves."[46]

Dio evokes the men of the past and their deeds, sometimes with remarkable detail,[47] but it is evident that this past is somewhat remote and not fully comprehensible.[48] Yet, it is not the past that he wants to re-construct. The past serves only as a background against which he sets his criticism of the citizens of Rhodes, and it is therefore not necessary for him to go into every detail.[49] More importantly, their disgraceful behaviour must necessarily become worse as the Rhodians move away from their glorious past:

"For even if they urge that now they follow this practice only in the case of the old statues, yet as time goes on, just as ever happens in the case of all bad habits (ὥσπερ ἐπὶ πάντων ἀεὶ συμβαίνει τῶν φαύλων ἐθῶν), this one, too, will, of necessity, grow worse and worse."[50]

While discourses of decadence tend to give a precise *caesura* that marks the starting-point for decline, Dio remains vague. He only contrasts a former way of behaviour with the actual one, highlighting that, despite "living in prosperity, you do what not a single one of the peoples in the past did".[51] This contrast becomes even more complex, in that honours were awarded in former times "in acknowledgement of a benefaction" (δι'εὐεργεσίαν) whereas now they are awarded "owing to political power" (δι'ἰσχὺν).[52] Here, Dio brings into play not only a contrast between Greeks and Romans, but he also makes it very explicit that εὐεργεσία (benefaction) and ἰσχύς (political power) have very different qualities:

---

46 Dio 31.75. Cf. 31.80, where Dio states that man of former times, even if they did not have something remarkable, can be considered semi-divine only because "of their remoteness in time". See, also, 31.93, 95, 124, 126; 12.27–28, 54; 21.1. For further evidence see Cohoon/Loeb 31.75 n. 1. The idea that the men of older times were superior to their descendants is very prominent in stoic philosophy: see, esp., Sen. Ep. 90.44: "Still, I would not deny that they were men of lofty spirit and—if I may use the phrase—fresh from the gods. For there is no doubt that the world produced a better progeny before it was yet worn out.—Non tamen negaverim fuisse alti spiritus viros et, ut ita dicam, a dis recentes; neque enim dubium est quin meliora mundus nondum effetus ediderit." (Transl.: Gummere/Loeb.)

47 For the use of historical examples in Dio's works, see Bost-Pouderon (2010), *Quelques considérations*.

48 See, e.g., Dio 31.90–92, 159–160.

49 See Dio 31.126–127.

50 Dio 31.99. See the teleological attitude in 31.129, 140–142.

51 Dio 31.68. Explicit comparisons with ancestors can also be found in 31.41, 46, 55, 93.

52 Dio 31.43.

"For all know how much more permanent a benefaction is than power, for there is no strength which time does not destroy, but it destroys no benefaction."[53]

Here, again, Dio ascribes a supratemporal quality to a distant past that is embodied in the statues of former times, but no longer exists. However, there is hope for the Rhodians:

"But you are left, for you alone still are believed actually to present something and not to be utterly despised. [...] Therefore, just as, when a prosperous and great family has been left desolate and only one male descendant survives, everything depends upon him, and if he errs in any way and bears a bad name, he destroys all the glory of his family and puts shame upon all those who preceded him, so too is your position now in respect to Hellas."[54]

But, Dio is well aware that the new political situation in the Greek world requires a different form of behaviour. Instead of "assuming the leadership over the others, in lending succour to the victims of injustice, in gaining allies, founding cities, winning wars",[55] the Rhodians are constrained to assume leadership over themselves, administer their city, honour and support distinguished men, to deliberate in the council, sit in judgment, offer sacrifice to the gods and to hold high festivals.[56]

In the eyes of Dio, not all is lost.[57] While he is fully aware that the past which he creates is gone, he still encourages the Rhodians to maintain the "antique and Hellenic character of their customs—τὸ ἐν τοῖς ἔθεσιν ἀρχαῖον καὶ Ἑλληνικόν".[58]

Dio's speech to the Rhodians is incredibly rich and covers a vast array of topics. From an archaeological point of view, this oration is an outstanding testimony to the re-use of statues and their interpretation. From a more historical perspective, the statues are also a means to an end. They

---

53 Dio 31.43.
54 Dio 31.158–159.
55 Dio 31.161.
56 Dio 31.162. Follows the translation of Cohoon.
57 See Dio 31.66: "I wish, moreover, to mention a deed of yours which took place not very long ago, and yet is commended by everyone no less than are the deeds of the men of old, in order that you may know by making comparison whether on principle it is seemly for people like you to be guilty of such behaviour as this."
58 Dio 31.163. See, also, 31.164. The term ἀρχαῖος is also used for men (75), statues (87) and personified statues (124). This can also be seen in the case of the unnamed philosopher, who is said to be "the only man who since the time of the ancients (μετὰ τοὺς ἀρχαίους) had lived most nearly in conformity with reason." (31.122: for the identity of the philosopher, see Amato (2014), *Traiani Praeceptor*, 68–69, n. 22).

help Dio to draw a picture of a Greek *polis* under Roman rule. The statues represent not only the glory of former times, they are symbols of good and appropriate behaviour as well. This makes them very explicit and visible testimonies of a past that fell into disrepair. While this past is, on the one hand, remote and lost, it nonetheless serves as a point of reference for the Rhodians in Dio's time. It is against this background that Dio portrays the degeneration of the Rhodian's behaviour. Although he is aware that the decay cannot be stopped and tends to expand from one field into another, he still encourages the Rhodians to regard the past that he creates in front of his audience as the very touchstone of good behaviour.[59]

III. Perversions or the Inverted World in Egyptian Pessimistic Literature

"It is unacceptable for the Egyptian to speak of matters negative, such as one's own mistakes or imperfections. For if he were to fix in speech or—worse yet—writing, characteristics or events which do not accord to the natural order, he would only grant them permanence and reality."[60]

This statement was made by Hellmut Brunner in 1966. And, indeed, there are no reports of failures or disasters which afflicted Ancient Egypt during its long history.[61] It is astonishing that there are various texts, which form a proper genre, that broach the issue of decline. This genre is known as "laments", "reflective discourse",[62] or "pessimistic literature".[63] The topic of

---

59 For this twofold function of the speech, see Bost-Pouderon (2009), *Prédication morale*, 240. She highlights that the speech can be read as as a συμβουλή as well as a ψόγος. For the obligation to not fall behind the ancestors, see 31.62–64.
60 "Negatives, also in diesem Fall eigene Fehler und Unvollkommenheiten auszusprechen, geht für den Ägypter nicht an, da durch die Fixierung in Wort oder gar Schrift solche aus der Ordnung fallenden Eigenschaften oder Vorkommnisse erst Dauer und Realität erhielten." Brunner (1966), *Grundzüge einer Geschichte*, 21.
61 For example, there are no reports of military defeats. Instead, many accounts of successions exist which may actually have been defeats. The most prominent example of that type is the Battle of Kadesh, which is known from several inscriptions in Egypt, where Ramesses II. presents the Egyptians as victorious. This contrasts with the Hittite references.
62 Parkinson (2010), *Poetry and Culture*, 193.
63 See, for example, Parkinson (2009), *Egyptian Poems*, 131; Gozzoli (2006), *Writings of History*, 164.

decline is typical of this genre, but appears in different forms. Although the date of origin of these texts is not certain, it is assumed that the texts did not originate before the Middle Kingdom (c. 2055–1650 BC). Hence, a relation to the First Intermediate Period seems likely.

1. The First Intermediate Period

The period between the Old and the Middle Kingdom, which means the time after the end of the sixth dynasty to the eleventh dynasty (c. 2160–2055 BC), is traditionally called the First Intermediate Period.[64] This time is not very well represented in the Egyptian sources on chronology, and differs in the records of rulers and the length of this period. The period was preceded by the so-called Old Kingdom (c. 2686–2160 BC), which essentially differs from the First Intermediate Period, because it was a unified kingdom, while, in the First Intermediate Period, various potentates fought for predominance until finally one of them succeeded and established the Middle Kingdom.[65] The First Intermediate Period had been regarded as a "Dark Age" or a phase of decline in Egyptology, mostly due to the lack of textual sources and archaeological records. Large buildings, such as the pyramids of the Old Kingdom, are not preserved from this time.[66]

The political upheavals and the loss of institutions such as central kingship are a central concern for the literature which emerged after the First Intermediate Period, because they brought with them a decisive shift in the self-conception of the king and his highest officials. In other words, the king's legitimacy was no longer exclusively derived from the gods, and, moreover, he had to justify his domination in a different manner than

---

[64] The term "First Intermediate Period" is problematical, because it implies impermanence and weakness. It is, however, the common name within the field of Egyptology and that is why I will use it throughout this section. For the German equivalent, "Erste Zwischenzeit", Ludwig Morenz recently suggested the alternative formulation "Zeit der Regionen" (Period of Regions). See Morenz (2010), *Zeit der Regionen*; Seidlmayer (2003), *First Intermediate Period*, 108.

[65] The words used are ascriptions of Egyptology. The Ancient Egyptians indeed maintained lists of kings, but did not sort them into Kingdoms and Intermediate Periods or dynasties.

[66] There are some records of the beginnings of the construction of pyramids, but only one of them seems to have progressed beyond the initial stage. Complete pyramids are preserved from the Middle Kingdom. See Theis (2010), *Pyramiden der Ersten Zwischenzeit*, 326 ff.

before. During the First Intermediate Period, it was shown that Egypt could exist without the figure of Pharaoh and that the king did not have the extensive power that he previously claimed for himself. In his essay on legitimation, John Baines concludes that the king never again held as much power as in the Old Kingdom.[67] This loss of power and the constraint for new forms of legitimation could be the reasons why the genre of the laments emerged. In addition to economic changes, social change must also have taken place.

It is not clear how the changes in the power structures, which marked the shift between the Old Kingdom and the First Intermediate Period, came about.[68] But it is nevertheless possible to describe in a very concrete manner the changes that occurred with the transition from the Old Kingdom to the First Intermediate Period. Obvious changes include the abolition of the central kingship and the strengthening of élites. Economic transformations accompanied these changes because the resources were no longer distributed centrally, but from within the single nomes.[69] These developments were accompanied by social and, to a certain extent, cultural change. Of fundamental importance is the fact that trade with other countries seems to have stopped completely and expeditions abroad were no longer undertaken. It remains unresolved why these developments occurred. In addition, no royal building projects seem to have taken place, and the only preserved monuments are the graves of the nomarchs. Furthermore, in the realm of material culture, pottery changed with regard to its shape. New designs such as vessels in bag or drop form originate from this period.[70]

New burial practices also emerged, including alterations in grave types and the quantity of funerary objects included. Generally, non-royal graves, *i.e.*, those of the "common people", increased in both size and number. Whereas in the Old Kingdom, mainly everyday items were given to the

---

67 Baines (1995), *Legitimation*, 11ff.
68 On this topic, see Bell (1971), *Dark Ages*; Gundlach (2004), *Grundgegebenheiten*; Hornung (1996), *Grundzüge*; Jansen-Winkeln (2010), *Untergang des Alten Reichs*; Müller-Wollermann (1986), *Krisenfaktoren*; Priglinger (2015), *Texte und ihre Interpretation*; 2015, Römer (2011), *Was ist eine Krise?*.
69 "Nomes" (sp3t) refers to the administrative units in Egypt, as they are known since the time of Djoser. In the First Intermediate Period, the nomes were ruled by the so-called nomarchs. See Helck (1977), *Gaue*, 386.
70 Seidlmayer (2003), *First Intermediate Period*, 113.

deceased official, we find funerary objects that were produced exclusively for this purpose in the First Intermediate Period.[71]

There was a change in the administrative system because of the dislocation of social centres. Previously, the state institutions such as the royal court were found in the capital, *i.e.*, the political and administrative centre of the land. At the end of the Old Kingdom, a shift to the provinces began and the different nomes were administered autonomously.[72]

It is because of these major changes that Elke Blumenthal, in her essay on the genre of the laments, comes to the conclusion that the descriptions in the pessimistic literature have their provenance in the time of the First Intermediate Period, even though some of the works can be dated to a subsequent time.[73]

2. The Pessimistic Literature

Various literary works are assigned to the genre "pessimistic literature", which are all concerned with a specific form of decline. In general, *The Words of Khakheperreseneb*, *The Teaching for King Merykara*, *The Words of Neferti*, *The Dialogue of Ipuur and the Lord of All*, *The Dialogue of a Man with his Soul*, *The Teaching of King Amenemhat*, and *The Tale of the Eloquent Peasant* are included in the genre of laments.[74] The commonality of the texts primarily consists of their contents, but there are also structural parallels between some of the texts. Thus, for example, *The Dialogue of a Man with his Soul*, as well as *Dialogue of Ipuur and the Lord of All*, are written in the form of a dialogue,

---

71 Seidlmayer (2003), *First Intermediate Period*, 114.
72 Seidlmayer (2003), *First Intermediate Period*, 113.
73 "Although [the laments] are written from a distance, they signal the collapse of an order that, up to that point, had been deemed the incontrovertible fundament and yardstick of the body politic. [...] There are, however, no grounds to doubt that the roots of the formulation of the unspeakable go back to Egypt's first pervasive crisis during the First Intermediate Period./Obwohl aus der Distanz formuliert, signalisieren sie den Zusammenbruch einer Ordnung, die bis dahin als unumstößliches Fundament und Maßstab des Gemeinwesens gegolten hatte. [...] Es gibt aber keinen Grund zu bezweifeln, daß die Wurzeln für die Formulierung des Entsetzlichen in die erste umfassende Krise Ägyptens in der 1. Zwischenzeit hinabreichen." Blumenthal (1996), *Verarbeitung der Übergangszeit*, 133.
74 Blumenthal (1996), *Verarbeitung der Übergangszeit*. The original Egyptian texts are untitled and were given names only in later scholarship.

while, for example, *The Words of Neferti*, like *The Teaching for King Merykara*, are embedded in a framework plot.

The different texts describe various aspects or forms of decay, sometimes referring to a lack of justice, a loss of faith, or to several of these and other aspects. For example, *The Words of Neferti* and *The Dialogue of Ipuur* describe a deterioration which manifests itself at the social, political, *and* spiritual level.

In these texts, the Egyptian world order, *Maat* is replaced by her antonym, *Isfet*. *Maat* describes the concept of the cosmic order, and the personification of *Maat* is the goddess of justice.[75] Jan Assmann sees the concept *Maat* as the central concept of ancient Egyptian culture (*"Zentralbegriff der altägyptischen Kultur"*).[76] The term is derived from the Egyptian word *m3ʿt*, which can roughly be translated as "to guide, to direct". This concept is important in the context of the pessimistic literature because it is denied for the time described. Instead, the world of description is dominated by *Isfet*. For the Egyptians, this meant the rule of chaos and injustice. In part, the loss of *Maat* is also articulated more directly. For example, *The Words of Khakheperreseneb* includes the sentence: "Justice (*Maat*) has been cast out, and evil (*Isfet*) is inside the shrine."[77] The pairing of *Maat* and *Isfet* is important, especially since it is also represented by many other reversals and/or perversions.

3. Perversions or the "Inverted World"

Texts in which so-called "perversions" are frequently used include *The Dialogue of Ipuur* and *The Words of Neferti*. The former is only preserved in a copy from the Ramesside Period, but originally came from the late Middle Kingdom or the Second Intermediate Period (c. 1650–1550 BC), and is the most elaborately text of this genre.[78] Richard Parkinson interprets it as a kind of spiritual complaint to the Creator God.[79] Within the text, various grievances are criticised, which affect the society of the time as well as the

---

75 For further information on the topic of Maat, see Assmann (2006), *Ma'at*.
76 Assmann (2006), *Ma'at*, 15.
77 Simpson (2003), *Literature*, 212.
78 Simpson (2003), *Literature*, 188.
79 Parkinson (2010), *Poetry and Culture*, 205.

"destruction" of the country. The beginning and the end of the text are not preserved because of the immense damage to the papyrus.

It is the speech of a man named Ipuur,[80] who speaks to a listener who, however, remains unnamed in the preserved part of the papyrus. It is thought that he must have been a king or even a god, since Ipuur addresses him with the title "Lord of All", which was common for these groups of persons.[81]

Firstly, the chaotic state in which the country finds itself is described in detail and with frequent repetitions. A dialogue unfolds, in the course of which the conditions of the time are contrasted with a golden past.

Particularly striking are the frequent reversals within the description of the country:

"Look, wealthy ladies are on boards; officials are in the workhouse; he who did not even sleep on a wall is a lord of a bed. Look, a lord of property goes to sleep thirsty; he who begged dregs for himself is a lord of strong beer. Look, the lords of robes are in rags; he who could not weave for himself is a lord of fine linen. [...] Look, a man without property is a lord of riches; the officials now favour him. Look, the beggars of the land have become rich; the lord of property is a have-not. Look, the butlers have become lords of cupbearers; he who was a messenger is sending someone else."[82]

In these verses, all social conventions and hierarchies are reversed. The members of the former élite have suffered the loss of all their possessions and their positions, their places having been "usurped", as it were, by "beggars, butlers, and cupbearers". It is noteworthy that these so-called perversions are directly related to one another, so that the contrast between the supposed upper and lower layers is even more distinct. From other texts, one can re-construct a self-perception of the group of scribes. This image is most clearly illustrated in the *The Instruction of Dua-Kheti*, also known as the *Satire of the Trades*. In this text, a fictitious student is asked to take the occupation of scribe, because it would be the only one desirable. In the text, the alleged disadvantages of other professions are markedly exaggerated and the advantages of the profession of scribe are stressed. The description of the profession of fisherman may serve as an example:

---

80 It is not clear whether this refers to an actual historical person since it is common in Egyptian literature to attribute texts to famous historical figures, even if they originated from another time.
81 Parkinson (2010), *Poetry and Culture*, 205.
82 Parkinson (2009), *Egyptian Poems*, 179–180.

"I'll speak of the fisherman also. His is the worst of all the jobs; he labours on the river, mingling with crocodiles. When the time of reckoning comes, he is full of lamentations; he does not say: 'There's a crocodile.' Fear has made him blind. [...] See, there is no profession without a boss. Except for the scribe; he is the boss."[83]

An increasing provincialisation and thus a gain of power by the local élites had already begun at the end of the Old Kingdom. This can be confirmed, for example, by the newly introduced title of the "Overseer of Upper Egypt" (*jmy r3 šmʿw*).[84] The local élites gained influence, so that the aristocracy of the former royal court might have lost influence, and one could speak of a crisis of these élites of the residence.[85]

Comparable descriptions such as the ones above can also be found in the Words *of Neferti*, a text preserved in a copy from the eighteenth dynasty and on some smaller fragments, referring to a king of the twelfth dynasty and thus probably to be dated to the Middle Kingdom. The text itself, however, is placed in the Old Kingdom at the court of King Snefru. In the framework story, a sage, Neferti, was summoned to entertain the king. The sage predicts the devastation of the country, which would ultimately be ended by King Ameny. The placement in the Old Kingdom is deliberately chosen. The Old Kingdom was often chosen as an ideal in the literature of the Middle Kingdom, because the kingship had not yet experienced any weaknesses, for example, in the form of rebellions. But also in the descriptions of Nefertis, a reference to a better past is given by contrasting it, in the form of pairs, with the present. In the text, reversals of possessions, as well as reversals of social position, are used. The statements are often arranged in parallel and sometimes antithetically:

"I shall show you the lord in sorrow, and the outsider at peace, the man who did nothing, helping himself, and the man who did something in want [...]. The man who followed after, now the man leading a generation. [...] I shall show you the lowermost uppermost, the man who followed after, now the man leading a generation. They will live in the necropolis. The wretches will make riches; the great will [beg] to exist. Only the poor will eat bread, while forced labourers are exultant."[86]

The topos of the inverted world has a long tradition and has been used in different spheres (outside of literature) and at different times. In the Greco-Roman world, for example, there existed several "saturnic" festivi-

---

83 Lichtheim (2006 [1973]), *Ancient Egyptian Literature*, 189.
84 Jones (2000), *Index of Ancient Egyptian Titles*, vol. 2, 246.
85 Seidlmayer (2003), *First Intermediate Period*, 111.
86 Parkinson (2009), *Egyptian Poems*, 137–138.

ties (the best-known being the annual *Saturnalia*), which were characterised by role reversals and licensed transgression of social norms. At the Thessalian Peloria, slaves were allowed to participate in the festival and to openly contradict their masters, who had to wait on them.[87] The Russian philosopher and literary theorist Mikhail Bakhtin (1895–1975) describes the phenomenon as "carnivalesque", but emphasises the aspect of humour ("*Lachprinzip*").[88] With the concept of carnival, he questions all structures, especially those which relate to power, and turns them upside-down, in order to stress their mutability. Whether this also applies to the Egyptian texts or not must be considered more closely. Various pictorial ostraca, which are preserved from the Ramesside period, are most likely to be attributed to the cult of laughter. They contain images, which, for example, show a kind of war between cats and mice, in which the mice attack a castle of the cats. These are in contrast with the above-mentioned examples of the literature discussed here, all of which appear to be a form of complaint.

4. Idealisation of the Past

The past was regarded as an ideal, whereas, in the present, institutions such as kingship, which had been regarded as irrevocable, were shaken. This is also reflected in the literature of the time; in particular, this phenomenon can be found in *The Words of Neferti*:

"Destroyed, indeed, are those things of happiness—the fish pools, which were full of people gutting fish, which overflowed full of fish and fowl; all happiness has fled and the land is laid down with pain, by those feeding Syrians who go throughout the pain."[89]

Interestingly, foreigners are mentioned here as the main reason for the decline. Thus, no own *responsibility is assumed*; *instead, it is ascribed to a foreign influence*. This is in accord with the Egyptian self-perception, since the Egyptians always saw themselves as superior to foreign peoples and countries.[90] In addition, a brilliant future under the predicted new King Ameny

---

[87] Gordon (2013), *Inversion, Codeverletzung, Spott*; Mili (2015), *Religion and Society*, 239 ff. The Peloria are possibly mythological.
[88] Bachtin (1987), *Rabelais und seine Welt*, 109.
[89] Parkinson (2009), *Egyptian Poems*, 138.
[90] Assmann (1996), *Fremdheit*, 88.

is described. This delineation contrasts with the description of the chaotic conditions in the country, which prevailed prior to the time of Ameny.

It is depicted that the bad conditions would be ended, and the order would be restored by the prospective king. This means that the ending of a predicted decline is also foreseen in this work. The text is shaped by the description of the contrast between periods of chaos and periods of order, thus between their personifications as *Isfet* and as *Maat*. These contradictions are clearly articulated at the end, when Neferti predicts: "Truth (*Maat*) will return to its proper place, with Chaos (*Isfet*) driven outside."[91]

Similar descriptions can also be found in *The Dialogue of Ipuur*. Narratives about the "present" conditions are contrasted with descriptions of the past and predictions of the future. The part with descriptions of the past is considerably shorter but formally related to the previous section on the present. This means that the individual statements are always initiated with the repeating word s *sḫ3* "remember" and are constructed as parallelisms. With regard to the content, it is particularly related to rituals and past prosperity. Some of the statements are in direct contrast to previously made images of the "current" time:

"Remember the flattened graylag-geese, the white-fronted and the pintail-geese, the donating of divine offerings to the gods!"

This sentence is directly related to a previous verse:

"Look, the colonial tenants are butchering graylag-geese; they are given to the Gods, instead of oxen."[92]

In one line, it is bewailed that private people make offerings, and that only offerings of inferior quality were used, while, in the next line, the earlier offerings to the gods were remembered.[93] Thus, there are strong antitheses in the comparison between the past and the present. In contrast to *The Words of Neferti*, which ends on a conciliatory note, since the predicted king will restore order, the end in *The Dialogue of Ipuur* is unclear, since the end of the papyrus is lost. In the last preserved part, the interlocutor of Ipuur, who is probably a divine being, makes humanity responsible for its own suffering.

---

91 Parkinson (2009), *Egyptian Poems*, 137–138.
92 Parkinson (2009), *Egyptian Poems*, 180, 184, 196.
93 Although praying was no longer a privilege of priests during the First Intermediate Period and the following periods, it was not a common practice for ordinary people ("colonial tenants").

The reasons for the emergence of this genre can be found in the First Intermediate Period. In this time, the worldview, which was unimpaired before, has been questioned. The king or the whole institution of kingship, which also referred to a divine legitimation, had not been able to prevail. This led to a change, one which also had an impact on the Middle Kingdom and was even sustained in the New Kingdom (c. 1550–1069 BC).

This change manifested itself in many different areas: for example, the king never again possessed such all-encompassing power as in the Old Kingdom. After the First Intermediate Period, the monarchy was re-introduced, but the time without a unified kingdom had left its marks. It can be assumed that the shock of the belief in the omnipotence of the monarchy also led to legitimation difficulties in the Middle and New Kingdom. Thus, the pessimistic literature could be read as a sort of propaganda for the re-established central kingdom. Moreover, other texts, such as one of the most famous Egyptian stories, *The Story of Sinuhe*, is said to have served "propagandistic" purposes.[94] This theory is supported by the frequent reference to and the location of the Old Kingdom in the pessimistic literature. The time of the Old Kingdom is idealised within the genre and staged as a Golden Age. Furthermore, the period without a king is characterised within the text as not referring to *Maat*, as opposed to the Egyptian world order. Accordingly, the period that has shattered the Egyptian worldview—at least that of the powerful part of the population—is skilfully processed by appealing to the fears of the potential readers, and is also reminiscent of the glorious times of the past.

IV. Federate or Perish—Decline Narratives and Paneurope after World War I

"Everything came to Europe, and everything came from it. Or almost everything. Now, the present day brings with it this important question: can Europe hold its pre-eminence in all fields? Will Europe become what it is in reality—that is, a little promontory on the continent of Asia? Or will it remain what it seems—that is, the elect portion of the terrestrial globe, the pearl of the sphere, the brain of a vast body?"[95]

---

94 Blumenthal (1997), *Sinuhe*, 886.
95 Valéry (1919), *Intellectual Crisis*, 279.

The ravages of World War I made it abundantly clear to contemporaries that the seemingly natural superiority of the European states and their culture had plunged into a grave crisis. Although—as Paul Valéry pointed out—a yawning gap between claim and reality had already existed for quite some time, the awareness of an acute crisis gained a new quality in Europe only after the war.[96] Before 1914, prophecies of doom had been a rather peripheral phenomenon, while, afterwards, an atmosphere of decay set the tone for public debates about the future of the "old continent" and developed into a Paneuropean debate. One look into the various books of writers, philosophers, politicians, economists and geographers shows, however, that Visions of Decline were usually accompanied by passionate appeals to stop the continent's downward trend. Indeed, the speeches on decline often aimed at legitimising new political orders by presenting them as necessary and sole remedies. Richard von Coudenhove-Kalergi demonstrated this when he reduced the "European question" to two options: "unite or perish."[97] The Paneuropean movement illustrates very vividly how narratives of decline were employed, how they worked, and the important role that historical references and metaphors played in this context. Finally, it has to be asked what kind of effect these narratives triggered.

On 3 October 1926, the first Paneuropean Congress took place in the Vienna *Konzerthaus*. Presided over by Richard von Coudenhove-Kalergi, who had previously articulated the principles of the Paneuropean Movement on several occasions, nearly 2,000 delegates proclaimed the necessity of a European union as the only way to maintain the old continent's status as a "luminaire of humanity".[98] Although the pursuit of peaceful unification was by no means unprecedented, but, in fact, had a long tradition in European history, the Paneuropean Movement in the interwar period revealed a number of particular characteristics. Combining the high ideals of the Enlightenment and pacifism with a decidedly realistic attitude, the Paneuropean Movement aimed to fulfil the Kantian vision of "eternal peace" as well as to protect the influence and status of the European nations which were being challenged by other world powers (such as the United States) and severely threatened by Stalinist Russia. Indeed, even the concert hall's decoration reflected this mind-set by the specific arrange-

---

96 Kaelble (2001), *Europäer über Europa*; Hewitson and d'Auria (2012), *Europe in Crisis*.
97 For "Paneurope", see, e.g., Ziegerhofer-Prettenthaler (2001), *Botschafter Europas*; Conze (2005), *Europa der Deutschen*; Orluc (2005), *Europe*; Schöberl (2008), *Europa*.
98 Coudenhove-Kalergi (1926), *Paneuropa-Kongreß*.

ment of portraits of famous historic predecessors.[99] While the German philosopher Immanuel Kant stood at the very centre, the variety of the other portraits symbolically combined the idealistic tradition (Friedrich Nietzsche, Victor Hugo, and Charles-Irénée Castel, abbé Bernadin de Saint-Pierre) with the rather practical approach of politicians and revolutionaries (Jan Amos Komensky, Giuseppe Mazzini, and, most notably, Napoleon Bonaparte). Despite this aspired balance, utopian thought played only a minor role in most of the speeches, which virtually shunned all sentiments inspired by high (but vague) hopes, and instead evoked the sheer practical need for the Paneuropean project. The difference between these two narrative modes—idealistic and realistic—is as obvious as it is revealing: whereas Victor Hugo, in particular, had articulated his dream of an united Europe in 1848 as the most desirable possibility to overcome war and hatred, after World War I, it was the nightmare of the ongoing continental decline that served to demonstrate the inevitability of unification.

In the "doom and gloom" atmosphere of the interwar period, it comes as no surprise that various notions of a "change for the worse" played a predominant role in the contemporary discussions on Europe in several ways. First, the widespread decline prophecies of Oswald Spengler's *Decline of the West* or Albert Demangeon's *Déclin de l'Europe* undoubtedly served as parts of the "ideological fundaments"[100] of the Paneuropean Movement. Moreover, some of the most eminent pessimist critics were either in contact with Coudenhove-Kalergi or even supported his cause publicly (or, at least, for a while): José Ortega y Gasset and Paul Valéry joined the so-called "committee of honour", with the author of *The European Crisis* (*Die Krisis der europäischen Kultur*, 1917), Rudolf Pannwitz, contributing to the committee's journal. The former Italian Prime Minister Francesco Nitti, whose critical Europe trilogy became a bestseller, supported the Pan-Europa idea personally.[101] Eloquent proponents of the "change for the worse", these authors also bear testimony to the need of European unification. In this regard, the Paneuropean motto "unite or perish" merged widely common perceptions of decline with the prospect of a possible remedy into a highly suggestive narrative. In the words of Coudenhove-Kalergi:

---

99 Coudenhove-Kalergi (1926), *Paneuropa-Kongreß*, 7–8.
100 Paul (2005), *A Man and a Movement*, 188.
101 Francesco Nitti's trilogy consists of "*L'Europa senza pace*" (1921), "*La decadenza dell'Europa*" (1922), and "*La tragedia dell'Europa*" (1924).

"Europe was a battlefield yesterday, today she is an anachronism, tomorrow she will be a federation. […] She stayed old and torn in a world re-organising itself far and outside from her and she does not realise sufficiently that the regime she has adopted sows the seeds of its own decadence. Nowadays, Pan-Europa is a categorical imperative, apart from which there is only decadence and death. Charlemagne, Napoleon, Bernadin de Saint-Pierre, Victor Hugo and many others dreamed of a European union. Today, the dilemma is here: unite or perish."[102]

These typical expressions reveal some characteristic elements of the argument and show how the narrative works. First, Coudenhove-Kalergi highlights the lamentable past and present of the continent as well as the future remedy. Remarkably, he does not refer to an ideal point in history in order to underline the dramatic scope of Europe's worsening situation. Instead, he simply recalls the recent war memories and remains rather vague in his explications. Second, although merely hinted at, the European decline is ascertained by comparison with other world regions that have overtaken the old continent's former status. Third, Europe is clearly depicted as having reached a turning-point where the ideals of the utopian tradition not only become a realistic, but even inevitable, option, since the decision to "perish" (or to "die", in other versions) is not an alternative to be seriously contemplated. The possibility of "perishing" is, instead, a rhetorical move to enhance the appellative effect of the narrative.

In this way, the comparatively simple plot structured along the deterioration from a higher status to a lower one, is not just combined with a specific remedy.[103] Moreover, the concrete narration follows the generic model of a tragedy in which the heroes and villains cannot be easily differentiated and the situation itself leads to a tragic end, evoking a cathartic effect.[104] Accordingly, the Pan-Europa Congress eschewed any debates about (war) guilt and instead focused on the vital questions of the present and the fate of the continent. Europe's future, as was explicitly argued, lay in her own hands:

"Europe is in control of its own destiny […]. Now, it is faced with the question that will determine its fate; Will it linger in its miserable existence, doomed to

---

102 Coudenhove-Kalergi, translated from the French version of his speech, EUI Florence, PAN/EU-13.
103 Hoffmann-Rehnitz (2016), *Unwahrscheinlichkeit der Krise*, 179–185, 181.
104 See the popular book by Francesco Nitti (1924), *"La tragedia dell'Europa"*.

degradation by incessant wars? Or blossom anew through solidarity between all states?[105]

From this point of view, the petty rivalry between its nations emerges as the true reason behind the decline of Europe. The German delegate Fritz Mittelmann referred to the times of the Nibelung saga to prove this very point:

"The era [of the Nibelungs], as well, was a Paneurope of sorts. For, in those days, it was paramount to save European culture from the vast hosts of Asia. Even today, this I cannot emphasise strongly enough, it is the fate of *all* of Europe that is at stake. It is a question but for dusty, ivory tower men of letters as to who in Europe lost the war. *All of Europe lost the war.* (Roaring applause.) All of Europe, every single part of her, may only be saved, if the collective European will as such is invigorated." [106]

While highlighting the current situation by evoking allegedly similar historical or even mythological precursors is hardly an innovative rhetorical move, the specific use of historical references at the congress is nonetheless quite remarkable. First, none of the speakers mentioned the—arguably—most ubiquitous historical case when treating processes of decline: the fall of the Roman Empire.[107] Unlike the widespread doom scenarios concerning the state of Europe at the time, dreadful visions based upon past events were noticeably uncommon (or, at least, not explicitly formulated) during the Paneuropean Congress. Although, for example, the theologian and humanitarian Albert Schweitzer had rejected the comparison with Rome since this move would belittle the present catastrophe, this kind of reservation was not universally shared in the Paneuropean context.[108] Historical references in the form of traditions and role models were utilised frequently and characterised unification not as an unprecedented act, but rather as an ever-recurring challenge. In this regard, European unification was largely supposed to follow the historical blueprints of national unification efforts in the nineteenth century, most notably that of the German *Zollverein* (the German Customs Union).[109] Aside from the talk by

---

105 Coudenhove-Kalergi (1926), *Paneuropa-Kongreß*, 44.
106 Coudenhove-Kalergi (1926), *Paneuropa-Kongreß*, 31.
107 See Demandt (2015), *Fall Roms*.
108 Schweitzer (2004), *Wir Epigonen*; see, also, Gutsche (2015), *Niedergang*, 225–226.
109 In this regard, Coudenhove-Kalergi's closing remarks adopted the perspective of Italian unification: "Vie amongst yourselves, which state may become the Piedmont [*i. e.*, the springboard of unification] of the united Europe! Vie amongst yourselves, which

Julius Wolf, who had propagated a Central European tariff union for over twenty years, a letter of greeting from the vice-president of the *Deutsche Bank* equally argued in favour of such an institution. He phrased his assessment rather bluntly:[110]

"The minor German Customs Union was the first step towards German unity and greatness. [...] European unity, likewise, will be based on a common tariff policy, or it will not be at all."[111]

Second, the Paneuropean gallery of ancestral portraits remained vague, open, and occasionally interchangeable. This, remarkably, is reflected in the ways in which several speakers held up Napoleon as a forerunner of a European federation. His merits and demerits were naturally highly disputed outside of France, and attitudes concerning him clearly reflected party boundaries.[112]

As mentioned above, the French emperor's portrait was part of the interior decoration, thus honouring his political legacy. Indeed, the former German chancellor Joseph Wirth spontaneously associated Napoleon with the Paneuropean idea when his eye caught the portrait. Moreover, Wirth mentioned the biography of Napoleon by Emil Ludwig, who personally participated in the congress and later stressed that Napoleon was "the only one [out of the portrayed thinkers] who could reflect and act at the same time".[113] In this sense, Napoleon was supposed to certify that a European federation was not simply the utopian goal of a group of noble idealists. Putting Bonaparte in the pantheon of role models was furthermore a visible sign of an attempt at French-German reconciliation, which was considered to be a first step to European unity.

Third, the origins of the motto "unite or perish" remain rather unclear. Ironically, it is likely to have been inspired by the American War of Independence, as is suggested by the American deputy Frederic H. Allen when he proposed "as the motto of the Pan-European Union our own American

---

statesman may become the Cavour [leading figure in the movement toward Italian unification] of his corner of the world! / Wetteifern Sie, welcher Staat zum Piemont des einigen Europas wird! Wetteifern Sie, welcher Staatsmann zum Cavour seines Erdteiles wird!" See: Coudenhove-Kalergi (1926), *Paneuropa-Kongreß*, 58.

110 See Kiesewetter (2008), *Julius Wolf*; Heilner, *Deutsche Wirtschaft und europäischer Zusammenschluss*, EUI Florence, PAN/EU-13.
111 Coudenhove-Kalergi (1926), *Paneuropa-Kongreß*, 71 (von Gwinner).
112 Coudenhove-Kalergi (1926), *Paneuropa-Kongreß*, 26 (Wirth); 44 (Ludwig); 48 (Dunan).
113 Coudenhove-Kalergi (1926), *Paneuropa-Kongreß*, 44.

motto: 'United we stand, divided we fall'".[114] Significantly, his words did not find their way into the official congress report. Another common version, attributed to Benjamin Franklin, was possibly the historical model for the French version: "s'unir ou mourir": "We must all hang together, or, most assuredly, we shall all hang separately."[115]

Against the background of these various, similar—but not identical—ways of envisioning the Paneuropean ideal, it becomes apparent that the images and metaphors used to articulate a "change for the worse" are hardly interchangeable. In fact, they bear a specific significance which is tightly interwoven with certain prefigurations and expectations that are essential for the persuasiveness and suggestive power of the vision itself.[116] This imaginative dimension often remains unconscious or unreflected by the historical actors. At the Paneuropean Congress, stressing the existential necessity of European unification by employing biological metaphors of life and death was somewhat uncommon. Instead, the focus lay on a gradual decline of European civilisation that was figuratively identified in the architectural image of ruins. Using this imagery, Edmund Stinnes drew a pessimistic sketch of the possible outcome of a new world war which would "create nothing but ruins among which later generations will conduct archaeological or historical research in much the same way as we dig for the rubble of the Forum Romanum".[117]

At first glance, this image might betray resignation. The prophecy, however, is part of an argument in favour of Paneurope as a means of preventing the continent's anticipated decline and fall. Moreover, it was also possible to see, in the predicted ruins, the potential for reconstruction, as Frederick Allen did:

"Prior to 1914, Europe stood like a great Reims cathedral and we of the outside world looked in admiration upon its strength and beauty. Devastated by the war, the first thought and effort must be for its material rebuilding, so that its Faithful may find therein protection [...]. But for this rebuilding the keystone is united effort."[118]

---

114 Speech by Frederick H. Allen, New York at the Paneuropean congress, EUI Florence, PAN/EU-2; Coudenhove-Kalergi (1926), *Paneuropa-Kongreß*, 40 f.
115 See e.g. Srodes (2011), *Franklin*, 282.
116 Nünning (2007), *Grundzüge*.
117 Sigmund Stinnes to Coudenhove-Kalergi, May 1925, EUI Florence, PAN/EU-3.
118 Speech by Frederick H. Allen, New York at the Paneuropean Congress, EUI Florence, PAN/EU-2.

Using cartographical means that showed Europe's "real" geographical dimension as a mere promontory of Asia was another way of illustrating the continent's weakness and inferiority. Against this background, Coudenhove-Kalergi provided a world map showing the future Paneurope at its centre (including the colonial possessions of Africa) and suggesting that a unified continent might compete with the existing world powers.[119]

An ascription of decline is, on the surface, merely *descriptive*. However, since such descriptions necessarily rely on metaphorical imagery, they also develop a narrative dimension. As these last examples make clear, metaphors and images employed in a Vision of Decline bear a particular quality that transforms the situational description of a weakness into an effective narrative; a story spun around diagnosed current deficits which will (allegedly) assuredly lead to a new or persistent "change for the worse", unless, of course, appropriate action is taken to counter them.[120]

In this sense, the Paneuropean federation was one possible remedy for the perceived decline of Europe, but not the only one. In the end, and in spite of having made every conceivable effort, Coudenhove-Kalergi did not succeed in preventing the continent's collapse and his plans remained unrealised until the enterprise of European integration in the wake of World War II. Nevertheless, the way in which he drew attention to the dreadful situation of Europe initiated a discourse, the dynamics of which became visible in the context of the "Study Commission for a European Union" initiated by Aristide Briand, who had spoken strongly in favour of a European union before the League of Nations on 5 September 1929. Although his plans certainly differed from the ideas of the Paneuropean Movement, he, too, used the highly suggestive motto "unite or perish". Lastly, we find the same formula after 1945 when the European project finally started to become a reality. One could argue that the narrative of European decline became part of the European Union's very "DNA" since it can be found in statements concerning the state of the EU to this day, especially following the Brexit decision.[121] Today, as well as in the interwar period, the narrative concerning European integration bears a distinctly appellative character. In it, European integration appears as a necessity that comes without any acceptable alternative. Nevertheless, there is a signifi-

---

119 See Coudenhove-Kalergi (1923), *Pan-Europa*.
120 See Klaus Seidl's chapter on "Representations of Weakness" in this volume for a more detailed discussion of the narrative quality of weakness ascriptions.
121 Tusk (2017), *United we stand*; see also Seidl (2018), *Kassandra*.

cant difference that particularly highlights the inherent ambivalence of decline narratives: whereas the Paneuropean Movement aimed for political change in the form of an unprecedented effort of unification in order to stop the continent's downfall, the current discourse, in contrast, focuses on maintaining a *status quo* threatened with disintegration. This suggests that Visions of Decline can conceivably provide stimuli for historical transformation as well as incentives for the perpetuation of a given order.

V. By Process of Elimination—Images of Ruin, Decay, and Struggle in China around 1900

"The state of Liang fell."

Question: The record [in the chronicle] has made no mention of an attack. Why now this reference to the fall of the state of Liang?
Answer: The state fell on its own.
Question: How did it fall on its own?
Answer: Like a fish, rotting from the inside out.
The "Gongyang Commentary" on the *Spring and Autumn Annals*, 19th year of Duke Xi's reign (*i.e.*, 641 BCE)[122]

In 1898, around the time when British Prime Minister Lord Salisbury gave his infamous "Dying-Nations-Speech" in front of the Primrose League,[123] late Qing China experienced a veritable "boom" of writings envisioning the impending "ruin (*wang*)" of the Chinese "nation/state (*guo*)",[124] not

---

[122] Miller (2015), *Gongyang Commentary*, 104. The "Gongyang Commentary" is composed in a question-and-answer format. It offers an almost word-by-word explanation of the *Spring and Autumn Annals*, the official chronicle of the state of Lu of pre-imperial China, allegedly written by Confucius.
[123] *The Times*, 5 May 1898, 17.
[124] The years between 1840 and 1949 have been called period of "nationalistic modernity" (Hon (2015), *Allure of the Nation*, 3) by some researchers. Nevertheless, correctly translating *guo* ("walled city," "realm," "country") or *guojia* in turn-of-the-century Chinese sources is not at all a straightforward matter. (Indeed, the same holds true for much of the "vocabulary of modernity.") As something like a Chinese national consciousness began to take shape in the course of the late nineteenth century, the word that had formerly designated a fluid territory without clearly demarcated borders (one notable exception being the Russian empire), inhabited by a great number of diverse peoples, and nominally belonging to the ruling Qing dynasty, came to stand for a united political

infrequently coupled with exhortations to guard against the danger of "racial extinction (*miezhong*)". Indeed, I would argue that, while the idea of the "dying nation" certainly gained some prominence in Euro-American discourse (having been, after all, coined by an eminent statesman), its influence there pales when compared to the ubiquity of the *wangguo* motif—one possible translation of which is "dying nation"—in the Chinese press between the reform era of roughly 1896–98 and the founding of the Chinese Republic in 1912 and beyond.[125] In other words, when Salisbury characterised China as "dying" (undoubtedly in order to legitimise a continued British presence in East Asia), a host of contemporaries in the Middle Realm did not at all disagree.[126] On the contrary, they voiced the same conviction even more vociferously than Salisbury himself had done. After all, the rhetorical motif owed its popularity in the Chinese context precisely to the fact that it pointed to a not wholly unrealistic scenario for the country's future. [127] *Wangguo* images thus constitute veritable "metaphors" in the

---

body which was culturally dominated by the Han ethnic group. The political fate of this polity was, however, contested and uncertain with visions ranging from outside (Western) domination, via the establishment of a constitutional monarchy, to the creation of a Han-Chinese nation-state. The key characteristic of a functioning *guo* was arguably its "sovereignty (*zhuquan*)" and "independence (*zili*)" as an equal participant in international relations (Svarverud (2007), *International Law*). However, as I will subsequently argue, political thinkers of that time became increasingly convinced that China's sovereignty as a state could only be ensured by forging the Chinese people into an indivisible community of common destiny; that is, a nation. This conviction became even more pronounced after the dynastic collapse in 1911 (Hon (2015), *Allure of the Nation*, 4). For Chinese "statism" around 1900 see Zarrow (2012), *After Empire*, esp. 89–118. On Liang Qichao's (a pivotal historical figure in this essay) views on "nation-state" and "nationalism:" Chang (1971), *Liang Ch'i-ch'ao*, 107–111; 164–167. The role of visions of failure and weakness in Chinese nation-building is discussed in Tsu (2005), *Failure*, Nationalism, and Literature, esp. 1–31. For a discussion of contemporary nationalism and racism, see Dikötter (2015 [1992]), *Discourse of Race*, 61–102; for critical appraisal, see Schneider (2017), *Nation and Ethnicity*, 390–391.

125 The *wang* ("there is not," "to lose," "to die") in the compound *wangguo* is just as troublesome conceptually as *guo* alone. As far as I can tell, all related Visions of Decline coalesce around the belief that the polity under discussion has ceased to function properly and independently—becoming eradicated from the world map being the most drastic outcome. Suffice it to say that *wang* around 1900 was no longer seen as a cosmological inevitability to occur after every period of bloom, but as a possible and preventable or redeemable outcome of politico-historical developments.

126 China was thus not only metaphorically rendered as a nation "asleep", as previous scholarship has emphasised. Wagner (2011), *China 'Asleep'*.

127 A contemporary assessment by a Western observer is provided by Reid (1900), *The Powers and the Partition of China.*

cognitive sense.[128] Their invocation in turn-of-the-century China is not a case of mere "Self-Orientalism" (*i.e.*, the act of framing one's own experience according to the prejudices of the Occident).[129] They are employed in order ultimately to stave off (further) decline, not to perpetuate it.

The same year, 1898, also saw the publication of *Tianyan lun* (On Evolution), written by the prolific translator and political commentator Yan Fu (1853–1921), and based upon Thomas Henry Huxley's *Evolution and Ethics*,[130] the first substantial work introducing Darwinian[131] ideas into the sinophone world. The notion of a "struggle for survival" (first mentioned in an essay by Yan written in 1895) provided the *wangguo* discourse with a new framework (supposedly based on science and natural principles) but also opened up a frightening scenario, namely, the possibility of China being "eliminated (*taotai*)" once and for all in the competition between the world's nations. In traditional Chinese historiography, "ruin" was always followed by "rise (*xing*)", most often of a new dynasty. Within the Darwinian framework, on the other hand, it is not only animal species that could become extinct, but also states or even entire civilisations.

Perhaps fuelled by the spread of Social Darwinian ideas, "national ruin" as a historical phenomenon was also explored in what I call "Ruination Histories", *i.e.*, monographs, essays, or serialisations in periodicals dedicated to the narration and analysis of the downfall of a given polity. Ruination Histories most prominently dealt with cases of national ruin in the recent past, such as Poland, India, Egypt, or the Ottoman Empire, but a large number dealt with ancient societies as well.[132] As a matter of fact, knowledge of these historical lessons was so widespread that a few names evolved into rhetorical commonplaces: "Poland (*Bolan*)", for instance,

---

128 In their cognitive theory of metaphors, Lakoff and Johnson stressed that living metaphors need to be grounded in experience. Metaphors thus simultaneous structure experience and are structured through it. Lakoff and Johnson (2003 [1980]), *Metaphors We Live By*, 19–21, 56–68.
129 The classic work on "Orientalism" is Said (1994 [1979]), *Orientalism*, esp. 4–28, 201–328.
130 The work is usually characterised as a *translation* of *Evolution and Ethics*. However, one needs to appreciate the significant alterations and additions made by Yan Fu to make Huxley "fit" the Chinese context as well as his own ideas. A critical evaluation of Yan as a translator is provided by Huang (2008), *The Meaning of Freedom*, 4–18.
131 I prefer to call these ideas "Darwinian" rather than "Darwinist" so as to circumvent the thorny (and in this context quite irrelevant) question of accuracy and ideology. It is of little concern to what degree Darwin was "misunderstood" by the likes of Yan and Liang and whether either of the two may be labeled a "true" Darwinist.
132 Karl (2002), *Staging the World*, 15–16; Zou (1996), *Qingmo wangguoshi bianyire*.

served as a virtual synonym for "partition (*guafen, fenge*)", and—due to the particularities of the Chinese language—was even readily turned into a verbal phrase: "*Bolan wo*" ([they will] poland (*i.e.*, partition) us). Stories about countries and peoples that had *failed* to meet the challenges of their time thus form a conceptual complement to the equally numerous (and generally better known) *success stories* of nations that had successfully "modernised", most notably, Japan.[133]

The question that I will tentatively explore in this section is how "ruination narratives" in turn-of-the-century China attribute *blame*, and wherein they locate the *causa ultima* of national failure. For this purpose, I will discuss one particularly dense and rich text in some detail, namely, "New Methods to Vanquish Nations (*Mieguo xinfa lun*)" of 1901, written by one Liang Qichao (1873–1929), arguably the most prominent figure in Chinese political discourse at that time, who offered opinions on virtually everything from from general politics, via history and literature, to new fields of knowledge such as logic and national debt.[134] In addition, he wrote the first (albeit brief) Ruination History of a non-Chinese country, "Record of the Blight of Poland (*Bolan miewang ji*)" (1896). However, in order to offer some context and allow a sense of the broader discussions of which these texts were part, I will draw on a few other sources as well.

To return to the research question, of whether a nation always fails because of the coincidence of "inner turmoil and outside threats (*neiyou waihuan*)", as a Chinese adage has it, which of the two is more critical? What, according to contemporary voices, should be addressed first? And wherein lies the root cause of China's weakness? As I will demonstrate below, the verdict is all but unequivocal in the sources under consideration here: "Ruin" (even if followed—or aggravated—by outside incursion) is, in the final consequence, always "self-inflicted (*ziqu*)". This notion already finds ex-

---

[133] This is not to say that the role of countries other than Japan to provide models for China's "road to modern statehood" is to be underestimated.

A recent comprehensive, albeit somewhat idiosyncratic, treatment of China's efforts to "change its models (*bianfa*)" is provided by Jenco (2015), *Changing Referents*, esp. 102–110. For Japan, see, among others, Fogel (2004), *Role of Japan*; Reynolds (1993), *Xinzheng Revolution*; Reynolds (2014), *East Meets East*, esp. 33–49, 404–411.

Reynolds (2014) is particular instructive for early nineteenth century exchanges between the two countries.

[134] Overview of Liang's thought: Chang (1971), *Liang Ch'i-ch'ao*, 73–295. Literature: Tsau (1980), Rise of 'New Fiction', 23–29. Logic: Kurtz (2011), *Discovery of Chinese Logic*, 260–276, 313–327. Journalism: Vittinghoff (2002), *Unity vs. Uniformity*. National debt: Amelung (2006), *Staatsanleihen*, 49–50. For Liang as a historian, see n. 154.

pression in a number of Chinese idiomatic expressions and is even discussed in certain canonical texts of wisdom and knowledge, such as the "Gongyang Commentary" quoted in the epithet. The text *Mengzi* (Book of Master Meng) of the late fourth century BCE puts it quite unambiguously:

"A man must demean himself, only then will others demean him. A family must ruin (*hui*) itself, only then will others ruin it. A state must attack itself, only then will others attack it."[135]

And the twelfth century thinker Zhu Xi, whose commentary on the *Mengzi* had become standard in late imperial China, concluded his explanation of said paragraph thus:

"Misfortune and good fortune are both things that one brings upon oneself."[136]

In other words: First, the wood has to rot, only then do the vermin emerge (*mu bi xian fu erhou chong sheng*).

1. Salisbury and China

Salisbury's speech was, to the best of my knowledge, not well-known in contemporary China. It is nonetheless instructive in analysing the Chinese *wangguo* discourse: first of all, what is commonly called the "China Question" served as Salisbury's key motivation behind the speech, which he held only weeks after the conclusion of the China crisis of 1897/98.[137] Second, the similarity in the choice of words is uncanny. And, as already mentioned, "dying nation" falls undoubtedly within the semantic scope of *wangguo*. Third, it was none other than Salisbury who led Britain during the Second Boer War, an event closely observed by Chinese reformers.[138] And finally, Salisbury also addressed the issue of "the attribution of blame", as I will show presently. Let us therefore turn to Salisbury for a moment.

---

135 *Mengzi* 4A.8. In: Jiao et al. (1987), *Mengzi zhengyi*, 500–501. Note also the closing summary statement provided in the "Significance of the Paragraph (*zhangju*)" which corresponds to Zhu Xi's interpretation.
136 Van Norden (2008), *Mengzi*, 93.
137 From the British point of view, the crisis had (temporally) been resolved by Britain's acquisition of Weihaiwei as a base of operations to keep German influence in East Asia in check. Otte (2007), *The China Question*, 83–132, 157.
138 Karl (2002), *Staging the World*, 117–148.

Salisbury does not actually provide his audience with a country-by-country division of the world along his two categories "living" and "dying". China, however, features prominently in his argumentation as the epitome of a "weak nation" that threatens to destabilise international relations and heaps ever more weight on "the White Man's Burden" by failing to provide regional leadership in East Asia.[139] A crucial point in Salisbury's argument is the insistence that the weakness of the dying nations developed *prior* to any encroachment via "the living" upon their sovereignty. In other words, China was not weakened by the interference of an outside foe, it became weak on account of internal decay and thus eventually grew dependent on outside aid:

"Decade after decade [the Dying Nations] are weaker, poorer, and less provided with leading men or institutions in which they can trust, apparently drawing nearer and nearer to their fate and yet clinging with strange tenacity to the life which they have got. In them misgovernment is not only not cured but is constantly on the increase. The society, and official society, the administration, is a mass of corruption, so that there is no firm ground on which any hope for reform or restoration could be based, and in their various degrees they are presenting a terrible picture to the more enlightened portion of the world—a picture which, unfortunately, the increase in the means of our information and communication draws with darker and more conspicuous lineaments in the face of all nations, appealing to their feelings as well as to their interests, calling upon them to bring forward a remedy."[140]

The current internal situation, as well as the political history of a country is conceptualised as a "black box" into which no outside intervention is possible. Domestic politics, in Salisbury's and similar arguments, in a way serves as a functional equivalent for *mutations* in biology: the occurrence of mutations is not the result of the struggle for survival—they are random, trial-and-error mechanisms. The historically grown internal constitution of a nation, too, is (mistakenly, of course) imagined to have developed (and continues to develop) somehow independently from international relations and external influences (good or bad). There is little to no regard for the necessary, inextricable mutual interdependency between the two. The spheres "internal" and "external" are neatly separated in the same way that

---

[139] The perceived "power vacuum" in East Asia was felt by Japanese contemporaries as well. This likely contributed to Japan's sense that it had to step-in and take leadership in the region in order to unite the "yellow race" against the "White Peril." Matten (2016), *Imagining a Postnational World*, 162–224.
[140] *The Times*, 5 May 1898, 17.

the neo-conservatives of our time imagine them to be. A state's inner *state* changes, to all intents and purposes, "randomly", in the sense that the other nations have neither the right nor an interest in having a stake in the "private" affairs of another nation[141]—as long as they have not deteriorated to a degree that makes interference (*i.e.*, "aid") politically and ethically (!) necessary. Whether historically grown, caused by recent unfortunate policy decisions, or due to certain allegedly flawed "national characteristics" or racial traits, the observed "un-fitness" (and eventual death) is not born out of the "international struggle for survival", it developed "naturally" and unprovoked within these nations. The struggle for survival merely serves as a process to eliminate that which is already weak. Indeed, it emerges almost as a truism that struggle makes things only stronger, never weaker.

We thus observe, around the year 1900, a transculturally observable preoccupation with two aspects of "national ruin": 1) Internal decay, which is seen as not ultimately caused by outside intrusion or aggression (which, in no way, implies, of course, that these are absent). 2) A competitive, warlike international system that eliminates "the weak", but only in the sense of "aiding" the "natural" and "inevitable" process of selection.

In its (early) East Asian recension, as has been argued repeatedly, the Darwinian vision tended to de-emphasise the potentially "beneficial" means of *intranational* competition (reducing poor relief, eugenics) which were regularly cited in Euro-America as measures to "strengthen the nation". Instead, it was the international stage that became the proper area for the struggle for survival, and it was nation states, not people, that were

---

141 Chinese intellectuals of the period in question were well aware of the blatant discrepancies between the lofty ideals of international law on the one hand, and the *realpolitik* of international relations on the other. The rules of international law do not, in fact, grant equal rights to all states. Certainly, they do not guarantee that these rights will actually be observed by the other nations. Liang Qichao, quoting an unnamed "Western philosopher" paraphrased the contemporary international situation thusly: "When two equals encounter each other, there is no power (*quanli*). [In this case,] reason (*daoli*) is power. When two unequals encounter each other, there is no reason. [In this case,] power is reason." Liang et al. (1999), *Liang Qichao quanji*, 470. The example that was closest to the heart of Liang and his peers were, of course the series of "unequal treaties" China had been subjected to ever since the Opium Wars. The term "unequal treaty (*bu pingdeng tiaoyue*)" itself, however, did not come into general use until much later (Dong (2003), *Unequal Treaties*, 401–407). The discourse on international relations in turn-of-the-century China thus had to negotiate ideas of progress (informed by both traditional and Western sources), the ideals of international law, and the realities of Darwinian evolution manifested in the struggle for survival among nations (Svarverud (2007), *International Law*, 195–221).

its key actors.¹⁴² In the service of nation-building and internal consolidation, any and all efforts that could lead to or compound internal strife were demonised, at least in the initial stage of the Chinese reception of Social Darwinism.¹⁴³ In Chapter 15 (*Zui zhi*, Key Pointers), which serves as a summary to the first part of *On Evolution*, Yan Fu comments:

"If I were to summarise the gist of the preceding 14 chapters, it would have to be that we must realise that the art of human selection may be applied to flora and fauna, but it must under no circumstances find employ within human society. This is not due to a lack of wisdom. Even if wisdom could be relied on, (human selection) would still cause sympathy and humanity to wane and such a society would disband. [...] Therefore I say, if one seeks strength by means of human selection, it will result only in weakness."¹⁴⁴

The "disbandment (*huan*)" of society (*qun*, lit.: "group")¹⁴⁵ constitutes—all imperialist encroachments notwithstanding—Yan's worst-case-scenario for China. Or rather, China's weakness lies in the fact that it lacks "group cohesion". He makes the relative dangers of "foreign incursions" and "group dispersion" even more clear in his essay "On Forces of Obstruction and Forces of Disintegration in China (*Lun Zhongguo zhi zuli yu lixinli*)", published in January of 1898:

"Presently, China extends over tens of thousands of *li* and has a few hundred million people. The people of the realm are in a state of profound unease, as if (China) was destined to die before her allotted time is up. If you ask them why,

---

142 Pusey (1983), *China and Charles Darwin*, 67–75, 110–112; Tikhonov (2010), *Social Darwinism*, 14–16.
Liang agreed in principal that in order for a whole to become strong, its individual units needed to compete against each other. China, however, was not yet at a point in its socio-political development where "internal competition" would be beneficial instead of detrimental. For the time being, he argued, "external competition", and (internal) integration had to take precedence in China (Chang (1971), *Liang Ch'i-ch'ao*, 245–250. A similar point is made in Tang (1996), *Global Space*, 123). His conviction that *inter-* rather than *intra-*national struggle was the way to progress as a society was shared, for example, by fellow reformer Mai Menghua (1875–1915) (Svarverud (2007), *International Law*, 195–197).

143 This "tolerant" state of affairs, however, changed quickly in the context of Revolution of 1911 and anti-Manchu racism had been a hallmark of the revolutionary camp even before 1900. On Anti-Manchuism at the turn of the century see Dikötter (2015 [1992]), *Discourse of Race*, 61–78; and Rhoads (2000), *Manchus and Han*, 187–205.

144 Yan et al. (2000), *Tianyan lun*, 194.

145 Vogelsang (2012), *Chinese "Society"*, 163–173. The word "*shehui*" (today, the word commonly used for "society" in Chinese) displaced *qun* at the beginning of the twentieth century (Vogelsang (2012), *Chinese "Society"*, 156, 173–185).

they will surely answer that [China's demise] will come by the obstruction of the strong countries of Europe. [As a matter of fact,] it does not matter about what subject you inquire, from the smallest issue to the biggest problem, all is because we are being wronged by the Westerners. They are actually correct in calling this "obstruction". However, let us delve into the question of why this obstruction is able to exert its force in our land [in the first place]. Is it honestly because we lack the strength to resist? We thus realise that the reason why (the Westerners can harm us) is because forces of disintegration (*lixinli*, lit.: centrifugal forces) are [rampant] in China."[146]

Yan goes on to elaborate that foreign aggressors as well as "traitors and usurpers within" (as devastating as their actions may be, even for centuries to come) may wreak havoc for a time, but only the prevalence of forces of disintegration between the "small particles" of society, will eventually lead to the "complete, utter and traceless disappearance of the race".

In a similar vein, the aforementioned Liang Qichao explained in 1896 ("On Groups (*Shuo qun*)") how one might go about destroying (*mie*) a nation (*guo*):

"He who wants to exterminate a nation (*guo*) may accomplish this by exterminating the nation's group (cohesion) (*qun*). If ruler and ruled do not communicate, and you and I do not care for each other, one can bring about ruin even to a Celestial Kingdom (*i.e.*, a perfect state). When wood gets infested with parasites and the wood thus infested had already withered, then the parasitic wood will waste away (completely)."[147]

A few sentences later, Liang quotes the very passage from the "Gongyang Commentary" mentioned above and concludes:

"National Ruin has been called by many names 'collapse of the land (*tubeng*)', 'shattering of roof tiles (*wajie*)', but what is meant is always 'societal disintegration (*liqun*)'."[148]

---

146 Yan et al. (2006), *Yan Fu wenxuan*, 112.
147 Liang et al. (1999), *Liang Qichao quanji*, vol. 1, 94.
  Yan's *Tianyan lun* was not published in full until two years later. However, Liang had seen a draft version prior to writing this essay, as he mentions in the first paragraph (Liang et al. (1999), *Liang Qichao quanji*, 93; Huang (2008), *The Meaning of Freedom*, 265).
148 Liang et al. (1999), *Liang Qichao quanji*, 95.

2. How to Vanquish Nations (and Save them)

Liang's essay "On Groups" appears to have never been finished. However, some years later, in 1901, he wrote a lengthy treatise dedicated to the second, external aspect of "national ruin" mentioned above: How can one go about *actively* destroying a *guo*, rather than waiting for its natural demise? According to Liang, "progress (*jinhua*)" has led to a number of methods (*fa*) by which this may be achieved and which had not existed previously.[149] The hallmark of the "new methods" is *subtlety*: destruction, nowadays, works by means of "coaxing and persuasion (*ao zhi, xiu zhi*)"; it is done "gradually (*jian*)", and "subtly (*wei*)". The tyranny and brute force of the tiger and the wolf has given way to the cunning of the fox.[150] Liang illustrates his analysis with five cases of national destruction in recent world history, namely, the fates of Egypt, Poland, India, the Boer Republics, and the Philippines. He in no way condones the aggressive actions of expansionist nations such as England, Prussia, France, and Russia, but it is evident that Liang holds *the victimised nations themselves* to be ultimately responsible for their destruction. He does so quite explicitly in a number of cases.

"By what means did the British manage to accomplish the great feat [of subjugating the Indian subcontinent]? Common sense would dictate that they could only have done so by levying a huge army and spending a vast amount of money on the military. Who knew that one would be entirely mistaken in supposing this! When the British annihilated India, this was not done by using Britain's strength; it was done by using India's strength."[151]

According to Liang's analysis, Britain built its invasion army of Indian recruits, trained by European military methods and led by European commanders. In addition, the sea power co-opted local overlords and chieftains into its colonial enterprise, using them as accessories. This second strategy corresponds to the interpretation offered by his teacher, Kang

---

149 Liang's virtual obsession with "the New" is well documented and researched. Among others, he preached the "renovation of the (Chinese) people (*xinmin*)", and called for a "new historiography (*xin shixue*)", as well as the "renovation of fiction" in the field of literature (Chang (1971), *Liang Ch'i-ch'ao*, 149–150; *Mieguo xinfa lun*, 467).
150 Chang (1971), *Mieguo xinfa lun*, 467.
151 Chang (1971), *Mieguo xinfa lun*, 469.

Youwei (1858–1927), who had blamed regional self-government and territorial fragmentation for India's downfall.[152]

Similarly, Poland was not so much partitioned by outside forces, as carved up by the Poles themselves and shared out among its stronger neighbours:

"When the Russians destroyed Poland, this was not due to the Russian's ability to do so. The nobles and bureaucrats, the rich and powerful of Poland made obeisance again and again, gave concessions again and again, and thus downright asked the Russians to destroy it."[153]

In the same vein, Liang deems Egypt's loss of sovereignty, especially in fiscal matters following the construction of the Suez-Canal, to have been a "self-inflected calamity (*ziqiuhuo*)".

Naturally, Liang is not primarily interested in world-historical abstractions.[154] His main concern is his own country, and, more specifically, the question as to what extent China can and should rely on foreign aid for its domestic reform project—a course of action which Liang objects to vehemently.[155]

There are two dangerous prevailing attitudes in China that just might, according to Liang, push the country "over the edge" and into utter destruction: first, the mistaken belief that China's precarious *status quo* with the country teetering on the brink of destruction might be preserved indefinitely; second, the fact that the Chinese people's confidence in their country's prospects (or lack thereof) depends on the prevailing attitude of the imperialist powers towards the Middle Realm.

"In the affairs of the world (*tianxia*), there is no such thing as neutrality. What is not extinguished, rises; what does not rise, is extinguished. When choosing what course (of action) to take, there is no room for the slightest mistake. And yet our 400 million people make no serious study of the policies (*ce*) by which one might rejuvenate (*xing*) the country (*guo*), but rather adhere to their pontifical ways, hop-

---

152 "Yu tongxue zhuzi Liang Qichao deng lun Yindu wangguo youyu ge sheng zili shu (A discussion about the downfall of India having been caused by the independence of its individual provinces held with Liang Qichao and other students)", May 1902. In: Kang et al. (2007), *Kang Youwei quanji*, 334–349.
153 Liang et al. (1999), *Liang Qichao quanji*, 472.
154 Liang as a "nationalist historian" is extensively discussed in Tang (1996), *Global Space*, 46–79.
155 He mentions the prominent and influential official Zhang Zhidong (1837–1909) specifically as a politician who allegedly condones securing foreign support to finance China's costly reform projects.

ing to avoid destruction (*miewang*). Herein lies the first root cause for (national) destruction.

Others will never love us as dearly as we love ourselves. Is it at all conceivable that someone sacrifices the interests of their own country in order for another country to pursue its interests? And yet our 400 million people, hearing that the powers (*lieqiang*) deliberate the partition of China, are stunned and cowed; hearing that the powers deliberate on the integrity of China, are carefree and at ease; and hearing that the Powers are going to lend China aid, are delighted and happy. Herein lies the second root cause for (national) destruction."[156]

It is thus not enough for China to realise its weakness in relation to Europe and the United States. In a world view governed by evolution and the constant need for change (*bian*, arguably, *the* watchword in turn-of-the-century Chinese political discourse), there can only be progress, or—through bad policies, inaction, or both—decline. Secondly, this "change for the better" must be accomplished self-sufficiently, since a call for aid is a sign of weakness, and weakness, in turn, invites outside aggression. Furthermore, from the earlier statements concerning "group cohesion", we may infer that, in the eyes of the two thinkers discussed here, uniting the "400 million" behind a common project of national rejuvenation would not only would not only serve to eradicate China's material deficits regarding industry, infrastructure, and the military, but foster "group cohesion"—believed to be the best indicator for national strength and, at the same time, its greatest safeguard. However, in the sources I have focused on for this article, neither Yan nor Liang provides a detailed *practical* strategy as to how this is to be achieved. Many of their ideas remain abstract. To answer this question, one would need to take a closer look at concrete reform measures, either at the local level or those enacted in nationwide programmes such as the New Policies (*Xinzheng*) begun in 1901.[157]

While Liang (among others) would have followed Salisbury in diagnosing weakness first and foremost as emerging "within" a nation, he most certainly did not believe in the West's professed "civilising mission", as we have seen. For Salisbury, the fact that a nation was dying necessitated outside intervention. For Liang, China had to lie in the proverbial bed it had

---

[156] Liang et al. (1999), *Liang Qichao quanji*, 470.
[157] For the late Qing reform movement in general, see Reynolds (1993), *Xinzheng Revolution* and, Esherick and Wei (2014), *China: How the Empire Fell*. Finances: Amelung (2006), *Staatsanleihen*. Education: Zarrow (2015), *Educating China*, 11–40. Military: Schillinger (2016), *The Body and Military Masculinity*, esp. 247–311. Reform at the local level: Rankin (1986), *Elite Activism*, 202–247.

made for itself.[158] This insistence on China's "national responsibility" was, of course, a two-edged sword. The *capacity* to solve its problems rests within the nation itself, but so does the *culpability* for these problems.

VI. The Problem of the Buddenbrooks—Images for the Rise and Decline of Lübeck in the Correspondence between Fritz Rörig and Thomas Mann

1. The Bourgeois Family as an Image for an Aristocratic Republic

In 1926, the "free imperial city (*Freie und Reichstadt*)" of Lübeck celebrated the 700th anniversary of its legal status as an immediate part of the German Empire. Emperor Frederick II had granted the right of "imperial immediacy (*Reichsunmittelbarkeit* or *Reichsfreiheit*)" to the city that rose on the Baltic Sea in 1226. For more than 700 years, the city had remained largely independent of imperial influence and did not become part of the territory of the rising territorial seigniors, but an immediate part of the federal empire. This status of a state within the empire survived both the proclamation of the German Empire in 1871 and the founding of the Weimar Republic in 1918/19. But the celebrations of 1926 were already clouded by ongoing negotiations over the dissolution of this legal status.[159] While earlier events of this nature were heavily influenced by the national movement of the nineteenth century (finding a place for Lübeck in national German history), the celebrations of 1926 had a completely different contemporary frame and referred to a different *"lieu de mémoire"*:[160] the self-perception of an aristocratic independent municipal republic and its position in modernity.[161]

The 700th anniversary celebrations may be regarded as a distinct orchestration of a "Vision of Decline". While the sovereignty of the Hanse towns of Hamburg and Bremen, both globally connected, logistic and

---

158 Svarverud (2007), *International Law*, 203–205.
159 Krogel (1994), *Die Stadt als bürgerliche Heimat*, 225–278; Lokers (2014), *Hansestädtische Erinnerungskultur im 19. und 20. Jahrhundert*, 307–309; Meyer (2008), *Vom Ersten Weltkrieg bis 1996*, 695–702; Hundt and Lokers (2014), *Ende des eigenständigen Lübecker Staates*.
160 For this concept, see Nora (1998), *Zwischen Geschichte und Gedächtnis*.
161 Krogel (1994), *Die Stadt als bürgerliche Heimat*, 231.

economic hubs with more than 500,000 inhabitants each, remained unchallenged, the comparable constitutional status of Lübeck, a town of less than 150,000 people, seemed to be an anachronistic relic of the medieval and early modern "German particularism" in the constitutional debates of the 1920s.[162] These ongoing debates shaped the character of the celebrations; municipal history was told as the history of an urban republic, the dignity of this history was evoked, while the city tried to renew its cultural and economic relations in Northern Europe.

On 6 July 1926, Fritz Rörig (1882–1952), professor for medieval history and former archivist of Lübeck, submitted his edition of the oldest German merchant's manual—in his words: "a supremely scientific (*schwerwissenschaftliche*) publication"—to the future winner of the Noble prize in literature and famous son of Lübeck, Thomas Mann.[163] Rörig seems to have been among the audience the previous evening, when Mann had held a public speech, entitled "Lübeck as a spiritual way of life (*Lübeck als geistige Lebensform*)",[164] as part of the anniversary celebrations. While Thomas Mann reacted kindly, but probably with little enthusiasm, to this gift—the arid business prose of fourteenth century merchants—it was very clear in the eyes of Rörig that he, as a medievalist, and Mann, as a writer, had essentially written the same story, albeit with different words.

In his letter to Thomas Mann, he explained this idea: during his extensive sociological studies in German medieval history, he had focused on the decline of particular notable families. And reading merchant manuals had allegedly enabled him to analyse the "economic, or, even better, psycho-economical (*wirtschaftspsychologischen*)" reasons for this decline. For Rörig, it was evident that this supported Mann's narrative in his novel *The Buddenbrooks*:

"The problem of the Buddenbrooks seems to be not only a contemporary general *bourgeois* problem but even the general problem of bourgeoisie merchants *per se*."[165]

To prove this, Rörig sent another article, entitled "Families and personages of Lübeck's early days (*Lübecker Familien und Persönlichkeiten aus der Frühzeit der Stadt*)" to Thomas Mann in December 1926. In his second letter to

---

162 Brandt (1979), *Das Ende der Hanseatischen Gemeinschaft*, 97–125.
163 AHL, *Nachlass Rörig*, n. 51, Fritz Rörig to Thomas Mann, 6 June 1926; Rörig (1925), Das älteste erhaltene deutsche Kaufmannsbüchlein, 12–66.
164 Thomas Mann gave this lecture on 5 June 1926 in the Stadttheater of Lübeck. It was published 1926. For the lecture, see Mann (1990), *Gesammelte Werke*, vol. 11, 376–398.
165 AHL, *Nachlass Rörig*, n. 51, Fritz Rörig to Thomas Mann, 7 December 1926.

Mann, Rörig not only postulated a "direct line from the end of the fourteenth century to the Buddenbrooks' Lübeck", but also asserted that the situation of the city had been significantly different in earlier times. Indeed, the article focused on the "before" and the "inner reasons" for the decline, as well as the "mode" of this historical change.[166] Thereby, Rörig transferred Mann's narrative of the "decline of a family" into a completely new context. He metaphorically grafted the fate of an individual *bourgeois* family onto the urban republic as a family-like organism.

2. Holistic Images—Lübeck and the Hanse as an Organism Formed by Family Ties

In some ways, the deconstruction of "historiographic narratives" has become the central concern for historians and scholars from related disciplines. Taking this idea seriously means analysing not only the context in which particular narratives arise, but also their inner semantics. For obvious reasons, historians are not only writing history but also narrating stories. They are weighing facts, structuring synchronous events into a linear narration, and shortening the temporal dimension of historical change. Writing history is, in the end, a literary pursuit.[167]

To what type of narrative did Fritz Rörig, whose name is closely associated with the socio-economic orientation of Hanse-scholarship in the 1920s,[168] refer when he addressed Thomas Mann? The anecdote concerning the correspondence between the historian of the Hanse and the "*bourgeois* bohemian (*Künstler-Bürger*)" Mann offers a fascinating perspective on a very particular type of narrative dealing with historical transformation. Narratives of decline are, as Reinhard Koselleck has argued, characterised by distinct semantics, which distinguish them from alternative modes of narrating historical transformation.[169] My aim is to focus on these semantics by a close reading of the conceptual metaphors[170] and images which

---

166 AHL, *Nachlass Rörig*, n. 51, Fritz Rörig to Thomas Mann, 7 December 1926.
167 See White (1973), *Metahistory*.
168 For Rörig's work, see Groth et al. (2018), *Unwiderstehliche Horizonte?*; Lambert (1999), *From Antifascist to Volkshistoriker*; Noodt (2007), *Fritz Rörig (1882–1952)*; Paulsen (2016), *Hanse und Europa*; Selzer (2016), *Nachgrabung auf dem Markt von Lübeck*.
169 Koselleck (2006), *Fortschritt und Niedergang*; Koselleck (1982), *Krise*, 617–650; Koselleck et al. (1980), *Niedergang*.
170 In the sense of Lakoff et al. (2003 [1980]), *Metaphors We Live By*.

Rörig uses to draw parallels between the decline of Lübeck and the decline of the élite families of this town, namely, the Buddenbrooks. I will argue that Rörig stylised Mann as a master narrator of Hanseatic history. But, while he did so, his and Mann's stories still differ markedly concerning the attributed alternatives and the estimated impacts of these narratives of decline. These differences are due to the fact that, while Rörig and Mann made use of a shared set of semantics, their respective narratives were part of completely different discourses.

Let us take a closer look at the "problem of the Buddenbrooks". Decline appears in Mann's novel not only as a decline of mentalities or psychological dispositions, but also as an inexorable organic process. After becoming a senator and having built a prestigious new home, representing his success, one of Mann's protagonists, Thomas Buddenbrook, reflects on this unstoppable process:

"What is success? A mysterious, indescribable power—a vigilance, a readiness, the awareness that simply by my presence I can exert pressure on the movements of life around me, the belief that life can be moulded to my advantage. [...] And the moment something begins to subside, to relax, to grow weary, then everything around us is turned loose, resists us, rebels, moves beyond our influence. And then it's just one thing after another, one setback after another, and you're finished. [...] [R]etreat, decline, the beginning of the end. [...] I know that the external, visible, tangible tokens and symbols of happiness and success first appear only after things have in reality gone into decline already."[171]

In this narration, the options for actions appear to be rather limited—success and failure are part of a process which neither individuals nor collectives can govern. In Mann's perspective—seeing Lübeck as an aristocratic-*bourgeois* republic and an important part of his identity as a "*Künstler-Bürger*"—this process of decline ultimately leads to death; that is the melding of a once unique and independent city with the insufferable normality of modernity.

But this death sentence also seems to be characterised by a particular type of dignity and nobility. And this nobility was, in Mann's perspective, represented by a close connection to death giving Lübeck (and its "sister" Venice) its uniqueness. The symbol for this close link to death was the "Dance of Death (or Dance Macabre)", a medieval genre of theatre and art. As early as 1921, Mann wrote to a friend that Lübeck was "the epitome

---

171 Mann (1994 [1901]), *Buddenbrooks*, 421–422. For the German original, see Mann (2002 [1901]), *Buddenbrooks*, 475–476.

of the Dance-Macabre-city (*überhaupt die Stadt des Totentanzes*)".[172] Medieval dances and dances of death were controversially discussed in early twentieth century and served as symbols for the psychology of the masses—a discussion in which Mann was also involved.[173] In Mann's imagination, the medieval gothic Lübeck appears as a cipher for the irrational Dionysian masses.[174] While Mann expressed sympathy for this symbol and what it represented in 1926, he had revised his analysis by the 1940s, now seeing irrationalism as part of the specific German way into National Socialism.[175]

Looking closer at the parallel narration of decline by Rörig, decline likewise appears as an organic and psychological process, in which individual decline serves as a representation of collective decline and *vice versa*. In the introduction to one of the articles that Rörig submitted to Mann in 1926, he distinctly characterises the city as an organic whole by focusing on the homogeneity and wholeness of its townscape: he mentions the "particular type of magic in the townscape of Lübeck even today", its "magnificent unity", the "gigantic rhythm of its church towers". And he explains the unity of the townscape not as random, but as the visible testimony of "a coherent social life process (*eines in sich geschlossenen sozialen Lebensprozesses*)", an "organism of mental unity", an organism, today, as it was in the past, distinguished by "inner unity" and "individual vitality", defending itself against any influences which would be alien to its character.[176]

The great strength of this organic social formation appears also as its biggest weakness: the city's unity and organic body protect it against—external—enemies, but it still runs the danger of being defeated should external influences become too strong. These external influences appear like bacteria or viruses infecting the body of the city. In this sense, Rörig's story of Lübeck reverts to metaphors which are close to immunology.

"Organic growth is surely the essential nature of a coherent, unified social body. It has its early period; it has its period of serene maturity. And it is doomed to meet the same end as any social organism: inner dissolution. This dissolution is induced by an excess of contrary points of orientation that no longer bear any relationship to its proper living conditions (*gegensätzlichen und nicht mehr im Zusammenhang mit den eigenen Lebensbedingungen stehenden Orientierungspunkten*). Self-alienation from within

---

172 Cited in Wißkirchen (2011), *Lübeck ist überhaupt die Stadt des Totentanzes*, 33.
173 Rohmann (2017), *Charisma, Bewegung und Exzess*.
174 Rohmann (2017), *Charisma, Bewegung und Exzess*, 25.
175 Rohmann (2017), *Charisma, Bewegung und Exzess*.
176 Rörig (1971 [1928]), *Lübecker Familien und Persönlichkeiten aus der Frühzeit der Stadt*, 134.

and foreign infiltration from without—these are more or less the two headings under which a process of decomposition (*Zersetzungsprozeß*) of this kind occurs."[177]

Rörig highlights three conditions for the rise and success of Lübeck in the thirteenth century. (1) The economic success of its citizens in international long distance trade: the decline starts when the merchants started to eschew risky enterprises and became *rentiers* (*i.e.*, began to live off their assets)—when, as Thomas Buddenbrook might say, their "inner tension" was gone. (2) The economic success of these proto-capitalistic, egoistic merchant-entrepreneurs qualifies them for membership in the city council and imbues them with political responsibility. The way to political power is open to those *homines novi* who are successful and whose business is expanding, but the weak *rentiers*, with hardly any motivation to foster their economic strength, are smartly thrown out of the city council if their business fails or shows signs of weakness. The last point is highly appreciated by Rörig, on account of his exceedingly liberal and aristocratic conception of history. And (3), the individual aim to earn money and to expand one's business seems to fit readily into a bigger united social structure. Rörig does not see any social conflicts, not even class struggle, arise from the ruthless fight for economic success and individual profit. Individual profit-orientation seems to be perfectly commensurable with the greater common good.

We have already seen how architecture and art reflect this mentality in the eyes of Rörig. In this sense, Lübeck's St. Mary's Church, with its "weight of brick stones, rising up into the sky", gives an impression of the "tremendous force of the *bourgeoisie* in early Lübeck".[178] In Rörig's imagination, the prototypical *bourgeois* city republic manifests itself in a particular, historical perception of space. As Groth and Höhn have shown, this appears not only as a process of perception and appropriation of political-economic and cultural spheres of action—the Baltic and North-Eastern-Europe, but also as the uniform manifestation of this perception in the townscape—represented in gothic architecture.[179]

Rörig distinguishes the prevailing mentality at the climax of Hanseatic history clearly from its initial rise to prosperity. And here, his images differ from those in older narratives in Hanse scholarship. While Ernst Daenell entitled his famous monograph, dealing with the 100 years between 1371

---

[177] Rörig (1971 [1928]), *Lübecker Familien und Persönlichkeiten aus der Frühzeit der Stadt*, 134.
[178] AHL, *Nachlass Rörig*, Nr. 110, 24.
[179] Groth et al. (2018), *Unwiderstehliche Horizonte?*

and 1474, *The Bloom of the Hanse* (*Die Blütezeit der Hanse*), Rörig saw only retarding moments in the decline of the Hanseatic League after 1370, where he located its climax. Rörig suggests that the first signs of decline began to appear after the Treaty of Stralsund (signed on 24 May of that year), a moment that he evokes by providing a fictional account of the inner thoughts of the "visionary" councillors of Lübeck who saw this decline appear. According to Rörig, a change in mental dispositions took place, allowing *rentiers* increasingly to control municipal politics, which he saw as a sign of a loosening of inner tension and verve. Alertness for political opportunities and business sense gave way to an omnipresent drive to remain modest. This new-found modesty, supposedly manifest in the manual of Johann Wittenborg, the mayor of Lübeck who was sentenced to death in 1363 following the defeat to the Danes in the Øresund strait, would have been, Rörig points out, completely alien to the preceding generations.[180]

In his never-published monograph on Lübeck, Rörig contrasted the expansive architecture of St. Mary's church (thirteenth and fourteenth century) with the architecture of the Holsten Gate (fifteenth century). While St. Mary's demonstrates the "enormous force and size" of expanding Lübeck, the Holsten Gate represents the primacy of comfort and attests to the contemporary concern to protect the wealth achieved. The stones of both buildings, Rörig asserts, tell in "mute, but urgent language of the different spirits of both periods of the history of Lübeck".[181]

For Rörig, then, decline, *i.e.*, dissolution, has its origins in a surplus of "points of orientation" which are not compatible with one's own conditions of living. "Self-alienation from within (*Selbstentfremdung von innen*)" and "foreign infiltration (*Überfremdung*)" appear as the conditions under which this process of dissolution takes place. While the images fit into the frame of "society as a body", the idea of a surplus of orientation should be seen as a hint at the problem of the complexity of modernity.

The discourse surrounding Lübeck's legal status had much more personal relevance for Fritz Rörig than for the cosmopolitan Thomas Mann, even though he was a local senator's son. Indeed, Rörig was deeply involved in the discussion about the federal structure of the "Reich". Two reasons, one professional, one academic, explain this involvement. First, Rörig (born in St. Blasien in the Black Forest and, having received his

---

180 Rörig (1971 [1925]), *Außenpolitische und innenpolitische Wandlungen*.
181 AHL, *Nachlass Rörig*, n. 110, 24.

doctorate from the University of Leipzig, archivist in Metz), came to Lübeck only in 1911. Here, his career as one of the most prominent German medievalists of the twentieth century began. He became second archivist, paradoxically not for his research on medieval constitutional history, but because he promised to finish his law studies in Göttingen and become a jurist (which he never did).[182] This promise made him attractive for the city council and enabled him to become one of the protagonists in one of the last battles for the independence of the state of Lübeck: Rörig wrote several legal reports for the law suit before the *Reichsgericht* (the supreme court of the German Empire as well as the Weimar Republic) between the state of Lübeck and the state of Mecklenburg-Schwerin and Oldenburg over the coastal waters and fishery rights in the bay of Lübeck. And in this sense, Rörig—in 1926, a professor in Kiel but still writing legal reports—was deeply involved in the discourse on Lübeck's constitutional position in the *Reich*.

The "baleful German particularism (*unheilvolle deutsche Partikularismus*)", *i.e.*, federalism perceived as political fragmentation, was, as it were, the proverbial golden thread in the *œuvre* of Fritz Rörig. He was a vociferous opponent of the dualistic structure between the *Reich* and the federal states, and saw it as the worst element in German history.[183] As legal advisor to the "*freie und Hansestadt Lübeck*", a town with a little more than 100,000 inhabitants, but which nonetheless enjoyed the privileges and autonomy of a federal state, he actually worked to uphold what was felt by many in the Weimar Republic to be the most anachronistic political structure within Germany. On the other hand, Rörig's history of the Hanseatic League and the German empire was based heavily upon the impression that the emperor and the princes had betrayed the German citizens—and that the representatives of the "*Kaiserreich*" and the "*Weimarer Republik*" were still doing so. The Hanseatic League appeared, in Rörig's eyes, as the *bourgeois* power in Germany fighting for the values and ideals of the empire, while the princes were only focused on their own individual, personal success. Lübeck and its autonomy became a *chiffre* for Rörig for a political power that, in spite of its peripheral status, nonetheless stood for unity and aristocratic-republican values. In this perspective, the decline of the city republic seems to have been unavoidable. At the same time, however, the decline of Lübeck was a sacrifice necessary for the rise of a unified political structure.

---

182 AHL, *Nachlass Rörig*, n. 8; AHL *„Dienstregistratur* 134.
183 Groth et al. (2018), *Unwiderstehliche Horizonte?*

In contrast, early Lübeck features in the writings of Rörig as the epitome of modern economy and politics. Let us summarise briefly the results of this comparison. Both Rörig and Mann employ similar metaphors and images, and refer to the same semantic field, although they operate in different discourses. The history of Lübeck is analysed in its parallels with the rise and decline of families, political formations are considered as an organic body, and buildings and architecture reflect a mentality of rising and declining formations. But while Lübeck appears as a rational and progressive political and economic space in Rörig's perception, Mann seems to have been fascinated by its backward-looking medieval townscape, its connection to death, and its ironic, broken dignity and nobility. Lübeck's irrationality—caught in the image of the Dance of Death—was originally intriguing for Mann but later featured among the reasons he saw behind the rise of fascism. In this sense, Rörig was completely misunderstanding Mann when he addressed him as a master narrator of the Hanseatic League. He saw the rise and decline of Lübeck as a mobilising example for political and social unification, and imbued it with clear political implications. Both were thinking in the same semantics, but they were not painting the same picture, and not for the same reasons.

VII. Conclusion and Outlook—Towards a "Critical Decline Analysis"

Sections II to VI of this chapter have approached the overarching phenomenon of decline from various angles. As we have argued in the introduction, it is insufficient to focus one's attention exclusively on certain linguistic items such as "*Auflösung* (dissolution)", "*Isfet* (chaos)", "*wangguo* (national ruin)", or "*déclin* (decline)". The identification of recurring verbal patterns—what we have called "images"—is but the first analytical step; and as the case studies amply demonstrate, this—in itself—is a formidable task. In order to reduce complexity further, and, in so doing, allow for a deeper investigation, each of the preceding sections coalesces around a narrowly (albeit not precisely) circumscribed segment of the semantic field labelled here as "decline". In other words, we need to expand our meta-language (which has—thus far—consisted of but one term) upon the basis of the five studies in the empirical part of this chapter, and, in so doing, "unfurl" the broad semantic category of "decline".

Based upon our findings, we propose the following more differentiated typology: "perversion", "decadence", "disintegration", "elimination", and "decay". In the first two cases, these tags represent the actual analytical concepts used in the first and second analysis, respectively. "Perversion" is decline due to a reversal of social roles or economic statuses. In the case of ancient Egypt, we even encounter the perversion of the entire cosmological order: a state of perfect order (*Maat*) transforms into its metaphysical antithesis (*Isfet*). "Decadence", on the other hand, manifests itself in the corruption of ethical, social, and aesthetic norms, or the perceived disappearance of certain "mind-sets" (such as industry, martial skills, or nobility) believed to underlie a functioning society. "Disintegration", refers to decline caused by the socio-political fragmentation of a polity that is imagined to have been a harmonious whole in the past. Again, Egypt's First Intermediate Period provides a good example, but it is also apparent in Fritz Rörig's admonition against that "baleful German particularism". Generally, however, the coming-about of disintegration itself has to be explained and the Vision of Decline will revert to one or more of the other modes of explanation. Furthermore, disintegration is equally likely to appear on the "solution-side" of a Vision of Decline: European *integration* is seen as a safeguard against the catastrophe of another continental war; social *cohesion* was deemed the pre-requisite for China's revitalisation. What the term "elimination" means is a process of decline primarily due to forces which are external to the historical formation: enemies, invaders, and outsiders. "Decay" describes decline as the dissolution of an organic whole. For the Hanse-historian Rörig, the deterioration of Lübeck's architecture was intrinsically linked to the general socio-psychological decay among the Hanseatic League's merchants. "Decay" is potentially the most devastating mode of decline, since all vital functions of the organism are imagined as being interconnected. "Organ failure" in one place will quickly spiral out of control as it directly affects even remote, seemingly unrelated areas. This may account for the preponderance of organic conceptions of society in Visions of Decline of the political right. (See below.) And finally, we reserve "ruin" for a "change for the worse" in terms of a loss of functionality. In contrast to "decay", the body politic remains essentially intact, but is rendered defunct on account of a missing vital component or piece of "hardware". (In this sense, "ruin" constitutes an important complement to "decadence".) Nineteenth-century Egypt, in the imagination of the Chinese thinker Liang Qichao, was a "ruined nation" even though the country was neither colonised nor partitioned nor morally corrupt. It had, however, no longer autonomous control over its finances. Thus, the various cogs and wheels of the social system were no longer able to function properly.

It should be noted that, while we offer five modes of decline, these are generally not congruent with any given case study. As should have become apparent, the underlying Vision of Decline in each of our investigations is always multi-faceted and more nuanced than any single "type" could aptly reflect. The terms proposed above should thus be treated as investigative focal points; that is, they are meant to highlight certain characteristics but not to the complete exclusion of all other aspects and tendencies. The notion of "strength in unity", for instance, was not only central to the discussions in the context of the Pan-Europa Congress of 1926, but also played a crucial role in early twentieth-century China, although, in China, the watchword was "nationalism", rather than "federalism". In Rörig's analysis of the downfall of the Hanse, "competition" (in the form of international trade) had been the guarantor of internal vitality and strength during the League's golden days. The decline began as the once venturesome Hanseatic merchants withdrew from competition and risky enterprises and took to a life of ease and leisure, living off their accumulated wealth.

To negotiate between the two fundamental factors of decline, internal conditions and external influences, is, as a matter of fact, a key component of Visions of Decline in general. Profound times of upheaval may lead a historical formation to question, or even to abandon, traditional self-perceptions of superiority, as happened in China in the wake of a series of humiliating events during the late nineteenth and early twentieth centuries that contemporaries in China experienced as humiliating.[184] However, established modes of thinking about one's place in the world can be remarkably enduring and can even survive prolonged periods of sociopolitical fragmentation, as Egypt's First Intermediate Period demonstrates. We will return to the issue of the relationship between internal and external factors below.

---

184 With China's "re-strengthening" in the late twentieth century, and its rise to become a global power, the traditional world-view has arguably made a comeback. French (2017), *Everything Under the Heavens*, 10–12 and passim.

The dread of perversion, that is, as previously defined, the reversal of the social order, is characteristic of highly hierarchical societies in general, both pre-modern and contemporary. However, we are well-advised not to conclude self-deceivingly that this tendency has somehow been overcome in present-day pluralistic societies, as political developments in Europe and the US during the mid-2010s amply demonstrate. Even if not as drastically (and poetically) phrased as in *The Dialogue of Ipuur*, perversion is a fear common to all ideological and political strands in which allegedly "traditional" hierarchies are romanticised and held up as ideals to be emulated in the interest of peace, security, and order. The issue behind any conservative agenda (*i.e.*, an agenda geared towards upholding a given hierarchical relationship) is, in the final analysis, not just the breakdown of a hierarchy. The absence of hierarchies, after all, results, first of all, in equality. The real "danger" is that, given equal opportunities, the former "haves" can become the future "have-nots" and *vice versa*, resulting in a *reversal of roles*. Perversion thus goes beyond an alleged aberration from a past ideal (see Lenk's "Decadence Theorem" cited in David Weidgenannt's contribution (Section II)). It is "decadence" that progresses past a "tipping-point" and into a situation that constitutes the inverse of the imagined ideal.

This ideal may be either sought in future developments or in past "experiences". We are usually inclined to associate the former with "progressive/revolutionary" and the latter with "conservative/reactionary" ideologies, but this is most probably an over-simplification.[185] The past, after all, cannot actually be experienced. It is just as malleable as the future, and equally subject to interpretative construction.[186] Rather, it would seem that, depending on historical setting and rhetorical purpose, it was the past, rather than the future, that has lent itself more readily as an empirical basis in the service of decline narratives. For the time being, suffice it to note that our understanding of decline allows for inferences from the past as well as projections into the future.

A Vision of Decline always commences with the depiction of a *status quo* that is regarded as deficient in comparison with a reference-point in either space or time. This first step thus coincides with the diagnosis of

---

[185] The history of the notion of "future" (in Europe) is delineated in Hölscher (1999), *Die Entdeckung der Zukunft*. For the decline of the conviction that the future is open and freely shapeable, see Hölscher (1999), *Die Entdeckung der Zukunft*, 219–229.

[186] The "(un)knowability" of the future is discussed in Chapter 4 by Linda Richter and Frederic Steinfeld in this volume.

weakness discussed elsewhere in this volume. Weakness assessment is the starting-point, the smallest common denominator, of Visions of Decline and Discourses of Weakness. Both are *relational* in nature.

Even if this diagnosis is not given numerical or quantitative form, we might call a diachronic or synchronic comparison "parametrical" in the sense that an observed or imagined difference is given a fixed value: "strong/weak (to a certain qualitative degree; to a quantifiable extent) with respect to X". "Weakness" is a non-dynamic, fixed (albeit not unalterable) status ascription: a *parameter*.

Once weakness is ascertained, a Vision of Decline takes the diagnosis a step further. It adds a *temporal dimension*. The ascription of decline is concerned not only with the *status quo* in relation to another, more (or less) favourable status, but with the narration of a negative tendency or *trend* (Burke's "change for the worse") along at least two "data points". The vision, as stated above, either commences in the past and is narrated until the present, or takes the present as its starting-point and reaches into the future. Mathematically speaking, "decline" is a *vector*. It needs a value as well as a direction.

Crucially, many Visions of Decline include an element of inevitability. A weakness will never be redeemed, let alone, turned into strength, if it is not counteracted in an appropriate fashion. However, it does not necessarily grow more dramatic, either. In a Vision of Decline, the ascertained downward trend may be projected into the future—unless it is claimed that one has already "hit rock bottom". In a state of decline, an initial weakness, left unattended, is a sure path to certain doom. It is only a matter of time. Let us recall, for instance, the battery of escalations and comparative forms in the quotation from Salisbury: "weaker", "poorer", "nearer to their fate", "darker". Similarly, the Greek orator Dio asserted that "as time goes on, [...] bad habits [...] will, of necessity, grow worse and worse". We would therefore assert that Visions of Decline, especially if they operate with an extremely short timeline, have a greater appellative potential than diagnoses of weakness. However, this is a point that warrants further investigation and discussion.

Above, we have made room for the possibility that a Vision of Decline ends in the present. The "change for the worse" has here turned into a "change for the worst", so to speak. In our opinion, this second scenario ought to occasion careful critical scrutiny on the part of researchers. After all, a Vision of Decline typically lowers the bar for a "change for the better". The more convinced a historical formation is of its impending doom, the less likely it is to assess critically the offered "ways out"; demands and restrictions imposed on legitimate means are probably going to be lowered or not going to be strictly observed. At the nadir, there is only one way, which is up.[187] The end increasingly justifies the means. For example, take an Egyptian nomarch who makes elaborate proclamations to the fact that his people still have food, while they are dying of starvation everywhere else. In this example, the ability to feed one's populace, which ought to be a *sine qua non* for legitimate rulership, has somehow become a point of pride. Voices of dissent ("more food", "equal distribution") may always be scotched by pointing to the "fact" that they could be much (much) worse off.

The aforementioned tendency to lower standards of legitimacy is inherent to Visions of Decline. It is therefore warranted to pose the question of where Visions of Decline are to be located on the political spectrum. Conceptually, they are political chameleons; infinitely malleable to serve any political agenda. Empirically, however, there is strong evidence that Visions of Declines "list" to the political right and appear more commonly in conservative, rather than liberal or left wing, discourses.[188] The "Decline of the West", the erosion of this undetermined, yet ostensibly clearly bounded entity by decadence and perversion as well as foreign invasion seems to be part and parcel of the mythological arsenal of right-wing ideologies. Beyond this, this vision of occidental decline provides an array of expedient images which can be adapted according to the nature and cause of the perceived weakness. The Staufer emperor Barbarossa, waiting for his reawakening beneath the Kyffhäuser hill range in order to save the German fatherland one day is as much part of this imagery as the last stand of the 300 Spartans at the Thermopylae who defied an overwhelming force of invading Persians from the East.[189]

---

187 We witnessed a particularly disconcerting example of such a "vision" on 20 January 2017 when newly-inaugurated President Donald J. Trump painted an unreservedly devastating picture of US society. Against such a backdrop, it is fairly easy to market virtually any new measure as a major improvement.
188 For the long tradition of conservative and right-wing visions of decline until today, see Weiß (2017), *Die autoritäre Revolte*.
189 For the long tradition of the (mis-)use of the Battle at Thermopylae from Hermann Goering/Göring to the Alt-Right in the USA and the Idenitarian Movement, see Rebenich (2006), *Leonidas und die Thermopylen*, 193–215; Weiß (2017), *Die autoritäre Revolte*, 106–110.

This affinity of the political right for Visions of Decline can perhaps be explained by its portrayal of society (or "the nation") as a uniform natural organism. In this conception, the notion of martyrdom, *i.e.*, of an individual sacrificing himself or herself in order to avert dangers to the political "body", plays a central role. The necessary recontextualisations and (mis-) usages of existing images seem to be inconsistent or even paradoxical, not least because the Visions of Decline under discussion here do not point to actions to be taken to alleviate or overcome the observed decline. Accordingly, decline appears to be irreversible. Nonetheless, the demise of the self-sacrificing hero is not an end, but a new foundation for the continuing survival of the historical formation –that is, its renovation.

From a defensive position, the figure of the defender appears as the one who stops or delays the decline before it brings about its destruction. He is the "withholder" of the apocalypse, the *katechon*. Carl Schmitt, the controversial "principal jurist of the Third Reich" (*Kronjurist des Dritten Reichs*), elevated the *katechon*, who is mentioned in Second Thessalonians (Chapter 2: verses 6–7), to the central *motif* of medieval *Reichsgeschichte* (imperial history).[190] His argument in the book *Nomos of the Earth* (1950) is based upon the twelfth century liturgical drama "*Ludus de Antichristo*" and the historiographical works of Otto of Freising (1114–1158). He writes:

"The empire of the Christian Middle Ages lasted only as long as the idea of the katechon was alive. I do not believe that any historical concept other than katechon would have been possible for the original Christian faith. The belief that a restrainer holds back the end of the world provides the only bridge between the notion of an eschatological paralysis of all human events and a tremendous historical monolith like that of the Christian empire of the Germanic kings."[191]

The idea of the *Reich* (*i.e.*, empire) as a "restrainer", that is, a delaying force in a transcendent design of salvation, operates along the lines of an implicit theory of *translatio* (transfer [of rule]), which enables Schmitt to fit ancient Greece, the Roman Empire, the German tribes of the Migration Period (middle of the first millennium CE), the Carolingian, and the Hohenstaufen Empire into the same long continuity.[192] This way of conceptualising the empire (*Reichsdenken*) draws its legitimacy, in Schmitt's perspective, first and foremost, from the empire's struggle against the Antichrist. This very

---

190 Schmitt (2010), *Der Nomos der Erde*, 28–32; see, also, Meuter (1994), *Der Katechon*; Palaver (2007), *Carl Schmitt's ‚Apocalyptic' Resistance against Global Civil War*, 69–94.
191 Schmitt (2003), *The Nomos of the Earth*, 61.
192 See Goez (1958), *Translatio Imperii*.

argument was instrumentalised in the 1940s and 1950s by Schmitt and other conservative and right-wing thinkers not only in their opposition to Bolshevism, but also to Western capitalism.

In the case of Visions of Decline as characterised above, it is of crucial importance to realise that these do not actively encourage ventures to shape the future. And, within their scope, it is simply inconceivable that uncertainty may actually increase one's options for action. On the contrary, it is their proponent's sole concern to impede, in true *katechon* fashion, a contingent future that they feel to be apocalyptic. Thus, these Visions of Decline limit possible courses of actions by postulating a future that offers either survival and preservation, or death and doom.

In the light of the observations above, we need to consider seriously the nature of the societal impact that a given Vision of Decline may have or have had. Otherwise, we run the danger of either excluding from consideration or—still worse—romanticising those historical changes which, with hindsight, should have taken a different path. As historians, we would be stepping far outside our jurisdiction if we were to take it upon ourselves to analyse the populist movements of our present. Instead, "inspired" by our time, we saw the necessity of consciously reflecting on the possible pitfalls of the analytical approach outlined in this chapter. It is stereotypically said of historians that they are "trapped" in the present, and that their research says more about them than it does about the topic that they are researching. In a way, we embrace our own time-boundedness here and direct our critical gaze, sharpened by the exposure to current events, back towards our actual field of interest. With this in mind, we shall offer a brief sketch of a "critical decline analysis" informed by the above-mentioned lessons from the present.

As a tentative first step, we can broadly distinguish between Visions of Decline and utopian visions, conceding that a Vision of Decline may very well contain a utopian thrust. The former, as previously noted, evokes *inevitabilities*, whereas utopias create *possibilities*.[193] Or, to put it differently, decline serves as a mechanism of contingency reduction. The exact course of future developments remains unknowable, the present remains incalcu-

---

[193] Rutger Bregman argues that utopian thought ought to be differentiated into (true) utopias and what he calls "blueprints". The latter "force us into a straitjacket" (however well-intentioned and benevolent). Only utopias "inspire us to change" as they offer "guideposts" rather than ready-made solutions. Bregman (2016), *Utopia for Realists*, 15–17; see Sargent (2010), *Utopianism*, 102 ff.

lable, but the general (negative) trend, nevertheless, provides a degree of certainty. At the level of emotion, or "crowd psychology", Visions of Decline seem to be geared towards fomenting fear and unease, while utopias, in contrast, offer hope.[194] In an effective narrative of decline, the two need to be productively combined, otherwise the end result would either be stagnation (no "fear"), or fatalism and apathy (no "hope").[195] The point is that we ought to pay close and critical attention to the ratio between the two in order to sort and distinguish platitudes, empty slogans, and fear-mongering from constructive agendas. Accordingly, the "utopian side" has to be scrutinised with respect to *specificity* and *practicality*.

The most "unsound" Vision of Decline will combine a short timeframe and great extent (that is, a drastic change in development) with unspecified goals ("greatness", "strength"), ready-made solutions, and easily visible, tangible causes. Along these very tentative and assuredly expandable criteria, a critical analysis of Visions of Decline may base itself upon: timeframe, scope/magnitude, goals, means, and alleged causes. Succinctly phrased, one has to examine how the *diagnosis* relates to the *prognosis*.

A second aspect in this regard, which might be subsumed under "causes" but which strikes us as so central that we wish to dedicate a proper paragraph to it, we call "internalisation" (or the degree of internalisation). This refers to the issue explored in Sebastian Riebold's contribution (Section V), namely, the question of whether the root causes for weakness and decline are attributed *internally* or *externally*. In our opinion, an entirely (or, at least, predominantly) external cause attribution disqualifies a given Vision of Decline as a productive Discourse of Weakness. By "productive", we mean the ability to re-configure a historical formation's Resource Regime in a manner which can be sustained. Briefly put, if a historical formation ultimately blames "others" for its deficiencies, and sees little or no fault with the norms and institutions upon which it relies to dispose of its resources, it removes itself from both the *responsibility* to tackle as well as the *possibility* of actually tackling its resource issues. The only conceivable course of action triggered by such an "unproductive"—for want of a better word—Discourse of Weakness must be some form of outward aggression;

---

194 On the history of "fear" as a political concept—and a rebuttal that fear may properly function as a viably tool of political change—see Robin (2004), *Fear*, esp. 3–25.
195 We admittedly discount here the possibility of "progress for progress' sake". This is the logical consequence of the focus on "weak" historical formations as we regard the detection of weakness as the necessary initial step of social change.

polemics and sanctions, shaming, and, in the last extreme, resorting to violence or war. The most obvious example, for such a course, can be found in attempts to sidestep tackling deep-rooted, structural problems within society by restricting access to limited resources in favour of a select sub-group. From the point of view of this (smaller) group, the resource issue has been alleviated, at least temporarily. This exclusion of others has the additional function of strengthening cohesion within the in-group, as their privileged access to the resources in question now becomes part of their group identity. We thus conclude that the processes leading to the identification of "in-groups" and "out-groups" in the context of a Vision of Decline (or Discourse of Weakness) need to be taken into consideration as well.

With these last remarks, we hope to have shown the potential profit inherent in analyses of Visions of Decline both in the context of historical research in particular, and as a scholarly pursuit in general. In future research, the typology outlined above will undoubtedly have to be revised and refined. In addition, we need to elucidate further the "social life" of Visions of Decline and elaborate on their relationship to the core concept Discourses of Weakness. Secondly, and no less important, we hope to have made a case that historical inquiries of the kind provided by the authors of this chapter bear strongly on the engagement with the troubling political developments that we are currently witnessing and may contribute to the "critical toolbox" of social theory in general.

Archival Sources

Archiv der Hansestadt Lübeck (AHL), Nachlass Fritz Rörig.
Archiv der Hansestadt Lübeck (AHL), Dienstregistratur.
European University Institute, Florence, Archives, International Paneuropean Union (PAN/EU).
The Times, "The Primrose League: Speech by Lord Salisbury", May 5th 1898, 17.

Literature

Amato, Eugenio (2014). *Traiani Praeceptor. Studi su biografia, cronologia e fortuna di Dione Crisostomo.* Besançon: Presses Universitaires de Franche-Comté.

Amelung, Iwo (2006). Zu den Staatsanleihen während der späten Qing-Zeit. In Raimund T. Kolb and Martina Siebert (eds.). *Über Himmel und Erde. Festschrift für Erling von Mende,* 21–54. Wiesbaden: Harrassowitz.

Arnim, Hans F. A. von (1898). *Leben und Werke des Dio von Prusa. Mit einer Einleitung: Sophistik, Rhetorik, Philosophie in ihrem Kampf um die Jugendbildung.* Berlin: Weidmann.

Assmann, Jan (1996). Zum Konzept der Fremdheit im Alten Ägypten. In Meinhard Schuster (ed.). *Die Begegnung mit dem Fremden. Wertungen und Wirkungen in Hochkulturen vom Altertum bis zur Gegenwart,* 77–99. Stuttgart/Leipzig: Teubner.

— (2006). *Ma'at. Gerechtigkeit und Unsterblichkeit im Alten Ägypten.* Munich: C.H. Beck.

Bachtin, Michail M. (1987). *Rabelais und seine Welt. Volkskultur als Gegenkultur.* Frankfurt/M.: Suhrkamp.

Bailey, Colin (2015). 'Honor' in Rhodes: Dio Chrysostom's Thirty-First Oration. *Illinois Classical Studies,* 40, 45–62.

Baines, John (1995). Kingship, Definition of Culture and Legitimation. In David O'Connor and David Silverman (eds.). *Ancient Egyptian Kingship,* 3–47. Leiden: Brill.

Beck, Ulrich (1986). *Risikogesellschaft. Auf dem Weg in eine andere Moderne.* Frankfurt/M.: Suhrkamp.

Bell, Barbara (1971). The Dark Ages inAncient History. I. The First Dark Age in Egypt. *American Journal of Archaeology,* 75, 1–26.

Biesinger, Benjamin (2016). *Römische Dekadenzdiskurse. Untersuchungen zur römischen Geschichtsschreibung und ihren Kontexten (2. Jahrhundert v. Chr. bis 2. Jahrhundert n. Chr.).* Stuttgart: Franz Steiner.

Blanck, Horst (1969). *Wiederverwendung alter Statuen als Ehrendenkmäler bei Griechen und Römern.* Rome: «L'Erma» di Bretschneider.

Blumenthal, Elke (1996). Die literarische Verarbeitung der Übergangszeit zwischen Altem und Mittlerem Reich. In Antonio Loprieno (ed.), *Ancient Egyptian Literature. History and Forms,* 105–35. Leiden: Brill.

— (1997). Die Erzählung des Sinuhe. In Otto Kaiser et al. (eds.). *Texte aus der Umwelt des Alten Testamentes Bd. III. Weisheitstexte, Mythen und Epen,* 884–911. Gütersloh: Gütersloher Verlagshaus.

Bost-Pouderon, Cécile (2010). Quelques considérations sur le traitement de l'exemple historique chez Dion Chrysostome. In Pierre-Louis Malosse, Marie-Pierre Noël, and Bernard Schouler (eds.). *Clio sous le regard d'Hermès. L'utilisation de l'histoire dans la rhétorique ancienne de l'époque hellénistique à l'Antiquité tardive. Actes du colloque international de Montpellier (18–20 octobre 2007),* 93–118. Alessandria: Edizioni dell'Orso.

— (2009). Entre prédication morale, parénèse et politique. Les discour 31–34 de Dion Chrysostome (ou: la subversion des genres). In Danielle van Mal-Maeder, Alexandre Burnier, and Loreto Nuñez (eds.). *Jeux de voix. Énonciation, intertextualité et intentionnalité dans la littérature antique*, 225–56. Berlin: Peter Lang.

Brandt, Ahasver von (1979). Das Ende der Hanseatischen Gemeinschaft. Ein Beitrag zur neuesten Geschichte der Hansestädte. In Klaus Friedland and Rolf Sprandel (eds.). *Lübeck, Hanse, Nordeuropa. Gedächtnisschrift für Ahasver von Brandt*, 97–125. Cologne: Böhlau.

Brunner, Hellmut (1966). *Grundzüge einer Geschichte der altägyptischen Literatur*. Darmstadt: Wissenschaftliche Buchgesellschaft.

Brush, Stephen G. (1987). *Die Temperatur der Geschichte. Wissenschaftliche und kulturelle Phasen im 19. Jahrhundert*. Braunschweig: Vieweg+Teubner.

Burke, Peter (1976). Tradition and Experience: the Idea of Decline from Bruni to Gibbo. *Daedalus*, 105, 134–52.

Chang, Hao (1971). *Liang Ch'i-ch'ao and Intellectual Transition in China, 1890–1907*. Cambridge MA: Harvard Univeristy Press.

Chaunu, Pierre (1981). *Histoire et Décadence*. Paris: Perrin.

Conze, Vanessa (2005). *Das Europa der Deutschen. Ideen von Europa in Deutschland zwischen Reichstradition und Westorientierung*. Munich: De Gruyter.

Coudenhove-Kalergi, Richard N. (1923). *Pan-Europa*. Vienna: Amalthea.

— (1926). 1. Paneuropa-Kongreß. *Paneuropa*, 13/14.

Demandt, Alexander (2015). *Der Fall Roms. Die Auflösung des römischen Reiches im Urteil der Nachwelt*. Munich: C.H.Beck.

Diamond, Jared (2006). *Kollaps: Warum Gesellschaften überleben oder untergehen*. Frankfurt/M.: Fischer.

Dikötter, Frank (2015 [1992]). *The Discourse of Race in Modern China*. New York: Oxford University Press.

Eco, Umberto (1994). Apocalyptic and Integrated Intellectuals: Mass Communications and Theories of Mass Culture. In Umberto Eco (author) and Robert Lumley (ed.). *Apocalypse Postponed*, 17–35. Bloomington IN: Perspectives.

Eco, Umberto, and Stephen Jay Gould, Jean Claude Carriére, Jean Delumeau (2000). *Conversations about the End of Time*. London: Penguin Books.

Eder, Walter (ed.). (1995). *Die athenische Demokratie im 4. Jahrhundert v. Chr.: Vollendung oder Verfall einer Verfassungsform? Akten eines Symposiums, 3.–7. August 1992, Bellagio*. Stuttgart: Franz Steiner.

Esherick, Joseph, and Wei, C. X. George (eds.). (2014). *China: How the Empire Fell*. New York: Routledge.

Fechner, Fabian, and Tanja Granzow, Jacek Klimek, Roman Krawielicki, Beatrice von Lüpke, Rebekka Nöcker (2014). „We are gambling with our survival." Bedrohungskommunikation als Indikator für bedrohte Ordnungen. In Ewald Frie and Mischa Meier (eds.). *Aufruhr—Katastrophe—Konkurrenz—Zerfall. Bedrohte Ordnungen als Thema der Kulturwissenschaften*, 141–73. Tübingen: Mohr Siebeck.

Finley, Moses I. (1977 [1963]), *The Ancient Greeks: An Introduction to their Life and Thought*. London: Viking.

Fischer-Lichte, Erika (2004). *Ästhetik des Performativen*. Frankfurt/M.: Suhrkamp.

Fogel, Joshua A. (ed.). (2004). *The Role of Japan in Liang Qichao's Introduction of Modern Western Civilization to China*. Berkeley CA: Institute of East Asian Studies, Center for Chinese Studies, University of California.

French, Howard W. (2017). *Everything Under the Heavens. How the Past Helps Shape China's Push for Global Power*. New York: Alfred A. Knopf.

Fuhrer, Therese (2014). Das Interesse am menschlichen Scheitern—Antike Konstruktionen des 'Niedergangs' einer Kultur. In Marco Formisano and Therese Fuhrer (eds.). *Décadence. "Decline and Fall" or "Other Antiquity"?*, 19–33. Heidelberg: Winter.

Gangloff, Anne (2013). Le langage des statues. Remploi et resémantisation des statues grecques sous le Haut-Empire (Dion de Pruse, Or. XII et XXXI). *Mêtis*, 11, 303–326.

Gnirs, Andrea (2006). Das Motiv des Bürgerkriegs in Merikare und Neferti. Zur Literatur der 18. Dynastie. In Gerald Moers and Heike Behlmer (eds.). *Festschrift für Friedrich Junge*, 207–65. Göttingen: Seminar für Ägyptologie und Koptologie.

Goez, Werner (1958). *Translatio Imperii. Ein Beitrag zur Geschichte des Geschichtsdenkens und der politischen Theorie in Mittelalter und früher Neuzeit*. Tübingen: Mohr Siebeck.

Gordon, Richard (2013). Inversion, Codeverletzung, Spott. „Karnevaleske Elemente" im antiken Griechenland. In Dominik Fugger (ed.). *Verkehrte Welten. Forschungen zum Motiv der rituellen Inversion*, 39–71. Munich: Oldenbourg.

Gozzoli, Roberto B. (2006). *The Writing of History in Ancient Egypt during the First Millennium BC (ca.1070–180 BC)*. London: Golden House.

Groth, Carsten, and Philipp Höhn (2018). Unwiderstehliche Horizonte? Zum konzeptionellen Wandel von Hanseraum, Reich und Europa bei Fritz Rörig und Carl Schmitt. *Historische Zeitschrift*, 306, 321–353.

Gundlach, Rolf (2004). Grundgegebenheiten der nationalen und internationalen Situation des ägyptischen Reiches. Ein Krisenmodell. In Rolf Gundlach and Andrea Klug (eds.). *Das ägyptische Königtum im Spannungsfeld zwischen Innen- und Außenpolitik im 2. Jahrtausend v. Chr.*, 73–91. Wiesbaden: Harrassowitz.

Gutsche, Verena (2015). *'Niedergang'. Variationen und Funktionen eines kulturkritischen Diskurselements zwischen 1900 und 1930. Großbritannien und Deutschland im Vergleich*. Würzburg: Königshausen & Neumann.

Harland, Philip A. (2006). The Declining Polis? Religious Rivalries in Ancient Civic Context. In Leif E. Vaage (ed). *Religious Rivalries in the Early Roman Empire and the Rise of Christianity*, 21–49. Waterloo: Wilfrid Laurier University Press.

Harter-Uibopuu, Kaja (2013). Auf dass Ehren ewig währen. Epigraphische Zeugnisse zum Schutz von Auszeichnungen. In Rupert Breitwieser, Monika Frass, and Georg Nightingale (eds.). *Calamus. Festschrift für Robert Graßl zum 65. Geburtstag*, 245–260. Wiesbaden: Harrassowitz.

— (2014). Rechtshistorische Überlegungen zu Dio Chrysostomus Rede an die Rhodier. In Michael Gagarin and Adriaan Lanni (eds.). *Symposion 2013. Vorträge zur griechischen und hellenistischen Rechtsgeschichte (Cambridge, MA, 26.–29. August 2013)*, 439–69. Vienna: Verlag der österreichischen Akademie der Wissenschaften.

Hausteiner, Eva M. (2015). *Greater than Rome: Neubestimmungen britischer Imperialität 1870–1914.* Frankfurt/M.: Campus.

Helck, Wolfgang (1977). Gaue. In Wolfgang Helck (ed.). *Lexikon der Ägyptologie*, vol. 2, 385–408. Wiesbaden: Harrassowitz.

Henschel, Gerhard (2010). *Menetekel: 3000 Jahre Untergang des Abendlandes.* Frankfurt/M.: Eichborn.

Herman, Arthur (1998). *Propheten des Niedergangs. Der Endzeitmythos im westlichen Denken.* Berlin: Propyläen.

Hewitson, Mark, and Matthew d'Auria (eds.). (2012). *Europe in Crisis. Intellectuals and the European Idea 1917–1957.* New York: Berghahn Books.

Hölscher, Lucian (1999). *Die Entdeckung der Zukunft.* Frankfurt/M.: Fischer.

Hoffmann-Rehnitz, Philip (2016). Zur Unwahrscheinlichkeit der Krise in der Frühen Neuzeit. Niedergang, Krise und gesellschaftliche Selbstbeschreibung in innerstädtischen Auseinandersetzungen nach dem Dreißigjährigen Krieg am Beispiel Lübecks. In Rudolf Schlögel et al. (eds.). *Die Krise in der Frühen Neuzeit*, 169–208. Göttingen: Vandenhoeck & Ruprecht.

Hon, Tze-ki (2015). *The Allure of the Nation. The Cultural and Historical Debates in Late Qing and Republican China.* Leiden: Brill.

Hornung, Erik (1996). *Grundzüge der ägyptischen Geschichte.* Darmstadt: Primus.

Huang, Max (2008). *The Meaning of Freedom. Yan Fu and the Origins of Chinese Liberalism.* Hong Kong: Chinese University Press.

Hundt, Michael, and Jan Lokers (eds.). (2014). *Das Ende des eigenständigen Lübecker Staates im Jahre 1937. Vorgeschichte, Ablauf und Folgen einer stadtgeschichtlichen Zäsur.* Lübeck: Schmidt-Römhild.

Jansen-Winkeln, Karl (2010). Der Untergang des Alten Reiches. *Orientalia*, 79.3, 273–303.

Jenco, Leigh (2015). *Changing Referents. Learning across Space and Time in China and the West.* Oxford: Oxford University Press.

Jiao Xun (author) and Shen Wenchao (ed.). (1987). *Mengzi zhengyi* (Correct meaning of the Book of Master Meng), 2 vols. Beijing: Zhonghua shuju.

Jones, Christopher P. (1978). *The Roman World of Dio Chrysostom.* Cambridge MA: Harvard University Press.

Jones, Dilwyn (2000). *An Index of Ancient Egyptian Titles, Epithets and Phrases of the Old Kingdom*, 2 volumes. Oxford: Oxford University Press.

Jung, Theo (2012). *Zeichen des Verfalls: semantische Studien zur Entstehung der Kulturkritik im 18. und frühen 19. Jahrhundert.* Göttingen: Vandenhoeck & Ruprecht.

Kaelble, Hartmut (2001). *Europäer über Europa. Die Entstehung des europäischen Selbstverständnisses im 19. und 20. Jahrhundert.* Frankfurt/M.: Campus.

Kang Youwei (author), and Jiang Yihua, Zhang Ronghua (eds.). (2007). *Kang Youwei quanji* (The Complete Works of Kang Youwei). 12 vols. Beijing: Renmin chubanshe.
Karl, Rebecca (2002). *Staging the World. Chinese Nationalism at the Turn of the Twentieth Century*. Durham NC: Duke University Press.
Kasperson, Roger E. et al. (2005). The Social Amplification of Risk: A Conceptual Framework. In Jeanne X. Kasperson and Roger E. Kasperson (eds.). *The Social Contours of Risk: Volume 1: Publics, Risk Communication and the Social Amplification of Risk*, 99–114. London: Earthscan.
Kiesewetter, Hubert (2008). *Julius Wolf 1862–1937. Zwischen Judentum und Nationalsozialismus. Eine wissenschaftliche Biographie*. Stuttgart, Franz Steiner.
Koselleck, Reinhart (1982). Krise. In Otto Brunner, Werner Conze, and Reinhart Koselleck (eds.). *Geschichtliche Grundbegriffe. Historisches Lexikon zur politisch-sozialen Sprache in Deutschland*, 3, 617–50. Stuttgart: Klett-Cotta.
— (2006). 'Fortschritt' und 'Niedergang'. Nachtrag zur Geschichte zweier Begriffe. In Reinhart Koselleck. *Begriffsgeschichten: Studien zur Semantik und Pragmatik der politischen und sozialen Sprache*, 159–81. Frankfurt/M.: Suhrkamp.
Koselleck, Reinhart, and Paul Widmer (eds.). (1980). *Niedergang. Studien zu einem geschichtlichen Thema*. Stuttgart: Klett-Cotta.
Krogel, Wolfgang G. (1994). Die Stadt als bürgerliche Heimat. Eine Untersuchung zum Geschichtsbild der mittelalterlichen Stadt in der 700-Jahrfeier der Reichsfreiheit Lübecks. *Zeitschrift des Vereins für Lübeckische Geschichte und Altertumskunde*, 74, 225–78.
Kuczynski, Jürgen (1984). *Gesellschaften im Untergang: Vergleichende Niedergangsgeschichte vom Römischen Reich bis zu den Vereinigten Staaten von Amerika*. Berlin: Pahl-Rugenstein.
Kurtz, Joachim (2011). *The Discovery of Chinese Logic*. Leiden: Brill.
Le Goff, Jacques (1978). Decadenza. In Ruggiero Romano (ed.). *Enciclopedia*, vol. 4, 389–420. Turin: Einaudi.
Lenk, Kurt (1989). *Deutscher Konservatismus*. Frankfurt/M.: Campus.
Lakoff, George, and Mark Johnson (2003 [1980]). *Metaphors We Live By*. Chicago IL: University of Chicago Press.
Lambert, Peter (1999). From antifascist to Volkshistoriker. Demos and ethnos in the political thought of Fritz Rörig, 1921–1945. In Stefan Berger, Mark Donovan, and Kevin Passmore (eds.). *Writing National Histories. Western Europe since 1800*, 137–49. London: Routledge.
Liang Qichao (author), and Wang Xiangyi, Yang Gang (eds.). (1999). *Liang Qichao quanji* (The Complete Works of Liang Qichao), 10 volumes. Beijing: Beijing chubanshe.
Lichtheim, Miriam (2006 [1973]). *Ancient Egyptian Literature. A Book of Readings. Volume I: The Old and Middle Kingdoms*. Berkeley CA: University of California Press.

Lokers, Jan (2014). Selige Jubelfeiern? Lübeck gedenkt seiner Stadtgründung. Hansestädtische Erinnerungskultur im 19. und 20. Jahrhundert. In Michael Hundt and Jan Lokers (eds.). *Hanse und Stadt. Akteure, Strukturen und Entwicklungen im regionalen und europäischen Raum. Festschrift für Rolf Hammel-Kiesow zum 65. Geburtstag*, 295–312. Lübeck: Schmidt-Römhild.

Mann, Thomas (1990). *Gesammelte Werke*, vol. 11. Frankfurt/M.: Fischer.

— (1994). *Buddenbrooks. The Decline of a Family*. Translated from German by John E. Woods. London: Vintage International.

— (2002). *Buddenbrooks. Verfall einer Familie*. Frankfurt/M.: Fischer.

Matten, Marc A. (2016). *Imagining a Postnational World. Hegemony and Space in Modern China*. Leiden: Brill.

Messner, J. J., and Nate Haken, Hannah Blyth, Christina Murphy, Amanda Quinn, George Lehner, Daniel Ganz (2017). *Fragile States Index 2017*. Washington, D. C.: Fund for Peace.

Meuter, Günter (1994). *Der Katechon. Zu Carl Schmitts fundamentalistischer Kritik der Zeit*. Berlin: Duncker & Humblot.

Meyer, Gerhard (2008). Vom Ersten Weltkrieg bis 1996. Lübeck im Kräftefeld rasch wechselnder Verhältnisse. In Antjekathrin Graßmann (ed.). *Lübeckische Geschichte*, 695–702. Lübeck: Schmidt-Römhild.

Mili, Maria (2015). *Religion and Society in Ancient Thessaly*. Oxford: Oxford University Press.

Miller, Harrison (2015). *The Gongyang Commentary on the Spring and Autumn Annals. A full translation*. New York: Palgrave Macmillan.

Morley, Neville (2004). Decadence as a Theory of History. *New Literary History*, 35(4), 573-585.

Müller-Wollermann, Renate (1986). Krisenfaktoren im ägyptischen Staat des ausgehenden alten Reichs. PhD Dissertation, Tübingen.

Noodt, Birgit (2007). Fritz Rörig (1882–1952). Lübeck, Hanse und Volksgeschichte. *Zeitschrift des Vereins für Lübeckische Geschichte und Altertumskunde*, 87, 155–80.

Nora, Pierre (1998). *Zwischen Geschichte und Gedächtnis*. Frankfurt/M.: Fischer.

Nünning, Ansgar (2007). Grundzüge einer Narratologie der Krise. Wie aus einer Situation ein Plot und eine Krise (konstruiert) werden. In Henning Grundwald and Manfred Pfister (eds.). *Krisis! Krisenszenarien, Diagnosen und Diskursstrategien*, 48–71. Munich: Fink.

Orluc, Katiana (2005). Europe Between Past and Future: Transnational Networks and the Transformation of the Pan-European Idea in the Interwar Years. PhD Dissertation, European University Institute.

Otte, Thomas G. (2007). *The China Question. Great Power Rivalry and British Isolation, 1894–1905*. Oxford: Oxford University Press.

Palaver, Wolfgang (2007). Carl Schmitt's ‚Apocalyptic' Resistance against Global Civil War. In Robert Hammerton-Kelly (ed.). *Politics & Apocalypse*, 69–94. East Lansing MI: Michigan State University Press.

Parkinson, Richard (2009). *The Tale of Sinuhe and other Egyptian Poems 1940–1640 BC.* Oxford: Oxford University Press.

Parkinson, Richard (2010). *Poetry and Culture in Middle Kingdom Egypt. A Dark Side to Perfection.* London: Continuum.

Paul, Ina U. (2005). A Man and a Movement—Neuerscheinungen zu Richard Nikolaus Coudenhove-Kalergi. *Jahrbuch für europäische Geschichte,* 6, 183–93.

Paulsen, Reinhard (2016). *Schifffahrt, Hanse und Europa im Mittelalter. Schiffe am Beispiel Hamburgs, europäische Entwicklungslinien und die Forschung in Deutschland.* Cologne/Weimar/Vienna: Böhlau.

Platt, Verity (2007). Honour Takes Wing: Unstable Images and Anxious Orators in the Greek Tradition. In Zahra Newby and Ruth Leader-Newby (eds.). *Art and Inscriptions in the Ancient World,* 247–71. Cambridge: Cambridge University Press.

Priglinger, Elisa (2015). Texte und ihre Interpretation zum Niedergang des Alten Reiches. In Gregor Neunert et al (eds.). *Text: Wissen—Wirkung—Wahrnehmung, Beiträge des Vierten Münchner Arbeitskreises Junge Aegyptologie (MAJA 4), 29.11. bis 1.12.2013,* 179–90. Wiesbaden: Harrassowitz.

Pross, Caroline (2013). *Dekadenz: Studien zu einer großen Erzählung der frühen Moderne.* Göttingen: Wallstein.

Pusey, James R. (1983). *China and Charles Darwin.* Cambridge MA: Harvard University Press.

Rankin, Mary B. (1986). *Elite Activism and Political Transformation in China: Zhejiang Province, 1865–1911.* Stanford CA: Stanford University Press.

Rebenich, Stefan (2006). Leonidas und die Thermopylen. Zum Sparta-Bild in der deutschen Altertumswissenschaft. In Andreas Luther, Mischa Meier, and Lukas Thommen (eds.). *Das frühe Sparta-Bild,* 193–215. Stuttgart: Franz Steiner.

Reid, Gilbert (1900). The Powers and the Partition of China. *The North American Review,* May, 634–641.

Reynolds, Douglas R. (1993). *China, 1898–1912: The Xinzheng Revolution and Japan.* Cambridge MA: Harvard University Press.

— (2014). *East Meets East. Chinese Discover the Modern World in Japan, 1854–1898. A Window on the Intellectual and Social Transformation of Modern China.* Ann Arbor MI: Association for Asian Studies.

Rhoads, Edward (2000). *Manchus and Han. Ethnic Relations and Political Power in Late Qing and Early Republican China 1861–1928.* Seattle WA: University of Washington Press.

Rifkin, Jeremy (1982). *Entropie—ein neues Weltbild.* Hamburg: Hoffmann und Campe.

Robin, Corey (2004). *Fear. The History of a Political Idea.* Oxford: Oxford University Press.

Römer, Malte (2011). Was ist eine Krise? oder: Wie ist das Alte Reich (nicht) untergegangen? *Göttinger Miszellen,* 230, 83–101.

Rörig, Fritz (1971 [1925]). Außenpolitische und innenpolitische Wandlungen in der Hanse nach dem Stralsunder Frieden. In Fritz Rörig and Paul Kaegbein (eds.).

Die Wirtschaftskräfte im Mittelalter. Abhandlungen zur Stadt- und Hansegeschichte, 147–166. Cologne: Böhlau.

Rörig, Fritz (1971 [1928]). Das älteste erhaltene deutsche Kaufmannsbüchlein. In Fritz Rörig and Paul Kaegbein (eds.). *Die Wirtschaftskräfte im Mittelalter. Abhandlungen zur Stadt- und Hansegeschichte*, 167–215. Cologne: Böhlau.

Rörig, Fritz (1971 [1928]). Lübecker Familien und Persönlichkeiten aus der Frühzeit der Stadt. In Fritz Rörig and Paul Kaegbein (eds.). *Die Wirtschaftskräfte im Mittelalter. Abhandlungen zur Stadt- und Hansegeschichte*, 134–46. Cologne: Böhlau.

Rohmann, Georg (2017). Charisma, Bewegung und Exzess. Die ‚Krise des Spätmittelalters' in Georg Wilhelm Pabsts Film ‚Paracelsus' (1943). In Brigitte Burrichter and Dorothea Klein (eds.). *Exzess. Formen der Grenzüberschreitung in der Vormoderne*, 327–62. Würzburg: Königshausen & Neumann.

Said, Edward W. (1994 [1979]). *Orientalism. Western Conceptions of the Orient*. New York: Vintage Books.

Sargent, Lyman T. (2010). *Utopianism. A Very Short Introduction*. Oxford: Oxford University Press.

Schillinger, Nicolas (2016). *The Body and Military Masculinity in Late Qing and Early Republican China. The Art of Governing Soldiers*. Lanham MD: Lexington Books.

Schmitt, Carl (2011). *Der Nomos der Erde im Völkerrecht des Jus Publicum Europaeum*. Berlin: Duncker & Humblot.

Schmitt, Carl (author), and G. L. Ulmen (trans.). (2003). *The Nomos of the Earth in the International Law of the Jus Publicum Europaeum*. New York: Telos Press.

Schneider, Julia C. (2017). *Nation and Ethnicity: Chinese Discourses on History, Historiography, and Nationalism (1900s-1920s)*. Leiden: Brill.

Schöberl, Verena (2008). *„Es gibt ein großes und herrliches Land, das sich selbst nicht kennt ... Es heißt Europa". Die Diskussion um die Paneuropaidee in Deutschland, Frankreich und Großbritannien 1922–1933*. Münster: LIT.

Schweitzer, Albert (2004). *Wir Epigonen: Kultur und Kulturstaat*. Munich: C. H. Beck.

Seidl, Klaus (2018). Kassandra und Europa. Niedergangsdiskurse und Europäisierung im 20. Jahrhundert. In Landry Charrier, Fanny Platelle, and Hélène Roth (eds). *Le déclin dans le monde germanique. Mots, discours et représentations (de 1914 à nos jours)*. Reims: EPURE. [Forthcoming.]

Seidlmayer, Stephan (2003). First Intermediate Period (c. 2160–2055 BC). In Ian Shaw (ed.). *The Oxford History of Ancient Egypt*, 108–136. Oxford: Oxford University Press.

Selzer, Stephan (2016). Nachgrabung auf dem Markt von Lübeck: Fritz Rörigs ‚Gründungsunternehmerthese' in der deutschen Geschichtsforschung der ersten Hälfte des 20. Jahrhunderts. *Zeitschrift für Lübeckische Geschichte*, 96, 9–51.

Shambaugh, David (2016). *China's Future*. Cambridge: Polity Press.

Sidebottom, Harry (1992). The Date of Dio of Prusa's Rhodian and Alexandrian Orations. *Historia*, 41, 407–19.

Simpson, William K. (2003). *The Literature of Ancient Egypt. An Anthology of Stories, Instructions, Stelae, Autobiographies, and Poetry*. New Haven CT/London: Yale UP.

Srodes, James (2011). *Franklin. The Essential Founding Father.* Washington, D.C.: Regnery Publishing.

Swain, Simon (1996). *Hellenism and Empire. Language, Classicism, and Power in the Greek World AD 50–250.* Oxford: Clarendon Press.

Tang, Xiaobing (1996). *Global Space and the Nationalist Discourse of Modernity. The Historical Thinking of Liang Qichao.* Stanford CA: Stanford University Press.

Theis, Christoffer (2010). Die Pyramiden der Ersten Zwischenzeit. Nach philologischen und archäologischen Quellen. *Studien zur altägyptischen Kultur,* 39, 321–39.

Tikhonov, Vladimir (2010). *Social Darwinism and Nationalism in Korea: the Beginnings (1880s-1910s): Survival as an Ideology of Korean Modernity.* Leiden: Brill.

Tiersch, Claudia (ed.). (2016). *Die athenische Demokratie im 4. Jahrhundert. Zwischen Modernisierung und Tradition.* Stuttgart: Franz Steiner.

Tsau, Shu-ying (1980). The Rise of 'New Fiction'. In Milena Doleželová-Velingerová (ed.). *The Chinese Novel at the Turn of the Century.* Toronto: University of Toronto Press

Tsu, Jing (2005). *Failure, Nationalism, and Literature. The Making of Modern Chinese Identity, 1895–1937.* Stanford CA: Stanford University Press.

Tusk, Donald (2017). United We Stand, Divided We Fall: Letter by President Donald Tusk to the 27 EU Heads of State or Government on the Future of the EU before the Malta summit.
URL: http://www.consilium.europa.eu/en/press/press-releases/2017/01/31-tusk-letter-future-europe/ [2018-01-14].

Valéry, Paul (1919). The Intellectual Crisis. *The Athenaeum,* 4644, 279–90.

Van Norden, Bryan W. (trans.) (2008). *Mengzi. With Selections from Traditional Commentaries.* Indianapolis IN: Hackett Publishing.

Vittinghoff, Natascha (2002). Unity vs. Uniformity: Liang Qichao and the Invention of a "New Journalism" for China. *Late Imperial China,* 23.1, 91–143.

Vogelsang, Kai (2012). Chinese "Society": History of a Troublesome Concept. *Oriens Extremus,* 51, 155–92.

Wagner, Rudolf G. (2011). China 'Asleep' and 'Awakening'. A Study in Conceptualizing Asymmetry and Coping with it. *Transcultural Studies,* 1, 4–139.

Wang, Dong (2003). The Discourse of Unequal Treaties in Modern China. *Pacific Affairs,* 76.3, 399–425.

Weiß, Volker (2017). *Die autoritäre Revolte. Die Neue Rechte und der Untergang des Abendlandes.* Stuttgart: Klett-Cotta.

Widmer, Paul (1983). *Die unbequeme Realität. Studien zur Niedergangsthematik in der Antike.* Stuttgart: Klett-Cotta.

White, Hayden (1973). *Metahistory. The Historical Imagination in Nineteenth-Century Europe.* Baltimore MD: Johns Hopkins University Press.

Wißkirchen, Hans (2011). 'Lübeck ist überhaupt die Stadt des Totentanzes'. Mittelalterliches im Lübeck-Bild Thomas Manns. *Thomas-Mann-Jahrbuch,* 24, 27–39.

Yan Fu (author/trans.), and Feng Junhao (ed.). (2000). *Tianyan lun* (On Evolution). Zhengzhou: Zhongzhou guji chubanshe.

Yan Fu (author), and Niu Yangshan (ed.). (2006). *Yan Fu wenxuan* (Selected writings by Yan Fu). Tianjin: Baihua wenyi chubanshe.

Zarrow, Peter (2015). *Educating China: Knowledge, Society, and Textbooks in a Modernizing World, 1902–1937*. Cambridge: Cambridge University Press.

Zou Zhenhuan (1996). Qingmo wangguoshi bianyire yu Liang Qichao de Chaoxian wangguoshi yanjiu (Research into the Ruination History-craze and Liang Qichao's history of the ruin of Korea), *Hanguo yanjiu luncong*, 2, 325–55.

Ziegerhofer-Prettenthaler, Anita (2001). *Botschafter Europas. Richard Nikolaus Coudenhove-Kalergi und die Paneuropa-Bewegung in den zwanziger- und dreißiger Jahren*. Vienna: Böhlau.

Chapter 4
Counting Weakness? The Institutionalisation of Data Collection in the Nineteenth Century German Chemical Industry and Meteorology

Linda Richter and Frederic Steinfeld

I. Introduction

Should I pack an umbrella before leaving for work today? Should a company invest in a new production line for a factory? Should a ship leave port today despite the forecast of a storm? Or should it wait for a few days, thereby risking a delayed delivery and a breach of contract?

Common sense suggests that, because they have not yet happened, our knowledge of future events is inherently weak and the decisions upon which we base it are consequently insecure. While this may be true, trying to know the future, or engaging with it, is, arguably, an equally common and old human practice. Certainly, there are many ways to do it: you can confer with your court astrologer, read tea leaves, calculate a weather forecast or commission a detailed market survey—depending on the time available, the location, and the specificity of your interest. Our lives are structured by the decisions that we make, which depend on the number of choices available to us. If there are several options, we choose the one that integrates, subjectively, most benefits, based upon our predictions of the future. Whether, in this process, the forecast comes true or not is as hard to measure as it is probably irrelevant: it plays an important role on an individual, group or societal level as a means to inspire and guide actions—regardless of its accuracy.[1] Of the many ways in which projections of the future figure into discourses of weakness and subsequent shifts in resource regimes, we wish to examine one more closely in this chapter: to wit, historical actors who identified a weakness in the historic present, tried to

---

1 Minois (1998), *Geschichte der Zukunft*, 18–19.

react to their diagnosis, and drew their conclusions as to whether they deemed this reaction successful or not.

The idea for this chapter came about as we realised that very different historical formations have tried to predict processes of particular complexity. Admittedly, the circumstances are very different (one being the market for synthetic dyestuffs, the other being meteorology), as are the complex processes (market dynamics, the weather) predicted. In addition, a company such as *Bayer* is an institutional actor confronted with the necessity of making business decisions which not only anticipate the future, but also affect it. The heterogeneous group of (proto-) meteorologists[2] were (unlike farmers, for example), for the most part, *not* in a position in which their success or failure at forecasting the weather affected them in an economic way. And, without suggesting that business and science in nineteenth-century Germany were necessarily organised in the same structures, we would nevertheless argue that the analytical stance of discourses of weakness in particular can provide a framework for comparing the two in a meaningful way. It has emerged, for example, that the actors reacted to the perceived uncertainty of the future with ambitious efforts of data collection—which yielded the desired result in one case, but remained futile in the other. In order to grasp a complex process, and perhaps reduce its complexity in the long run, the construction of a comparatively complex corpus of data was deemed the appropriate response. To account for the differences between the two groups of actors involved, we are both going to provide glimpses into our respective more comparable counterparts, *i.e.*, nineteenth century economic theories of market dynamics and predictability, on the one hand, and the individual actors who depend on weather forecasts to make concrete decisions, on the other. As a set, however, the case studies are intended to be complimentary to each other.

---

2 When referring to "meteorology" or "meteorologists", it must be noted that we use this term to talk quite broadly about people who published their thoughts on meteorological phenomena. These men could be of diverse social and professional backgrounds, including preachers, professors of astronomy or physics, monks, medical professionals or teachers. It was not until the latter half of the 19th century that Meteorology as a scientific discipline was institutionalised in European countries—both as government weather services and in university or state research institutions. The relationship of the two differs from state to state. In a more detailed analysis of the field between 1750 and 1850, distinctly different forms of knowledge about the weather can be distinguished, including different actors who were also critical of the meteorological methods described and suggested competing epistemic structures. A more detailed analysis of these dynamics will follow in Linda Richter's PhD thesis.

Identifying these discourses and describing the reactions that they brought about (be they in the form of subsequent changes in the resource regime or otherwise) can reveal developments that have been hitherto concealed to historians. The nature of this chapter is to be understood as exploratory, both in terms of the comparability of the two very different predictive processes carried out by the very different actors involved, and in terms of the source material included.[3] In one case, the diagnosis of a certain weakness led to a successful transformation of the resource regime in question, while, in the other case, the historical actors succumbed to the complexity of atmospheric processes.

II. Diagnosing Weakness

In 1881, *Bayer* joined a cartel that had been created in order to control the sales volume and price of the synthetic dyestuff alizarin.[4] The so-called *Alizarinkonvention* had been established in response to the fact that the price of alizarin had dramatically fallen during the 1870s when many companies began producing this particular dyestuff and the leading companies—along with Bayer, these were *Badische Anilin- und Sodafabrik* (BASF) and *Farbwerke Meister, Lucius & Brüning* (Hoechst)—aimed to secure their market shares. While there were also other companies involved in the cartel, *Bayer*, *BASF* and *Hoechst* held the biggest share with each of them providing 19 per cent of the total quantity of sales.[5] For *Bayer*, this favoured position was remarkable, as the company was much smaller compared to its two major competitors. As alizarin had been the most lucrative dyestuff in the 1870s, *Bayer* had focused its product portfolio mainly on this product and thus produced large quantities of the dyestuff.

Despite the existence of the cartel, the price for alizarin decreased even after its establishment in 1881. Outside the cartel, numerous companies also produced the dyestuff. The aim of the *Alizarinkonvention* was not to

---

3 All historical sources cited in the following text are in German originally. If direct quotations are given in the text, they have been translated by us into English to ensure the readability of the text for a wider audience.

4 For more details about the alizarin dyestuff, see Osteroth (1985), *Soda, Teer und Schwefelsäure*, 92–100.

5 For the Alizarinkonvention, see: Pinnow (1938), *Werksgeschichte*, 63–64.

unify all individual producers of the dyestuff, but to bring together the most important ones that accounted for the vast majority of the market shares. As it was impossible to patent alizarin, since its discovery dated before the passing of the first consistent German patent law in 1877, companies could legally produce alizarin very easily.[6] In addition, the production of the dyestuff did not require particularly big investments in machinery as tubs sufficed for most of the chemical reactions.[7] Thus, both the dyestuff itself as well as the required production process was easy to acquire and to set up, and the barriers for other competitors to enter the alizarin market were comparatively low. As soon as the companies outside the cartel were able to compete with the *Alizarinkonvention*'s prices, the cartel reacted with repeated price reductions. These reductions hit *Bayer* especially hard as, between 1881 and 1885, up to 70 per cent of the company's total revenue originated from the alizarin dyestuff, whereas it only accounted for around 40 per cent of *BASF*'s turnover.[8] Due to this high dependence on the alizarin dye, the *Bayer* management initially refused to follow the reduction in prices, but eventually had to accept the demands made by the still far bigger *BASF* and *Hoechst* companies as they repeatedly threatened to leave the cartel. When these two companies pushed for a significant markdown in May 1885, the *Bayer* supervisory board instructed its delegation to the cartel to "avoid a price reduction in any way possible".[9] In the middle of 1885, *Hoechst* and *BASF* had reached a point of company development that was no longer compatible with the cartel. Both companies sold a far lower quantity of alizarin than they could have produced as the *Alizarinkonvention*'s quotas were outdated.[10] In addition, *BASF* had already fabricated a significant number of the precursors needed for the production of alizarin—a diversification that could not be found at *Bayer*. In August 1885, the cartel broke up. At this point, the dyestuff still accounted for 60 per cent of Bayer's net profit.[11] By the time of the cartel's dissolution, *Bayer*'s economic success largely depended on a product that its major competitors were not only able to produce in larger quantities, but also able to produce at lower prices. Surprisingly, the Bayer executives

---

6 See Streb et al. (2007), *Knowledge Spill-Over from New to Old Industries*, 205.
7 See Duisberg (1918), *Selbsterlebtes und Schlussbetrachtungen*, 587–644.
8 Numbers from Bayer taken from BAL 15/BA.2 (own calculation). Numbers from BASF taken from Abelshauser et al. (2004), *BASF*, 94.
9 BAL 11/3, 42. Aufsichtsraths Sitzung am 15. Mai 1885.
10 See Abelshauser et al. (2004), *BASF*, 90–91.
11 BAL 15/BA.2.

decided to follow the competitors in their post-cartel pricing. The supervisory board gave the management the instruction "to keep the Alizarin sales at the regular level of 11,000 kilos for the following three months and during this time to follow the competitors' pricing in order to achieve this goal, as it is impossible to determine any limit either in quantum or in the price".[12] The *Bayer* leadership apparently perceived an urgency to maintain its market share after the dissolution of the cartel, even though it was uncertain how far the price for alizarin would fall.

While *Bayer*'s major competitors had already begun to establish laboratories for basic research in the 1870s and held several popular products in their portfolios, *Bayer* focused on the efficient production of a few profit-building dyes. When the company entered the *Alizarinkonvention*, there was barely any incentive for further product improvement or the diversification of the product portfolio, as *Bayer* could count on a constant and high profit. This profit was not re-invested in the company but almost entirely distributed to the shareholders, preventing any investment in long-term strategies of growth.[13] On closer consideration, the company did not operate in a traditional competitive market, as Bayer was not forced to compete against other companies with its most important product by far.[14] In traditional market competition, the permanent discourse of weakness will force the competitors to adapt repeatedly to their environment. This diagnosis of weakness finds its expression in the fact that companies tend to observe the actions undertaken by their competitors, such as the pricing of products and changes in production portfolios.[15] The underlying assumption is that companies need to perceive their position as weak or threatened in order to trigger decision-making processes that will eventually lead to adaptation.[16] The perceived weakness can be reduced by a strong market position, as can be found in the case of monopolists, or, as in this case study, in a cartel. The repeated adaptation is related to both current and future changes in the business environment, mostly those influenced by their

---

12 BAL 11/3, 44. Aufsichtsraths Sitzung am 4. August 1885.
13 Between 1882 and 1884, the paid dividends accounted for between 88 and 72 percent of the net profit. For numbers, see: BAL 15/BA.2.
14 This was also the case of Dow Chemical as shown by Levenstein (1991), *The Use of Cost Measures*, 76–77.
15 Bayer, for instance, kept several records of dyestuffs produced by its competitors and their prices, as well as detailed information about their balance sheets, see: BAL 1/5.2, BAL 15/D.11.
16 See Plumpe (2016), *Wie entscheiden Unternehmen?*, 147–152.

competitors. While the current changes can directly be observed, for example, by monitoring their competitors' pricing, expected future changes are far more difficult to adapt to. Companies need to create certain future scenarios, predicting or forecasting the actions that will occur in their environment while never knowing precisely what may or will actually happen.[17] Both this modelling and the day-to-day observations are triggered by the permanent discourse of weakness, which is inherent to market competition. In the *Bayer* case, these mechanisms of adaptation were more or less abolished through the cartel. The lack of this adaptation eventually led to the company not collecting information about the efficiency of its own production. However, when the cartel fell apart, the discourse of weakness was reactivated, resulting in processes of adaptation and information procurement at Bayer.

With regard to knowledge about the weather, between 1750 and 1850, contemporaries explicitly acknowledged it to be a resource of potentially high economic value. Learned authors frequently pointed out that it could come in useful in maritime endeavours (for example, trade and connected branches of the economy), in medical treatment of human beings and animals, and in agriculture. If a heavy storm was on the way, the crew aboard a trade ship could decide not to leave the port to avoid endangering their lives and their cargo.[18] Knowing what weather changes lay ahead would also be relevant for industries not immediately dependent on sea travel, for example, the winemaker whose harvest or crop would be either damaged or, if well protected from cold, might increase in price after a night of frost because of damage to other competitors.[19] Most of the authors who propagated that meteorology needed to become an exact science stressed the possible benefits to agriculture in particular, surmising,

---

17 For further research on economic decision-making and modeling of the future, see Knight (1921), *Risk, Uncertainty and profit*; Simon (1955), *A Behavioral Model of Rational Choice*; Cyert/March (1992), *A Behavioral Theory of the Firm*; Williamson (1975), *Markets and Hierarchies*; Greve (1998), *Performance, Aspirations, and Risky Organizational Change*; Lamoreaux (2001), *Reframing the Past*; and Beckert (2016), *Imagined Futures*.

18 See Eicke (1752), *Von der Beobachtung des Wetters*, 186–187 or Böckmann (1778), *Wünsche und Aussichten*, 5.

19 Pilgram (1788), *Untersuchungen über das Wahrscheinliche der Wetterkunde*, 2. One should not assume, however, that these promises of utility were based upon needs articulated by agricultural and trade actors when uttered by meteorologists. Pilgram's example of the wine tradesman, for example, is remarkably similar to an example used by Jakob Bernoulli as cited by Schneider (1979), *Die Mathematisierung der Vorhersage künftiger Ereignisse*, 105.

for example, that one could possibly even double the yields of farming and cattle breeding.[20] However, should a farmer rely on a false prognosis, the damage could be devastating, as the East Hessian parish priest Friedrich Anton Fresenius described: if he sowed at the wrong time for fear of an upcoming frost, he could compromise his crops; being overly confident about the fertility of the upcoming season, he might rashly sell all his stock of fodder and grains for fear of a decrease in prices, only to be confronted with a shortage of supplies himself; he could also sow too much or too little of a specific crop.[21] It must be stressed that we mostly need to rely on learned authors who ascribed these knowledge needs to social groups whose actual needs and practices regarding foreknowledge of the weather were not necessarily familiar to them. To point out the potential for economic gain could, therefore, also have been a strategy to gain support for their own scientific interests. However, contrary to claims that the utility of meteorological knowledge, particularly prognosis, was only realised in the second half of the nineteenth century,[22] the hope of reliable forecasts for economic purposes was much older among scholars.

Meteorology as a science, as has been pointed out by historians of science, lent itself very neatly to the Enlightenment ideals of rationally describing, understanding, and predicting natural phenomena and processes. However, given the complexity of the subject matter in question, the limits of this approach became apparent very clearly.[23] Enlightenment scholars of meteorology praised the potentials of practical meteorology, but this praise was often followed by complaints about the weak state of the meteorological knowledge available. Throughout the eighteenth and nineteenth centuries, both in the German territories and beyond, learned attempts to understand atmospheric processes physically competed with traditional bodies of knowledge such as astrometeorology and the so-called farmers' rules, which they deemed to be superstitious.[24] The academic discipline which these early meteorologists aimed to emulate was astronomy: just as astronomers had rid themselves of astrology, they thought astrometeorology could be converted into an equally rational science that would observe the

---

20 Eicke (1752), *Von der Beobachtung des Wetters*, 186–187.
21 Fresenius (1799), *Praktische Wetterkunde*, 80.
22 See Emeis (2006), *Das erste Jahrhundert*, 40; Wege (2002), *Die Entwicklung der meteorologischen Dienste in Deutschland*, 38.
23 Golinski (2007), *British Weather*, xiii.
24 See Golinski (2007), *British Weather*, xiii and Anderson (2005), *Predicting the Weather*; Anderson (1999), *The Weather Prophets*.

weather, calculate regularities and enable prediction with mathematical precision. Johann Lorenz Böckmann, a teacher and church official in Karlsruhe, and founder of the short-lived Badisch Weather Institute in the 1770s, summarised his ideas for improving meteorology poignantly in 1778. Surely what had worked for the superlunary sphere should also be possible for the sublunary atmosphere because both were governed by laws of nature.[25] Epistemically, wrote Böckmann, the quality, range and coherence of regular instrumental observations left much to be desired, which led to a deficient empirical basis. The observers were often not qualified and their instruments of different quality, and, for this reason, presumably incongruous. Meteorology also lacked a uniform (sign-) language, a fact which hindered data exchange across language borders. Furthermore, proper observations would have to be collected in one place, where "a few astute men" would compare them amongst themselves and apply the laws and rules of meteorology in order to affirm, modify or disregard the latter.[26] With regard to its social situation, Böckmann lamented that meteorology did not enjoy royal patronage in any way comparable to that of astronomy. If this were to change, he promised, meteorology would soon produce results of similar certainty and quality.[27] Only when they could rely on a corpus of coherent data could meteorologists attribute weather phenomena to definite causes, recognise periodical recurrences, and eventually predict similar weather events, thus overcoming the practical weaknesses of meteorology. Concretely, he maintained, one could then compile a reliable calendar for farmers and other groups. The "meteorological calendar" that Böckmann envisioned, however, was nonetheless relatively modest: instead of predictions, it should include "the most important results of the previous year" as well as "the practical rules and cautions that the observations seem to suggest".[28]

---

25 Böckmann (1778), *Wünsche und Aussichten*, 12.
26 Böckmann (1778), *Wünsche und Aussichten*, 20.
27 Böckmann (1778), *Wünsche und Aussichten*, 10–12.
28 Böckmann (1778), *Wünsche und Aussichten*, 21.

III. Reacting to Weakness

These diagnoses of weakness, framed by Böckmann in relation to astronomy, suggest that his suggestion to overcome these weaknesses was to copy the method employed by astronomy method (observations, periodic regularities, predictions) and seek the same kind of courtly patronage that astronomy enjoyed. The learned monk Anselm Ellinger argued in a similar vein during a talk at the Bavarian Academy of Sciences in 1815 that, if this were achieved, one could find "empirical prognostics" which would mainly be the "expectations of similar events". Events of the future could be foretold through a proper understanding of the past.[29] Following in astronomy's footsteps, however, was easier said than done.

For one thing, the notion that atmospheric processes unfolded as regularly as planetary movements proved to be fallacious. Weather phenomena were highly complex for at least two reasons: 1) cause and effect were very difficult to distinguish at any given point, and any effect might have been the cause of another effect, *etc.*;[30] 2) as cause and effect could also be spread out over a large geographical area, it could be very hard to determine their linkage in the first place. Comparing the atmosphere to a distillation flask, the famous naturalist Georg Christoph Lichtenberg allegedly described it as:

"a continuous, big, chemical process, conducted within an immeasurable vessel. When the spherical part of the retort lies in Africa, its neck may reach across Europe and pour out into the receiving flask that is Siberia."[31]

As opposed to other natural sciences, this meant that, in meteorology, it was very difficult to reduce the complexity of these processes in a way that would translate into an experiment in which the individual parts of the process could be manipulated.[32] Singular, narrowly defined parts (for example the electricity in the air or its chemical make-up) were accessible through experiments, but were of very limited value for greater atmospheric processes.[33]

---

29 Ellinger (1815), *Von den bisherigen Versuchen*, 3.
30 Kämtz (1831), *Lehrbuch der Meteorologie*, 7; see, also, the only slightly paraphrased statements in Mahlmann (1850), *Meteorologie*, 150.
31 Cited in: Hufeland/Göttling (1793), *Vorrede*, n. p.
32 Kämtz (1831), *Lehrbuch der Meteorologie*, 6.
33 Kämtz (1831), *Lehrbuch der Meteorologie*, 6.

These insights were not necessarily new and had resulted in a gradual withdrawal from the search for laws which began in the early eighteenth century and increasingly shifted, as Böckmann exemplified, the attention to observations, instruments, and uniform visual representation in tables and symbols.[34] The belief, however, that, eventually, if only observations were continued long enough, regularities would be revealed, was remarkably persistent. Again, Lichtenberg was quick to point out in the late eighteenth century that, although there were piles of meteorological observations by entire academies, it remained just as difficult to predict whether the day after tomorrow would be sunny or not.[35] Notwithstanding this, he continued to believe that the atmosphere was "a mere machine" whose "engine" humankind would certainly be able to understand at some point.[36] This resulted in a data frenzy that was all about publishing table upon table of instrumental data, insisting rather stubbornly that there was no way that regularities would *not* reveal themselves eventually. As late as 1850, the first director of the Prussian Meteorological Institute, Wilhelm Mahlmann, argued for ever more published data: certain observatories should publish not just averages, minima and maxima of their recordings, but all individual readings.[37] And so, just like in other social arenas, the "avalanche of printed numbers" grew,[38] along with the insecurity of the dismayed meteorologists because the only things that showed up time and time again were more irregularities.[39] The point at which the data entries were to be transformed into rules was repeatedly postponed indefinitely.[40] Observation series conducted with several daily readings of various instruments in a number of places over a number of years quickly produced a significant amount of data in tables—a fact that was also criticised, and not just because consistency could only seldom be guaranteed.[41] The possible reasons

---

34 Daston (2008), *Unruly Weather*, 235–236.
35 Lichtenberg (1801), *Über Physiognomik*, 433–434.
36 Lichtenberg (1801), *Über Physiognomik*, 433–434.
37 Mahlmann (1850), *Meteorologie*, 154.
38 Cf. Hacking (1990), *The Taming of Chance*; Porter (1995), *Trust in Numbers*.
39 This had hardly changed since the early 18th century, see Daston (2008), *Unruly Weather*, 247.
40 Golinski (2007), *British Weather*, 79.
41 Muncke (1837), *Meteorologie*, 2044. A notable exception for many is the Societas Meteorologica Palatina, which gathered weather data from many stations in Europe and beyond measured by identical instruments. The results were published between 1783 and 1795. For further information, see Cassidy (1985), *Meteorology in Mannheim*, or Traumüller (1885), *Die Mannheimer Meteorologische Gesellschaft* (1780–1795).

for the inconsistency of the observational data were numerous, even if one only takes the meteorological instruments into account: Who produced them and from what material, how often (if at all) they were calibrated, which scale they used and how it was divided up, whether they were installed inside a house or outside, in the shade or in the sun, how many times a day they were read?—all of this had a significant impact on the data produced during the observations.[42]

Aside from astronomy, there was another body of knowledge against which physical meteorology felt inferior in terms of practical success: the traditional weather wisdom of agricultural and seafaring workers. For everyone who tried to approach meteorology from a more theoretical point of view, wrote the Swiss naturalist Horace-Bénédict de Saussure in 1784, it was "very humiliating" that a "seaman or farmer who has neither instruments nor theory can predict changes in the weather many days ahead with admirable success, which the naturalist with all his scholarship and art would not have surmised".[43] If we accept this feeling as true, then the naturalists believed their knowledge not only to be in direct competition with the knowledge of farmers and seamen, but they were reminded of their own comparative weakness time and time again through the success of that body of knowledge. What picture did a naturalist like de Saussure paint of that knowledge? Firstly, he claimed, that these groups were economically dependent on the accuracy of their own predictions—if one waited a day too long to gather the dried hay, rain might come and the whole hay harvest would rot. According to de Saussure, farmers and seamen collected "many small events" to develop a "premonition", comparable to the instinct of an animal. In addition, they had a collection of personal experiences, so-called "local signs" that were indicative of certain weather conditions to come, for example, a gathering of clouds draped around a mountain in a certain way.[44] This was also tied to the main weakness that de Saussure attested, in turn, to that body of knowledge: it was inherently bound to the spot where it was acquired, it was locally situated

---

[42] One only needs to look at the observation instructions sent out, for example, by the Societas Meteorologica Palatina, an extract of which is printed in Schneider-Carius (1955), *Wetterkunde, Wetterforschung*, 127–129. In a similar vein, many of aspects that Böckmann wants to improve in meteorology were concerned with the coherence of observers, instruments, and observations; see Böckmann (1778), *Wünsche und Aussichten*, 16–22.

[43] Saussure (1784), *Versuch über die Hygrometrie*, 403.

[44] Saussure (1784), *Versuch über die Hygrometrie*, 404.

and non-transferable. Were one to take a farmer, move him to a spot 10 miles down the road, his knowledge would be useless. In that case, hoped de Saussure, the farmer would realise the actual inferiority of his local knowledge and seek the advice of the naturalist.[45] Because, once the naturalist had gained insights into atmospheric processes, they would be universal "like the theory they are based upon". His concepts and the signs could be clearly explicated.[46] The knowledge of the naturalists was thus epistemically superior, at least potentially, over agrarian semiotics because it produced rules that could—theoretically, anyway—easily be transferred to other people and locations. In addition, the knowledge of naturalists would not be a fuzzy feeling based upon sensual experience, but explicable and rational.

How accurately de Saussure viewed agricultural practices of weather prognosis at the time is anyone's guess. With written sources being the main tool of any historian, it is difficult to judge from today's point of view how responsive farmers were to Enlightenment efforts to reform their forecasting, because, presumably, much of this was indeed based upon oral tradition and sensory experience. But one option to find out whether, and, if so, how forecasting played a role in their daily lives is to look at diaries and chronicles compiled by farmers and their families, some of which reveal surprisingly long-term observations. The members of the Hüßner family in northern Franciona, for example, listed grain prices, crop yields, and weather developments from 1750 to 1893. There are no hints in the diary as to whether they attempted forecasting, but instead we find meticulous record-keeping of the beginning and duration of particularly relevant times. In the "beautiful and graceful" spring of 1775, the Hüßners could even begin sowing in March, whereas in 1780, winter lasted until April, and even then, it rained so frequently that it was not until the end of that month that they could start working in the vineyards "because of the wet and cold".[47] Instead of quantifying the weight, temperature and humidity of the air, they identified the state of the atmosphere in more general terms. Their observations do not seem to have been aided by instruments and were focused on the influence of the weather on the timing of agricultural activities. The diary does not convey how the Hüßner family used their written records to guide future activities, but it seems at least possible

---

45 Saussure (1784), *Versuch über die Hygrometrie*, 404.
46 Saussure (1784), *Versuch über die Hygrometrie*, 404.
47 Glaser et al. (1991), *Die Hauschronik*, 20–22.

that they consulted the observations to infer appropriate times for certain actions.

As the weakness of the meteorologists was relative to the (perceived) strength of the astronomers, in *Bayer*'s case as well, the company's weakness became apparent to the management in comparison with others. During the *Alizarinkonvention*, the company had relied on steady sales of the alizarin dyestuff, not considering any change in strategy for as long as it guaranteed attractive returns. As mentioned earlier, the *Bayer* management found its previously successful strategy to be relatively weak as soon as the cartel had disbanded. Other companies had already invested both in research and in the production of own primary products and now benefited from these investments. Bayer's response to the problematical situation was to collect information about the company's productivity. In addition, Bayer began to consider producing the primary products needed for the production of the dyestuffs on its own in the middle of the year 1884 in order to obtain competitive prices for their end products. In the protocol of a meeting of the supervisory board in August 1884, Friedrich Bayer jr., son of the company founder, stated:

"For the next possible competitive battle, Mister Bayer emphasises the major importance of optimizing the factory's revenue by achieving savings in unmanufactured material."[48]

The decision to produce their own primary products required a calculation of fictional production prices. These fictional prices were then compared with the actual market prices for the products in question, in order to examine the benefits of in-house production. In 1884, for example, the *Bayer* executives considered the integration of the production of causticized soda, an important basic substance. After the supervisory board had discussed the purchase of a so-called *"Thelen'sche Apparat"* for causticizing soda, it also approved the building of a factory around this machine in order to secure their own production of this product. The engineers involved in this make-or-buy decision assured that the price for the home produced soda would not exceed 20.5 Marks.[49] After several experiments in the following weeks, the expected price turned out to be accurate.[50] As

---

48 BAL 11/3, 34. Aufsichtsraths Sitzung am 30. August 1884.
49 BAL 11/3, 35. Aufsichtsraths Sitzung am 3. Oktober 1884.
50 BAL 11/3, 36. Aufsichtsraths Sitzung am 22. November 1884.

the soda could not be bought from the market at a cheaper price, the construction of the factory began in late 1884.

Understanding a discourse of weakness as a trigger for future change and adaptation, the example of a make-or-buy decision illustrates the procedures that can be induced by a perceived weakness, such as the lack of self-production of primary materials. A similar process was also put in motion when the meltdown of the *Alizarinkonvention* became apparent. Since the middle of the year 1884, an increasing number of discussions regarding the in-house production of primary products can be observed in the advisory board's protocol: besides the case of causticized soda cited above, the construction of a facility for the regeneration of chrome had been discussed numerous times between 1884 and 1886 and was finally decided upon in July 1886.[51]

In addition, the company's already existing factories were to be revised. As will be detailed below, one of the methods of this revision consisted of a broad acquisition of information on unnecessary costs in the individual production units. The company executives had apparently identified numbers as a measure to reduce uncertainty in decision-making by accurately identifying the processes taking place within their own factories. This quantitative acquisition of the company's data was not solely a reaction to the firm executives' demands, it had also become necessary due to changes in the law on stock companies. In 1884, a new amendment of the law on stock companies became effective with the aim of making businesses more transparent regarding their economic efficiency and formulated rules about business administration.[52] The focus of this transparency was to provide shareholders with detailed information about the stock companies' economic performance and was an immediate result of the Panic of 1873 and its aftermath.[53] While the amount of data gathered at *Bayer* clearly increased in the second half of the 1880s, the establishment of the *"Statistisches Bureau"* (bureau for statistics) in 1892 was another landmark. Here, data from all of the company's products were collected and accredited to the countries to which they were sold. Also, various statistics about the company's facilities, workers, clerks and welfare institutions were collected.[54] At *Bayer*,

---

51 BAL 11/3, 56. Aufsichtsraths Sitzung am 30. Juli 1886.
52 See Plumpe (2006), *Unternehmen*, 68.
53 See Wischermann et al. (2004), *Die institutionelle Revolution*, 259–267.
54 See Messner (1918), *Geschichte der Buchhaltung*, 489.

the 1890s therefore bear resemblance to the "avalanche of printed numbers" observed in mid-nineteenth century Prussian meteorology.[55]

The new law on stock companies had a major impact on *Bayer*. There had not been a consecutive gathering of the manufacturing costs of dyestuffs before, as the costs were only calculated "when the product was newly introduced or the management wished to re-evaluate the manufacturing cost of an old product".[56] The law on stock companies now forced *Bayer* to evaluate all supplies of semi-finished and finished products "according to the law on stock companies" as well as to "calculate precise manufacturing costs".[57] These manufacturing costs were, however, mostly focused on the actual efficiency of production and looking at the input-output relation, while the calculation of overhead costs did not yet play an important role. By 1886, the new relevance of production costs even resulted in institutional changes at the *Bayer* company. Special "factory books" were introduced in which the works managers were to note the daily consumption of raw materials as well as the factories' actual yields. Referring to data collected in these books, quarterly reports were compiled with the intention of defining the exact worth of the goods produced.[58] The information gathered in the factory books was then transferred to the newly installed "*Rohmaterial-Kontrolle*" (department for raw material control) where the data collected in the factory books were audited and the efficiency of production was evaluated. Confronted with an economically critical situation, *Bayer* reacted by establishing control mechanisms and practices of recording that were based upon quantitative data collected within the company.

In addition to the quantitative gathering of accurate production costs, the *Bayer* management also ordered a thorough inspection of the actual conditions of production found in the individual factories. For the alizarin factory, the inspection recorded that numerous things were not found to be in order "considering the hard times". Furthermore, it was noted that the alizarin was not handled economically and that the machinery was in very poor condition. The inspectors were also confident that the factory could operate with 20 per cent fewer workers and that larger sums could be saved by thrift and tidiness. However, it was also stated that the factory

---

55 See Hacking (1990), *The Taming of Chance*, 2.
56 Nobbe (1918), *Die technische Buchhaltung*, 493.
57 BAL 11/3, 44. Aufsichtsraths Sitzung am 4. August 1885.
58 Nobbe (1918), *Die technische Buchhaltung*, 493.

had made good progress recently. Along with the optimisation of production, *Bayer* also evaluated the possibility of replacing old machinery with newer, more efficient models.[59]

The wrong handling of the production goods ultimately resulted in higher costs of manufacturing. For this reason, the revision of the factories would inevitably serve an optimised and more effective production. Combined with the more general idea of a differentiated cost approach, the diagnosis of weakness eventually led to more efficient production which was now controlled by newly installed organisational additions, such as the department for raw material control. The large profits guaranteed by the *Alizarinkonvention* had not made it necessary for *Bayer* to evaluate the complex connections of the production by economic measures. When this security was gone, the company reacted with a comprehensive quantification of the manufacturing processes.

This quantification, which could also be described as the first steps towards management accounting, was motivated both internally and externally, and could also be observed in other German and international industries.[60] While entrepreneurship certainly always focused on numbers, the big wave of statistics and quantification at *Bayer* did indeed precede the first true institutionalisation of business administration and thereby accounting that found its expression in the establishment of the *Handelshochschule Leipzig* in 1898 (school of commerce). This institutionalisation should not, however, be seen as the act of foundation for business administration as a scientific discipline. Instead, it was a terminal-point of a scientific debate that had treated different aspects of business management from the early modern period and made use of references and ideas that cameralism had produced between the early eighteenth and nineteenth century.[61] It is thus difficult to determine whether the growing importance of businesses in the second half of the nineteenth century influenced the development of business administration as a discipline or whether it was the discipline that enabled business to use more nuanced methods of management.

---

59 BAL 11/3, 49. Aufsichtsraths Sitzung am 30./31. Januar 1886.
60 Johnson et al. (1987), *Relevance Lost*, 6–13. For the German companies Krupp, Scheidt and Farina, see Pleitgen (2005), *Die Entwicklung des betriebswirtschaftlichen Rechnungswesens*.
61 See Schneider (1999), *Geschichte der Betriebswirtschaftslehre*, 1–24.

IV. Acting towards the Future

Bayer recovered remarkably quickly from its crisis in the years around 1885. The increasing accuracy in the calculation of prices led to an overall more efficient production which was used on the next generation of synthetic dyestuffs, the so-called azo dyes, after 1886. While information had been gathered about the processes, a second major part of Bayer's production was still left more or less untouched: the overhead costs. In this category, costs that could not be directly attributed to a certain product were summarised, such as wages, the cost of repairs, or the consumption of the cooling water that was needed in several factories. The overheads were calculated as a percentage markup that was defined by comparing the sum of the yearly total consumption of raw material with the total sum of operating costs.[62] This percentage was then counted towards the production costs of the individual products. For a company, the accurate calculation of the overhead costs was an important factor for evaluating the real production costs of individual products and thereby their actual margin.

As Bayer had identified the gathering and control of information as a best practice, it is not surprising that, in 1889, the *"technische Buchhaltung"* (department for technical accounting) was installed in order to tackle the problem of the still rudimentary calculation of overhead costs. The department played a significant role for the company. Being part of market competition, *Bayer* always had to adjust product prices to those of other companies in order not to risk its competitive edge. The only way to continue to generate increasing profits then was by reducing the costs of production. The department for technical accounting began to allocate the company's total costs at the different fabrication units. In a next step, these costs should allow the exact production costs for individual products, now including the overhead costs, to be calculated. In addition, the department was instructed to calculate the construction costs of new facilities and allocate these costs to particular new buildings and devices.[63]

When the collection of information was finally institutionalised, further improvement focused on the methods employed by the individual departments. In the following years, the collecting of data was simplified, even though, the ultimate goal—the exact attribution of every cost to the particular products—had still not been achieved. In the 1890s, costs for steam,

---

62 Nobbe (1918), *Die technische Buchhaltung*, 493–494.
63 See Nobbe (1918), *Die technische Buchhaltung*, 493.

gas, water and transportation were still totalled and then allocated to the individual factories by the end of the year. The task of accurately gathering all the necessary information required both personnel and time, and could thus not be accomplished by the existing departments. *Bayer*'s management reacted by creating a new department whose task it was to continue the calculation from where the older departments had terminated them. The new *"Kalkulation II"* department first attributed overhead costs to the individual factories and then to the individual products. As this process was complex, it was not conducted continuously, but was instead evaluated by samples. However, the process was still so labour-intensive that the department published its report only once a year.[64] As the controlling tasks became routine and the departments more efficient, the publishing interval increased from yearly to quarterly and finally to monthly, a change that "was of major importance for the economic development of the company".[65]

The demand for detailed information also correlated with the company's growth. While *Bayer* employed some 555 workers in 1885, the number had more than doubled five years later.[66] At the same time, its revenue had almost quadrupled. It seems likely that, in the early years of the *Alizarinkonvention*, the company's management could have gathered information about the company's performance more easily as it was still a small company. Later, when the management was more separated from the operating activities, information became more important and laid the foundation for "management by numbers".[67] The collection of information was again expensive, both in terms of monetary costs as well as the time it took to set up the infrastructure. When the gathering of information had been institutionalised in the form of departments, both types of costs could be reduced as soon as the processes within the department were routinised.[68] Processes for information collection were then adapted and implemented into the production itself, resulting in clear standards regarding the constant control and monitoring of both consumption and output. While the

---

64 See Nobbe (1918), *Die technische Buchhaltung*, 494.
65 Nobbe (1918), *Die technische Buchhaltung*, 494.
66 BAL 1/5.2.
67 Johnson et al. (1987), *Relevance Lost*, 15. The "alienation" of management and day-to-day business through accounting is also discussed in Porter (1995), *Trust in Numbers*, 89–113 and for the case of Carnegie in Chandler (1977), *The Visible Hand*, 267–269.
68 This is a point also made by the economic perspective of New Institutional Economics. For an overview, see: Hesse (2002), *Im Netz der Kommunikation*, 31–47.

Bayer management had not expressed a lot of interest in the quantitative understanding of the company both before and during the *Alizarinkonvention*, the collapse of the cartel made the importance of information clear to the *Bayer* executives. In the end, this reaction triggered a quantitative penetration of the entire company, ultimately leading to a scheme for information gathering that could be easily applied to any existing and future production unit. Internally gathered information thus became a crucial factor for decision-making.

Meteorologists developed at least two strategies in order to cope with numerous uncertainties of a related kind. One was to qualify forecasts by terming them "probable". As we will soon see, this is not to be confused with mathematical probability theory which formed around the same time, but was not applied to meteorological matters until later. But authors such as the above-mentioned Fresenius attempted to collect weather lore, evaluate whether the rules conformed to experience, and inform his readers which rules were indeed valid. Unfortunately, he did not convey exactly how he examined the rules.[69] Similarly, in a 1770 agrarian calendar, the Swabian teacher and priest Balthasar Sprenger printed "conjectures of a learned friend" that chose to remain anonymous.[70] After roughly outlining the course of each month's weather, the "learned friend" emphasised that his projections usually came true, save for "exceptions" due to multiple possible causes which disturbed the month's regular weather.[71] This shows that the emphasis on "probability" was both a confession of weakness as well as an insurance measure against successive claims when the prognoses were falsified—after all, the forecasts had been qualified as probable, not as certain. "Naturally," concluded the astronomer Johann Elert Bode, such "probable conjectures" were much more likely to be true in some way than to fail.[72] As long as it was not possible to view atmospheric processes from above the clouds safely or have "weather couriers" transmit observational

---

69 Fresenius (1799), *Praktische Wetterkunde*. Vgl. auch Pilgram (1788), *Untersuchungen über das Wahrscheinliche der Wetterkunde*.
70 These conjectures, however, bear close resemblance to the astrometeorological predictions Sprenger published in subsequent calendar volumes (1772–1774) which were sent in by the renowned Swabian priest and instrument maker Philipp Matthäus Hahn. Hahn also published a summary of how accurate his predictions had been for the year before in which he admitted to very mixed results. Sprenger then ceased to publish Hahn's predictions after his calendar's 1775 volume.
71 Sprenger (1770), *Allgemeiner öconomischer oder Landwirthschafts-Kalender*, 1.
72 Bode (1819), *Gedanken über den Witterungslauf*, 4–5.

data quickly over long distances, these kinds of predictions would have to suffice because there could be none on the grounds of physical laws.[73] Until then, people would need to make do with what "attentive naturalists and farmers" knew or suspected about their local weather, that is, with statistical, locally valid experience.[74] Without a way of predicting with certainty, this was the next best solution:

"So long as something certain can be seen, it is foolish to rely on something probable; but if nothing is certain, human wisdom demands to choose the *most* probable from a selection of probable events."[75]

Compared to the mathematical probability theory developed by scholars Jakob Bernoulli and Pierre Simon Laplace, however, the "probable" statements that we find in these meteorological texts appear to be rather crude: based upon arithmetic means from the observations with no expressions of numerically quantified probability yet.[76] As Lorraine Daston pointed out, the belief in a calculable natural world, developed in the seventeenth century, was the necessary metaphysical pre-condition for the believing in the possibility of predicting events in the classical theory of probability that emerged between 1650 and 1840.[77] Regarding the course of the weather, this required the establishing of what was the "normal" weather through long-range observation and retrospectively identifying factors that led to exceptions to the rule, as fellow astronomer Anton Pilgram suggested in 1788. It would be a quite respectable accomplishment to know at least the average weather because unusual weather is rarer more or less by definition.[78] However, Pilgram's and Bode's pleas appear not to have been realised consistently because, even in the 1830s, the physical scientist Ludwig Kämtz complained that meteorologists tried to follow the methods of astronomers, who, said Kämtz, calculated the path of a planet generally without taking into consideration the disturbances caused by the neighbouring planets. Meteorologists, on the other hand, invested too much

---

73 Bode (1819), *Gedanken über den Witterungslauf*, 61–62.
74 Bode (1819), *Gedanken über den Witterungslauf*, 75–76.
75 Pilgram (1788), *Untersuchungen über das Wahrscheinliche der Wetterkunde*, 3.
76 Though the mathematical tools were invented, the first meteorologist to actively work toward introducing probability theory into the discipline toward the middle of the 19th century was the Belgian astronomer and statistician Adolphe Quetelet,; Sheynin (1984), *On the History of the Statistical Method in Meteorology*, 76; Anderson (2005), *Predicting the Weather*, 134.
77 Daston (1988), *Classical Probability*, xv.
78 Pilgram (1788), *Untersuchungen über das Wahrscheinliche der Wetterkunde*, 3.

effort into explaining singular and unusual events while disregarding the normal course of weather for a given place.[79] If we follow Daston's idea that "quantification" was a "process of mutual accommodation between mathematics and subject matter to create and sustain the analogies that make applications possible", the conception of weather needed to be changed first in order to lend itself to mathematical treatment.[80]

A second way of coping with this shortcoming was to withdraw from forecasts altogether. While it was still commonplace in the eighteenth century to insist, as seen above, on meteorology's potential for practical applications, the plea for practical utility was noticeably downplayed in the first half of the nineteenth century. One way to read this is that meteorologists were striving for scientific autonomy by disregarding the wishes of society and practising a pure, theoretical science that was not contaminated by expectations of applicability. Kämtz, who had written one of the first comprehensive textbooks of meteorology, thought the demands for forecasts was utterly "ridiculous", a great misconception of the true tasks of a meteorologist. Instead, he put forward the idea that meteorologists were "historians of weather" whose only goal was to discover the laws of past events—and, just as historians were not expected to foretell the future, according to Kämtz, you could not expect a meteorologist to foretell the weather.[81] His impression was that society did not demand applicable knowledge from other scholars, and, therefore, meteorology was also not to be practised for its own sake, instead of trying to satisfy those that reproached meteorologists for merely piling up numbers. In a dictionary entry on meteorology, published in 1850, the first secretary of the Prussian Meteorological Institute claimed that, for this reason, every meteorologist had the right to "reject such demands resolutely" and to

"abstain from prophesying in his research altogether, so long as the necessary means are discovered or made applicable. This science cannot pursue any other goal than to collect all available observations, examine them critically, put them in order and compare them in order to achieve more or less general results."[82]

It is due to this logic that, in the same dictionary, there was a separate entry dedicated to weather prediction ("*Meteoromantie*") as opposed to weather

---

79 Kämtz (1831), *Lehrbuch der Meteorologie*, 6.
80 Daston (1988), *Classical Probability*, xvi.
81 Kämtz (1840), *Vorlesungen über Meteorologie*, vii.
82 Mahlmann (1850), *Meteorologie*, 154.

science ("*Meteorologie*")[83]. One of the reasons for this separation, cited in another dictionary, mirrored the laudatory yet condescending tone of de Saussure: while it was remarkable how well short-term local predictions worked, this ability could not be learned theoretically from a textbook, but only from practical experience—it was a skill, rather than a science.[84]

Based upon the evidence just laid out, another interpretation of this withdrawal from the practical application of meteorological science seems worthy of further investigation. Perhaps this road was taken not—or not only—to enable meteorologists to practise their science free from immediate societal demands—to improve it by purifying it. Perhaps it was, instead, a confession of practical weakness. Faced with this failure to keep the promise of predictability, initially, meteorologists sought refuge in their observatory at the top of the ivory tower. In the first half of the nineteenth century, the theory and practice of meteorology were dissociated, as though they did not—and should not—be two faces of the same coin, as had been so natural in the eighteenth century. Demanding that meteorology be of practical use for society had become presumptuous. Ironically, this opened the door for actors deemed less scientific to fill the void, and was—at least in part—responsible for astrological and semiotic prediction remaining a strong competitor.[85] Whereas the need to predict the weather provided great impetus to the development of meteorology in Great Britain,[86] the separation of theory and practice was to have a permanent effect on the institutionalisation of meteorology in the German territories. Before all the different regional weather services were unified in Nazi Germany 1934 to form the *Reichswetterdienst* (subordinated to the Ministry of Aviation), the meteorological field was scattered, with a great number of public or private actors who focused on issuing forecasts while research was kept tightly in the hands of a few state institutions.[87] This development of a knowledge élite was not only met with understanding but also produced the need for a new literary genre, meteorological books which were explicitly designed to be popular. Hermann Hager, for example, explained that his book was an effort to work against meteorology remaining the "property of the learned" and remaining unknown to most people, particularly

---

[83] Mahlmann (1850), *Meteoromantie*.
[84] Muncke (1837), *Meteorologie*, 2044.
[85] Golinski (2007), *British Weather*, 79–80; Anderson (2005), *Predicting the Weather*, 42–46.
[86] Anderson (2005), *Predicting the Weather*, 2–8.
[87] See Wege (2002), *Die Entwicklung der meteorologischen Dienste in Deutschland*, 37–61.

farmers. It was because of this fact that no use could be made of this science. All the available books that were for sale were too expensive and too hard to understand for someone without a background in physics.[88]

V. Conclusion

Although the two case studies described actors in very different situations, their reactions to weak knowledge about the future show some similarities. Whether we look at the development of German meteorology between 1750 and 1850 or at a chemical company in the late nineteenth century, a diagnosis of weakness is answered by collecting vast amounts of data—the complexity of the processes to be predicted was mirrored in the complexity constructed. While, in the case of meteorology, however, it was for a long time unclear how and where to collect the data, the problem for *Bayer* was rather whether this practice would be beneficial at all. The company had been successful and its success was protected by a cartel. The collection of information as an exit strategy was, in both cases, triggered when a comparative weakness became apparent. When the *Alizarinkonvention* collapsed in 1885, *Bayer* was immediately put into an economically dangerous position *vis-à-vis* its competitors, while German meteorologists never seemed to stand a chance against astronomy's successful empirical method and the benefits that were thus granted by the patronage of the nobility. Not only did the meteorologists see themselves as inferior to astronomers, even the traditional weather wisdom of agricultural and seafaring workers appeared to be more precise than the predictions presented in the naturalists' theories.

In both cases, the scope shifted from the outside to the inside. The answers to the comparative weakness were, in both cases, to be found within the resource regime itself, and, as a result, modified the existing resource regime. This was done by re-evaluating the method of data collection or tweaking the kinds of questions that could be answered with the data collected. The meteorologists no longer searched for laws but for regularities in the data that would allow them to formulate probable weather. The company executives were on the hunt for as precise a quantification of

---

88 Hager (1845), *Wetter und Witterung*, iv.

production processes as possible with the aim of using this knowledge for future production as well. Both the price as well as the weather data led to an institutionalisation of collecting. While, for the meteorologists, the search for regularities resulted in a data frenzy that posed more questions than it answered, *Bayer* set up more and more departments that helped monitoring the production and thereby optimised the production by utilising the collected data. For the meteorologists, the failure to make theoretical sense out of the huge amount of data that they had collected resulted in two coping strategies. As the data did not allow them to formulate general rules about the weather, they used the information at least to determine the probabilities of the weather, although not yet in a mathematical sense. The withdrawal to merely chronicling and averaging observations was both a confession of weakness with regard to the claim to formulate a theory, as well as an insurance measure in case the prognoses should fail.

For *Bayer*, the collection of data and the in-detail quantification of production costs can be identified as a successful measure to overcome comparative weakness. In addition, a new focus on a better quantitative understanding of the actual processes took place in a lot of other companies and industries at about the same time, leading to a more or less coherent economic body of knowledge. Whereas economic knowledge became more and more coherent, knowledge about the weather, confronted with its weakness, remained in its fragmented state. The practical weakness stressed in the chapter can be linked to the core distinction between the two case studies which lies in complex processes: meteorologists dealt with natural phenomena, the interplay, causation and scope of which were quite unclear, whereas arguably, the emergence of an economic market in the abstract sense was a more recent, man-made invention, and, perhaps, for this reason, easier to understand. Eventually, it appears that the permanent discourse of weakness that is inherent to any prediction of the future led to very similar strategies of coping in two very different historical formations and thereby presented itself as a powerful tool for comparison.

Literature

Unpublished Material

Bayer Archiv Leverkusen (BAL)
1/5.2, Geschichtliche Entwicklung der Farbenfabriken von 1863–1906
11/3, Aufsichtsrat: Schriftwechsel, Einladungen, Protokolle
15/BA.2, Gewinn und Verlustkonto der Farbenfabriken vorm. Friedr. Bayer & Co.
15/DA.1.1, Umsätze der Bayer AG

Published Material

Abelshauser, Werner et al. (eds.). (2004). *German Industry and Global Enterprise. BASF: The History of a Company*. Cambridge: Cambridge University Press.

Anderson, Katharine (1999). The Weather Prophets. Science and Reputation in Victorian Meteorology. *History of Science*, 37, 179–216.

— (2005). *Predicting the Weather: Victorians and the Science of Meteorology*. Chicago IL: Chicago University Press.

Beckert, Jens (2016). *Imagined Futures: Fictional Expectations and Capitalist Dynamics*. Cambridge MA: Harvard University Press.

Böckmann, Johann Lorenz (1778). *Wünsche und Aussichten zur Erweiterung und Vervollkommnung der Witterungslehre*. Karlsruhe.

Bode, Johann Elert (1819). *Gedanken über den Witterungslauf*. Berlin.

Cassidy, David (1985). Meteorology in Mannheim: The Palatine Meteorological Society, 1780–1795. *Sudhoffs Archiv*, 69, 8–25.

Chandler, Alfred D. Jr. (1977). *The Visible Hand*. Cambridge MA: Harvard University Press.

Cyert, Richard M, and James G. March (1992). *A Behavioral Theory of the Firm*. 2nd edition. Cambridge: Wiley-Blackwell.

Daston, Lorraine (1988). *Classical Probability in the Enlightenment*. Princeton NJ: Princeton University Press.

— (2008). Unruly Weather. Natural Law Confronts Natural Variability. In Lorraine Daston and Michael Stolleis (eds.). *Natural Laws and Laws of Nature in Early Modern Europe. Jurisprudence, Theology, Moral and Natural Philosophy*, 233–248. Farnham/Burlington: Ashgate.

Duisberg, Carl (1918). Selbsterlebtes und Schlussbetrachtungen. In Farbenfabriken vorm. Friedr. Bayer & Co. (ed.). *Geschichte und Entwicklung der Farbenfabriken vorm. Friedr. Bayer & Co. Elberfeld in den ersten 50 Jahren*, 585–644. Munich: Meisenbach Riffarth & Co.

Eicke, L. B. (1752). Von der Beobachtung des Wetters. *Hannoverische Gelehrte Anzeigen*, 185–224.

Ellinger, Anselm (1815). *Von den bisherigen Versuchen über längere Voraussicht der Witterung.* Munich.

Emeis, Stefan (2006). Das erste Jahrhundert deutschsprachiger meteorologischer Lehrbücher. *Berichte zur Wissenschaftsgeschichte*, 29, 39–51.

Fresenius, Friedrich Anton (1799). *Praktische Wetterkunde nach alten Bauernerfahrungen.* Gotha.

Glaser, Rüdiger, and Winfried Schenk (eds.). (1991). *Die Hauschronik der Wiesenbronner Familie Hüßner: Ihre Aufzeichnungen zu Wirtschaft, Geschichte, Klima und Geographie Mainfrankens von 1750–1894.* Sondheim v. d. Rhön: Hartmann.

Golinski, Jan (2007). *British Weather and the Climate of Enlightenment.* Chicago IL: Chicago University Press.

Greve, Heinrich R. (1998). Performance, Aspirations, and Risky Organizational Change. *Administrative Science Quarterly*, 43, 1, 58–86.

Hacking, Ian (1990). *The Taming of Chance.* Cambridge: Cambridge University Press.

Hager, Hermann (1845). *Wetter und Witterung, ihre Ursachen, Kennzeichen und Vorzeichen.* Glogau.

Hesse, Jan-Otmar (2002). *Im Netz der Kommunikation. Die Reichs-Post und Telegraphenverwaltung 1876–1914.* Munich: C.H.Beck.

Hufeland, Christoph Wilhelm, and Johann Friedrich August Göttling (1793). Vorrede. *Aufklärungen der Arzneywissenschaft*, 1, n. p.

Johnson, H. Thomas, and Robert S. Kaplan (1987). *Relevance Lost. The Rise and Fall of Management Accounting.* Boston, MA: Harvard Business School Press.

Kämtz, Ludwig Friedrich (1831). *Lehrbuch der Meteorologie*, 1. Leipzig.

— (1840). *Vorlesungen über Meteorologie.* Halle.

Knight, Frank (1921). *Risk, Uncertainty, and Profit.* Boston MA: Houghton Mifflin Company.

Lamoreaux, Naomi R. (2001). Reframing the Past: Thoughts about Business Leadership and Decision Making under Uncertainty. *Enterprise & Society*, 2, 4, 632–59.

Levenstein, Margaret (1991). The Use of Cost Measures. The Dow Chemical Company, 1890–1914. In Peter Temin (ed.). *Inside the Business Enterprise. Historical Perspectives on the Use of Information*, 71–112. Chicago IL: University of Chicago Press.

Lichtenberg, Georg Christoph (1801). Über Physiognomik. In Ludwig Christian Lichtenberg and Friedrich Kries (eds.). *Vermischte Schriften*, 3, 425–526. Göttingen.

Mahlmann, Wilhelm (1850). Meteorologie. In Ernst Friedrich August et al. (eds.). *Handwörterbuch der Chemie und Physik*, 3, 150–155. Berlin.

— (1850). Meteoromantie. In Ernst Friedrich August et al. (eds.). *Handwörterbuch der Chemie und Physik*, 3, 155–157. Berlin.

Messner, Georg (1918). Geschichte der Buchhaltung. In Farbenfabriken vorm. Friedr. Bayer & Co. (ed.). *Geschichte und Entwicklung der Farbenfabriken vorm. Friedr. Bayer & Co. Elberfeld in den ersten 50 Jahren*, 485–90. Munich: Meisenbach Riffarth & Co

Minois, Georges (1998). *Geschichte der Zukunft. Orakel, Prophezeiungen, Utopien, Prognosen*. Düsseldorf: Artemis & Winkler.

Muncke, Georg Wilhelm (1837). Meteorologie. In Heinrich Wilhelm Brandes et al. (eds.). *Johann Samuel Traugott Gehler's Physikalisches Wörterbuch*, revised ed., 6, 3, 1817–2083. Leipzig.

Nobbe, Fritz (1918). Die technische Buchhaltung. In Farbenfabriken vorm. Friedr. Bayer & Co. (ed.). *Geschichte und Entwicklung der Farbenfabriken vorm. Friedr. Bayer & Co. Elberfeld in den ersten 50 Jahren*, 491–96. Munich: Meisenbach Riffarth & Co.

Osteroth, Dieter (1985). *Soda, Teer und Schwefelsäure. Der Weg zur Großchemie*. Hamburg: Rowohlt Taschenbuch Verlag.

Pilgram, Anton (1788). *Untersuchungen über das Wahrscheinliche der Wetterkunde*. Vienna.

Pinnow, Hermann (1938). *Werksgeschichte. Der Gefolgschaft der Werke Leverkusen, Elberfeld und Dormagen zur Erinnerung an die 75. Wiederkehr des Gründungstages der Farbenfabriken vorm. Friedr. Bayer & Co.*. Munich: Bruckmann.

Pleitgen, Verena (2005). Die Entwicklung des betriebswirtschaftlichen Rechnungswesens von 1890 bis 1940 am Beispiel der Firmen Krupp, Scheidt und Farina. PhD Dissertation, Cologne University.

Plumpe, Werner (2006). Unternehmen. In Gerold Ambrosius (ed.). *Moderne Wirtschaftsgeschichte. Eine Einführung für Historiker und Ökonomen*, 61–94. 2nd edition. Munich: Oldenbourg.

— (2016). Wie entscheiden Unternehmen? *Zeitschrift für Unternehmensgeschichte*, 61, 2, 141–59.

Porter, Theodore M. (1995). *Trust in Numbers: The Pursuit of Objectivity in Science and Public Life*. Princeton NJ: Princeton University Press.

Saussure, Horace-Bénédicte de (1784). Versuch über die Hygrometrie. Leipzig.

Schneider, Dieter (1999). Geschichte der Betriebswirtschaftslehre. In Michael Lingenfelder (ed.). *100 Jahre Betriebswirtschaftslehre in Deutschland*, 8–36. Munich: Vahlen.

Schneider, Ivo (1979). Die Mathematisierung der Vorhersage künftiger Ereignisse in der Wahrscheinlichkeitstheorie vom 17. bis zum 19. Jahrhundert. *Berichte zur Wissenschaftsgeschichte*, 2, 101–12.

Schneider-Carius, Karl (1955). *Wetterkunde, Wetterforschung. Geschichte ihrer Probleme und Erkenntnisse in Dokumenten aus drei Jahrtausenden*. Freiburg/Munich: Karl Alber.

Sheynin, Oscar B. (1984). On the History of the Statistical Method in Meteorology. *Archive for History of Exact Sciences*, 31, 1, 53–95.

Simon, Herbert A. (1955). A Behavioral Model of Rational Choice. *The Quarterly Journal of Economics*, 69, 1, 99–118.

Sprenger, Balthasar (1770). *Allgemeiner öconomischer oder Landwirthschafts-Kalender auf das Jahr 1770*. Stuttgart.

Streb, Jochen et al. (2007). Knowledge Spill-over from New to Old Industries: The Case of German Synthetic Dyes and Textiles (1878–1913). *Explorations in Economic History*, 44, 2, 203–23.

Traumüller, Friedrich (1885). *Die Mannheimer Meteorologische Gesellschaft (1780–1795). Ein Beitrag zur Geschichte der Meteorologie*. Leipzig.

Wege, Klaus (2002). *Die Entwicklung der meteorologischen Dienste in Deutschland*. Offenbach/M.: Selbstverlag des Deutschen Wetterdienstes.

Williamson, Oliver E. (1975). *Markets and Hierarchies. Analysis and Antitrust Implications. A Study in the Economics of Internal Organization*. New York: Free Press.

Wischermann, Clemens, and Anne Nieberding (2004). *Die institutionelle Revolution. Eine Einführung in die deutsche Wirtschaftsgeschichte des 19. und frühen 20. Jahrhunderts*. Stuttgart: Franz Steiner.

Chapter 5
Resources—A Historical and Conceptual Roadmap

Daniel Hausmann and Nicolas Perreaux

I. Introduction

In the past decades, resources became a growing, important field of research within the humanities and social sciences.[1] Nowadays, resources are everywhere in the mass media, and everything, at least so it seems, could, potentially, be a resource. However, the significance of the term and concept of "resource(s)" for research in the humanities remains unspecific, and an accurate explanation of the term and its history is still nowhere to be found.[2] Treading along this path without a conceptual map may, indeed, leave historians or social scientists unmindful of their position in relation to this trend. In fact, most research on resources comes from the field of economics, and, by appropriating this concept from economics, social

---

1 This chapter has benefited from the feedback of several researchers, including Iwo Amelung, Alain Guerreau, Hartmut Leppin, Christian A. Müller and Joseph Morsel. We are grateful to them for their ideas. Naturally, there had already been popular research about resources in the past decades, for example, the resource-mobilisation approach in the 1970s: McCarthy et al. (1977), *Resource Mobilization and Social Movements*. Nevertheless, the amount of research into "resources" has grown quickly during the 1990–2018 period. Two recent cases in History include: Flachowsky et al. (2017), *Ressourcenmobilisierung* and Bührer-Thierry et al. (2017), *Acquérir, prélever, contrôler: les ressources en compétition (400–1100)*.

2 Outside of Economics, none of the dictionaries of human or social sciences that we have consulted contain an entry for the word "resource": Lacey (1996), *A Dictionary of Philosophy*; Wilczynski (1981), *An Encyclopedic Dictionary*; Seymour-Smith (1986), *Macmillan Dictionary of Anthropology*; Iannone, *Dictionary of World Philosophy*; Boudon et al. (1989), *A Critical Dictionary of Sociology*; Audi, *The Cambridge Dictionary of Philosophy*; Bunnin et al. (2004), *The Blackwell Dictionary of Western Philosophy*; Atkinson et al. (2005), *Cultural Geography: A Critical Dictionary of Key Concepts*; Protevi (2005), *The Edinburgh Dictionary of Continental Philosophy*; Bruce et al. (2006), *The Sage Dictionary of Sociology*; Turner (2006), *The Cambridge Dictionary of Sociology*; Morris (2012), *Concise Dictionary of Social and Cultural Anthropology*; Foulquié et al. (1969), *Dictionnaire de la langue philosophique*; Lalande (1926/1992), *Vocabulaire technique et critique de la philosophie*; Bröckling et al. (2004), *Glossar der Gegenwart*.

scientists and historians might bring undesired implications into their own fields. The goal of this chapter is thus, first, roughly to sketch the history of the term "resource(s)", and second to analyse how an economic understanding of the term came to dominate by the twentieth century. Our objective is in no way to present a definitive solution to the problem that we wish to address; it is more a matter of showing that the analysis of the multiple concepts used in the human and social sciences very often opens perspectives, and that the history of "resource(s)" is particularly interesting. This short chapter therefore invites other studies, which could focus not only on the term alone, but also on the words which form its semantic *entourage* (*i.e.*, collocations); hence, the concept necessarily draws its meaning and strength.[3]

This essay traces the conceptual history of "resource(s)", in order to clarify its implication and possible usages.[4] A brief probing into the development of the term and its current usages shows that the period of the industrial revolution (eighteenth–nineteenth centuries)[5] marks a significant shift in the understanding of the term "resource" as well. With the spread of industrial capitalism, the notion of "resources" came to denote primarily "exploitable nature",[6] whereas previously it had meant an inner strength. From the late nineteenth century, economics aspired to be a rigorous science, a trend which intensified in particular after WWII because of its mathematisation, in particular because of the invention of game theory around 1944.[7] Then, after WWII, the concept of "resource" was step-by-step extended literally to all areas of human and social life by means of terms such as "human capital" or "social capital". By thus extending the term "resources", economics was presented as the most suitable candidate to unify the social sciences and the humanities. Edward Lazear (b. 1948), for instance, claims that "the goal of economic theory is to unify thought

---

3 Trier (1931), *Der Deutsche Wortschatz im Sinnbezirk des Verstandes*; Schmidt (1973), *Wortfeldforschung*; Klemperer (1947), *LTI*.
4 For paradigmatic works in conceptual history, see Koselleck (1979), *Historische Semantik und Begriffsgeschichte*; Koselleck (2006), *Begriffsgeschichten*; Gumbrecht (2006), *Dimension und Grenzen der Begriffsgeschichte*; Morsel (forthcoming), *La production circulation d'un concept*.
5 Verley (1997), *L'Échelle du Monde*.
6 About the concept of "nature" in our contemporary thought (which he describes as a "Naturalist Ontology"), see Descola (2013), *Beyond Nature and Culture*, Chapter 8: "The Certainties of Naturalism".
7 The classic reference is Neumann et al. (1944), *The Theory of Games and Economic Behavior*. For a critical history of game theory in economics, see Amadae (2015), *Prisoners of Reason: The Cold War Origins of Rational Choice Liberalism*.

and to provide a language that can be used to understand a variety of social phenomena".[8] Some economists even argued that this constitutes an "invasion" or a sort of "economic imperialism".[9] It is, of course, useful that the human and social scientists become aware of the role played by the term in economics, in order to give a more global, but nevertheless precise, definition of the concept, proper to the analyses of "resources" in the other scientific fields. This chapter serves the purpose of sketching its dynamics and historical background. Its core features are two crucial shifts: first, the re-location of resource(s) from the inner self to the outer world, and the concomitant shift from the singular (resource) to the plural (resources); and second, the expansion of the economic understanding of the term to virtually all domains of society and life following the experiences of the post-WWII period.

II. Resource, a Historical Semantics

1. Latin Etymology and the *Resurrectio* (Antiquity–Twelfth century)

Without going back unnecessarily to the Indo-European roots of the term, the etymology of *resource* refers to the Latin verb *resurgo (-ere)*, which means to arise from, to resurrect, to get up, or to recover.[10] In contemporary French, many verbs still derive from it, including "*sourdre*" (to rise up) or "*surgir*" (to arise). Naturally, *resurgo* is not an uncommon Latin word, especially during the Middle Ages. First, the term appears up to 70 times in its different forms of conjugation in the *Vulgata*.[11] This score should be com-

---

8 Lazear (2000), *Economic Imperialism*, 142. On the opposite side, for historical and anthropological perspectives about the role of economy in societies, see Polanyi (1944), *The Great Transformation*; Godelier (1972), *Rationality and Irrationality in Economics*; Sahlins (1974), *Stone Age Economics*; Baschet (2014), *Adieux au capitalisme*. Becker (1976), *The Economic Approach*; Hirshleifer (1985), The Expanding Domain of Economics; Swedberg (1990), *Economics and Sociology*; Grossbard-Shechtmanet al. (2002), *The Expansion of Economics*.
9 Fine et al. (2009), *From Economic Imperialism*.
10 Gaffiot (1934), *Dictionnaire*, 1355; Parisse et al. (2006), *Lexique latin-français*, 583; Baier et al. (2012), *Der Neue Georges*, 4164–4165; Lewis et al. (1879), *A Latin Dictionary*.
11 With these numbers of occurrences: *resurrexit* (16), *resurget* (11), *resurgere* (7), *resurgunt* (7), *resurgent* (6), *resurgat* (4), *resurgant* (3), *resurrexeit* (3), *resurrexint* (2), *resurrexero* (2), *resurrexisse* (2), *resurrexisse* (2), *resurgam* (1), *resurgemus* (1), *resurgens* (1), *resurrecturos* (1), *resurrexistis* (1) Regarding the role of the Bible for Medieval Latin, see Lobrichon et al. (1984), *Le Moyen Âge et la Bible*; Lourdaux et al. (1979), *The Bible and Medieval Culture*; Fontaine et al. (1985),

pared with another one obtained from a corpus of ancient/classic texts which contains more than six million words, 8.5 times larger than that of the *Vulgata*.[12] It ranges from the third century BC (with, for example, Plautus [254 BC–184 BC] and Marcus Porcius Cato [234 BC–149 BC]) to the first and second centuries AD (with Juvenale [c. 60–127] or Apuleius [124–170]).[13] In this database, there are only 74 mentions of *resurgo*.[14] The verb is associated and/or connotated[15] with war (*bellum*), especially with the Trojan War (*Troy*), astronomy, cycles, and time (*rursum, iterum, etc.*).[16] Famous Roman poets seem to have used the term first, including Horace [65 BC–8 BC], and then Virgil [70 BC–19 BC], Titus Livius [c. 64 BC–17 AD], Propertius [c. 50 BC–c. 15 BC], and Ovid [43 BC–c. 18 AD].[17]

Even so, the term *resurgere* becomes more frequent only in the Vulgata, especially in the New Testament. Of the total biblical references only 13 are found in the Old Testament, compared to 67 in the New Testament.[18]

Le monde latin antique; Guerreau (2001), *Vinea*; Kuchenbuch et al. (2006), *Textus im Mittelalter*; Dahan, *Lire la Bible au Moyen Âge*; Nelson et al. (2015), *Reading the Bible*.

[12] These texts have been drawn from various websites, mostly The Latin Library (http://www.thelatinlibrary.com/) and the Classical Latin Texts (http://latin.packhum.org/). This corpus contains 948 files.

[13] The Vulgata is about 730,000 words.

[14] All the corpora used here have been lemmatised using the TreeTagger software and the parameters generated by the ANR Omnia (http://www.glossaria.eu/treetagger/, see Bon (2009), OMNIA (1); Bon (2010), OMNIA (2); Bon (2011), OMNIA (3)).

[15] These associations are revealed by the computation of co-occurrences, *i.e.*, the lemmata that appear in the same context as resurgere. The calculation has been made via the TXM software. See Heiden (2010), *TXM Platform*. Heiden et al. (2010), *TXM* used a span of 5 words before and after resurgere.

[16] Marcus Velleius Paterculus, *Historiarum Libri Duo* 2.87: "*Hic speculatus est per summam quietem ac dissimulationem precipitis consilia iuuenis et mira celeritate nullaque cum perturbatione aut rerum aut hominum oppresso Lepido inmane noui ac resurrecturi belli ciuilis restinxit initium.*"; Seneca, *Cons. Helun* 9.8: "*[...] donec fratre eius capto regressus est, properantius tamen quam ex utilitate sociorum, relictis per quos resurgeret bellum*"; Tacitus, Ann. 3.74: "*Nunc ecce trahit illum ad se Africa resurgentis belli minisplena [...]*"; Ovidus, Rem. am. 281–282: "*Que tibi causa fuge ? non hic noua Troia resurgit, Non aliquis socios rursus ad arma uocat*".

[17] Horace, *Odes* 2.17.13–14: "*Me nec Chimaerae spiritus igneae, si resurgat centimanus gigas, diuellet umquam*"; Virgil, *Aeneid* 1.203–206: "*Per uarios casus, per tot discrimina rerum tendimus in latium; sedes ubi fata quietas ostendunt; illic fas regna resurgere troie.*"; Livius, *Historiarum* 24.45.3: "*Quia res romana contra spem uotaque eius uelut resurgere ab stirpibus uideatur, nouam referre proditionem proditis polliceatur*"; Propertius, *Elegies* 4.85–88: "*Quid moueant pisces animosaque signa leonis, lotus et hesperia quid capricornus aqua. dicam: "Troia cades, et Troica Roma, resurges" et maris et terre longa sepulcra canam.*"; Ovid, *Metamorphoses* 2.453: "*Orbe resurgebant lunaria cornua nono, cum de uenatu fraternis languida flammis, nacta nemus gelidum dea, quo cum murmure labens ibat et attritas uersabat riuus harenas*".

[18] With 31 occurrences within the Four Gospels alone.

If *resurgere* still remains a relatively rare lemma (for example, *terra* and *aqua* are met 3,153 and 707 times, respectively), it expands considerably during the first and second century AD, in direct relation to the resurrection of Jesus Christ.[19] The main collocations of *resurgere* are then *mortuus* (32 co-occurrents), *dies* (14), *Christus* (13), *tertius* (10), *morior* (6), *occido* (5), and *cado* (5).[20] This lexical shift, occurring during the early rise of Christianity, inaugurates a new semantic era due to last for centuries, in which the verb is no longer associated with war and/or cycles, but first with a character (Christ) and his resurrection, as well as the ascending movement that allows his terrestrial death.[21]

Co-occurrent	Frequency	Co-frequency	Co-efficient	Average Distance
mortuus	435	32	46	1,2
tertius	222	10	12	0,9
christus	604	13	12	1,8
resurrectio	51	4	6	2,8
dies	2655	14	5	0,9
oporteo	122	4	4	3,8
adicio	43	3	4	1
morior	481	6	4	2,5
occido	334	5	4	4,4
surdus	14	2	3	3
cado	429	5	3	2,4

---

19 Léon-Dufour (1970), *Vocabulaire de théologie biblique*, 1100–1109; Hamman (1975–76), *La résurrection du Christ*, 292–318 and 1–24; Stubenrauch (2006), *Auferstehung des Fleisches?*, 147–156; Leclercq (1948), *Résurrection de la chair*; Guilbert (1975), *Résurrection*; Villette (1957), *La resurrection*; Mainville et al. (2001), *Résurrection*.
20 Some examples: *"Ceci vident, claudi ambulant, leprosi mundantur, surdi audiunt, mortui resurgunt, pauperes evangelizantur et beatus est, qui non fuerit scandalizatus in me."* (Matt 11:5); *"Et coepit docere eos quoniam oportet Filium hominis pati multa, et reprobari a senioribus, et a summis sacerdotibus et scribis, et occidi et post tres dies resurgere."* (Mar 8:31); *"et dixit eis quoniam sic scriptum est et sic oportebat Christum pati et resurgere a mortuis die tertia."* (Luc 24:46), etc.
21 *"et nemo ascendit in caelum nisi qui descendit de caelo Filius hominis qui est in caelo."* (Jn 3:12).

dormio	227	4	3	3,2
dispario	19	2	3	4,5
nubo	24	2	3	3,5
immuto	31	2	3	3,5
postquam	182	3	2	0,3
discipulus	186	3	2	4,3
euangelizo	47	2	2	2
crucifigo	50	2	2	4

Figure 6: Main collocations for resurgo in the Vulgata (TXM-Textométrie)

This christic meaning remained dominant in the Latin literature of the Middle Ages. Within the corpus of the *Patrologia latina*, which is still the largest collection of digitised medieval texts to date,[22] *resurgo* refers mainly to the resurrection of Christ, but it also refers to that of Lazarus and the rise of the bodies during the Last Judgment. A semantics analysis of the 17,000 references to this lemma in this heterogeneous but nonetheless representative corpus reveals three main groups of collocations, and thus meanings: first, Christ himself (*Christus, crucifixus, crucifigo, etc.*), then flesh and its corruptible or incorruptible nature (*corpus, caro,* but also *mortalis/immortalitas, corruptibilis-corruptio/incorruptibilis-incorruptio, etc.*), and, finally, the possibility of rising from the dead (*Lazarus, surgo, sepulcrum, dormio, resuscitatio, infernum*).[23] While the frequency of the lemma is relatively stable in *Patrologia latina,* with only two noticeable, but slow declines during the fourth-fifth and ninth-eleventh centuries, man (*homo*), soul (*anima*), and sin (*peccatum*) become increasingly important in the semantic neighbourhood of *resurgere.* The resurrection thus progressively became a personal stake: it was a matter of saving one's soul, of spiritual rebirth, of emerging from an internal crisis.[24]

---

22 The *Patrologia Latina* contains about 100 million of words, with texts ranging from Tertullian [c. 155–c. 240] to Pope Innocent III [1198–1216 for his papacy].
23 Guilbert, *Résurrection*, 998, insists on the following themes that gravitate around the resurrection of Christ in the Christian thought: death/life, flesh/spirit, earth/sky, bottom/up, and presence/absence.
24 Walker Bynum (1995), *The Resurrection of the Body in Western Christianity, 200–1336*; Brown (2015), *The Ransom of the Soul.*

2. Vernacular Evolutions (twelfth–seventeenth centuries)

It was in this context that the first vernacular occurrences of a derivative of *resurgo*, that is to say, *"ressource"*, slowly appear around the twelfth-thirteenth centuries in Old French and then in Middle French.[25] A first reference can be found in the *Chronicle of the Dukes of Normandy* written by the troubadour Benoît de Sainte-Maure around the year 1174.[26] The text relates to a critical situation between feudal lords and the lack of means to overcome it.[27] It also appears in the *Roman de la Rose* by Guillaume de Lorris and Jean de Meung, c. 1230/1235–c. 1275/1280 and evokes the idea of personal treasures.[28] At the same time, a few words deriving from *resurgo* appear: *ressours* (substantive), *ressourdre* (verb), *ressourte* (substantive), *résurrexi* (verb), *resordre* (verb), *resordement* (substantive), *resorce* (substantive), and, finally, *resors* (adjective).[29] What they all have in common is that they evoke actions or other means that permit one to recover from a crisis, or for one to emerge/re-emerge, to rise, and sometimes even to fly.[30] The dictionary of Old French by Godefroy gives the following definition:

"RESOURS, ress., s. m., jaillissement (breakthrough), abondance (abundance), [...] renouvellement (renewal)."[31]

---

25 For this question, see Auroux et al. (2001), *History of the Language Sciences*; Ernst et al. (2003–2009), *Romanische Sprachgeschichte*.
26 For the edition of the Chronicle, see: Fahlin (1951), *Chronique des ducs de Normandie par Benoît*; Michel (1836-1844), *Chronique des ducs de Normandie par Benoît*. It is probable that the Chronicle was ordered by Henry II of England [1154–1189 for his reign]. See also: Blumenfeld-Kosinski, Benoît de Sainte-Maure.
27 *"Que de France n'avoit resorse, Force n'aie ne rescosse."*, in Michel (1836-1844), *Chronique des ducs de Normandie par Benoît*, 92, v. 17984–17985.
28 *"Car ainz que soit vuiz mes tresors, denier me vienent a resours."*, in Lecoy (1965–1970), *Guillaume de Lorris et Jean de Meun*, v. 11532–11533.
29 In order to define this list, we have used: Godefroy (1891–1902), *Dictionnaire*; Godefroy (1898–1901), *Lexique*; De la Curne de Sainte-Palaye (1875–1882), *Dictionnaire*; Greimas (2012), *Dictionnaire*, but also Wartburg (1922-1967), *Französisches Etymologisches Wörterbuch*. The following websites were also very useful: http://www.atilf.fr/dmf/ (*Dictionnaire du Moyen Français, 1330–1500*); http://www.cnrtl.fr (*Centre National de Ressources Textuelles et Lexicales*). A very rich database of Old French texts was also used for our research: http://bfm.ens-lyon.fr/ (*Base de français medieval*, TXM).
30 For example: *"Deus est prodom, qui nos governe et paist, S'en conquerront enfer qui est punais, Le malvais puiz, dont ne resordront mais."*, in an anonymous text of the XIIth century: *Le Couronnement de Louis. Chanson de geste publiée d'après tous les manuscrits connus*, Langlois, 1888, IV:35.
31 Godefroy (1891–1902), *Dictionnaire*, vol. VII, 108, col. 1.

The vernacular term *ressource* is thus originally a term designating the possibility of using personal capacities in order to overcome a crisis and to renew oneself. The Latin idea of resurrection has thus evolved into *ressource*, but the word still retained part of its original Biblical meaning: "resource" carried the meaning of a personal character, appeared predominantly in the singular form, and very often remained linked to a moment of weakness.

This meaning appears to have been more or less stable during the period from the thirteenth to the sixteenth centuries,[32] even though references to coins and money progressively developed during this period. For instance, in his *Quadrilogue invectif* (1422), Alain Chartier [c. 1390–c. 1430] used the word on several occasions, most of the time in relation to the question of rebirth and salvation.[33] Nevertheless, the semantics of the word was also progressively extended to institutions, communities, and social groups. At the end of this period, for example, Agrippa d'Aubigné (1552–1630) wrote in his *Histoire universelle* (1616–1630) of the "*resource de l'Eglise* (the resource of the Church)".[34] However, even during the sixteen century, the semantics of the term remained strongly linked to its Christian roots.

3. From singular to plural (mid-eighteenth c.–mid-twentieth c.)

It is during the eighteenth century that a radical change took place in the meaning of the term and where its contemporary significations appeared. In order to analyse this phenomenon, we have used the Google NGram Viewer based upon the Google Books database.[35] It allows the generation of chronological charts showing the usage of a term or a group of terms in

---

32 Huguet (1925–1967), *Dictionnaire*, vol. VI, 550–551 indicates these main semantics elements for the sixteen century: "Relèvement, redressement, renaissance", "renaître", "salut", "revanche, reparation", "soulagement, guérison", "reprise de ce qu'on a dépensé", "celui qui relève", "source", "rebondissement".

33 "[M]ais aux travaillans saiges et curieux adviennent de don des cieulx et de leur pourchaz les prosperitez et les ressourses" (Chartier (1422), *Le Quadrilogue invectif*, 13); "[E]n querant vostre ressource et relievement" (Chartier (1422), *Le Quadrilogue invectif*, 14); "Haa, Dieu tout puissant, se tous ceulx qui a ce se soubtillent joignissent ensemble leurs entendemens a cherchier la ressourse de leur seigneurie, ilz gaignassent a la prosperité comme le salut de leurs estas et de leurs vies" (Chartier (1422), *Le Quadrilogue invectif*, 32).

34 "Toutes ces choses maintenues dans les conciles, dans les prisons et dans les feux, le livre des tesmoins de la verité a esté facile jusques à la première resource de l'Eglise par les Albigeois.", in Aubigné (1553–1559), *Histoire universelle*, t. II, 5.

35 https://books.google.com/ngrams

a given language during a specific time frame (see Figures 1, 2 and 3).[36] The existence of national corpora (here: English, French, German) makes it possible to compare specific trends and correlate them to the intellectual and social conditions peculiar to these countries.[37] The corpus used by Google Ngram was generated in 2008 and 2012: it contains more than 450 million words.

The NGram-Viewer carries different well-known biases that must be addressed first.[38] Initially released in December 2010, the database used non-proofread digitised texts (known as dirty OCR).[39] These *optical character recognition* (OCR) programmes induce mechanical errors, which can sometimes distort the interpretation of lexical trends.[40] In the case of the concept of "resource", the margin of error is indeed slim: the word is so frequently used that these errors do not influence the systematic structure of the graphs. The second bias is related to the documentary typology itself. Since Google has built its collection by digitising libraries, the structure of the corpus depends on the book sample. Nevertheless, the sample is large enough to allow for a statistical generalisation. The last bias is probably the most serious for our survey: the recording of metadata and particularly the metadata concerning chronology. An analysis of the data generated by our request shows that some works are sometimes poorly indexed, especially in or for the fifteenth to eighteenth centuries. In our case, however, this problem plays a minor role: first, because the analysis for the oldest period of our survey has been achieved with other corpora/databanks (see above); secondly, because the observed trends are so obvious that they remain valid, granting a generous error margin.

An examination of the Google Books corpora (English, French, and German) reveals two main lexical structures: (a) a considerable development of references to "resources" (in general) during the period from the

---

36 Moretti (2005), *Graphs, Maps, Trees*; Moretti (2013), *Distant Reading*.
37 The Spanish use is different and would merit a special treatment which cannot be achieved in this chapter: the vernacular word for '*resource*' is '*recurso*' which derives from the Latin "*recursus*".
38 Michel et al. (2011), *Quantitative Analysis of Culture*; Lin et al. (2012), *Syntactic Annotations*; Pechenick et al. (2015), *Characterizing the Google Books Corpus*; Hellrich et al. (2016), *Bad Company*.
39 Price-Wilkin (1997), *Just-in-time Conversion*; Guerreau (2011), *Pour un corpus de textes latins*; Willett (2004), *Electronic Texts*; Strange et al. (2014), *Mining for the Meanings of a Murder*; Price (2016), *Social Scholarly Editing*; Cordell (2017), *'Q i-jtb the Raven'*; Schreibman et al. (2015), *A New Companion to Digital Humanities*.
40 Especially in the case of the letter "s", which can sometimes be turns into "f" or "l" by the OCR (for example in the case of 17th-18th typographies).

eighteenth to the twenty-first century, albeit with considerable chronological and national variations, and (b) the emergence and the growing importance of the plural form (*resources*) over the singular one (*resource*), starting from the eighteenth century in the French and English corpora. Indeed, the ratio between the singular and the plural forms of "resource(s)" does not cease to diverge in favour of the latter, especially after the Second World War (*Figure 1–4*).

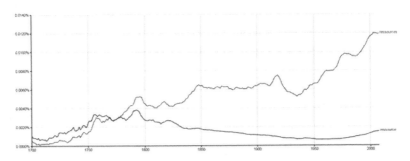

Figure 7: Corpus Google Books "French". Frequencies for ressource and ressources, 1700–2002 (smoothing of 3)

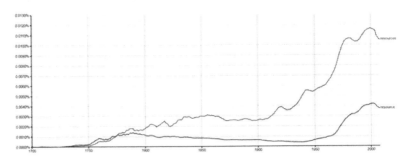

Figure 8: Corpus Google Books "English". Frequencies for resource and resources, 1700–2002 (smoothing of 3)

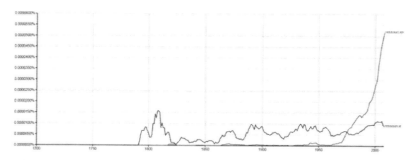

Figure 9: Corpus Google Books "German". Frequencies for ressource and ressourcen, 1700–2002 (smoothing of 3)

This change from the singular to the plural form corresponds to a new massive shift in the meaning of "resource(s)". First, let us look closely to what happend during the eighteenth century. As a symbol of the Enlightenment, the *Encyclopédie* (1751–1772)[41] edited by Denis Diderot (1713–1784) and Jean-Baptiste le Rond d'Alembert (1717–1783) contains 795 occurences of the lemma *ressource* (of which 457 are in the singular and 338 in the plural form). An entire entry is devoted here to the singular form:

"(1). RESSOURCE, s. f. (Gram.) est un moyen de se relever d'un malheur, d'un désastre, d'une perte, d'une maniere qu'on n'attendoit pas; car il faut entendre par ressource un moyen qui se présente de lui-même; cependant quelquefois il se prend pour tout moyen en général. Ce marchand a de grandes ressources, il lui reste encore du crédit & des amis. Sa derniere ressource fut de se jetter dans un couvent. Le galimathias de la distinction est la ressource ordinaire d'un théologien aux abois. (2). Ressource, (Maréchal.) un cheval qui a de la ressource, est la même chose qu'avoir du fond. Voyez Fond."

It differs only slightly from the medieval meaning, which prevails until the seventeenth century: the resource is a force that allows, at a crucial moment, to overcome a personal/internal weakness.[42] The list of the main collocations in the *Encyclopédie* reveals then several categories related to the "*resource*": 1. Its importance and its quantity (*grande, aucune, faible, assez*); 2. Its availability (*dernière, reste, seule, unique, toujours, infinie*); and 3. Its qualities

---

41 Diderot et al. (1751–1772), *Encyclopédie*. The *Encyclopédie* is now available on the website of the ARTFL Project (by Robert Morrissey, Glenn Roe): http://encyclopedie.uchicago.edu/. See also the project ENCRE (by Alexandre Guilbaud, Marie Leca-Tsiomis, Irène Passeron, and Alain Cernuschi): http://enccre.academie-sciences.fr/encyclopedie/.

42 The article above clearly evokes the context of weakness, in which the resource appears as a possibility of salvation: "*malheur*", "*désastre*", "*perte*", "*derniere(ressource)*", "*abois*", etc.

and object (*état, nature, pays, contre, vertu, mauvaise*). The "resource" therefore appears to be associated with the quality, the "*nature*" of a thing or a being, which it defines.

However, an examination of the occurrences in the plural form shows that the term then refers to something very different. Whereas, in the singular form, "*ressource*" means the structural quality of a thing or a being, "*ressources*", in the plural form, are things external to oneself, which can be tapped, but, above all, accumulated, for various activities. These resources may be related to the spirit (in the Germanic sense of *Geist*), but could also be related to "nature" (the environment) or consist of economic capital.

The emergence of the contemporary meanings of "resource" was thus accompanied, as early as from the eighteenth century, by a transformation from the singular to the plural, which corresponds to a semantic shift. Previously designating a personal or internal attribute that enabled the individual to escape from a crisis, "resource(s)" became mainly a set of external objects, which could be manipulated and multiplied. In France and England, this semantic evolution took place in the decades from 1760 to 1790. The English corpus saw a transformation in the 1750s while the French corpus had already witnessed this a few years before. This periodisation relates to the historical context: it correlates with the massive transformation of European societies.[43] The change in both the meaning and the form of the word did, indeed, concur with the emergence of capitalism and with industrialisation in particular. We believe that this transition from "resource" (singular) to the "resources" (plural) thus correlates with a change in social organisation, in which the accumulation of resources defined capital.

III. Towards a Resource "Imperialism"?

This historical survey indicates that the notion of "resources" correlates with the rise of industry and capitalism. During its development between the eighteenth and the twenty-first century, there occurred an integration

---

[43] Labrousse (1990/1994), *La crise de l'économie française*; Crouzet (1966), *Angleterre et France au XVIIIe siècle*; Hobsbawm (1999), *Industry and Empire*; Hobsbawm (1962), *The Age of Revolution*; Braudel et al. (1970–1982), *Histoire économique et sociale*; Cullen (2000), *La crise économique*; Legay (2010), *Capitalisme, crises de trésorerie*; Legay et al. (2009), *Retour sur les origines financières*; González Enciso (2016), *War, Power and the Economy*.

not only of the hitherto unexploited resources into the global capital, the concept of resources was also enlarged and made to encompass new domains, namely, culture, knowledge, the environment, and, above all, social relations. The history of the concept of resource(s) is, indeed, a history of expansion, from the internal resource to economic (*i.e.*, external) resources, and then to many diverse fields. Ben Fine (b. 1948) has termed this invasion of other disciplines as "economic imperialism", and has diagnosed a conceptual reduction that was harmful to the disciplines concerned.[44] In parallel, Marshall Shalins (b. 1930) spoke, in 2013, of "zombie economic ideas that refuse to die",[45] which poison our non-ethnocentric appreciation of social systems. He even claims: "Economics, as constituted, is an anti-anthropology."[46] However, whether the situation is as critical as Ben Fine and Marshall Shalins diagnose is a question which this short chapter does not aspire to answer. Nonetheless, it still provides some particulars which throw a critical light on this trend.

Furthermore, to pose the question of resources historically in the early twenty-first century might be no accident. For one, academia has become more and more enmeshed in economic networks since the 1980s and 1990s. Sheila Slaughter (b. 1945) and Gary Rhoads (b. 1955) claim, for instance, that universities have entered the age of "academic capitalism".[47] The implications of this scientific trend thus remain uncertain.[48]

Acceptance of economical thinking may lead to the imposition of methodical individualism, rational choice theory, and the logic of the market onto domains that do not necessarily rely on economic relations, at least in pre-capitalist societies.[49] For example, if a social field such as culture is economically-depended in our system—and, in this perspective, seems explainable by highly restrictive economic models—was it systematically the case in the past? This problem is especially thorny when dealing with

---

[44] See Fine et al. (2009), *From Economic Imperialism*; see, also, Lazear (2000), *Economic Imperialism*.

[45] Sahlins (1974), *On the Culture of Material Values* 163, and also 164: "Problem is, of course, with the commodification of everything, thus mystifying cultural facts as pecuniary values, the notion that the cultural order is the effect of people's economizing, rather than the means thereof, became the native bourgeois common sense as well as its social science."

[46] Sahlins (1974), *On the Culture of Material Values*, 167.

[47] Slaughter et al. (2004), *Academic Capitalism and the New Economy*. See, also, Radder (2010), *The Commodification of Academic Research*.

[48] Compare the quotations collected in Fine et al. (2009), *From Economic Imperialism*, 14–15.

[49] Guerreau (1990), *Politica/derecho/economìa/religiòn*; Godelier (1972), *Rationality and Irrationality*.

non- or pre-capitalist societies, which did not separate what we nowadays call resources, and especially *natural* resources, from other conceptual or even social fields.[50] For instance, the extension of the term to Medieval Europe or late imperial China is difficult, since there is no straightforward correspondence to any of these notions. As shown above, the term "resource" emerged only late in the Middle Ages, namely, in the twelfth century, and, for several centuries, denoted an inner force to overcome a crisis.

1. The Overlaps between "Capital" and "Resources"

Most dictionaries of sociology, history or philosophy[51] do not contain an entry on "resource(s)". It could refer to the so-called "factors of production", or it could constitute the object of the recent research field of resource economics. Most of the time, the former capture fairly well what common sense understands by the term. Classical economists, such as Adam Smith or David Ricardo, distinguished three factors of production: a) land; b) labour; and c) capital.[52] Recently, the interest in natural resources has been growing, in the form of resource economics, which commonly distinguishes between different types of resources, to wit: a) current reserves (known resources, which can be profitably extracted); b) potential reserves (known resources, which could only be extracted at higher prices); and c) resource endowment (all the resources on the earth). Furthermore, exhaustible resources, which do not replenish themselves, are set apart from recyclable resources.[53] Natural resources have also been labelled "natural capital".[54]

Some influential research sets natural resources clearly apart from capital, defined as equipment to produce goods.[55] However, there is a consid-

---

50 Descola (2011), *L'écologie des autres*, 55–56.
51 See fn 2.
52 Smith (1776), *The Wealth of Nations*, Book I, Chapter 6: "Of the component Parts of the Price of Commodities": "In every society the price of every commodity finally resolves itself into someone or other, or all of those three parts; and in every improved society, all the three enter more or less, as component parts, into the price of the far greater part of commodities. In the price of corn, for example, one part pays the rent of the landlord, another pays the wages or maintenance of the labourers and labouring cattle employed in producing it, and the third pays the profit of the farmer. These three parts seem either immediately or ultimately to make up the whole price of corn."
53 See Tietenberg (1984), *Environmental and Natural Resource Economics*, 120–21.
54 Schumacher (2011), *Small is Beautiful*, 3–4.
55 Meadows et al. (1993), *Beyond the Limits*.

erable overlap between the concepts of "capital" and "resources", especially since some authors apparently use the terms often interchangeably.[56] Even though the terms "capital" and "resources" are, of course, not equivalent, the latter is rather flexible. The progressive extension of the term "capital" during the past decades to both humans and social relations also means, we contend, that these are treated as economic resources. In the following, we would like to focus on three central aspects: human, social, and natural capital.

2. Human Capital and Human Resources

The theory of human capital came to the fore in the late 1950s and early 1960s (see Figure 5 below). Jacob Mincer (1922–2006) and, in particular, Theodore Schultz (1902–1998) and Gary S. Becker (1930–2014) contributed to its rise. Schultz published the first textbook on this subject in 1963, but it rose to public prominence only in the early 1970s. A flood of articles on the topic, and several textbooks and anthologies were published from that point.[57] The basic idea of human capital theory is surprisingly simple: it is roughly conceived as the sum of the knowledge, attributes and habits that someone can use to perform specific tasks. Thereby, human capital is perceived as an investment made on someone or on a group of persons, which could presumably produce value in the end or long term. For example, an investment in higher education may result in higher wages. Individuals, families, institutions, firms and even states are then considered as capitalist elements that are interested in maximising their rate(s) of return on investments. From this perspective, for instance, a rational person first calculates the investment necessary for schooling, meaning the loss of time which could be spent wage earning and the necessary expenditure, such as schoolbooks, stationery, fares for commuting, *etc*. A rational state will also calculate the costs for investments in schools relative to the expected rates of return before deciding upon a certain policy.[58]

With this theory in mind, the passage from the "human capital" to the "human resource" becomes easier. Since persons or human groups are

---

[56] See Schultz (1961), *Investment in Human Capital*, 3; Field (2008), *Social Capital*, 1, Fine (2010), *Theories of Social Capital*, 30, 43.
[57] See Becker (1964), *Human Capital*; Schultz (1961), *Investment in Human Capital*. For an overview, see Blaug (1976), *The Empirical Status of Human Capital*.
[58] See Becker (1964), *Human Capital*; Schultz (1961), *Investment in Human Capital*.

considered as investments that should be managed, it becomes possible to perceive them as "resources" that could be used to produce value under certain conditions. A simple examination of the chronological evolution of the two syntagms ("human resources"/"human capital") clearly shows that they are strongly correlated, with a strong increase after WWII:

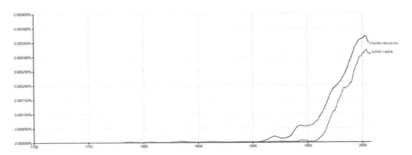

Figure 10: Corpus Google Books "English. Frequencies for "human resources" and "human capital", 1700–2002 (smoothing of 3)

However, the theory of human capital has not been unchallenged. For instance, in 1975, Samuel Bowles [b. 1939-] and Herbert Gintis [b. 1940-] claimed that human capital theory was the last step of neoclassical economic theory in eliminating the concept of class from economic analysis.[59] This is mirrored by Ben Fine's (b. 1948) commentary that social capital theory succeeded in eschewing all categories, such as class, gender, ethnicity and globalisation, which allow for critical reflection.[60] Moreover, Stephen Steinberg (b.1940) stated that human capital theory served reactionary and racist agendas.[61] By abstracting this from its context, it engaged in correlating education and culture with economic success, while it failed in specifying education and culture as independent variables. According to Steinberg, it thus not only ended up in explaining economic success by economic success, but it also went one step further: economic success was rooted in cultural backgrounds taken to be essences. For instance, the economic success of American Jews allegedly flourished in the fertility of Jewish culture, whereas the poverty of many blacks in America was alleged-

---

59 Bowles et al. (1975), *The Problem with Human Capital Theory*, 74. For the impact of this criticism see Blaug (1987), *The Economics of Education*.
60 Fine (2010), *Theories of Social Capital*, 126. Compare Bowles et al. (1975), *The Problem with Human Capital Theory*, 82.
61 Steinberg (1985), *Human Capital*.

ly caused by their cultural background, for instance, in slavery.[62] Thus, Bowles, Gintis and Steinberg all found that human capital theory was conceptually impoverished because it abstracted from categories which were vital to critical social analysis. Moreover, not only is "every worker now treated as capitalist",[63] but every person's reasoning and planning on culture and education is assimilated to rational choice models. According to Bowles and Gintis, this reduction also served reactionary and even racist agendas.

3.   How about Social Capital?

A considerable amount of debate about the term "social capital" has taken place in recent years, although the term had already been used in the early twentieth century by the philosopher and psychologist John Dewey (1859–1952) and an educator from West Virginia, called Lyda J. Hanifan (1879–1932), who is now credited for its invention.[64] Despite James Farr's claims to the discovery of a continuous history of social capital dating at least back to Karl Marx (1818–1883), who would—ironically—become the "patron saint"[65] of contemporary neo-liberalism, Ben Fine's argument that social capital emerged in the 1990s—or at least totally changed in terms of meaning at that time—seems to be much more plausible.[66] Again, a quick look at the chronological development of the syntagma "social capital" in the Google Books database shows a massive take-off around the 1990s (Figure 11).

---

[62] Steinberg (1985), *Human Capital*.
[63] Bowles et al. (1975), *The Problem with Human Capital Theory*, 74. This is expressed explicitly by Schultz (1961), *Investment in Human Capital*, 3.
[64] Putnam (2000), *Bowling Alone*; Farr (2004), *Social Capital*.
[65] Farr (2004), *Social Capital*, 25.
[66] Farr (2004), *Social Capital*, 25; Fine (2007), *Eleven Hypotheses*; Fine (2010), *Theories of Social Capital*, 13 f. On the Farr-Fine controversy, see Fine (2007), *Eleven Hypotheses*; Farr (2007), *In Search of Social Capital*.

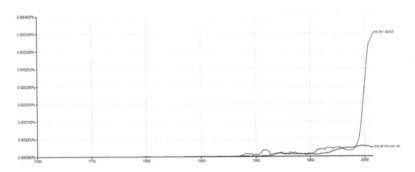

Figure 11: Corpus Google Books "English". Frequencies for "social capital" and "social resources", 1700–2002 (smoothing of 3)

In some ways, the theory of social capital is a successor to tht of human capital.[67] Chronologically speaking, this is at least what Figures 5 and 6 show, with a few decades between the rise of the two concepts. Thus, "social capital" could be considered as an extension of the concept of "capital" to a broader social field. In comparison, the concept of "social resources" has remained thin, probably because of the dominance of "social capital".

In contrast to the notion of human capital, the theory of social capital escaped the rather narrow bounds of rational choice theory.[68] According to Robert Putnam, social capital embraces social relations which have value, that is to say, which contribute positively to production. Putnam comments that this is close to a civic virtue.[69] It is an important asset of society which indicates a general tendency of deterioration or amelioration, and his main objective was to amass evidence to prove the following point: that social capital in America has declined since the 1960s and was thus also responsible for the declining growth rates and the quality of life in general in these years.[70] Putnam's theory of social capital has solicited severe criticism. Ben Fine, for instance, has compared Putnam to Ronald McDonald fostering the McDonaldisation of social science.[71] More to the point, Fine makes the criticism that, on the one hand, the definition of social capital is vague and too permissive, while, on the other, it figures in reductive corre-

---

67 Field (2008), *Social Capital*, 3–4.
68 Field (2008), *Social Capital*, 23–24, 36; Fine (2010), *Theories of Social Capital*, 158.
69 Putnam (2000), *Bowling Alone*, 18–19, see, also, Field (2008), *Social Capital*, 32 ff.
70 Field (2008), *Social Capital*, Chapter 19.
71 Fine (2010), *Theories of Social Capital*, 161.

lations which are presented as causal relationships, without taking other contextual variables into account. The toolkit for analysis is thus deprived of several important social concepts, such as class or gender, and social capital theory falls back onto a neoliberal set of categories, idealising the rational individual and connecting the ideal market to the rise of democracy.[72] Moreover, Steven Durlauf [b. 1958–] has highlighted several important methodological shortcomings in Putnam's argument, and was sceptical about the allegedly benign function of social capital.[73] Thus, the impact of social capital theory resulted in a gross reduction of genuinely social concepts, such as class, power relations, and gender.

4. Nature between Resources and Capital

Another field in which the concept of "resources" has been extensively used is that of "natural resources". Resource scarcity and environment protection gained a lot of popularity in the 1960s and 1970s. After the famous Brundtland Report of 1987,[74] the term "sustainable development" passed into scientific, popular and policy discourses. Its main aim was to combine economic growth with the protection of the environment, that is, to merge and extend the free market to nature and resources. In contrast to the report, *The Limits to Growth* by the Club of Rome, which conceptualised environmental risks in relation to resource scarcities and stressed the importance of limits, the Brundtland Commission stressed growth, the importance of technology, and the alleviation of living standards. Sustainable development was then defined as "development that meets the needs of the present without compromising the ability of future generations to meet their own needs".[75] Its aim is to sustain the natural stock of resources or the "critical natural capital". One of the main ideas of the Brundtland Commission was to combine the ideas of economic growth while preserving the amount of critical natural capital.[76] It thus continued a tradition of economic thinking, which goes back to Lionel Robbins [1898–1984], who defined economics in the early 1930s as *the science analysing the allocation of*

---

72 Fine (2010), *Theories of Social Capital*, 23 ff., 42 ff., 158, 176 ff.
73 Durlauf (2002), *Bowling Alone*.
74 Brundtland Commission (1987), *Our Common Future*.
75 Brundtland Commission (1987), *Our Common Future*, 41.
76 For a business perspective on environmental protection, see Schmidheiny (1992), *Changing Course*.

scarce resources between competing ends. Despite critiques and alternative approaches, the mind-set of the neoclassical economy still dominates the approaches to sustainable development.[77]

The neoclassical authors' approach treats the "environment" like a commodity in order to analyse it like other commodities. They claim that the environment is undervalued and thus exploited without paying any fees.[78] Environmental protection thus mainly consists in bestowing the right price on the environment.[79] Neoclassical economists develop supply-and-demand curves of the environment, relying again on methodological individualism and the assumption of an economically rational person operating in a competitive market.[80] This does not mean, however, that the neoclassical approach relies upon a notion of minimal government. On the contrary, the government influences the market by imposing taxes or providing subsidies.[81] Be that as it may, the important consequence of this approach for the argument presented here is that the whole environment is turned into a cluster of commodities with prices attached. This means that the environment enters the capitalist logic not by being exploited, but by being left to itself, for instance, in order to guarantee biodiversity.[82] The enormous development of the notion of "natural resources" is probably a result of this social shift. According to our survey, this rise starts during in the early twentieth century, probably in direct link with the First World War, but is also because of the increasing interest in the conservation of nature since the 1970s.[83]

The first and most intuitive critique of this approach is that large parts of the environment are not a commodity like potatoes or soap. For instance, part of it is not owned in any straightforward sense, and, in contrast to real markets, individuals do not express preferences about the environment, which could be used as a basis for constructing supply and demand curves.[84] Secondly, and most importantly, the anthropologist Arturo Escobar (b. 1952) argued that the sustainability discourse operates in fa-

---

77 Jacobs (1994), *The Limits to Neoclassicism*, 67.
78 Jacobs (1994), *The Limits to Neoclassicism*, 69; McCauley (2006), *Selling out on Nature*, Redclift (1987), *Sustainable Development*. See, in particular, Schmidheiny (1992), *Changing Course*, 14–33.
79 Jacobs (1994), *The Limits to Neoclassicism*, 70.
80 Jacobs (1994), *The Limits to Neoclassicism*, 71.
81 Jacobs (1994), *The Limits to Neoclassicism*, 68.
82 Escobar (1996), *Construction Nature*, 47.
83 See, for example, Pinchot (1908), *The Conservation of Natural Resources*.
84 Jacobs (1994), *The Limits to Neoclassicism*, 74–78.

vour of the first world, which thus tries to impose parsimony and a decrease in population growth on the third world.[85] In sum, the discourses on human, social and natural capital show that economics encroached on other disciplines, sociology in particular, and that, in all three cases, this trend has resulted in a neglect of social issues.

IV. Concluding Reflections

Before concluding, the limits of our study should be underlined once again. To sketch the development and semantic changes of "resource(s)" over roughly 2,000 years, in order to discuss the current developments within the human and social sciences critically, is, to say the least, a tall order. In inquiring quantitatively into the term "resource(s)", we should also chart the development of associated terms, and, in order to do this, we relied on non-homogenous data-sets which leave many questions open. As historians outside their comfort zones, probing into contemporary economics and social theory is a necessary, but ambitious, task. Despite all these difficulties, we hope that this effort shows the deep interest of a history of the concept of resource. In this perspective, this contribution is also conceived as a call for future reflections on the topic.

This chapter proposes two working hypotheses, which should be tested and detailed by latter research. First, the notion of "resources", as we know it today, emerged in the eighteenth century and matured over the following two centuries. By the twentieth century, it became predominant in economics from where it spread first to the social and then to the human sciences. This might correlate with the rise of industrial capitalism in the eighteenth and nineteenth centuries, and the growing dominance of economic approaches to many aspects of social life and nature in the second half of the twentieth century. Second, this economic encroachment into the human sciences fosters the appearance that nearly all aspects of our life world are within the grasp of methodological individualism, be it moral values, educational choices, friends and family, or the protection of the environment. This also means that these domains allegedly fall within the scope of economic rationality to the detriment of many contextually relevant aspects, in particular power, hierarchies and cultural representations.

---

85 Escobar (1996), *Construction Nature*.

Literature

Amadae, S.M. (2003). *Rationalizing Capitalist Democracy: The Cold War Origins of Rational Choice Liberalism.* Chicago IL: University of Chicago Press.

Amadae, S.M. (2015). *Prisoners of Reason: Game Theory and Neoliberal Political Economy.* Cambridge: Cambridge University Press.

Atkinson, David, and Peter Jackson, David Sibley, Neil Washbourne (eds.). (2005). *Cultural Geography: A Critical Dictionary of Key Concepts.* London/New York: Palgrave Macmillan.

Aubigné, Agrippa d' (1553–1559). *Histoire universelle.*

Audi, Robert (ed.). (1995). *The Cambridge Dictionary of Philosophy.* Cambridge: Cambridge University Press.

Auroux, Sylvain, and Konrad Koerner, Hans-Joseph Niederehe, Kees Versteegh (eds.). (2001). *History of the Language Sciences: An International Handbook on the Evolution of the Study of Language from the Beginnings to the Present. Geschichte der Sprachwissenschaften: ein internationales Handbuch zur Entwicklung der Sprachforschung von den Anfängen bis zur Gegenwart*, 2 volumes. Berlin/New York: Walter de Gruyter.

Baier, Thomas, and Tobias Dänzer, Karl Ernst Georges (eds.). (2012). *Der neue Georges. Ausführliches Handwörterbuch Lateinisch Deutsch.* Darmstadt: Wissenschaftliche Buchgesellschaft.

Baschet, Jérôme (2014). Adieux au capitalism. Paris: La Découverte

Becker, Gary S. (1964). *Human Capital.* New York: Columbia University Press.

— (1976). *The Economic Approach to Human Behavior.* Chicago IL: Chicago University Press.

Blaug, Mark (1976). The Empirical Status of Human Capital Theory: A Slightly Jaundiced Survey. *Journal of Economic Literature*, 14–3, 827–55.

— *The Economics of Education and the Education of an Economist.* New York: University Press, 1987.

Bon, Bruno (2009). OMNIA—Outils et Méthodes Numériques pour l'Interrogation et l'Analyse des textes médiolatins (1). *Bulletin du Centre médiéval d'Auxerre*, 13, 291–92.

— (2010). OMNIA—Outils et Méthodes Numériques pour l'Interrogation et l'Analyse des textes médiolatins (2). *Bulletin du Centre médiéval d'Auxerre*, 14,251–52.

— (2011). OMNIA—Outils et Méthodes Numériques pour l'Interrogation et l'Analyse des textes médiolatins (3). *Bulletin du Centre médiéval d'Auxerre*, 15.

Boudon, Raymond, and François Bourricaud (1989). *A Critical Dictionary of Sociology.* Chicago IL: Chicago University Press.

Bourdieu, Pierre (1997). Marginalia: Some additional notes on the gift. In Alan D. Schrift (ed.). *The Logic of the Gift: Toward an Ethic of Generosity*, 231–41. New York: Psychology Press.

Bowles, Samuel, and Herbert Gintis (1975). The Problem with Human Capital Theory. A Marxian Critique. *The American Economic Review*, 65–2, 74–82.

Braudel, Fernand, and Ernest Labrousse (1970–1982). *Histoire économique et sociale de la France*. 3 volumes. Paris: Presses Universitaires de France.

Bröckling, Ulrich, and Susanne Krasmann, Thomas Lemke (eds.). (2004). *Glossar der Gegenwart*. Frankfurt/M.: Suhrkamp.

Brown, Peter (2015). *The Ransom of the Soul: Afterlife and Wealth in Early Western Christianity*. Cambridge MA: Harvard University Press.

Bruce, Steve, and Steven Yearley (2006). *The Sage Dictionary of Sociology*. London: Sage.

Brundtland Commission (1987). *Our Common Future*. Oxford: Oxford University Press.

Bührer-Thierry, Geneviève, and Régine Le Jan, Vito Loré (eds.). (2017). *Acquérir, prélever, contrôler: les ressources en compétition (400–1100)*, Turnhout: Brepols.

Bunnin, Nicholas, and Yu Jiyuan (2004). *The Blackwell Dictionary of Western Philosophy*. Malden, MA: John Wiley & Sons.

Chartier, Alain (1422), *Le Quadrilogue invectif*.

Chaurand, Jacques (2006). *Histoire de la langue française*. Paris: PUF.

Cordell, Ryan (2017). 'Q i-jtb the Raven'. Taking Dirty OCR Seriously. *Book History*, 20, 188–225.

Crouzet, François (1966). Angleterre et France au XVIIIe siècle : essai d'analyse comparée de deux croissances économiques. *Annales ESC*, 21–2, 254–91.

Cullen, Louis (2000). La crise économique de la fin de l'Ancien Régime. In *L'économie française du XVIIIe au XXe siècle. Perspectives nationales et internationales*, 581–601. Paris: PUF.

De la Curne de Sainte-Palaye, Jean-Baptiste (1875–1882). *Dictionnaire historique de l'ancien langage François ou Glossaire de la langue françoise depuis son origine jusqu'au siècle de Louis XIV*. 10 volumes. Niort: L. Favre.

Descola, Philippe (1994). *In the Society of Nature: A Native Ecology in Amazonia*. Cambridge: Cambridge University Press.

— (1996). *The Spears of Twilight: Life and Death in the Amazon Jungle*. New York: Harper and Collins.

— (2011). *L'écologie des autres. L'anthropologie et la question de la nature*. Paris: Editions Quæ.

— (2013). *The Ecology of Others*. Chicago IL: Chicago University Press.

— (2013). *Beyond Nature and Culture*. Chicago IL: Chicago University Press.

Diderot, Denis, and Jean-Baptiste Le Rond D'Alembert (eds.). (1751–1772). *Encyclopédie ou Dictionnaire raisonné des sciences, des arts et des métiers*, 17 volumes, Paris: Briasson & al.

Durlauf, Steven N. (2002). Bowling Alone: A Review Essay. *Journal of Economic Behavior & Organization*, 47–3, 259–73.

Duval, Frédéric (2009). *Le Français médiéval*, Turnhout: Brepols.

Ernst, Ehrhard, and Martin-Dietrich Gleßgen, Christian Schmitt, Wolfgang Schweickard (eds.). (2003–2009). *Romanische Sprachgeschichte*. Berlin: De Gruyter.

Escobar, Arturo (1996). Construction Nature. Elements for a post-structuralist political ecology. *Futures*, 28/4. 325–43.

Farr, James (2007). In Search of Social Capital: A Reply to Ben Fine. *Political Theory*, 35-1, 54–61.

— (2004). Social Capital: A Conceptual History. *Political Theory*, 32-1, 6–33.

Fahlin, Carin (ed.). (1951). *Benoit de Sainte Maure, Chronique des Ducs de Normandie, édité par C. Fahlin*. Uppsala: Almqvist och Wiksell.

Field, John (2008). *Social Capital*. London/New York: Routledge.

Fine, Ben (2007). Eleven Hypotheses on the Conceptual History of Social Capital: A Response to James Farr. *Political Theory*, 35-1, 47–53.

— (2010). *Theories of Social Capital: Researchers Behaving Badly*. London, New York: Routledge.

Fine, Ben, and Dimitris Milonakis (2009). *From Economics Imperialism to Freakonomics: The Shifting Boundaries between Economics and Other Social Sciences*. London, New York: Routledge.

Flachowsky, Sören, and Rüdiger Hachtmann, Florian Schmaltz (eds.). (2017). *Ressourcenmobilisierung: Wissenschaftspolitik und Forschungspraxis im NS-Herrschaftssystem*. Göttingen: Wallstein.

Fontaine, Jacques, and Charles Pietri (eds.). (1985). *Le monde latin antique et la Bible*. Paris: Editions Beauchesne.

Foucault, Michel (2002). *Archaeology of Knowledge*. London-New York: Routledge.

— (1977). *Discipline and Punish: The Birth of the Prison*. New York: Vintage.

— (2002). *The Order of Things: An Archaeology of the Human Sciences*. London-New York: Routledge.

Foulquié, Paul, and Raymond Saint-Jean (eds.). (1969). *Dictionnaire de la langue philosophique*. Paris: Presses Universitaires de France.

Gaffiot, Félix (1934). *Dictionnaire abrégé latin-français illustré*. Paris: Hachette.

Georges, Karl Ernst, and Thomas Baier, Tobias Dänzer, Heinrich Georges (eds.). (1913/2013). *Der Neue Georges. Ausführliches lateinisch-deutsches Handwörterbuch: aus den Quellen zusammengetragen und mit besonderer Bezugnahme auf Synonymik und Antiquitäten unter Berücksichtigung der besten Hilfsmittel*. 2 volumes. Darmstadt: Wissenschaftliche Buchgesellschaft.

Godelier, Maurice (1972). *Rationality and Irrationality in Economics*. London: NLB.

— (1999). *The Enigma of the Gift*. Chicago IL: Chicago University Press.

— (1986). *The Mental and the Material: Thought Economy and Society*. London: Verso.

Godefroy, Frédéric (1891–1902). *Dictionnaire de l'ancienne langue française et de tous ses dialectes du IXe au XVe siècle*. 9 volumes. Geneva: Slatkine.

— (1898–1901). *Lexique de l'ancien français*. Paris: H. Welter.

González Enciso, Agustín (2016). *War, Power and the Economy: Mercantilism and State Formation in 18th-century Europe*. London/New York: Routledge.

Goody Jack (2000). *The European Family: An Historico-anthropological Essay*. Oxford: Blackwell.

— (2006). *The Theft of History*. Cambridge: Cambridge University Press.

Greimas, Algirdas Julien (2012). *Dictionnaire de l'ancien français.* Paris: Larousse.
Grossbard-Shechtman, Shoshana, and Christopher Clague (eds.). (2002). *The Expansion of Economics: Toward a more Inclusive Social Science.* New York/London: Armonk/M.E. Sharpe.
Guerreau, Alain (1990). Politica / derecho / economìa / religiòn: còmo eliminar el obstàculo?. In Reyna Pastor (ed.), *Relaciones de poder, de producciòn y parentesco en la edad media y moderna. Aproximaciòn a su estudio,* 459–65. Madrid: Consejo superior de investigaciones cientìficas.
— (1998). L'étude de l'économie médiévale : genèse et problèmes actuels. In Jacques Le Goff and Guy Lobrichon (eds.). *Le Moyen Âge aujourd'hui. Trois regards contemporains sur le Moyen Âge : histoire, théologie, cinéma,* 31–82. Paris: Le Léopard d'Or.
— (2001). Avant le marché, les marchés: en Europe, XIIIe-XVIIIe siècle. *Annales. Histoire, Sciences sociales,* 56 (6), 1129–75.
— (2001). *Vinea.* In Monique Goullet and Michel Parisse (eds.). *Les historiens et le latin médiéval,* 67–73. Paris: Publications de la Sorbonne.
— (2011). Pour un corpus de textes latins en ligne. *Bulletin du Centre médiéval d'Auxerre (Collection CBMA).* URL: https://cem.revues.org/11787 [2018-03-16]
Guerreau-Jalabert, Anita (2015). Occident médiéval et pensée analogique: le sens de *"spiritus"* et *"caro".* In Jean-Philippe Genet (ed.). *La légitimité implicite : actes des conférences organisées à Rome en 2010 et en 2011 par SAS en collaboration avec l'École française de Rome,* 457–476. 2 volumes. Paris/Rome: Publications de la Sorbonne/École française de Rome.
— (1995). *Spiritus* et *caritas.* Le baptême dans la société médiévale. In Françoise Heritier-Augé, Elisabeth Copet-Rougier (eds.). *La parenté spirituelle,* 133–203. Paris/Bâle: Éditions des Archives contemporaines.
— (2013). *Spiritus* et *caro.* Une matrice d'analogie générale. In: Frédéric Elsig, Pierre-Alain Mariaux and Brigitte Roux (eds.). *L'image en questions: pour Jean Wirth,* 290–295. Geneva: Droz.
Guilbert, Pierre (1975). *Résurrection de Jésus et message pascal.* Paris: Centurion
Gumbrecht, Hans Ulrich (2006). *Dimension und Grenzen der Begriffsgeschichte.* Munich: Wilhelm Fink.
Gunder-Frank, Andre, and Barry K. Gills (eds.). (1993). *The World System: Five Hundred Years or Five Thousand?.* London/New York: Routledge.
Hamman, Adalbert (1975–1976). La résurrection du Christ dans l'Antiquité chrétienne. *Revue des Sciences Religieuses,* 49 (4) / 50 (1), 292–318 / 1–24.
Heiden, Serge (2010). The TXM Platform: Building Open-Source Textual Analysis Software Compatible with the TEI Encoding Scheme. In Ryo Otoguro, Kiyoshi Ishikawa, Hiroshi Umemoto, Kei Yoshimotoand Yasunari Harada. *24th Pacific Asia Conference on Language, Information and Computation, Nov 2010, Sendai, Japan. Institute for Digital Enhancement of Cognitive Development,* 389–398. Tokyo: Waseda University.

Heiden, Serge, and Jean-Phlippe Magué, Bénédicte Pincemin (2010). TXM: Une plateforme logicielle open-source pour la textométrie – conception et développement. In Sergio Bolasco, Isabella Chiari and Luca Giuliano. *10th International Conference on the Statistical Analysis of Textual Data—JADT 2010, Jun 2010, Rome, Italy*, 1021–1032. Milano: Edizioni Universitarie di Lettere Economia Diritto.

Hellrich, Johannes and Udo Hahn (2016). Bad Company. Neighborhoods in Neural Embedding Spaces Considered Harmful. In: *Proceedings of COLING 2016, the 26th International Conference on Computational Linguistics*, 2785–2796. Osaka.

Hirshleifer, Jack (1985). The Expanding Domain of Economics. *American Economic Review*, 75 (6), 53–68.

Hobsbawm, Eric (1962). *The Age of Revolution. 1789–1848*. Worthing: Littlehampton Book Services.

Hobsbawm, Eric (1999). *Industry and Empire. From 1750 to the Present Day*. London: Penguin.

Huguet, Edmont (1925–1967). *Dictionnaire de la Langue Française du XVIe Siècle*. Paris: Classiques Garnier Numérique.

Iannone, A. Pablo (2001). Dictionary of World Philosophy. London/New York: Routledge.

Jacobs, Michael (1994). The limits to neoclassicism: towards an institutional environmental economics. Social theory and the global environment. In Michael Redclift and Ted Benton (eds.). *Social Theory and the Global Environment*, 67–91. London/New York: Routledge.

Kesselring, Wilhelm (1973). *Die französische Sprache. Band VII, Die Französische Sprache im Mittelalter von den Anfängen bis 1300. Handbuch des Altfranzösischen: Äussere Sprechgeschichte, Phonologie, Morphosyntax, Lexik, Dokumente*. Tübingen: Fotodruck Präzis B. v. Spangenberg.

Klemperer, Victor (1947). *LTI—Notizbuch eines Philologen*. Berlin: Aufbau.

Kocka, Jürgen (2013). *Geschichte des Kapitalismus*. Munich: C. H. Beck.

Koselleck, Reinhart (ed.). (1979). *Historische Semantik und Begriffsgeschichte*, Stuttgart: Klett-Cotta.

— (2006). Begriffsgeschichten. Frankfurt/M.: Suhrkamp.

Kuchenbuch, Ludolf and Uta Kleine (eds.). (2006). *'Textus' im Mittelalter. Komponenten und Situationen des Wortgebrauchs im schriftsemantischen Feld*. Göttingen: Vandenhoeck & Ruprecht.

Labrousse, Ernest (1994/1990). *La crise de l'économie française à la fin de l'Ancien Régime et au début de la Révolution*. Paris: Presses Universitaires de France.

Lacey, Allan R. (1996). *A Dictionary of Philosophy*. London/New York: Routledge.

Lalande, André (1926/1992). *Vocabulaire technique et critique de la philosophie*. 2 volumes. Paris: Presses Universitaires de France.

Lazear, Edward P. (2000). Economic Imperialism. *Quarterly Journal of Economics*, 115 (1), 99–146.

Leclercq, H. (1948). Résurrection de la chair. *DACL*, XIV/2, 2393–2398.

Lecoy, Félix (1965–1970). *Guillaume de Lorris et Jean de Meun, Le Roman de la Rose, éd. par Félix Lecoy*. Paris: Champion

Legay, Marie-Laure (2010). Capitalisme, crises de trésorerie et donneurs d'avis: une relecture des années 1783–1789, *Revue Historique*, 655 (3), 577–68.

Legay, Marie-Laure, and Joël Félix, Eugene White (2009). Retour sur les origines financières de la Révolution française. *Annales historiques de la Révolution française*, 356, 183–201.

Léon-Dufour, Xavier et al. (eds.). (1970). *Vocabulaire de théologie biblique*. Paris: Ed. du Cerf.

Lewis, Charlton T., Charles Short (1879). *A Latin Dictionary*. Oxford: Clarendon Press.

Lin Yuri et al. (2012). Syntactic Annotations for the Google Books Ngram Corpus. In *ACL 12 Proceedings of the ACL 2012 System Demonstrations*, Stroudsburg, 169–174.

Lobrichon, Guy, and Pierre Riché (eds.). (1984). *Le Moyen Âge et la Bible*, Paris: Editions Beauchesne.

Lourdaux, Willem, and Daniel Verhelst (eds.). (1979). *The Bible and Medieval Culture*, Leuven: Leuven University Press.

Mainville, Odette, and Daniel Marguerat (2001). *Résurrection. L'aprés-mort dans le monde ancien et le Nouveau Testament*. Paris: Labor et fides.

McCarthy, John D., and Mayer N. Zald (1977). Resource Mobilization and Social Movements. *American Journal of Sociology*, 82, 1212–41.

McCauley, Douglas J. (2006). Selling out on Nature. *Nature*, 443, 27–28.

Meadows, Donella, and Dennis Meadows, Jorgen Randers (1993). *Beyond the Limits. Confronting Global Collapse, Evisioning a Sustainable Future*. White River Junction: Chelsea Green Publishing.

Michel, Francisque (ed.). (1838). Chronique des ducs de Normandie par Benoît.

Michel, Jean-Baptiste et al. (2011). Quantitative Analysis of Culture Using Millions of Digitized Books, *Science*, 331 (6014), 176–82.

Moretti, Franco (2013). *Distant Reading*, London/New York: Verso.

— (2005). *Graphs, Maps, Trees: Abstract Models for a Literary History*, London/New York: Verso.

Morris, Mike (2012). *Concise Dictionary of Social and Cultural Anthropology*, Malden MA/Oxford/Chichester: John Wiley & Sons.

Morsel, Joseph (forthcoming). La production d'un concept: le *Geschlecht* (lignage). Contribution à l'approche critique de la *Begriffsgeschichte*. Paris.

Nelson, Jinty, and Damien Kempf (eds.). (2015). *Reading the Bible in the Middle Ages*. London et al.: Bloomsbury.

Neumann, John von, and Oskar Morgenstern (1944). Theory of Games and Economic Behavior. Princeton NJ: Princton University Press.

Parisse, Michel, and Monique Goullet (2006). *Lexique latin-français: Antiquité et Moyen Âge*. Paris: Picard.

Pechenick, Edith A., and Christopher M. Danforth, Peter S. Dodds (2015). Characterizing the Google Books Corpus: Strong Limits to Inferences of Socio-Cultural and Linguistic Evolution. *PLoS One*, 10 (10), 2015, available at: http://journals.plos.org/plosone/article?id=10.1371/journal.pone.0137041

Pierenkemper, Toni, and Richard H. Tilly (2004). *The German Economy during the Nineteenth Century*. New York: Berghahn Books.

Pinchot, Gifford (1908). *The Conservation of Natural Resources*. Washington DC: Doubleday.

Polanyi, Karl (1944). *The Great Transformation: The Political and Economic Origins of our Time*. New York: Farrar & Rinehart Inc.

Price, Kenneth (2016). Social Scholarly Editing. In Susan Schreibman, Ray Siemens, John Unsworth (eds.). (2015). *A New Companion to Digital Humanities*, 137–146. Malden: John Wiley & Sons.

Price-Wilkin, John (1997). Just-in-time Conversion, Just-in-case Collections. *D-Lib Magazine*: http://www.dlib.org/dlib/may97/michigan/05pricewilkin.html [2018-03-16].

Protevi, John (2005). *The Edinburgh Dictionary of Continental Philosophy*. Edinburgh: Edinburgh University Press.

Putnam, Robert D. (2000). *Bowling Alone: The Collapse and Revival of American Community*. New York: Simon & Schuster.

Radder, Hans (ed.). (2010). *The Commodification of Academic Research: Science and the Modern University*. Pittsburgh PA: Pittsburgh University Press.

Redclift, Michael (1987). *Sustainable Development. Exploring the Contradictions*. London: Methuen.

Sahlins, Marshall (1974). *Stone Age Economics*. London, New York: Routledge.

Schmidheiny, Stephan (1992). *Changing Course: A Global Business Perspective on Development and the Environment*. Cambridge: Harvard University Press.

Schmidt, Lothar (ed.). (1973). *Wortfeldforschung: zur Geschichte und Theorie des sprachlichen Feldes*. Darmstadt: Wissenschaftliche Buchgesellschaft.

Schreibman, Susan, and Ray Siemens, John Unsworth (eds.). (2015). *A New Companion to Digital Humanities*, Malden MA: John Wiley & Sons.

Seymour-Smith, Charlotte (ed.). (1986). Macmillan Dictionary of Anthropology. Basingstoke: Palgrave Macmillan.

Schultz, Theodore W. (1961). Investment in Human Capital. *The American Economic Review*, 51-1, 1–17.

Schumacher, Ernst F. (2011). *Small is Beautiful: A Study of Economics as if People Mattered*. New York: Random House.

Slaughter, Sheila, and Gary Rhoades (2004). *Academic Capitalism and the New Economy: Markets, State, and Higher Education*. Baltimore MD: JHU Press.

Smith, Adam (1776). *An Inquiry into the Nature and Causes of the Wealth of Nations*. London: William Strahan & Thomas Cadell

Steinberg, Stephen (1985). Human Capital: A Critique. *The Review of Black Political Economy*, 14-1, 67–74.

Strange, Carolyn, and Daniel McNamara, John Wodak, Ian Wood (2014). Mining for the Meanings of a Murder: The Impact of OCR Quality on the Use of Digitized Historical Newspapers. *Digital Humanities Quarterly*, 8 (1) http://www.digitalhumanities.org/dhq/vol/8/1/000168/000168.html [2018-03-16].

Sterx, Sigrid (2010). Knowledge Transfer from Academia to Industry through Patenting and Licensing: Rhetoric and Reality. In Hans Radder (ed.). *The Commodification of Academic Research: Science and the Modern University*, 44–64. Pittsburgh PA: Pittsburgh University Press.

Stubenrauch, Bertram (2006). Auferstehung des Fleisches? Zum Proprium christlichen Glaubens in Motiven christlicher Theologie. *Römische Quartalschrift für christliche Altertumskunde und für Kirchengeschichte*, 101, 147–56.

Swedberg, Richard (1990). *Economics and Sociology. Redefining Their Boundaries: Conversations with Economists and Sociologists*. Princeton NJ: Princeton University Press.

Sweezy, Patrick M., and Maurice Dobb, H.K. Takahashi (eds.). (1954). *The Transition from Feudalism to Capitalism: A Symposium*. New York: Science and Society.

Tietenberg, Tom (1984). *Environmental and Natural Resource Economics*. London: Longman Higher Education.

Trebilcock, Clive (1981). *The Industrialisation of the Continental Powers 1780–1914*. London/New York: Routledge.

Trier, Jost (1931). *Der Deutsche Wortschatz im Sinnbezirk des Verstandes: Die Geschichte eines sprachlichen Feldes. Band 1: Von den Anfängen bis zum Beginn des 13 Jahrhunderts*. Heidelberg: C. Winter.

Turner, B.S. (2006). *The Cambridge Dictionary of Sociology*. Cambridge.

Verley, Patrick (1997). *L'Échelle du Monde. Essai sur l'Industrialisation de l'Occident*. Paris: Edition Gallimard.

Villette, Jeanne (1957). *La Résurrection du Christ dans l'art chrétien du IIe au VIIe siècle*. Paris: H. Laurens.

Walker Bynum, Caroline (1995/2017). *The Resurrection of the Body in Western Christianity, 200–1336*. New York: Columbia University Press.

Wallerstein, Immanuel (1974–2011). *The Modern World-System*. 4 volumes. Oakland: University of California Press.

Von Wartburg, Walther (ed.). (1922-1967). *Französisches Etymologisches Wörterbuch. Eine Darstellung des galloromanischen Sprachschatzes*. Basel: R.G. Zbinden.

Weber, Max (1904–5/2004). *Die protestantische Ethik und der Geist des Kapitalismus*. Munich: C.H.Beck.

Willett, Patrick (2004). Electronic Texts: Audiences and Purposes. In Susan Schreibman, Ray Siemens, and John Unsworth (eds.). *A Companion to Digital Humanities*, 240–253. Malden MA: Blackwell Publishing.

Wilczynski, Josef (1981). *An Encyclopedic Dictionary of Marxism, Socialism and Communism: Economic, Philosophical, Political and Sociological Theories, Concepts, Institutions and Practices*. Berlin/New York: Springer.

Walker Bynum, Caroline (1995). *The Resurrection of the Body in Western Christianity 200–1336*. New York City: Comubia University Press.

Woolcock, Michael (1998). Social Capital and Economic Development: Toward a Theoretical Synthesis and Policy Framework. *Theory and Society*, 27 (2), 151–208.

Wu, Silas (1969). *Communication and Imperial Control in China*. Hong Kong: Chinese University Press.

Zink, Gaston (2007). *L'ancien français: XIe-XIIIe siècle*. Paris: PUF.

Chapter 6
Perspectives of a Resource History: Actions—Practices—Regimes

Christian A. Müller

I. Introduction

Resources are an ambivalent subject of research.[1] At the *Meeting of German Historians* in 2012, which was about *Resource Conflicts*, the environmental historian Frank Uekoetter noted that it is not easy to "bring intellectual tension into the topic".[2] This observation is inspiring and is easy to spell out. Questions about the history of resources formulate—one could argue—the merely obvious: resources are always important, scarce, and, therefore, contested. In modern times, we continue to practise a to-date unprecedented waste of resources that could only be stopped by promptly resorting to economics of sustainability. Exaggeratedly, whoever wants to write a history of resources already knows the results of his or her work and only has to deal with the details, or, respectively, has to write a predictable epoch-specific "prologue". In summary, why should there be research about resources if the dramaturgy of the research is largely known?

For actors, the use of resources is inevitable. Actors of all epochs have had to use resources. How exactly and under which circumstances this happened is historically highly variable and demands exploration. But what exactly is the epistemological interest in researching resources, especially from a historic point of view? And what would a "history of resources" look like from a disciplinary dimension, meaning a historical approach in where resources are not the quintessence, but a basic term of explanation? Resources are frequently seen as raw commodities of central importance,

---

1 This article profited from feedback and critique. Thanks to Iwo Amelung, Hans Peter Hahn and Hartmut Leppin. Also, I have to thank Christian Scheidler and Frederic Steinfeld for insights into their research. Carl Rumpeltes helped with the translation.
2 As stated in a "virtual discussion" in preparation for the Meeting of German Historians: Uekötter (2012), *Ressourcen*.

since they are the starting-point for economic processing and therefore influenced societies in all aspects of everyday life.[3] We are surrounded by composed resources. Since the twentieth century at least, however, the always existing necessity to use resources became a downright resource fixation, in which the future was solely dependent on the availability of resources.[4] Two points stick out: on the one hand, there are comparatively few concepts of resources that reveal the high importance of the topic.[5] Until deep into second half of the twentieth century, the German encyclopaedia *Große Brockhaus*, for example, defines resources merely as "*Hilfsquellen*" or "*Geldmittel*".[6] On the other hand, a rise in scepticism in terms of a too one-dimensional fixation on resources can be observed. A prominent example can be found in the so-called "resource curse", which points out the disastrous consequences for countries with a concentrated reserve of resources.[7] But there is another line of criticism of a strict view of resources. For the question of living, that is to say, how we live, an exclusive orientation on resources is said to be counter-productive.[8] Surviving and good living—so to speak—are not the same. To sum up, resources are comparatively important for the understanding of societies, but comparatively unclear in the sense of a research design.

The question of resources becomes even more complex when the well-known resources (education, fossil fuel, *etc.*) are set to one side and historic- or geographically-removed landscapes are put into focus, instead: How can one coherently talk about resources when dealing with the sixth century A.D., or with the growth of a chemical company in the nineteenth century, or with current African developmental topics? What criteria can be listed to identify resources? Is a resource simply everything that is important to actors or something to which they attribute a certain worth? In the following, the term "resource" will be considered as a theoretical term, meaning a term that constructs a certain research object without deeming

---

3 Reith (2010), *Ressourcennutzung*.
4 Reder et al. (2012), *Kampf um Ressourcen*.
5 But see the CRC 1070 "RecourceCultures" in Tübingen, where, since 2013, the dimension of a "resource turn" has been investigated: Hardenberg et al. (2017), *Resource Turn*, 13–23.
6 Der Große Brockhaus (1956), *Ressourcen*, 691.
7 See: Auty (1993), *Sustaining Development*. Today there is also a debate not about a determining resource curse but rather about open-ended resource challenges. For example: Heinrich et al. (2012), *Resource Challenges*, 443–477.
8 From a sociological point of view, see Rosa (2016), *Resonanz*, 16.

the accompanying research superfluous. Conceptualising resources within our research cluster means establishing two general alterations: the framing of resources in regimes as well as the opening of the understanding of resources for discourses about weaknesses and strengths.[9] In concrete practice, however, such research questions require containments: thus, this article will focus only on how to specify the concept of a regime. Since they can only answered in the long-term, questions about the concrete embodiment and change of regimes will not be included.

From a conceptual standpoint, it quickly becomes obvious that it is not sufficient to describe resources merely as a means, because then a boundless topic of research would arise. Instead of this, it is necessary to focus on the *extent* of the embeddedness of the means in question: resources show a specific *situatedness* with regard to the regulations and rules under which they become accessible.[10] This opens up a new view on resources: if one looks, for example, at the acts of war in the East-Roman Empire in the sixth century, one can observe the appropriation of sacred objects for military purposes, a phenomenon highly relevant to modern day conflicts.[11] This begs the question of how to measure such phenomena. The perspective on regimes has the option of not putting the objects themselves at the centre of the explanation, but the regulations determining the handling of these objects, instead: Under what conditions were they announced? Who could use them and who could not? Who was blamed for the absence of the impact? Who was allowed to vary the use of the objects (normally or in an exceptional state)? Such questions of availability are more extensive than the objects themselves and cannot be deduced from them. They give reasons for a perspective that is not grounded in phenomena such as materiality, scarcity, allocation or distribution.[12] To capture such regulations, a vocabulary has to be created because the embeddedness of a specific means can refer to different aspects: bodies of knowledge, power relations, discourses, or spatial structures are all examples that could be named. This text will illustrate the embeddedness of means upon the

---

9 See the Introduction to this volume.
10 The term "situatedness" is borrowed from the research design of the history of science projects. See the project: Situated Knowledge: Forms and Functions of Weak Bodies of Knowledge (Moritz Epple/Annette Imhausen) (www.sfb1095.net).
11 See the project: Sacral Objects as Military Resources in the Eastern Roman Empire from Justinian to Heraclius (Hartmut Leppin) (www.sfb1095.net).
12 These are typical approaches in economics: See: Müller-Christ (2011), *Sustainable Management*.

basis of their diffusion: *Was a means individual (action), was it common (practice), or was it a part of a set of regulations and rules (regime)*? The different answers lead to different action contexts whose differentiation could be useful to obtain a conceptual view on resources.

II. Resources as a Means to an End?

To obtain a minimal consensus, one could define that resources, as a means, refer to the pure instrumental dimension of an action context.[13] The accompanying scope then ranges from the classic raw material to the fluid phenomena of trust. As a result, the understanding of resources becomes inflationary and, in the end, artificial: since actors are always a part of not-completely-manageable relationships and conditions, such an understanding of resources means a significant reduction in complexity. It focuses actors on the, to some extent, "molecular" dimension of actions within which they have distinct intentions and for which they need the "right" means, but it ignores pre-conditions, backgrounds and parameters. Therefore, it is optimistically assumed that aims and means are abundantly clear and can be extracted and analysed separately from their situations. Nevertheless, the concept of means will be maintained, albeit in a modified way: when resources are everything which actors integrate into their actions in order to reach a goal, then it becomes necessary to make a clear differentiation between resources and mere means.

In its most simple form, the idea of a means refers to a means/purpose-relation whose explaining power for a line of action is seen sceptically by researchers.[14] The concept of an aim-choosing and means-seeking actor may seem artificial to many. In response to this, it can be said that means and purposes are neither isolated nor clearly separated phenomena, and, additionally, that actors are not completely informed or completely autonomous beings. This emphasises the fluid character of social processes that do not oppose actors but are continuously intertwined with them. This indication should be conceptually accounted for in any

---

13 A pragmatic definition is used in many approaches. See, for example, Deppe-Schmitz et al. (2016), *Ressourcenaktivierung*; Opp (1998), *Ressourcenmobilisierung*, 96.
14 Welskopp (2014), *Dualität von Struktur und Handeln*, 63.

perspective on resources, which is why a dynamisation of the action situation is a pre-requisite in the following.

Valuable suggestions for models beyond schematic purpose/means-relations can be found in the action theory approach of the social scientist Hans Joas,[15] who develops a decidedly pragmatic view on actions, in which the goals and means of an action are rooted in action situations. The goals could be so general (for example, to win a battle, to develop a new product, *etc.*) that there is no distinct or solely right choice of the means. This choice could also not be established from the beginning, but follows the course of action and changes throughout it. What was considered necessary to attain a goal and what was actually deployed to achieve it is understood as the result of the action situation. From such an action theory approach, it would be ill-advised to assume that actors have a great clarity and transparency in both their goals and the means by which they wish to achieve them.[16] The action situation is not only the place where actors implement their plans and look for suitable means, but is also a place where the forming of purposes and means is actually taking place: existing goals change in the face of the available means and *vice versa*—goals that were previously not considered are formulated according to the means currently available.[17] In particular, the idea of a strictly rational relation between means and purposes that centres on the concept of an ideal choice of means is counter-productive, since, besides other aspects, not all the required information can be extracted from an action situation.[18] The thoughts presented by Hans Joas are naturally not of an empirical, but of a conceptual, nature. Although they say nothing about an actual action, they nonetheless provide reasons for a shift of attention: individual means/purpose-relations are replaced by the situations in which they emerged. In short, a historisation of means-purpose-relations which explains the status of a given means emerges. The clear separation of goals and means is naturally of an analytical character because they are inseparably intertwined in practice: only goals create the measures to evaluate means, which, in turn, are a benchmark for something that is achievable. And, of course, there is always a normative dimension which frames the

---

15 Joas (1992), *Kreativität des Handelns*.
16 Joas et al. (2001), *Action Theory*, 273.
17 Instead of "goals" you can also use "problem solution". See Ash (2017), *Ressourcenansatz*, 544 f.
18 Beckert (2011), *Pragmatismus*.

relationship between goals and means (in the sense that we or somebody *should* do this or that). As a preliminary summary, it can thus be noted that, starting from an action theory approach, the phenomenon of a means is highly dynamic, which mirrors the characteristics of acting.

III. Is Every Means to an End a Resource?

Under what circumstances does a mean become a resource? Means differ with regard to their diffusion: they can appear *sporadic*, *increasingly* or even *frequent*. All these cases mirror—to put it technically—the different levels of their generalisation. If, as in the middle of the sixth century, sacred objects became military objects not just a few but several times, then this shows two different historical phenomena. This expresses a diffusion of means which leaves an increasingly rule-based and regulated use of the objects to be expected. Such changes in reach are probably frequent, but often are not documented in historic sources, so the degree to which this observation can be clearly observed strongly depends on the actual type of source that we are dealing with. For a sound conceptualisation of resources, such processes of the generalising of a means should still be taken in to account, because they can show important *caesurae*: as the use of sacred objects in the fourth century pointed to individual incidents, the importance of the objects increased overtime and recorded, especially in the middle of the sixth century, a dramatic leap, which illustrates that a single incident of military defence *turned into a proven course of action*. Another—and completely different example—can be found in the implementation of accounting in the chemical company *Bayer* from the 1880s.[19] In view of a very dynamic economic situation (the change to a stock company, the new reporting obligations, the increasing size of the company), the role of information at *Bayer* changed radically. Information had always been important for companies, but, in 1889, a specific accounting department (*"Technische Buchhaltung"*) was created to improve the observation of the cost structure. In particular, the quantification of the cost of individual products (in contrast to the production costs as a whole) was of interest.

---

19 See the project: The Use of Resources and Economic Calculation: Perception, Structures of Decisions and Practices of Adaption in the German Chemical Industry between 1860 and 1960 (Werner Plumpe) (www.sfb1095.net).

What followed was a continuous development of cost accounting within *Bayer*. At the beginning of the twentieth century, *Bayer* finally made use of an internal handbook of accounting that contained a detailed regulation of the collection and processing of information (who has to collect it, who has to fill in such - and - such a form, which were the various steps in the procedure and so forth). The case of *Bayer* provides a vivid example of the realisation of a regime: information was not merely a means for the management, but also became a resource, as part of an embeddedness in a system of rules and norms, for overcoming the changing environment. The difference between the sacred objects in the fourth and sixth century respectively, and between economic information in the 1880s and 1910s, was their different situatedness, or involvement within a specific context: first, as a means in a sporadic way, then as a means in a frequently used system of rules and regulations. An exact and detailed explanation of these processes of generalisation is clearly still needed, since the mere observation of the military applicability does not make it plausible as to *why* sacred objects could be deployed militarily in the first place, just as the mere fact of the applicability of newly gathered data within *Bayer* does not make it plausible as to *why* data became such an important factor of success.

IV. Resources as an Impact of Practices

Actors setting goals for themselves and employing the means to attain them is empirically well comprehensible. The question about the generalisation of means, however, is harder to answer, because it asks for categories in which their level with regard to the extent of their usage can be validly formulated. But what vocabulary is available for this? An important indicator for *generalisation* is that a phenomenon is explicable *without* reference to actors. In contrast to a decision, which can be strongly influenced by individual-related aspects, the specific feature of generalised behaviour is its indifference towards actors. For example, not giving a tip in a canteen is so routine that its performance does not need any reference to concrete actors. Naturally, it is possible to offer a tip in a canteen, but then it collides with the *practice* of not giving a tip. In our daily routine, such generalised phenomena are normally procedures such as "taking the bus" or "going to the supermarket". "Taking the bus" and its constitutive elements, such as "waiting for the bus" (but only at bus stops), "getting on, one after another" (or jumping the queue, which can be socially sanctioned) and "paying the fare" (albeit at a reduced price as a child or student) do not depend on the actors involved, their motives or their convictions. Sacred objects—to take again an example from our research cluster—have, in their military function, a generalised character when their use is not tied to specific actors, but nonetheless remain available *as a proven course of action* to any actor. In the case of *Bayer*, the collection of data has a generalised character when a bureaucratic system determines the rules, procedures and operations of the data-collection. A vivid indicator for such a rule-based handling can be seen in the high significance of forms, reports, and written documentation that can be seen as typical for regime structures.

How can such phenomena of generalisation be broken down methodically? From a social sciences perspective, phenomena, which are about activeness, but not, primarily, actors can be described with the term "practices". A practices-based perspective is currently being tested in many places within history and the social sciences.[20] For the present case, only one aspect that is interesting for the handling of resources will be taken into consideration. As Andreas Reckwitz put it, a practice refers to a "routinised type of behaviour".[21] Therefore, practices are more than actions, because the former can be—analytically—subdivided into the latter. Following Theodore Schatzki, practices add up to entanglements of various activities.[22] In the case of taking the bus, these are waiting, getting on, paying, waiting again, and getting off. So practices—in the present argument—do not simply refer to what actors do, but to what *can* be done *independently* of actors. In contrast to the single action, practices make it possible to identify more distinct stabilised activities. Notwithstanding this, the value of actors and their convictions is not eliminated. Actors remain a central category that is tremendously valuable especially in the emergence, variation and vanishing of practices. But a focus on practices makes a more differentiated description possible, one that does not sort every social event into actors or structures, but categorises them as an interjacent practice. The everyday practice of "taking the bus" or, citing historical examples from our research cluster, the practice of using sacred objects or collecting data all distinguish themselves by having, from a certain time

---

20 Brandes et al. (2017), *Praxeologische Perspektiven*.
21 Reckwitz (2002), *Social Practices*, 249.
22 Schatzki (2016), *Materialität*, 69.

onwards, a generalised character, meaning that they take place in a world in which the efficacy of the course of action is expected: the usage of sacred objects took place—at least since the sixth century—in a world that knew about the effects of such objects in military conflicts; the collection of data in the chemical industry happened—at least from the 1880s—in a world that was economically calculating with data, *etc*. Even if the research of such practices is, because of the sources, more difficult, it should be adhered to in order to reach the goal of an understanding of the appropriation of means and their transformation into resources.

V. Resources in Regimes

Practices can—conceptually—be the starting-points of regime-building, within which the resource status constitutes itself. Regimes are, therefore, in contrast to actions and practice, the most distinct handling of means. The term "regime", however, is connotated negatively and is normally associated with undemocratic and non-Western types of rule. In political sciences, the term "regime" is used to analyse international relations in the sense of modes of co-operation between states and other international actors. A regime in this understanding refers to:

"implicit or explicit principles, norms, rules, and decision-making procedures around which actors' expectations converge in a given area of international relations. Principles are beliefs of fact, causation, and rectitude. Norms are standards of behaviour defined in terms of rights and obligations. Rules are specific prescriptions or proscriptions for action. Decision-making procedures are prevailing practices for making and implementing collective choice."[23]

In the research programme of the CRC 1095 regimes are also used neutrally as regulations, rules and norms that determine the availability of resources. From this perspective, resources have regime-character and are only understandable by acknowledging the processes of making them available. The individual type of regime, its scale and its relation to other regimes is, of course, only empirically determinable. So, at this point, only a conceptual distinction between regimes and distribution systems is to be made because both share characteristics. Distribution systems are histori-

---

23 Krasner (1983), *Regime as Intervening Variables*, 2.

cally imaginable in a lot of ways because they regulate the distribution of both the necessary or wanted goods, and therefore describe a very general circumstance.[24] In contrast to distribution systems, regimes contain a deeper dimension of the availability of resources and therefore aim to identify the phenomena that can contain distribution systems. Regimes refer to arrangements *vis-à-vis* availability, which consist of authorisations, qualifications, limitations, obligations, detentions, and exclusions, within which the handling of the resource takes place.[25] Thus, regimes focus on the fundamental aspect of the creation of a resource, whereas distribution assumes the status of a resource.[26] The historically-changing, shaping-power of regimes refers to correlations that constitute, with regard to their capacities and impacts, more than actions or practices, and also more than distribution systems for scarce goods.

VI. Why this Extravagant Theoretical Effort?

Resources can commonly be structured by perspectives on their materiality (e.g., wood), immateriality (e.g., trust), sustainability (e.g., conservation), scarcity (e.g., coltan) or debates (e.g., "The limits of growth").[27] Such approaches can reveal interesting case studies but run the risk of neglecting the resource perspective systematically. Thus, this article has tried to unfold means as a part of regimes. To avoid an inflation of terms, two proposals were made: because of pragmatic considerations, means are conceptualised dynamically. The emergence of a concrete relation of purposes and means has a genuine historic character and should not be understood as a previous process, but as an ongoing process during action situations. The second aspect attempted to identify the varying situatedness of a means, which was demonstrated with the example of sacred objects and economic information: the objects were not only instruments of warfare but were so with *varying intensity*: first, in the fourth century (action), later increasingly

---

24 Wehler (2013), *Umverteilung*, 54 ff.
25 This dynamic is—without using the term *regime*—explicated in: Lessenich (2016), *Sintflut*, 56–63.
26 Resource regimes so far mostly were understood as institution, see Young (1984), *Resource Regimes*, 15 or Hübner (2015), *Soziale Ungleichheit*, 150.
27 These aspects were often used in discourses on sustainability: See: Grunwald et al. (2006), *Nachhaltigkeit*.

(practice), and, at least in the sixth century, as a result of continuous regulations (regime). Only when they established themselves as a regime could they be considered as a resource, because their usage became a calculable military strategy, independently of how they were applied, by whom, or with what success.[28] This generalisation of sacred objects indicates a new dimension of practical relevance. The collection of data within the chemical company *Bayer* shows a similar characteristic: from the 1880s, data became a means in an increasingly regulated system which operated independently of the concrete stuff within *Bayer*. This regime became a stable part of the organisation. In this way, means always raise the question of their embeddedness, which itself is subject to historical change. The analysis of such regime dynamics is promising and constitutes an important research goal of the CRC 1095. For an understanding of the emergence of regimes, a vocabulary which focuses on practices seems the best suited: if a means inserts itself in a practice, a more general phenomenon can be expected. But if a means inserts itself into a regime, then this signals an even more stable inventory of regulations, rules and norms of accessibility. Only in the latter case, which, conceptually, is "late", should resources be discussed. Practices and regimes make it methodically possible to illustrate different levels of generalisation, which, in turn, makes it possible to identify different grades of social effectiveness.

Theoretical thoughts of this nature are always under scrutiny for their applicability. How can such terms be dealt with in empirical research, and what is the end result in the face of often fragmentary sources? The approach to analyse not only the means, but also its situatedness (Action—Practice—Regime) will, in many cases, lead to the situation in which only those regimes, meaning developed modes of regulation, can be detected in sources and research data whose emergence cannot be fully reconstructed with the sources. Practices are methodically difficult to detect, something that is stressed in discussions about practices.[29] But it is still both possible and meaningful to utilise practices in order to explain that the emergence of regimes was exemplarily shown with both the sacred objects and the

---

[28] Variations of the regimes remain, of course, possible: for example, sacred objects became mobile in the 580s because their former use in cities was expanded to usage on the battle field (which, in turn, made a re-regulation of the object administrations necessary because only bishops were allowed to use them).
[29] Reckwitz (2008), *Praktiken und Diskurse*, 197.

economic information, which serve to emphasise the characteristics of a regime-focused perspective on resources.

Literature

Ash, Mitchell G. (2017). Reflexionen zum Ressourcenansatz. In Sören Flachowsky and Rüdiger Hachtmann, Florian Schmaltz (eds.). *Ressourcenmobilisierung. Wissenschaftspolitik und Forschungspraxis im NS-Herrschaftssystem*, 535–53. Göttingen: Wallstein.

Auty, Richard (1993). *Sustaining Development in Mineral Economies. The Resource Curse Thesis*. London/New York: Routledge.

Beckert, Jens (2011). Pragmatismus und wirtschaftliches Handeln. In Bettina Hollstein, Matthias Jung, Wolfgang Knöbl (eds.). *Handlung und Erfahrung. Das Erbe von Historismus und Pragmatismus und die Zukunft der Sozialtheorie*, 247–69. Frankfurt/M.: Campus.

Brandes, Sören, and Malte Zierenberg (2017). Doing Capitalism. Praxeologische Perspektiven. *Mittelweg 36* (1), 3–24.

Deppe-Schmitz, Uta, and Miriam Deubner-Böhme (2016). Auf die Ressourcen kommt es an. Praxis der Ressourcenaktivierung. Göttingen: Hogrefe.

Der Große Brockhaus (1956). Art. Ressourcen. 16., new edition in 12 volumes. Volume 9. Wiesbaden: Brockhaus, 691.

Grunwald, Armin, and Jürgen Kopfmüller (2006). *Nachhaltigkeit*. Frankfurt/M.: Campus.

Hardenberg, Roland, and Martin Bartelheim, Jörn Staecker (2017). The 'Resource Turn'. A Sociocultural Perspective on Resources. In Anke K. Scholz, Martin Bartelheim, Roland Hardenberg, Jörn Staecker (eds.). *ResourceCultures. Sociocultural Dynamics and the Use of Resources—Theories, Methods, Perspectives*, 13-23. (RessourcenKulturen 5). Tübingen: Universität Tübingen.

Heinrich, Andreas, and Heiko Pleines (2012). Resource Challenges. Die politische Dimension von Ölbooms. *Neue Politische Literatur* 75, 443–77.

Hübner, Jonas (2015). Soziale Ungleichheit in einem ländlichen Ressourcenregime der Frühen Neuzeit. *Jahrbuch für Geschichte des ländlichen Raumes*, 12, 150–162.

Joas, Hans (1992). *Die Kreativität des Handelns*. Frankfurt/M.: Suhrkamp.

Joas, Hans, and Jens Beckert (2001). Action Theory. In Jonathan H. Turner (ed.). *Handbook of Sociological Theory*, 269–85. New York: Springer.

Krasner, Stephen D. (1983). Structural Causes and Regime Consequences. Regime as Intervening Variables. In Stephen D. Krasner (eds.). *International Regimes* (Cornell Studies in Political Economy). Ithaca NY/London: Cornell University Press.

Lessenich, Stephan (2016). *Neben uns die Sintflut. Die Externalisierungsgesellschaft und ihr Preis*. Munich: Hanser Berlin.

Müller-Christ, Georg (2011). *Sustainable Management*. Berlin/Heidelberg/New York: Springer.

Opp, Karl-Dieter (1998). Die Perspektive der Ressourcenmobilisierung und die Theorie kollektiven Handelns. Eine Anwendung zur Erklärung der Ökologiebewegung in der Bundesrepublik. In Kai-Uwe Hellmann, Ruud Koopmans (eds.). *Paradigmen der Bewegungsforschung: Entstehung und Entwicklung von Neuen Sozialen Bewegungen und Rechtsextremismus*, 90–109. Opladen: Westdeutscher Verlag.

Reckwitz, Andreas (2002). Toward a Theory of Social Practices. A Development in Culturalist Theorizing. *European Journal of Social Theory* 5(2), 245–65.

— (2008). Praktiken und Diskurse: Eine sozialtheoretische und methodologische Relation. In Herbert Kalthoff, Stefan Hirschauer, Gesa Lindemann (eds.). *Theoretische Empirie. Die Relevanz qualitativer Forschung*, 188–209. Frankfurt/M.: Suhrkamp.

Reder, Michael, and Hanna Pfeifer (eds.). (2012). *Kampf um Ressourcen. Weltordnung zwischen Konkurrenz und Kooperation*. Stuttgart: W. Kohlhammer.

Reith, Reinhold (2010). Art. Ressourcennutzung. In Friedrich Jaeger (eds.). *Enzyklopädie der Neuzeit*, vol. 11, 122–134. Stuttgart/Weimar: J. B. Metzler.

Rosa, Hartmut (2016). *Resonanz. Eine Soziologie der Weltbeziehung*. Berlin: Suhrkamp.

Schatzki, Theodor (2016). Materialität und soziales Leben. In Herbert Kalthoff, Torsten Cress, Tobias Röhl (eds.). *Materialität. Herausforderungen für die Sozial- und Kulturwissenschaften*, 63–88. Paderborn: Wilhelm Fink.

Uekötter, Frank (2012). H-Soz-u-Kult Debatte zu "Ressourcen" in den Geschichtswissenschaften: 1. Teil. *H-Soz-Kult*, 20.09.2012 URL: http://www.hsozkult.de/debate/id/diskussionen-1876) [2018/03/21]

Wehler, Hans-Ulrich (2013). *Die neue Umverteilung. Soziale Ungleichheit in Deutschland*. Munich: C.H. Beck.

Welskopp, Thomas (2014). Die Dualität von Struktur und Handeln. Anthony Giddens' Strukturierungstheorie als "praxeologischer" Ansatz in den Geschichtswissenschaften. In Thomas Welskopp. *Unternehmen Praxisgeschichte. Historische Perspektiven auf Kapitalismus, Arbeit und Klassengesellschaft*. 55–76. Tübingen: Mohr Siebeck.

Young, Oran R. (1982). *Resource Regimes. Natural Resources and Social Institutions*. Berkeley: University of California Press.

Chapter 7
Resources in a Social World

Otto Danwerth, Teresa Dittmer, Seto Hardjana, Daniel Hausmann, Nicolas Perreaux, Linda Richter, Christian Scheidler, Frederic Steinfeld, and David Weidgenannt

I. Introduction

Resources seem to be ubiquitous today, and almost anything may appear to be a resource. This is a recent trend, and it goes hand in hand with the economisation of thought in the twentieth century, as an earlier chapter in this volume has argued.[1] However, in many ancient, pre-capitalist and non-Western cultures and societies, the concept of "resource", in the modern sense, is not known and has to be applied by contemporary observers.[2] Past societies also relied on resources, albeit in a different way, so the crucial question is to sketch a social and cultural framework for understanding resources, one which is valid not only for the narrow sphere of the modern economy, but also for past societies and non-material and religious contexts. In order to identify a common ground for resources and their functions, this essay relies on a comparison of different cases.

After a brief discussion of historical comparison, this chapter will present five case studies from various fields: Ancient Near Eastern history, Late Antiquity, the European Middle Ages, early modern Spanish America, and China in the late Qing Dynasty. At the core of the argument there seems to be a contradiction: on the one hand, "resource(s)" actually is an "etic" category in most cases; on the other hand, we claim that resources should be addressed from each society's "emic" point of view. This tension, in fact, is typical of any comparative and transdisciplinary research

---

[1] See Chapter 5 in this volume; for the resurgence of the concept of capitalism, see Kocka et al. (2016), *Capitalism*.

[2] On "resources", as an analytical category, see Hardenberg et al. (2017), *The "Resource Turn"*. On the history of concepts, see Koselleck (2006), *Begriffsgeschichten*.

which not only aims to be relevant for various historical and cultural contexts, but which also strives to share a common language.[3] Instead of treating "resource(s)" as a lucid and definite category, our reasoning begins with specific objects which can easily be identified as resources without distorting the cultural and social context in question. These cases inductively contribute to the notion of "resource(s)", rather than the other way around.

Based upon this empirical evidence, the final part of the chapter will propose a preliminary model of how to approach resources in the humanities. They are always embedded in larger systems which we call resource regimes. These systems, in turn, were profoundly shaped by power relations, social hierarchies, dominant discourses, cosmologies, and mythologies. The suggested model thus moves away from picturing resources as external factors of competition and accumulation which imping upon or constrain society—a perspective typical for macro-sociology or economy—or from explanations addressing the issue from the point of view of a tool-using agent. Instead, we analyse resources with respect to their social context.

II. Historical Comparison and its Problems

Before turning to the case studies, a few problems concerning the role and method of comparison should be addressed. Comparison in history is quite popular among historians who are influenced by the social sciences, but many others are more cautious.[4] Indeed, history as a scientific endeavour emerged as a national discipline in the nineteenth century, and most researchers relied on nationalistic cultural elements (for example, "borders", "nations", "peoples", "origins", *etc.*) as basic units, at least until the second half of the twentieth century.[5] However, comparison has always been within the reach of historians, since anthropology, a discipline in constant dia-

---

3 Detienne (2008), *Comparing the Incomparable*.
4 See Aymard (1990), *Histoire et Comparaisons*; Kaelble (1999), *Der historische Vergleich*; Osterhammel (2001), *Geschichtswissenschaft jenseits des Nationalstaats*; Siegrist (2006), *Comparative History of Cultures and Societies*.
5 See Detienne (2000), *Comparer l'incomparable*, 26–28; Kaelble (1999), *Der historische Vergleich*, 9; Werner et al. (2006), *Beyond Comparison*, 31–32, 48–49; Guyot-Bachy et al. (2015), *La Naissance de la médiévistique*; Wood (2013), *The Modern Origins*.

logue with history, provided abundant material for comparison and emerged at about the same time.[6]

Despite the difficulties, the comparatist challenge nevertheless persisted in the twentieth and twenty-first centuries: comparing societies based upon very different technical systems, social mechanisms, and mythologies implies having to find common ground(s) for comparison. Indeed, the increasing force of globalisation spurs comparative studies,[7] but it also generates complex puzzles that make comparison harder. Criticising a study on marriage in 350 different cultures, Francis Galton had already stressed in 1888 that comparison would be meaningless for cases of strong mutual influence.[8] In the early twenty-first century, globalisation has intensified interdependence and renders comparison even more problematical. On the other hand, this phenomenon also challenges identities, which makes the definition of stable units of comparison more and more difficult.[9] It thus seems to be no accident that approaches such as *"histoire croisée"*, "entangled history", "world history" and "connected histories" emerged in the late twentieth century as alternatives to comparative history in its classical form.[10]

Moreover, historical comparison, as such, is fraught with methodological problems.[11] The thorniest difficulties seem to be twofold: in the first place, the units, and thus also the scale of comparison, and, secondly, the categories used for the analysis.[12] In 1984, Charles Tilly suggested four different scales of historical studies: world history, world-system,[13] macro history, and micro history.[14] However, a neat delineation of units which corresponds to these scales is almost impossible, since even the comparison of narrowly circumscribed aspects tends to rely on the relevant histori-

---

6 Detienne (2000), *Comparer l'incomparable*, 17–41, esp. 22, 30.
7 Diamond (1997), *Guns, Germs, and Steel*; Harari (2011), *Sapiens*.
8 Giraud (2012), *Les défis de la comparaison à l'âge de la globalisation*, 95–96.
9 Giraud (2012), *Les défis de la comparaison à l'âge de la globalisation*, 97.
10 Randeria (2002), *Entangled History*; Subrahmanyan (1997), *Connected Histories*; Werner et al. (2006), *Beyond Comparison*; Duve (2014), *Entanglements in Legal History*.
11 A good discussion of the problems in classical comparisons is found in Tilly (1984), *Big Structures*, 23–59.
12 Espagne (1994), *Sur les limites du comparatisme en histoire culturelle*.
13 Wallerstein (1974–2011), *The Modern World System*; Shannon (1989), *An Introduction to the World-system Perspective*; Frank et al. (1996), *The World System: Five Hundred Years or Five Thousand?*.
14 Tilly (1984), *Big Structures*, 61; see also Kaelble (1999), *Der historische Vergleich*, 36–41.

cal context, which might quite simply not overlap with the object of analysis.[15]

It is also difficult to find suitable concepts for comparison as well as the adequate terminology. Ethical issues loom large, as can be seen in the following example: Is the use of concepts which have emerged in the context of European history an act of epistemic imperialism (including the concept of "history"),[16] or does the translation of empirical findings in a scientific Euro-American context automatically repeat colonial practices?[17] Moreover, finding the right terms of comparison is a theoretical and empirical challenge. The classical approach not only takes the dualism of concept, on the one hand, and reality, on the other, as given, but simultaneously disregards the influence of concepts on that very reality. It also neglects the dynamics underlying the configurations analysed. In particular, the historical influence of the concepts used in comparison on the emergence of the entities compared is often disregarded.[18]

In view of such major difficulties, it seems prudent to set our sights on a humbler aim: we understand comparison as a process. The distinction between classical sociological comparison and the more dynamic approaches recently advanced by Marcel Detienne and Olivier Giraud might help us to illustrate our perspective for this chapter. Classical approaches clearly distinguished between theory and object. The objects of comparison had to be subsumed under theoretical concepts, but there was no creative tension between the two.[19] By contrast, dynamic approaches take the confrontation with the objects to be a creative process, which leads to a reconfiguration of the key concepts. That is, the finding of data transforms key concepts, and they can no longer be neatly distinguished as belonging to two completely different realms.[20] Any abstraction made is thus to be seen in relation to the cases presented before. If societies universally relied in one way or another on resources, an analysis of a wide range of different cases might unfold an explanatory potential which closely related cases

---

[15] See also Werner et al. (2006), *Beyond Comparison*, 34.
[16] Randeria (2006), *Entangled History*, 291–292; Said (1978), *Orientalism*.
[17] Calame (2002), *Interprétation et traduction des cultures*.
[18] Werner et al. (2006), *Beyond Comparison*, 34–35.
[19] For two very different overviews about classical approaches, see Kaelble (1999), *Der historische Vergleich*; Tilly (1984), *Big Structures*.
[20] Detienne (2000), *Comparer l'Incomparable*; Giraud (2012), *Les défis de la comparaison à l'âge de la globalisation*; Werner et al. (2006), *Beyond Comparison*.

could not achieve. We thus aim at a heuristic and explorative comparison which delineates the main lines of tension.[21]

III. Case Studies

1. Precious Things: Glass in the Ancient Near East (Late Bronze Age)

Glass seems to have been known in the Ancient Near East for almost a thousand years before it was tapped in the sixteenth century BCE and large-scale glass production slowly developed in various locations. The production reached its peak in the fourteenth and thirteenth century BCE and almost vanished around the first millennium BCE before it redeveloped from the nineteenth century BCE onwards.[22] The archaeological and textual sources[23] indicate that, from the very beginning, glass, and any other vitreous material,[24] mainly functioned as an imitation of semiprecious stones.[25] Andrew Shortland has suggested that either a scarcity or

---

21 Our understanding is close to "pragmatic induction" as defined by Werner et al. (2006), *Beyond Comparison*, 46–47.
22 On the history of glass in the Ancient Near East, see Moorey (1994), *Ancient Mesopotamian Materials and Industries*, 189–215; Saldern (2004), *Antikes Glas*; Henderson (2013), *Ancient Glass*.
23 On the archaeological findings, see Barag (1985), *Catalogue of western Asiatic glass in the British Museum*; Moorey (1994), *Ancient Mesopotamian Materials and Industries*, 190–201; Saldern (2004), *Antikes Glas*. On the textual evidence, see Oppenheim et al. (1970), *Glass and glassmaking in ancient Mesopotamia*.
24 Such as glazed stone, faience and glazed ceramics.
25 Schuster-Brandis (2008), *Steine als Schutz- und Heilmittel*, 7–8. The ambiguous and sparsely attested terminology makes it very difficult to identify glass in written sources. The Akkadian term for glass is "stone" (*abnu*). Sometimes stones are specified as "from the kiln" (*ša kūri*), which is interpreted as glass, in contrast to "from the mountain" (*ša šadî*) which denotes a genuine stone. In addition, Oppenheim et al. (1970), *Glass and Glassmaking in Ancient Mesopotamia*, 87–96, identifies other terms for primary glasses. In this case study I restrict the focus on terms for glass attested in the Amarna correspondence: West Semitic *mekku* and Hurrian *eḫlipakku* ("raw glass"), and NA₄ *bušlu* ("molten stone"). But many Amarna letters also distinguish between "Lapis Lazuli" (NA₄.ZA.GÌN) and "genuine Lapis Lazuli" (NA₄.ZA.GÌN KUR) within each letter. An investigation of this differentiation and the comparison of glass and other vitreous materials might render a clearer picture of glass as a resource. On the terms *mekku* and *eḫlipakku*, see Oppenheim (1973), *Towards a History of Glass in the Ancient Near East*. On the differentiation of "Lapis Lazuli" and "genuine Lapis Lazuli", see Mynářová (2012), *From the Mountain or from the Kiln?*.

an increasing demand for the said stones might have triggered the experimentation with glass-making and glass-working techniques.[26] Thus, it would have been the tapping of a not fully developed resource that led to its unfolding.

Focusing on its golden age, we can see that glass was utilised in the same social fields and with the same culturally-ascribed properties as genuine stones.[27] During the Amarna period,[28] it was part of the circulation of luxurious objects within the diplomatic gift exchange.[29] This gift exchange functioned on different levels: at an economical level, it secured the supply of scarce raw materials such as copper; at a symbolic level, it represented the power of kings and equality between them thus strengthening their reciprocal ties. The Amarna correspondence[30] bears textual witness to this practice between Egypt and Mitanni, Hatti, Assyria and Babylonia, which were temporally equally powerful competitors. Within the hierarchically[31] organised lists of gifts, glass was used either as an application in golden objects,[32] or, unlike gold, silver and bronze, left unworked as a raw materi-

---

26 Shortland (2012), *Lapis Lazuli from the Kiln*, 46. Lapis Lazuli, the most valued mineral, for example, came from the region of Badakhshan in north-eastern Afghanistan. A possible change in trade routes may have caused a lack in supply. See Mynářová (2012), *From the Mountain or from the Kiln?*, 64.

27 This draws attention to the colours and colour density of glass. In fact, Ancient Near Eastern finds show that opaque glass was very popular, despite the difficulty to opacify glass.

28 Around 1355–1330 BCE.

29 The letters use terms for gift (*šulmu, qištu*), special gifts such as dowries and bride prizes (*mulūgu, terḫatu*) or paraphrase gift-giving situations. In the context of diplomatic gift exchange, there was a reciprocal obligation and asking for or complaining about a gift was an accepted practice. As the value of a gift is usually not given, it creates an imbalance that keeps a relationship going. On gift exchange in the Amarna period, see Cohen et al. (2000), *Amarna Diplomacy*; Cochavi-Rainey et al. (1999), *Royal Gifts*; Liverani (1990), *Prestige and Interest*. For an outline of general concepts of exchanges, see Quadflieg (2014), *Tauschen und Geben*, 117–124.

30 For a translation, see Rainey (2015), *The El-Amarna Correspondence*. Letters which mention glass are EA 14, EA 25, EA 37, EA 64, EA 148, EA 314, EA 323, EA 327, EA 331. In EA 13, lines 8, 10, 13, 15, and 18, Rainey translated *tarabbanu* "coloured glass", with *tarabbanu* as the only indication for glass. Within the glass recipes the term refers to a raw material for glassmaking. See Oppenheim et al. (1970), *Glass and Glassmaking in Ancient Mesopotamia*, 42, 80.

31 From most valuable materials like gold and special objects like oils, chariots and boats to less valuable materials like wood and everyday goods like furniture.

32 Rainey (2015), *The El-Amarna Correspondence*, EA 13, EA 25. As a worked object its total value in weight was never given, unlike gold, silver and bronze.

al.[33] The Egyptian vassal states from the Levantine coast of the Eastern Mediterranean also delivered raw glass as a tribute, and seem to have used its transfer to request military protection in time of need.[34]

But glass was not just a decorative prestigious material. The medical and ritual literature of the first millennium BCE illustrates that, together with genuine stones, it had also been used for protective and healing amulets.[35] It might well have been these culturally ascribed properties in a time of economic and intercultural exchange that led to the separation of the knowledge of glass-making and the actual material, and, as a consequence, the disentanglement from the workshop context.[36] The oldest preserved formula for glass, dated between the fourteenth and the twelfth century BCE,[37] seems—at least partly—to be codified in a traditional text form.[38] Thus, practical knowledge became a valuable resource for medical scholars and scribes.

Glass mainly served as an imitation of another highly valued resource, although it did not take over as a substitute, but was used simultaneously as an alternative, or even as an addition, to semi-precious stones. The connection with semi-precious stones clearly shows that resources cannot be considered as isolated objects, but must instead be seen as part of a resource regime. The temple and palace administration dominantly controlled this resource regime, including, at least part of glass production,[39] the circulation of glass and semi-precious stones, and the medical and ritual knowledge.

---

33 Rainey (2015), *The El-Amarna Correspondence*, EA 37, EA 14.
34 Rainey (2015), *The El-Amarna Correspondence*, EA 64, EA 148, EA 314, EA 323, EA 327, EA 331. EA 64 is the exception, for it mentions the production of female figurines made of glass.
35 In Schuster-Brandis (2008), *Steine als Schutz- und Heilmittel*, 105 (Kette 55), 154 (Kette 183), and 164 (Kette 204) *mekku* is listed as part of the amulets.
36 Robson (2001), *Society and Technology in the Late Bronze Age*, 52–54.
37 BM 120960 currently displayed in the British Museum. For a translation, see Oppenheim et al. (1970), *Glass and Glassmaking in Ancient Mesopotamia*, 59–65.
38 This procedural form can be found in mathematical, legal, medical and divinatory texts.
39 For example, the supply of difficultly procurable raw materials like antimony, copper, *etc.*

2. Sacred Objects: The Battle of Solachon and the acheiropoieton

When Emperor Maurice (582–602 AD) ascended the throne of the Eastern Roman Empire in 582, the military situation was critical. The Empire was beset by Avars and Slavs, who had been raiding and pillaging the western provinces for decades. Roman forces were struggling to defend the western periphery.[40] At the same time, the Empire was at war with the Sasanid Persians in the east. Roman military resources were overstretched and thin. Fighting on two fronts meant that the Romans were unable to concentrate sufficient fighting power to achieve any lasting successes. The armies not only lacked manpower, but the troops had also been demoralised by the recent defeats. During this time of crisis, relics came to take on a new role as military resources that could boost the morale of the Roman soldiers.

Relics were venerated because of the Christian belief that a part of the holy soul of the saints was present in their earthly remains, giving them the same power to work miracles that the saints had had during their lives.[41] This belief was even stronger with objects that were related to Christ or the Virgin Mary, such as pieces of the True Cross or the so-called *acheiropoieta*, or icons not made by human hands.[42] Since Christianity had become the predominant religion of the Roman Empire after its legalisation by Constantine the Great in 312, relics had begun to play an important role in the local communities in which they were kept. When a city in a border region was besieged and the imperial armies were unable to come to its aid, people would sometimes turn to relics in the hope of divine protection through the intercession of the saints. Stories about cities being miraculously saved by relics emerged, especially in the eastern provinces, which were constantly threatened by the powerful Persian Empire. This intensified during the 540s, when most Roman troops were tied down in other conflicts and the eastern frontier was left almost defenceless. Several cities were said to have been saved from conquest by divine intervention, supposedly caused by the presence of relics. Instead of the Emperor, it was

---

[40] Theophylactus Simocatta (1887), *Historiae*, I, 3–8.
[41] See Klein (2010), *Himmlische Schätze*, 371; Pfister (1912), *Der Reliquienkult im Altertum*, 617–618.
[42] From the Greek ἀχειροποίητον = "not made by human hands"; see von Dobschütz (1899), *Christusbilder*.

these relics that came to be the defenders of Roman cities.[43] This belief was not fabricated by political or religious leaders, but originated from the inhabitants of threatened cities in border regions, who sought the protection of God when the government failed to provide it.[44] Its diffusion was furthered by reports from church historians, such as Evagrius Scholasticus, who included stories about miraculously saved cities in their works.

In 584, the Roman general Philippicus asked the patriarch Gregory of Antioch for a relic of Saint Simeon Stylites, who was buried there, hoping that it would serve as "protection of the eastern expeditionary forces".[45] He probably hoped that the presence of the relic and the miraculous protection that it promised would boost the damaged morale of his troops. And it seemed to work: in 584 and 585, Philippicus led successful raids into Persian territory.[46] In 586, Philippicus intercepted an invading Persian army on the plain of Solachon in order to face them in battle. Before the battle commenced, he showed his troops an even more potent relic: the image of Camuliana,[47] believed to be an *acheiropoieton*, created by Christ himself and displaying his divine features. Philippicus gave a rousing speech, "thereby inspiring the army with a greater and irresistible courage".[48] After a hard-fought battle, the Romans won the day and prevailed. This was the first time that the use of a relic as a military resource was explicitly described.

The reasons why relics gained their new role as military resources during this time of crisis are evident. They already existed, so they did not have to be produced and could be acquired easily. Belief in their supernatural powers was already accepted and widespread, both in civil and in military contexts. Philippicus' initial successes further legitimised the practice of using sacred objects as military resources. Their efficiency was mainly due to the positive impact that the presence of relics had on the morale of

---

43 See Cameron (1978), *The Theotokos in Sixth-century Constantinople*, 81–82; Haldon (1997), *Byzantium in the Seventh Century*, 405–406.
44 Meier (2009), *Der christliche Kaiser zieht (nicht) in den Krieg: "Religionskriege" in der Spätantike?*, 263–264.
45 "Φιλιππικοῦ δεηθέντος παραφυλακῆς ἕνεκα τῶν ἑῴων ἐκοστρατευμάτων τίμια λείψανά οἱ ἐκπεμφθῆναι." Evagrius Scholasticus, *Historia ecclesiastica*, I, 13.
46 Theophylactus Simocatta, *Historiae*, I, 13–14.
47 On the Image of Camuliana, see Rist (2014), *Das Bild von Kamuliana und seine Bedeutung für das frühe Byzanz*.
48 "κρείττονος καί ἀνανταγωνίστου θράσους ἐντεῦθεν μεταδιδούς τῷ στρατεύματι." Theophylactus Simocatta (1887), *Historiae*, II, 3, 6.

the troops. Especially in the ethnically diverse Eastern Roman Empire and army, symbols of the common religion could have a unifying effect which strengthened cohesion between soldiers from different cultural backgrounds both within and outside the empire.[49]

The Battle of Solachon marked the start of a development that was to become increasingly important during the following decades. Earlier, military conflicts were mainly seen as struggles between political entities. While religious symbols, practices and rituals played a role even before the Christianisation of the empire, they were not seen as the decisive factors for victory.[50] But, with the usage of relics, to which the Romans attributed the power to work miracles and thus change the outcome of battles, the focus shifted towards the religious aspect of war.

3. Donating Land: Spiritualising Land in the Middle Ages

The Church, as the main institution of Medieval Europe, was a huge collector of resources, following complex mechanisms that involved kinship, ecclesiastic communities, land and saints. As a certain Berthold Roseli said when he gave all his earthly possessions to the hospital of Esslingen in 1297: "What a happy action it is, to have learned how to exchange earthly things for celestial ones."[51] Throughout the Early and High Middle Ages, clerics produced various types of discourses of weakness, not only about the corruptible nature of man (*homo*), earthly time (*sæculum, tempus*) and space (*mundus*), but also about their own status. These discourses, based upon the Bible, were, of course, omnipresent in exegetical and hagiographical texts,[52] but were also dominant in diplomatic documents, or charters. Written after frequent transactions involving donations of land, from lay people to ecclesiastical institutions, these charters, especially their preambles, were, indeed, an appropriate place for this specific expression. Here, men appear as weak and corruptible, the current century labile and uncertain, and finally, the monks are seen as fragile, isolated, at the mercy

---

49 On the possibility of relics creating identity, see Carlà (2014), *Exchange and the Saints*, 407; Fowden (1999), *The Barbarian Plane*, 67.
50 Lee (2007), *War in Late Antiquity*, 176–177.
51 "O quam felix industria, que terrena didicit pro celestibus permutare", in Königliches Haus- und Staatsarchiv (1849–1913), *Württembergisches Urkundenbuch*, here vol. XI, no 5031, 64–65 (Esslingen, August 1, 1297).
52 Magnani (2010), *Un trésor dans le ciel*, 51–68.

of time. At the heart of these preambles lies the injunction that earthly possessions, that is to say, resources, should be transformed into heavenly things:

"Divina pietate legumque auctoritate sanctitum est, ut de terrenis rebus celestia adquirantur, dicente scriptura: 'Date helemosinam, et ecce omnia munda sunt vobis.' [Luke 11:41]."[53]

These preambles were very widespread all across Medieval Europe, from the Empire[54] to what are nowadays France,[55] Spain,[56] and the British Isles.

Since the Church was the institution that issued most of the charters, the *ecclesia* was creating and expressing an orthopraxy of distribution of resources. Paradoxically for our contemporary thought, these discourses on the weakness of earthly goods, and the need to transform them into ecclesiastical things, led, in consequence, to an acceleration of the flow of donations to the Church. Indeed, from 500 to 1300, hundreds of thousands of charters documenting the giving of gifts to the Church were written,[57] resulting in the giant growth of Church property.[58]

Other discourses of weakness generated by the *ecclesia*, such as that on kinship, appear in the *cartae*, and contributed to a specific distribution of resources. Indeed, the medieval system distinguished between two forms of kinship: the carnal (*carnalis*) and the spiritual (*spiritualis*). While the carnal kinship was devalued in discourses because of its association with the flesh

---

53 Bernard et al. (1884), *Recueil des chartes de l'abbaye de Cluny*, vol. 3, no 2262, in June 994. ("Divine piety and the holy authority of the law require the use of earthly things to acquire heavenly ones, as the Writings say: 'Give alms: and behold, all things are clean unto you.' [Luke 11:41]", English translation by Nicolas Perreaux.)

54 "Et pro terrenis adquirit celestia optimum sibi lucrum adquirit [...]", Stavelot abbey (Belgium), in 991. In the databases *Thesaurus diplomaticus*, no 1563 or *Diplomata Belgica*, no 1311. Arnoul and Gautelinus gave their properties located in Kröv to the abbey of Stavelot.

55 "Ut ex rebus transitoriis et terrenis adquirere possent mansiones in celestibus gaudiis.", in: Doniol (1864), *Cartulaire de Sauxillanges*, no 520, in 994.

56 "Cum pro transitoriis manencia et pro terrenis adquiruntur celestia, illud quam illud quam maxime recto oculo cordeque deuoto considerantes quod in magna egestate sunt diuites, iustitie opes et sapientie tesauros non habentes.", Cathedral of Barcelona, in 1055: Baucells i Reig *et al.* (2006), *Diplomatari de l'Arxiu Capitular de la Catedral de Barcelona—Segle XI*, 2006, vol. 3, no 888.

57 For a review of a chrono-geographical distribution of half a million of charters, see Perreaux (2015), *L'écriture du monde*; Perreaux (2015), *Des structures inconciliables?*.

58 Algazi et al. (2003), *Negotiating the Gift*; Magnani (2007), *Don et sciences sociales*; Davies et al. (2010), *The Languages of Gift in the Early Middle Ages*.

(*caro*), the Fall, and original sin, the spiritual one was highly valued, as it was seen as being close to the divine kinship and certain exemplary forms of social organisation. Accordingly, monasteries followed some forms of spiritual organisation, since the monks were brothers (*fratres*) and had a spiritual father, the abbot (*pater*). The result of these discourses was a devaluation of filiation and of some forms of transfer linked to this form of kinship. Gifting earthly resources not to one's children but to the Church, so the institution could make almost heavenly things out of them, was seen as something very positive. As a matter of fact, this transformation process was considered as one of the main ways to attain salvation. Thus, the *ecclesia* organised the flow of resources through the production of discourses of weakness which worked in different directions: 1. Towards the clerics themselves ("we are without resources"); 2. Towards the laymen, and especially the lay aristocracy ("flesh is weak; the gift could save your soul"); and 3. Towards resources—defined as *carnalis* or *spiritualis*—depending on the relationships from which they emerged. This orthodoxy of resource distribution was based upon a global theory of social organisation structured around the concept of charity (*caritas*), an ethics of giving.[59] Thus, we can conclude that the production of discourses of weakness about what was "carnal" and what was not organised both the flow and the distribution of resources.

4. Knowledge as a Resource: The Circulation of Pragmatic Normative Literature in Spanish America (16th-17th c.)

By the third decade of the sixteenth century, once the first settlements had been built in Central and South America, the Spanish monarchy had to confront the task of establishing its dominion over a huge population and across vast distances, notwithstanding its limited human and material resources. In the light of this scarcity, great importance was accorded to implementing codes of conduct among European settlers as well as the indigenous population. By this time, "pragmatic normative literature" gained significance in the remote *frontier* contexts of an early modern empire, as this body of works—confessional writings, catechisms, moral theo-

---

[59] Jussen (1991), *Patenschaft und Adoption im frühen Mittelalter*; Jussen (2000), *Spiritual Kinship as Social Practice*; Heritier-Augé et al. (1995), *La parenté spirituelle*; Mathieu et al. (2007), *Kinship in Europe*; Johnson et al. (2013), *Blood and Kinship*.

logical instructions—contained condensed knowledge. In imperial peripheries where the reach of law was limited, these adaptable texts, addressed, in particular, to religious practitioners, were instrumental for the implementation and notions of "proper" behaviour.[60]

However, the dissemination of books in colonial Spanish America was subject to a "knowledge regime", *i.e.*, "the structured and (more or less) stabilised interrelation of practices, rules, principles and norms concerning knowledge and different forms of knowledge".[61] The Castilian Crown created a system of controlled exportation, trade, and circulation of books in its overseas territories. The *Casa de la Contratación* (House of Trade), founded in 1503 in Seville, aimed at a complete supervision of the transatlantic traffic of ships, people, and goods.[62] Books had to be registered before exportation since they were considered to be ambivalent resources: sources of useful knowledge, which, at the same time, could spread heretical ideas to the overseas territories.[63]

In 1550, Emperor Charles V decreed that each and every book to be exported to the New World had to be specifically mentioned in the records individually—and not in a collective manner.[64] However, it was only with the publication of Quiroga's *Index of Prohibited Books* in 1583 that this norm came to be obeyed more regularly, and homogenous series of book lists started to be drafted until about 1620.[65] In order to prevent the transit of prohibited texts, the *Casa de la Contratación* co-operated with the Inquisition.[66] Book merchants had to submit to the Secretary of the Holy Office detailed lists of books which were to be sent to America; friars had to approve the cargo lists. However, since the inquisitorial censors did not always perform rigid examinations of the book inventories, and due to the lack of vigilance in the overseas ports, the knowledge regime became permeable.

---

60 See Danwerth (2017), *La circulación de literatura normativa pragmática*.
61 Wehling (2007), *Wissensregime*, 704.
62 The classic manual about the Trade House was written by Veitia Linage (1672), *Norte de la Contratación*. See García-Baquero (1992), *La Carrera de Indias*; Acosta Rodríguez et al. (2003), *La Casa de la Contratación y la navegación entre España y las Indias*.
63 See González Sánchez (2011), *New World Literacy*, 54–57.
64 *Recopilación de leyes de los reynos de las Indias*, 1681, lib. I, tít. XXIV, ley V: "De los libros que se imprimen y pasen a las Indias."
65 See González Sánchez (2011), *New World Literacy*, 47–53. The basic sources are ship registers, conserved in the *Archivo General de Indias* (AGI).
66 Rueda Ramírez (2005), *Negocio e intercambio cultural*, 61–80.

Despite restrictions and control measures exercised by civil and ecclesiastic authorities, the transatlantic book-trade was a booming enterprise. At least 85 per cent of the books circulating in America were imported and of European origin. Due to the fast-growing immigration to Spanish America, the market for books was expanding, too. Archival records reveal that certain manuals of moral theology written by Martín de Azpilcueta and Manuel Rodríguez became "best sellers" in the second half of the sixteenth century.[67] About 15 per cent of the circulating books in the New World were supplied by the few printing presses that had received a royal licence in early colonial Spanish America: they operated in Mexico City (1539), Lima (1581/84), Puebla de los Angeles (1640), and Guatemala (1660).[68] As the printing presses of Mexico and Lima had been founded to help the missionaries, they produced many catechetic texts, including translations into indigenous languages.[69]

In order to know more about the ownership and dispersion of the books in America, one has to consult other sources, for example, inventories of goods that individuals or institutions owned. Early colonial library catalogues and personal book inventories as well as archival sources from Peru and Mexico show that manuals and compendia of moral theology, catechisms and other genres, used especially in missionary contexts, not only reached cities and convents, but also rural areas and mission zones.[70] Such books and manuscripts were central resources for the diffusion of normative orders in the emerging empire. The circulation and use of these religious pragmatic works helped to establish normative concepts and codes of conduct in places where "official" legal sources did not arrive.

---

67 See González Sánchez (2011), *New World Literacy*, 112; Rueda Ramírez (2005), *Negocio e intercambio cultural*, 309–312.
68 A good overview on the vast historiography is provided by Calvo (2003), *The Politics of Print*.
69 See only Jiménez (2007), *Los libros en lenguas indígenas*, 65–117; Guibovich Pérez (2001), *The Printing Press in Colonial Peru*, 167–188.
70 Some examples might suffice here: Leonard (1992), *Books of the Brave*; Hampe Martínez (1996), *Bibliotecas privadas en el mundo colonial*; Guibovich Pérez (2010), *Los libros de los doctrineros*, 97–132.

5. Procuring Legitimacy: Grain Distribution and State Legitimacy in the late Qing Dynasty

In the Qing dynasty (1644–1911), grain was not only a form of nourishment, it also had symbolic value. First and foremost, grain was the main staple food. However, it was also offered to some gods and used in rituals, and grain-cherishing societies (*xiguhui*) regarded it as a holy item to be treated with care and respect. Moreover, as government aid for destitute persons, grain embodied imperial virtue (*de*) and thus featured as a stabilising cosmic force.[71] Grain came in many forms: rice, wheat, millet, and sorghum. Peasants normally cultivated grain, sold it for copper cash, and finally exchanged it into silver taels in order to pay their taxes. Grain was not only the basis for peasants to pay their taxes, but the state also stored it in the so-called "ever normal granaries" (*changpingcang*) throughout the imperial territory.[72]

The Qing state was mainly agrarian. It was organised into districts at the lowest level, then prefectures and provinces, with the central court at its summit, with each level extracting taxes from the people, retaining part of it to cover their running costs and forwarding the remaining part to the next level up. In theory, major decisions were sanctioned by the court, but, in fact, routines and local decision-making determined much of the political realities.[73] However, many political thinkers acknowledged the indebtedness of the government to the peasant, and they argued that either the state "took root" (*ben*) in the people, or that it was the state's duty to repay the peasants for their duties. Thus, the state could simply not flinch from involving itself in famine relief, one of its major paternalist duties.[74]

In the eighteenth century, famines in Qing China can roughly be defined in two complementary ways. On the one hand, they were character-

---

71 On grain cherishing societies, see for instance Sun Nianqu (1800), *Quanren juyue*, 3/43a-45b; the philosophical basis for the thinking on the double nature of grain is found in the *Daxue* (Zhu Xi (2011), *Sishu zhangju*, 13), it was famously expressed by Zhu Xi (Zhu Xi (2010), *Zhuzi yulei*, 3467) and then often repeated in disaster handbooks or palace memorials.
72 On the *changpingcang* system, see Will et al. (1991), *Nourish the People*.
73 On the structure of the government, see Metzger (1973), *The Internal Organization Workings*; Qu Tongzu (1969), *Local Government*; on famine administration in particular, see Will (1990), *Bureaucracy and Famine*; on the memorial system and decision making, see Bartlett (1994), *Monarchs and Ministers*; Wu (1969), *Communication and Control*.
74 This view on famines is well expressed in Wei Xi (2010), *Jiuhuang ce*.

ised by bad weather, mostly droughts, but sometimes excessive rainfall, by a growing grain scarcity, an increase in grain prices, the dissolution of social sedentary communities, the emergence of a large number of famine refugees, and, finally, by the consumption of substitute aliments such as tree bark, roots, *etc.*, as well as cannibalism.[75] Moreover, famines were also characterised by their relation to legitimate rule. Famine indicated bad rule by the court and the provincial and local governments, and it was a sign that imperial virtue did not suffice to hold the realm together and that the Heavenly mandate (*tianming*) legitimising the current dynasty had been revoked. This allegedly resulted in a degeneration of local morals, which, in turn, angered Heaven. Heavenly punishments in the guise of famines followed suit.[76]

The most important feature to note is that famines were causally overdetermined: on the one hand, they were seen as a result of bad weather in conjunction with bad governance; on the other, they were interpreted as heavenly punishment resulting from moral decay. The Great North China Famine (1876–78) was one of the most devastating famines in world history causing approximately 9.5 million people to die of starvation. Partly caused by the so-called El Niño–Southern Oscillation, which triggered a prolonged drought in China, it was also perceived as the sad reflection of impoverished communities and the result of a central government that had set its eyes on modernisation or on quelling rebellions.[77]

A decade before the famine, a group of officials in the Hanlin Academy had entered their office as an elite, but they were not promoted at all, which would normally have been the case. They were frustrated. Many of them reacted to the accession of the Guangxu emperor to the throne in 1875 by intensifying their criticism of court politics in general. These actions were furthered by the empress dowager, but they were also a counter-reaction to the former emperor's stern silencing of criticism and reliance on the higher strata of officialdom. In addition, these Hanlin officials also reacted to the mounting crisis which was represented by frequent natural disasters and irregular occurrences (*yi*). Thus, they posed as virtuous offi-

---

75 For a stereotypical but concise description of this process, see Tu Long (2010 [1690]), *Huangzheng kao*, 105.
76 An introductory synthesis of this view is found in Will et al. (1991), *Nourish the People*.
77 On this famine, see Hao Ping (2012), *Ding Wu qihuang*; He Hanwei (1983), *Guangxu*; Edgerton-Tarpley (2008), *Tears from Iron*.

cials who did not fear punishment and who spoke sincerely (*cheng*) about the administration.

The Great North China Famine was another opportunity for the Hanlin officials to voice several of their views. In conjunction with other "unusual" phenomena such as the appearance of comets, and occurrence of earthquakes and other disasters, it indicated that Heaven had revoked its mandate and that imperial governance was seriously flawed. They memorialised to the court about the dysfunctional aspects of promotions and career patterns, the general lack of talent, the leaks in the financial administration, and they impeached allegedly corrupt high officials whom they thought responsible for this disaster. However, they did not care much about the actual famine situation. They exploited the double nature of the famine as an economic disaster, on the one hand, and as a Heavenly punishment, on the other, and translated it into a resource crisis of talents, which was hardly related to the actual famine at all: they exposed the alleged causes of the famine in the central court, in the officialdom and governance, that is, the corruption of high officials and the lack of talents in general.

In sum, this case suggests that the symbolic dimensions of grain, relief and famine became more important under certain conditions of state failure. This shift marks a clear break with the eighteenth century Qing dynasty, but it does not discard its general cultural framework. Moreover, the utter failure of the central state to provide relief, despite its claims to the contrary, challenged its legitimacy and provided the basis for some officials to link state failure to the lack of talent.

IV. Resources in a Social World

These five cases presented different uses of resources, in various periods and geographical contexts. The last section of the chapter sketches a model for understanding resources and their dynamics in the humanities and social sciences. Our empirical survey suggests that there are several alternative ways and frameworks for analysing resources. However, we would first like to stress that resources are always embedded in social, political, symbolic and discursive contexts.[78]

Second, there are two dimensions of the embedding of resources in society. We emphasise that resources are things, either abstract or material or both, which a society accesses, *i.e.*, which are tapped, and which are transformed by production in a wide sense. On the other hand, resources circulate. While they are not ontologically transformed by exchange—in a very narrow sense of the word "matter"—they still only become resources in the full sense when they are actually within a system of transfer. To date, the latter point has not, however, received much attention in the literature, which focuses either on the use, the social function, or the tapping processes.[79] Although—in contrast to goods, commodities and gifts—resources are much more determined by production and tapping, this should not divert attention from the fact that they are also conditioned by systems of transfer.

Resource Regimes

Roughly put, resources are things which groups or individuals in societies exchange within given patterns of exploitation, distribution or transfer, in order to reproduce themselves socially. These groups or individuals rely upon them to fortify their position in given hierarchies or to foster change.[80] Resources may be used actively, arguably in the majority of cases, but they do not always feature in action or exploitation patterns.[81] However, such a functional approach replaces a perspective on resources which essentialises them or perceives them solely as tools.[82] Thus, instead of focusing on the use of resources in "Robinson Crusoe settings"—situations in which a person acts solitarily outside of a social community—it is more appropriate to interrogate the *function* of resources in societies. In short, we regard resources as something essentially social.

---

78 See, also, Hardenberg (2016), *Beyond Economy and Religion*.
79 For a recent discussion, see Hardenberg et al. (2017), *Resource Turn*.
80 Godelier (1986), *The Mental and the Material*; Descola (1994), *In the Society of Nature*.
81 A telling example is the understanding of the rainforest as a resource in discourses on sustainable development; see Escobar (1996), *Constructing Nature*.
82 Karl Polanyi pioneered in presenting a similar argument, see Polanyi (1944), *The Great Transformation*, 171–209.

Resources always figure within organised systems and patterns, that is, resource regimes.[83] These regimes are determined by the norms, practices and discourses of given societies, but they are, on the one hand, and, in a narrower sense, systems of tapping and exploiting, which are interlocked and dependent upon the systems of exchange and circulation of resources, on the other.

On a very general level of abstraction, the two most important systems with respect to resources are: (a) exploitation, cultivation, (re-) production or the discovery of resources; and (b) their transfer, exchange and distribution, or accumulation.[84] Resources must figure in both of these systems. Put differently, we argue that, for anything to be considered as a resource in a specific historical setting, this society must make an effort to "introduce" this resource into itself; that is, there must be an endeavour to "obtain", "possess" or "acquire" it.

Moreover, resources must be transferable. This underscores their social character. Transfers may be of the purely economic kind, namely, exchanges, but they may also be gifts or even symbolic actions as in the case of the transfer of rights.[85] Whether a certain object is transferable, however, depends upon the society in which this transfer occurs. According to our contemporary standards, for instance, innate abilities such as intelligence, or even some acquired traits, such as beauty resulting from cosmetic surgery, cannot be transmitted. Other abilities, such as skills, can, however. The decisive criterion here is whether the society in question has a notion of transferability for the object in question.

The tapping and transfer of resources are related to the establishment of power structures, and we claim that no resource exists outside such constraints.[86] To exploit certain resources, to distribute them, or to transfer them, always takes place within given hierarchies and class relations. These activities lay claim to or fortify certain statuses, be they new or old, and they serve either to sustain a given system or to disrupt it. Thus, to ignore

---

83 For an analysis of contemporary resource regimes focusing on natural resources, see Young (1982), *Resource Regimes*.
84 On transfer, see Testart (2007), *Critique du Don*, 23–70.
85 On the distinction between economic exchange and gift, see Bourdieu (1997), *Marginalia*; Testart (2007), *Critique du Don*; Testart (1993), *Des Dons et des Dieux*, 85–93. On the distinction of gifts in sacred contexts and exchanges, see Godelier (1999), *The Enigma of the Gift*, esp. 179–180. A useful collection of writings on gifts can be found in Schrift (1997), *The Logic of the Gift*.
86 Harari (2011), *Sapiens*, Chapters 5 and 6.

constellations of power and hierarchies in analysing resources would remove nearly everything which makes them relevant.

The case of the controlled circulation of pragmatic literature in Spanish America in the sixteenth and seventeenth centuries is instructive. Books, considered ambivalent resources of knowledge, were introduced into the New World, but they were subject to a resource regime co-ordinated by a central state institution, the House of Trade, and by the Inquisition. The circulation of pragmatic religious works resulted in a wide distribution of these texts, even in remote regions of an emerging empire where secular institutions and traditional legal sources were often still absent. There are strong indications that this constellation of resources used by ecclesiastic institutions and clerics was responsible for generating the basic normative conceptions of social order and establishing a system of rule among both the European settlers and the indigenous population. Juridical normativity and secular institutions which were consolidated in a process of differentiation—*i.e.*, resources central to the formation of the early modern European state—were substituted by religious normativity and pragmatic literature in the frontier regions of early colonial Spanish America.

Resources as Symbols, Symbols as Resources

The circulation of resources is determined by more than their material qualities, and it would be a mistake to conceptualise them simply and exclusively as tangible objects. They have, of course, been identified as material things or products, but, in many cases, we can observe their so-called immaterial or symbolic resources, such as moral components, political agendas, and normative orders.[87] Symbolism itself is always related to a given culture or group. Consequently, the same material object could have different meanings in different socio-cultural and political contexts. This implies that an effort to understand resources should also include their symbolic dimension(s). However, this is not a one-way street: symbols themselves can become resources, and the symbolic aspect of resources may trump their material value.[88]

---

[87] The symbolic dimension has been of prime importance to Claude Levi-Strauss and Maurice Godelier. See Levi-Strauss (1964–1971), *Mythologiques*; Godelier (1999), *The Enigma of the Gift*.
[88] See, in particular, Bourdieu (1980), *Le Sens Pratique*, 191–207.

Clearly, during the Battle of Solachon, relics were only a resource because of their symbolic dimension. Something similar holds true for the donation of land to the *ecclesia* in order to create the City of God on earth. However, this interpretation should not conceal more profane aspects: the presentation of relics motivated the soldiers psychologically, and the donors of land to the *ecclesia* were keen to maintain good relations with the *ecclesia*, not least because the latter was instrumental in collecting taxes for the landlords. As with almost any analysis of symbols, the pitfall of exoticism, on the one hand, and outright reductionism, on the other, must be balanced against each other.

Tapping

All the cases discussed above address, be it explicitly or implicitly, a certain action of tapping, that is, of introducing or acquiring resources, which always involves a process of formation. Tapping of resources is always a strategical operation. A resource is tapped with a goal in mind, but these goals may vary and, in the end, can result in something very different but still very valuable. For instance, famine relief in the Qing dynasty was subject to two goals. First, it was conceived as an economic measure to ensure social stability and economic recovery. Second, it also displayed imperial virtue which served as a foundation for legitimate rule. A large part of the Qing dynasty tapping network of grain production, taxation and state granaries served these two purposes.[89]

Resources as things submit to a slightly different logic than other objects such as goods or commodities. The latter are all, in one way or another, destroyed by consumption, which is less relevant for resources outside the context of the economy. Whereas the standard view of commodities assumes cycles of production, exchange, and consumption, tapping resources in all the cases discussed here serves a goal belonging to a higher order: salvation in the case of land donation in the Middle Ages, the establishment of normative orders in early colonial Spanish America, legitimate rule in the Qing dynasty, and so forth. Whereas resources in an economic sense are shaped by processes of consumption, such as those of coal or oil, or production, such as in industry, where, for instance, iron is transformed into steel, resources in cultural contexts, which is the main object of this

---

89 On this network, see Will et al. (1991), *Nourishing the People*; Dunstan (2006), *State or Merchant?*

chapter, are not exhaustively understood by either consumption or production.

In addition, power is a constitutive element of these cultural processes. Be it land in the Middle Ages, or, more explicitly, the gifts of glass in the Amarna period (*circa* 1355–1330 BCE), all of these tapping practices are shaped by the use or presence of force. The use of force was also crucial in the case of land distribution in the Middle Ages, since the *ecclesia* advanced its claims to land upon the basis of a complex discourse on the sacred and sanctity. In this particular case, the strength of the Church was not based upon brute force at all, but upon the fact that it regulated morals, kinship, time and space, and thus the use of land in Medieval Europe. In other words, power enters here as a structural element into the tapping processes which are shaped by hierarchies or a spectrum of possibilities for articulating one's legitimate claims.

Transfer and Transferability

The examples of resource tapping show that practices of transfer were intertwined with tapping, but transfers or exchanges were highly relevant to the significance of resources as well. Sending glass as gifts played an important role in consolidating inter-monarchical relations in the Amarna period. The transfer of rights to land in the Middle Ages by donating them to the *ecclesia* not only fundamentally changed the agrarian production and social domination, but it also contributed to the formation of the City of God on earth. Even if the basic notion of transfer is material, most frequently it was symbolic or immaterial. Donating land to the *ecclesia* does not consist in the transportation of land to the Church but in a switch of property rights.[90] Although tapping and formation are the defining characteristics of resources, they acquire their significance only by being embedded within a system of social transfer or exchange relations.

For instance, resources could be transferred in gift exchange. They could serve to establish or consolidate social ties and thus be instrumental to the formation of communities. In addition, transfer of resources enforced loyalty or could serve as a basis to demand services.[91] Both aspects are lucidly shown, again, by the use of glass in the Amarna period. On the

---

90 This immaterial relation received much attention in the literature on gifts; see Gregory (1982), *Gifts and Commodities*; Testart (2007), *Critique du Don*.
91 See, in particular, Testart (2007), *Critique du Don*, 159–170.

one hand, vassal states donated glass to the Pharaoh, along with pleas for support, often military. On the other hand, giving glass to other competing kingdoms served to strengthen their relationship. The Amarna period case illustrates that glass had a value both as raw material and as a finished object, depending on the circulation context, be it a relationship between vassals and ruler, or a gift exchange between kings.

The final major mode of transfer is distribution. The examples from the use of land in the Middle Ages, the circulation of the books in Spanish America, and, most lucidly, the distribution of grain in the Qing dynasty, all suggest that the distribution of resources and, in particular, the management of this process is probably the major reason why larger political entities, such as states or the Church, remained in their position of power. Rather than fostering group cohesion or demanding services, the distribution of resources mainly serves to maintain stability and thus seems to be an inherently consolidating force in society.

All these examples show that it is impossible to detach transfer from tapping: glass in the Amarna period only became a resource for vassal states because it featured as an asset in inter-monarchical gift exchanges; it is also impossible to detach the accumulation of land by the *ecclesia* from charity donations and their imposed clerical discourse. Although this might be contra-intuitive to the miner's or the tool-using artisan's take on resources, to look at merchants, clerics, collectors, donors and distributors reveals much more clearly, in our view, the significance of resources in societies.

V. Conclusion

Resources relate closely to social and historical change by consolidating given hierarchies or by fostering change. As discussed above, resource regimes could sustain and invigorate the stability of a group, an institution or even a society. In other contexts, however, the identification, codification or recognition of new resources induced periods of crisis or instability. This might occur intentionally when certain groups tap or introduce new resources in order to trigger change, but it may also take place unintentionally. Moreover, the notions of limits and the patterns of transfer or circulation are particularly relevant in this context, since they set the framework wherein to situate resources in relation to change. Finally, change could have been triggered by the symbolic dimension of resources.

All these questions have to be answered specifically according to each case, and, as has been pointed out by Charles Tilly,[92] it is an almost impossible task to aim for theories of general social change. What, then, do we attempt to achieve with these conceptual considerations on resources? The bottom line was to sketch a perspective in broad strokes which is not reductive to economic reasoning. As has been emphasised by a previous chapter in this volume, thinking about resources in the humanities is closely tied to the rising dominance of economics. One feature of such a model is methodological individualism, which is imposed as a norm on rationality as such. However, we contend that this type of analysis sacrifices many important dimensions of historical complexity, and we therefore stress that resources are always embedded in social settings, that is to say, power, discourses and symbols, among other factors, all serve to counterbalance methodological individualism. But we risk throwing the baby out with the bathwater if we do not retain some aspects of instrumental rationality. It was Pierre Bourdieu, in particular, who stressed the importance of strategical thinking in relation to symbols and culture, and some of his insights should be retained,[93] but there is more than strategy to the handling of resources. Even though we propose a cultural and social perspective on resources, this should not lead to the discarding of the economic aspects of the phenomenon. Our essay has endeavoured to present arguments for a complementary vision.

Literature

Acosta Rodríguez, Antonio, and Adolfo González Rodríguez, Enriqueta Vila Vilar (eds.). (2003). *La Casa de la Contratación y la navegación entre España y las Indias*. Sevilla: Universidad de Sevilla.

Algazi, Gadi, and Valentin Groebner, Bernhard Jussen (eds.). (2003). *Negotiating the Gift: Pre-modern Figurations of Exchange*. Göttingen: Vandenhoeck & Ruprecht.

Aymard, Maurice (1990). Histoire et Comparaisons. In Hartmut Atsma and André Burguière (eds.). *Marc Bloch aujourd'hui. Histoire Comparée et Sciences Sociales*, 271–278. Paris: École des Hautes Études en Sciences Sociales.

---

[92] Tilly (1984), *Big Structures*.
[93] Bourdieu (1980), *Le Sens Pratique*; Bourdieu (1977), *Outline of a Theory of Practice*.

Barag, Dan (1985). *Catalogue of Western Asiatic Glass in the British Museum*, vol. 1. London: British Museum Publications Ltd.

Bartlett, Beatrice S. (1994). *Monarchs and Ministers the Grand Council in Mid-Ching China, 1723–1820*. Berkeley: University of California Press.

Baucells i Reig, Josep, and Ángel Fabrega i Grau, Manuel Riu i Riu, Josep Hernando i Delgado, Carme Battle i Gallart (eds.). (2006). *Diplomatari de l'Arxiu Capitular de la Catedral de Barcelona—Segle XI*, vol. 3. Barcelona: Fundació Noguera.

Bernard, Auguste and Alexandre Bruel (eds.). (1876–1903). *Recueil des chartes de l'abbaye de Cluny*. 6 volumes. Paris: Imprimerie Nationales.

Bourdieu, Pierre (1977). *Outline of a Theory of Practice*. Cambridge: Cambridge University Press.

— (1980). *Le Sens Pratique*. Paris: Éditions de Minuit.

— (1997). Marginalia: Some Additional Notes on the Gift. In Allan D. Schrift (ed.). *The Logic of the Gift: Toward an Ethic of Generosity*, 231–241. New York: Routledge.

Calame, Claude (2002). Interprétation et traduction des cultures. Les catégories de la pensée et du discours anthropologique. *L'Homme*, 163, 51–78.

Calvo, Hortensia (2003). The Politics of Print: The Historiography of the Book in Early Spanish America. *Book History*, 6, 277–305.

Cameron, Averil (1978). The Theotokos in sixth-century Constantinople: A City Finds its Symbol. *Journal of Theological Studies*, 29, 79–108.

— (1979). Images of Authority. Elites and Icons in Late Sixth-Century Byzantium. *Past and Present*, 84, 3–35.

Carlà, Filippo (2014). Exchange and the Saints. Gift-Giving and the Commerce of Relics. In Filippo Carlà, Maja Gori (eds.). *Gift Giving and the "Embedded" Economy in the Ancient World*, 403–437. Heidelberg: Winter.

Cochavi-Rainey, Zipora, and Christine Lilyquist (1999). Royal Gifts in the Late Bronze Age Fourteenth to Thirteenth Centuries B.C.E.: Selected Texts Recording Gifts to Royal Personages. Beer-Sheva: Ben-Gurion University Press.

Cohen, Raymond, and Raymond Westbrook (2000). *Amarna Diplomacy: The Beginnings of International Relations*. Baltimore MD: Johns Hopkins University Press

Danwerth, Otto (2017). La circulación de literatura normativa pragmática en Hispanoamérica (siglos XVI-XVII). In Thomas Duve (ed.). *Actas del XIX Congreso del Instituto Internacional de Historia del Derecho Indiano: Berlin 2016*, vol. I, 359–400. Madrid: Dykinson.

Davies, Wendy, and Paul Fouracre (2010). *The Languages of Gift in the Early Middle Ages*. Cambridge: Cambridge University Press.

Descola, Philippe (1994). *In the Society of Nature: A Native Ecology in Amazonia*. Cambridge: Cambridge University Press.

Detienne, Marcel (2008). *Comparing the Incomparable*. (Translation of *Comparer l'incomparable*, Paris 2000). Stanford CA: Stanford University Press.

Diamond, Jared (1997). *Guns, Germs, and Steel: The Fates of Human Societies.* New York: W.W. Norton & Company.
Diplomata Belgica (2015). *The Diplomatic Sources from the Medieval Southern Low Countries.* Eds. Thérèse de Hemptinne, Jeroen Deploige, Jean-Louis Kupper, and Walter Prevenier. Brussels: Royal Historical Commission URL: http://www.diplomata-belgica.be
Dobschütz, Ernst von (1899). *Christusbilder: Untersuchungen zur christlichen Legende.* Leipzig: J.C. Hinrichs.
Doniol, M. Henry (ed.). (1864). *Cartulaire de Sauxillanges.* Clermont-Ferrand, Paris: L'Académie des Sciences, Belles-Lettres & Arts de Clermont-Ferrand.
Dunstan, Helen (2006). *State or Merchant? Political Economy and Political Process in 1740s China.* Cambridge: Harvard University Press.
Duve, Thomas (ed.). (2014). *Entanglements in Legal History: Conceptual Approaches.* Frankfurt/M.: Max-Planck-Institut für europäische Rechtsgeschichte.
Edgerton-Tarpley, Kathryn (2008). *Tears from Iron: Cultural Responses to Famine in Nineteenth-century China.* Berkeley: University of California Press.
Escobar, Arturo (1996). Constructing Nature: Elements for a Postmodern Political Ecology. In Richard Peet and Michael Watts (eds.). *Liberation Ecologies: Environment, Development and Social Movements,* 46–68. London: Routledge.
Espagne, Michel (1994). Sur les limites du comparatisme en histoire culturelle. *Genèses. Sciences sociales et histoire,* 17, 112–121.
Evagrius Scholasticus (2007). *Historia ecclesiastica—Kirchengeschichte.* (Fontes Christiani 57). Ed. Adelheid Hübner. 2 volumes. Brepols: Turnhout.
Fowden, Elizabeth Key (1999). *The Barbarian Plane: Saint Sergius between Rome and Iran.* Berkeley CA: University of California Press.
Frank, Andre Gunder, and Barry K. Gills (eds.). (1996). *The World System: Five Hundred Years or Five Thousand?* London/New York: Routledge.
García-Baquero, Antonio (1992). *La Carrera de Indias: Suma de contratación y océano de negocios.* Sevilla: Algaida.
Giraud, Olivier (2012). Les défis de la comparaison à l'âge de la globalisation: pour une approche centrée sur les cas les plus différents inspirée de Clifford Geertz. *Critique internationale,* 57, 89–110.
Godelier, Maurice (1986). *The Mental and the Material: Thought Economy and Society.* London/New York: Verso Books.
— (1999). *The Enigma of the Gift.* Chicago IL: University of Chicago Press.
Goldhill, Simon, and Robin Osborne (1994). *Art and Text in Greek Culture.* Cambridge: Cambridge University Press.
González Sánchez, Carlos Alberto (2011). *New World Literacy: Writing and Culture Across the Atlantic, 1500–1700.* Lewisburg PA: Bucknell University Press.
Gregory, Chris A. (1982). *Gifts and Commodities.* London/New York: Academic Press.

Guibovich Pérez, Pedro (2001). The Printing Press in Colonial Peru: Production Process and Literary Categories in Lima, 1584–1699. *Colonial Latin American Review*, 10, 167–188.

— (2010). Los libros de los doctrineros en el virreinato del Perú, siglos XVI-XVII. In Wulf Oesterreicher and Roland Schmidt-Riese (eds.). *Esplendores y miserias de la evangelización de América. Antecedentes europeos y alteridad indígena*, 97–132. Berlin: Walter de Gruyter.

Guyot-Bachy, Isabelle, and Jean-Marie Moeglin (eds.). (2015). La Naissance de la médiévistique. Les historiens et leurs sources en Europe (XIXᵉ-début du XXᵉ siècle). Genève: Droz.

Haldon, John F. (1997). *Byzantium in the Seventh Century*. Cambridge: Cambridge University Press.

Hampe Martínez, Teodoro (1996). Bibliotecas privadas en el mundo colonial: la difusión de libros e ideas en el virreinato del Perú (siglos XVI-XVII). Frankfurt/M./Madrid: Vervuert, Iberoamericana.

Hao Ping (2012). Ding wu qihuang: Guangxu chunian Shanxi zaihuang yu jiuji yanjiu. Beijing: Beijing daxue chubanshe.

Harari, Yuval Noah (2011). *Sapiens: A Brief History of Humankind*. New York: Harper.

Hardenberg, Roland (2016). Beyond Economy and Religion. Resources and Sociocosmic Fields in Odisha, India. *Religion and Society: Advances in Research*, 7, 83–96.

Hardenberg, Roland, and Martin Bartelheim, Joern Staecker (2017). The 'Resource Turn': A Sociocultural Perspective on Resources. In Anke K. Scholz, Martin Bartelheim, Roland Hardenberg, Jörn A. Staecker (eds.). *Resource Cultures: Sociocultural Dynamics and the Use of Resources—Theories, Methods, Perspectives*, 13–24. Tübingen: Eberhard-Karls-Universität Tübingen.

He Hanwei (1983). *Guangxu chunian* (1876–79) *Huabei de da hanzai*. Hong Kong: Zhongwen daxue chubanshe.

Henderson, Julian (2013). *Ancient Glass: An Interdisciplinary Exploration*. Cambridge: Cambridge University Press.

Heritier-Augé, Francoise, and Elizabeth Copet-Rougier (1995). *La parenté spirituelle*. Paris: Editions des archives contemporaines (Ordres sociaux).

Jiménez, Norah Edith (2007). Los libros en lenguas indígenas como un género de las imprentas novohispanas entre los siglos XVI y XVII. In Norah Edith Jiménez and Martina Mantilla Trolle (eds.). *Colección de Lenguas Indígenas*, 65–117. Guadalajara: Universidad de Guadalajara, El Colegio de Michoacán.

Johnson, Christopher H., and Bernhard Jussen, David Warren Sabean, Simon Teuscher (eds.). (2013). *Blood and Kinship: Matter for Metaphor from Ancient Rome to the Present*. New York: Berghahn Books.

Jones, Christopher P. (1978). *The Roman World of Dio Chrysostom*. Cambridge MA: Harvard University Press.

Jussen, Bernhard (1991). Patenschaft und Adoption im frühen Mittelalter. Künstliche Verwandtschaft als soziale Praxis. Göttingen: Vandenhoeck & Ruprecht.

Jussen, Bernhard (2000). Spiritual Kinship as Social Practice: Godparenthood and Adoption in the Early Middle Ages. Newark: University of Delaware Press.

Kaelble, Hartmut (1999). Der historische Vergleich: eine Einführung zum 19. und 20. Jahrhundert. Frankfurt/M.: Campus.

Klein, Holger A. (2010). Himmlische Schätze, In Albrecht Weiland (ed.), *Münster Sonderheft 2010: Reliquien*, 371–381, Regensburg: Schnell & Steiner.

Kocka, Jürgen, and Marcel van der Linden (eds.). (2016). *Capitalism: The Reemergence of a Historical Concept*. London et al.: Bloomsbury.

Königliches Haus- und Staatsarchiv (ed.). (1849–1913). *Württembergisches Urkundenbuch*, 11 volumes. Stuttgart: Köhler.

Koselleck, Reinhart (2006). Begriffsgeschichten: Studien zur Semantik und Pragmatik der politischen und sozialen Sprache. Frankfurt/M.: Suhrkamp.

Lee, Alan Douglas (2007). *War in Late Antiquity: A Social History*. Malden: Blackwell.

Leonard, Irving Albert (1992). Books of the Brave. Being an Account of Books and of Men in the Spanish Conquest and Settlement of the Sixteenth-century New World. Berkeley CA: University of California Press.

Lévi-Strauss, Claude (1964–1971). *Mythologiques*. Chicago IL: University Chicago Press.

Liverani, Mario (1990). Prestige and Interest: International Relations in the Near East, ca. 1600–1100 B.C. (History of the Ancient Near East. Studies 1). Padua: Sargon.

Magnani, Eliana (ed.). (2007). *Don et Sciences Sociales. Théories et pratiques croisées*. Dijon: Presses Universitaires de Dijon.

— (2010). Un Trésor Dans Le Ciel. De la pastorale de l'aumône aux trésors spirituels (IVᵉ-IXᵉ siècle). In Lucas Burkart, Philippe Cordez, Pierre Alain Mariaux, and Yann Potin (eds.), *Le trésor au Moyen Âge: discours, pratiques et objets*, 51–68. Firenze: SISMEL-Edizioni del Galluzo.

Mathieu, Jon, and David W. Sabean, Simon Teuscher (eds.). (2007). *Kinship in Europe: Approaches to Long-term Development (1300–1900)*. New York, Oxford: Berghahn Books.

Meier, Mischa (2009). Der christliche Kaiser zieht (nicht) in den Krieg: "Religionskriege" in der Spätantike? In Andreas Holzem (ed.), *Krieg und Christentum. Religiöse Gewalttheorien in der Kriegserfahrung des Westens*, 254–278. Paderborn: Ferdinand Schöningh.

Metzger, Thomas A. (1973). The Internal Organization of Ch'ing Bureaucracy Legal, Normative, and Communication Aspects. Cambridge MA: Harvard University Press.

Moorey, Peter Roger Stuart (1994). Ancient Mesopotamian Materials and Industries: The Archaeological Evidence. Oxford: Clarendon Press.

Mynářová, Jana (2012). From the Mountain or from the Kiln? In Gregorio del Olmo Lete (ed.). *The Perfumes of Seven Tamarisks: Studies in Honour of Wilfred G. E. Watson* (Alter Orient und Altes Testament 394), 63–70. Münster: Ugarit-Verlag.

Oppenheim, Adolf Leo (1973). Towards a History of Glass in the Ancient Near East. *Journal of the American Oriental Society*, 93:3, 259–266.

Oppenheim, Adolf Leo, and Robert H. Brill, Dan Barag, Axel von Saldern (1970). Glass and Glassmaking in Ancient Mesopotamia: An Edition of the Cuneiform Texts, which Contain Instructions for Glassmakers; With a Catalogue of Surviving Objects (The Corning Museum of Glass Monographs 3). Reprinted in 1988. Corning: The Corning Museum of Glass.

Osterhammel, Jürgen (2001). Geschichtswissenschaft jenseits des Nationalstaats. Studien zu Beziehungsgeschichte und Zivilisationsvergleich. Göttingen: Vandenhoeck & Ruprecht.

Perreaux, Nicolas (2015). L'écriture du monde (I). Les chartes et les édifices comme vecteurs de la dynamique sociale dans l'Europe médiévale (VIIe-milieu du XIVe siècle). *Bulletin du Centre médiéval d'Auxerre*, 19:2. URL: http://journals.openedition.org/cem/14264.

Perreaux, Nicolas (2015). Des structures inconciliables? Cartographie comparée des chartes et des édifices "romans" (Xe-XIIIe siècles). In Marie-José Gasse-Grandjean, Laure Saligny (eds.). *Géolocalisation et sources anciennes? Actes des journées d'études de Dijon, Maison des Sciences de l'Homme, 13–14 novembre 2014*, Hors-série du *Bulletin du Centre médiéval d'Auxerre* no 9 URL: http://journals.openedition.org/cem/13817.

Pfister, Friedrich (1912). *Der Reliquienkult im Altertum*. Zweiter Halbband: *Die Reliquie als Kultobjekt*. Gießen: Verlag von Alfred Töpelmann.

Polanyi, Karl (1944). *The Great Transformation: The Political and Economic Origins of our Time*. New York: Farrar & Rinehart/Boston: Beacon Press.

Qu Tongzu (1969). *Local Government in China under the Ch'ing*. Stanford CA: Stanford University Press.

Quadflieg, Dirk (2014). Tauschen und Geben. In Stefanie Samida, Manfred K. H. Eggert, and Hans Peter Hahn (eds.). *Handbuch materielle Kultur: Bedeutungen, Konzepte, Disziplinen*, 117–124. Stuttgart: Metzler.

Rainey, Anson F. (2015). The El-Amarna Correspondence: A New Edition of the Cuneiform Letters from the Site of El-Amarna Based on Collations of All Extant Tablets. In William M. Schniedewind, Zipora Cochavi-Rainey (eds.). Handbuch der Orientalistik, Section 1, vol. 110. Leiden: Brill.

Randeria, Shalini (2006). Entangled History of Uneven Modernities: Civil Society, Caste Solidarities and Legal Pluralism in Post-Colonial India. In Yehuda Elkana, Ivan Krastev, Elísio Macamo, Shalini Randeria (eds.), *Unraveling Ties: From Social Cohesion to New Practices of Connectedness*, 284–311. Frankfurt/M.: Campus.

Recopilación de leyes de los reynos de las Indias (1681). 4 volumes. Madrid: Iulian de Paredes.

Rist, Josef (2014). Das Bild von Kamuliana und seine Bedeutung für das Frühe Byzanz. In Karlheinz Dietz, Christian Hannick, Carolina Lutzka, and Elisabeth Maier (eds.). *Das Christusbild: Zu Herkunft und Entwicklung in Ost und West*, 135–155. Würzburg: Echter.

Robson, Eleanor (2001). Society and Technology in the Late Bronze Age: A Guided Tour of the Cuneiform Sources. In Andrew J. Shortland. *The Social Context of Technological Change: Egypt and the Near East, 1650–1550 BC. Proceedings of a Conference Held at St. Edmund Hall, Oxford, 12–14 September, 2000*, 39–58. Oxford: Oxbow Books.

Rueda Ramírez, Pedro (2005). Negocio e intercambio cultural: El comercio de libros con América en la Carrera de Indias (siglo XVII). Sevilla: Universidad de Sevilla.

Said, Edward W. (1978). *Orientalism. Western Conceptions of the Orient*. London: Routledge & Kegan.

Saldern, Axel von (2004). *Antikes Glas* (Handbuch der Archäologie). Munich: C.H. Beck.

Schrift, Allan D. (1997). *The Logic of the Gift: Toward an Ethic of Generosity*. New York: Routledge.

Schuster-Brandis, Anais (2008). Steine als Schutz- und Heilmittel: Untersuchung zu ihrer Verwendung in der Beschwörungskunst Mesopotamiens im 1. Jt. v. Chr. (Alter Orient und Altes Testament 46). Münster: Ugarit.

Shannon, Thomas R. (1989). *An Introduction to the World-system Perspective*. Boulder CO: Westview Press.

Shortland, Andrew (2012). *Lapis Lazuli from the Kiln: Glass and Glassmaking in the Late Bronze Age* (Studies in Archaeological Sciences 2). Leuven: Leuven University Press.

Siegrist, Hannes (2006). Comparative History of Cultures and Societies. From Cross-societal Analysis to the Study of Intercultural Interdependencies. *Comparative Education*, 42:3, 377–404.

Simocatta, Theophylactus (1887), *Historiae*. Ed. Carl de Boor. Leipzig: Teubner.

Subrahmanyan, Sanjay (1997). Connected Histories: Notes Towards a Reconfiguration of Early Modern Eurasia. *Modern Asian Studies*, 31:3, 735–762.

Sun Nianqu 孫念劬 (1800). *Quanten juyue* 全人矩矱.

Testart, Alain (1993). Des Dons et des Dieux: Anthropologie religieuse et sociologie comparative. Paris: Armand Colin.

Testart, Alain (2007). Critique du Don: études sur la circulation non marchande. Paris: Syllepse.

Thesaurus diplomaticus (1997). Eds. by Paul Tombeur, Walter Prevenier, Philippe Demonty, Marie-Paul Laviolette. Turnhout: Brepols.

Tilly, Charles (1984). *Big Structures, Large Processes, Huge Comparisons*. New York: Russell Sage Foundation.

Tu Long (2010 [1690]). Huangzheng kao. In Li Wenhai, Xia Mingfang, and Zhu Hu (eds.). *Zhongguo huangzhengshu jicheng*, vol. 1, 103–114. Tianjin: Guji chubanshe.

Veitia Linage, Joseph de (1672). *Norte de la Contratación de las Indias Occidentales*. Sevilla: Iuan Francisco de Blas.

Wallerstein, Immanuel (1974–2011). *The Modern World-System.* 4 vols., New York, London: Academic Press.
Wehling, Peter (2007). Wissensregime. In Rainer Schützeichel (ed.). *Handbuch Wissenssoziologie und Wissensforschung,* 704–712. Konstanz: UVK Verlagsgesellschaft.
Wei Xi (17th century, 2010). *Jiuhuang ce.* In Li Wenhai, Xia Mingfang, Zhu Hu (eds.). *Zhongguo huangzhengshu jicheng,* vol. 1, 927–934, Tianjin: Guji chubanshe.
Werner, Michael, and Bénédicte Zimmermann (2006). Beyond Comparison: Histoire croisée and the challenge of reflexivity. *History and Theory,* 45, 30–50.
Will, Pierre-Etienne (1990). *Bureaucracy and Famine in Eighteenth-Century China.* Stanford: Stanford University Press.
Will, Pierre-Etienne, and Roy Bin Wong (1991). *Nourish the People: The State Civilian Granary System in China, 1650–1850.* Ann Arbor: Center for Chinese Studies, University of Michigan.
Wood, Ian (2013). *The Modern Origins of the Early Middle Ages.* Oxford: Oxford University Press.
Wu, Silas (1969). *Communication and imperial control in China.* Hong Kong: Hong Kong University Press.
Young, Oran R. (1982). *Resource Regimes. Natural Resources and Social Institutions.* Berkeley CA: University of California Press.
Zhu Xi (2010). *Zhuzi quanshu.* Zhu Jieren, Yan Zuozhi Liu Yongxiang (eds). Shanghai: Huadong daxue chubanshe.
Zhu Xi (2011). *Sishu zhangju jizhu.* Zhonghua shuju (ed.). Beijing: Zhonghua shuju.

Chapter 8
Power and Resource Regimes: A Study of the Impact of Social Relationships on the Function of Resources

Anna Dorofeeva and Alexander Krey
in collaboration with Nadine Eikelschulte, Lukas Jäger, Melina Kalfelis, Sebastian Riebold, Carla Thiel, and Marco Toste

I. Introduction

Any discussion of discourses of weakness and resource regimes—the key concepts of the Collaborative Research Center 1095 (CRC 1095)—must eventually confront questions related to power. This is simply because power, in all its practical and theoretical nuances, is at the heart of the issues that the CRC 1095 aims to investigate. The building and maintenance of discourses and regimes, of whatever sort, ultimately depends on the balance or imbalance of power. The interaction of these complex structures and ideas over time has barely begun to be explored. The aim of this chapter is to investigate the relationship between power and resource regimes. Firstly, it provides an overview and conceptualisation of the CRC's key terms, "resources" and "regimes", in relation to power, as well as an exploration of "power" as a historical, sociological and anthropological concept; and secondly, it explores the structures identified in the first section of this chapter as the drivers of transformation, using case-studies from the projects and general areas of expertise of those individual researchers who participated in the CRC 1095 working group on power. Throughout, the focus of the analysis is on the effects of power on the rule-based processes that arise from the use of resources by social groups. From this investigation, this chapter distils several key functions of power within resource regimes and assesses the implications of this new conceptual approach for future research.

This chapter does not attempt to arrive at a universal and binding definition of any of the key terms noted above, nor to explain the phenomenon of power in all its manifestations. Rather, it is a study of the tripartite social systems arising from discourses of weakness, resource regimes, and power. In particular, it is intended as an exploration of the effects of the presence and practice of power within these systems. As such, this chapter is the first of two consecutive chapters in this volume that examine power as a phenomenon by using case-studies: here, the authors examine resource regimes as social structures in which power is more or less balanced, using historical examples; while chapter nine, by David Rex Galindo, Melina Kalfelis and José Luis Paz Nomey, uses empirical examples to tackle the concept of agency in relation to power and resources. Its aim is to explore where power is created, taking, as its premise, that agency serves as a bridge between resources and resource regimes, as well as a means of understanding the power interface between the two. Chapters eight and nine are therefore separate but complementary studies of power from two key conceptual viewpoints.

II. The Theoretical Foundations of the CRC 1095: Resources, Regimes, and Historical Formations

Both resource regimes and discourses of weakness are relatively little-studied historical concepts whose scholarly applications have not yet been fully explored. Their component terms may easily be separated and understood. Resources and regimes, as well as discourses and weakness, can each be individually defined and used in the social sciences. Each of these terms possesses its own historiography. The strength of the CRC 1095 lies in the particular combination of these concepts, which enables it to focus not only on weakness, but also on the discourses that arise about weakness; and not on resources in isolation, but rather on the ways in which they are treated.

This chapter sets aside discourses of weakness,[1] which are discussed in chapters 1 to 4 of this volume, in order to focus on resource regimes. The below conceptual modelling of resource regimes is based upon the preliminary empirical results of eight projects conducted by CRC researchers, and is used as a means to examine the function of power in human networks.

---

1 On the concept, see Cordes et al. (2016), *Schwächediskurse und Ressourcenregime*, 170–177; Leppin et al. (2017), *Discourses of Weakness and Resource Regimes*, 48 f.

This framework makes it clear that resource regimes—that is, specific social arrangements that arise around attempts to control and apply resources—cannot be studied consistently and appropriately without taking power into account. This chapter does not aim to develop a full-scale theoretical paradigm by conceptualising power as a component of resource regimes,[2] but rather to sharpen our understanding of the key terms, and to suggest the potential for a new historical perspective on social structures by exploring them through a range of case studies.

1. Resources

The term "resources" is both commonplace and has a complex history grounded in economics. What precisely constitutes a "resource" in our current understanding is, however, difficult to define clearly. Certain key elements nevertheless become apparent when the term "resource(s)" is considered as a research tool, and when its features are extrapolated from their historical and social context. In doing this below, we do not aim for an abstract categorisation of resources. In his social model, for example, Anthony Giddens saw resources as structural elements,[3] classifying them as authoritative and allocative resources based on formal distinctions such as the distinction between material and immaterial resources.[4] This can be a very fruitful means of understanding societies, but is less useful for obtaining a clearer perspective on resources as such. For this reason, we have elected to follow a different path: namely, to draw the features of resources from situational studies. The following five defining elements of resources examine them within this empirical context, and are used, together with the discussion of regimes in Section II.2, as the practical foundation for the study of power in the second half of this chapter.

a. "Resource(s)" is a word that is used in everyday, business, and political speech, and it carries a range of connotations and related concepts ("resource curse", "scarcity of resources", "resource conservation" and "resource management", to name a few). As Daniel Hausmann and Nicolas Perreaux have discussed in chapter 5, the term itself has a long history

---

[2] On the concept, see Cordes et al. (2016), *Schwächediskurse und Ressourcenregime*, 177–192; Leppin et al. (2017), *Discourses of Weakness and Resource Regimes*, 48 f.
[3] Giddens (1984), *Constitution of Society*, 17.
[4] Giddens (1984), *Constitution of Society*, passim.

and is deeply problematical. It must, therefore, be defined before it can be properly applied here. This definition does not depend on whether or not past societies knew the term, but, as noted above, is a modern research tool that can be used to describe both past and current resource-related phenomena. Finally, in the context of the CRC 1095, resources (as well as regimes) are used to describe and analyse historical transformation. The term "resources" therefore points to the specific problem of discursively framed operational processes that can be examined structurally outside their particular historical context, though they take their features from this context.

b. Nothing is, *per se*, a resource. Resources are not an end in themselves, but are used by historical formations or by the actors within them in order to attain particular goals.[5] In this context, historical formations[6] are complex aggregates of regimes and actors, and, like the term "resources", are a conceptual research tool. A goal-oriented definition of resources is given by Wolfgang J. Koschnick, for example:

"Resources are [...] anything that a person or an organization uses in the course of his, her or its activities as a means of attaining some goal."[7]

We take this goal orientation further, however, by emphasising that goals may be defined within a historical formation and in a multiplicity of ways, rather than simply by persons or organisations. Two extremes of a scale can be used to represent this. On one end of the scale are societies that define their aims and negotiate resources in participative processes. On the other end of the scale are single actors that define goals and resources on behalf of the whole society or historical formation. A vivid example of this is Mao Zedong's Great Leap Forward, in which Mao almost singlehandedly made steel into an important resource by linking this material to the aim of industrialising China at any cost.[8] As a result, thousands of backyard furnaces were set up all over the country in 1958, and the population was forced to make steel instead of working in the fields. This fundamental revolution in an agrarian resource regime led to a catastrophic famine. However, it should be noted that, although Mao had autocratic power,

---

5 See Leppin et al. (2017), *Discourses of Weakness and Resource Regimes*, 47.
6 On the concept see Leppin et al. (2017), *Discourses of Weakness and Resource Regimes*, 46.
7 Koschnick (1993), *Resource*, 1312.
8 While Mao played a decisive role in the Great Leap Forward, the development strategy that underpinned it was not his sole invention.

there were discourses—for instance, among the members of the Central Politburo of the Communist Party—upon which his goal-setting was based, and which later led to amendments to, and the premature end of, the Great Leap Forward.[9] Although Mao was a single actor who deeply influenced his entire society, he did not and could not act in perfect isolation from social norms and discourses. Further empirical study could lead to a systematisation of this goal-setting process by working out in greater detail how exactly a resource is defined as a resource through combination with a goal (the discourses about resources are a separate question, as they are intricately interrelated, and are themselves usually contested), what sort of resources arise, which specific resources are not used and why, which trials and errors are associated with this process, which power struggles and bodies of knowledge play a role in it, and so on.

If we consider goals as the intended outcomes of action, we can further say that resources are the potential instruments of action. We can take sand as an example of this. Sand, in a wide variety of mineral compositions, is available all over the world in huge quantities. Yet sand, as such, is not a resource. This is the case even though sand is specifically associated with beaches, and human beings use beaches with the aim of bolstering physical and mental health. These aims are pursued at an individual level, but may also be traced to a societal or cultural level, in that the "beach" and the "coast" were discovered for social purposes at certain times and in particular places (rather than simply as *loci* from which one can access the fish in the sea, for example).[10] Our modelling is therefore particularly oriented towards the historical study of human society. In this context, however, what matters for determining beaches or coasts as resources is, above all, their location and climate. Sand remains passive—a "something", a "substance". However, the working of sand, so as to create artificial beaches, fill sandboxes or make glass,[11] is associated with a shift in our perception of it. When sand is purposefully removed, made transportable and put onto the market, it is thereby activated or appropriated, becoming a resource.[12] The actual use to which it is put is of secondary importance.

---

9 On the full historical context, see, for example, Dikötter (2010), *Mao's Great Famine*; Jisheng (2012), *Grabstein*; Wemheuer (2007), *Steinnudeln*.
10 See, for example, Corbin (1988), *Le Territoire du vide*.
11 Example taken from the work of Teresa Dittmer for the project "The Knowledgeable as a Resource in pharaonic Egypt and in Mesopotamia", led by Annette Imhausen.
12 In some contexts, the sand then ceases to be sand: the mineral composition is relevant for making glass, but not for artificial beaches, for example.

Human actors can process sand in order to sell it, but they can also fail to understand the market and so fail to sell the sand. Nevertheless, their appropriation of sand makes it into a resource.

Of course, historical formations, human actors or groups of human actors can also define resources in relation to goals that lie outside economic contexts. For example, from the tenth century onwards, ritualised forms of "punishment" or "humiliation" of saints were used in some Western monasteries to "penalise" relics or statues of saints for having "permitted" specific kinds of harm that it was their function to prevent. Outside the monastery walls, the custom was for the people to show violence towards the statues of those saints that had failed to fulfil their functions, by hitting or dismembering them.[13] The reverse custom has also been observed in China. River gods have, for a long time, been worshipped by people all along the Yellow River. From at least the middle of the nineteenth century, when a dyke is recorded as having broken, people prayed to these gods for help with repairs to water-related structures, and offered them rewards if the repairs were successful.[14] For our purposes, both the saints worshipped in medieval Europe through relics and statues, and the Chinese river gods, can be understood as resources. Worship of these saints and gods was clearly goal-oriented in that they were intended to avert specific dangers, as is evident in their punishment or reward. These examples also show that goal definition is regularly, though not necessarily always, linked to a particular kind of weakness that is taken seriously and from which a variety of discourses of weakness arise. From this regular link between goal definition and discourses of weakness, it follows that the goals must pass a certain boundary of relevance before they can "identify" a resource. This boundary, in turn, makes it possible to exclude single occurrences from our theoretical modelling. From a historical perspective, we consider this boundary to be a conceptual tool, rather than an empirical phenomenon. Further study of the boundary is required in order to determine its characteristics. The idea is that the goal becomes more than simply a causal link between events. Just because an individual who has lost his or her keys uses a tool to open their house door instead, does not automatically make the tool become a resource for opening house doors.

---

13 On the humiliation and punishment of saints, see, for example, Geary (1983), *Humiliation of Saints*, 123–140; Palazzo (2000), *La Liturgie dans la société médiévale*, 184–186.
14 Amelung (2000), *Der Gelbe Fluß in Shandong*, 314 f.

At the level of historical formations, we are faced with the problem that potential goals are often very open, more so than at the level of individual actors or resource regimes. Yet, they are not completely limitless. For example, the slogan "make the country rich and strong" was widely disseminated and recognised in China *circa* 1900. However, the strategies for implementing it were very diverse and the actors involved could work in opposition to each other. Some groups advocated for national defence and military infrastructure, others stressed the primacy of economic reforms, and others saw the "renovation" of China's intellectual heritage as the key to the country's survival.[15] The ubiquity of a certain rhetorical trope is thus not a sufficient criterion for identifying one of the "goals" of a historical formation. To "make the country rich and strong" becomes a goal only when it is tied to concrete options from which actors can choose. Otherwise, it has to be regarded simply as a slogan (although a powerfully endorsed one, in this instance).

In sum, we consider goal definition to be the key defining characteristic of a resource. Appropriation, as discussed above, is taken to be part of goal definition, as appropriation is always carried out with a goal in mind. Appropriation, as we define it, is more than the natural will to possess ("*Besitzbegründungswille*"). A person can, for example, have the natural will to possess an object such as a ball or a book, but may be unable to appropriate it. Human beings can also possess things with an indeterminate future function or for their sentimental value. In such cases, there is also no appropriation because there is no connected goal. Appropriation must have an aim, as in the sand example above. We must, however, also consider that resources can be limited or controlled. This is a concern for historical formations which seek to limit or control resources in order to attain their goals more efficiently. Equally, different resources may be differently rele-

---

15 Example taken from the work of Sebastian Riebold for the project "Visions of national weakness in the late 19th and the first half of the 20th century", led by Iwo Amelung. On the various ways in which social Darwinist imagery was used to support widely diverging political views, see Pusey (1983), *China and Charles Darwin*, 179–433. Margherita Zanasis, in her study on Chinese "economic modernity", makes the same observation for the 1930s: Wang Jingwei and Jiang Jieshi (Chiang Kai-shek), leading figures of the Chinese Nationalist Party (KMT), employed strikingly similar language (they both invoked the spectre of "national perdition" and referred to the ideology of their predecessor Sun Yat-sen, for example), but differed drastically in their vision for China's "salvation", with the former favouring economic reforms and the latter popular militarisation. See Zanasi (2006), *Saving the Nation*, 12–20, 25–51.

vant. This inherent potential in resources to be controlled or limited can, in social contexts, result in actors or groups of actors progressively perceiving "limitation", "scarcity[16] of resources",[17] and, finally, "weakness".[18] The idea of limitation or weakness is therefore relational, in that it arises through discourses within specific social contexts, and further study is required to be able to describe it clearly. Society's access to resources can exceed—not necessarily objectively, and is, perhaps, simply perceived as exceeding—the actual resources available. Such perceptions of weakness are part of discourses of weakness. Strictly speaking, nothing, not even sand or air, is available in endless quantities on our planet; but, in social terms, it is the historical formations, and the human actors within them, that perceive or generate scarcity. Knowledge, for example, may—theoretically and independently of its bearer—be available without limit, but is, in every practical case, both limited and limitable. The bearers of knowledge, be they "human resources" or man-made data carriers, are important, for it is through them that knowledge is made accessible as well as limited by historical formations.

c. Resources are never merely material or merely intangible.[19] This is clearly reflected in the above example of the humiliation of saints. The statues or relics in this example are material, but both the religious beliefs and the goal definitions associated with them are intangible. Only when both of these material and intangible components are present do they form a resource. In the same way, animal bones can be a material resource, as they are (among other uses) utilised in the soap-making industry. But in the medieval imagination, such a bone can become an indirect contact relic when attached to a holy relic.[20] The animal bone becomes loaded with religious significance.[21] As another goal is defined, so a new resource is created from a combination of tangible and intangible components. However, even knowledge, which seems at first glance to be intangible, is hardly ever, if at all, made into a resource without material data carriers, which

---

16 There exists a wide range of sociocultural research on this subject; see, for example, Tauschek et al. (2015), *Knappheit, Mangel, Überfluss*.
17 Leppin et al. (2017), *Discourses of Weakness and Resource Regimes*, 47, and Luhmann (1988), *Die Wirtschaft der Gesellschaft*, 178.
18 Leppin et al. (2017), *Discourses of Weakness and Resource Regimes*, 46.
19 See Leppin et al. (2017), *Discourses of Weakness and Resource Regimes*, 51 f., and chapter 5 by Nicolas Perreaux and Daniel Hausmann in this volume.
20 See the reference book on relics, Angenendt (1997), *Heilige und Reliquien*.
21 See, especially on the material aspect, Röckelein (2015), *Mittelalterliche Sakralobjekte*.

encompass a very wide range of materials—from bones and bark to books and USB sticks—and can also include, in pre-modern societies, certain people able to pass on memorised knowledge. Equally, intangible knowledge plays an important role in resources that are, at first glance, purely material. In Hanseatic trade, sheep wool was an important commodity, exported from England to Flanders where it was processed. For this trade, knowledge of market conditions, consumer expectations and technical processes was essential.[22] What we understand to be a resource is, in the end, less a question of its tangibility or intangibility, but rather a result of complex discourses and practices in historical formations and their sub-systems. This is evident in the treatment of land as a resource.[23] Real estate seems at first to be a simple tangible resource. Yet the allocation and ownership of land is determined by legal systems which are much more strongly applicable to immovable than to movable goods; unlike the latter, immovable goods cannot normally be appropriated simply by picking them up, and the applicable legal systems are intangible and can be part of the norms that are the foundation of a resource regime. The identification of resources can therefore also be influenced by resource regimes. This demonstrates that a strict differentiation between tangible and intangible resources would result in an essentially meaningless distinction with little intellectual potential.

d. Resources can be recognised and defined as resources on different levels. Two basic levels of goal definition are discernible. The first of these is the level of historical formations or their sub-systems, which can identify resources both discursively and practically, in that a substance is associated with a goal. For example, coal and oil have been defined as resources at this level in the past. Both substances were available on the planet before the evolution of mankind, but, for a long time, they were not identified as resources and were therefore not relevant to society. It is, however, also clear that goal definition at the level of historical formations is generally represented by a set of possible goals, which are fed inductively into the process of goal definition. These possible goals are held in a kind of reser-

---

22 Example taken from Cordes et al. (2016), *Schwächediskurse und Ressourcenregime*, 69.
23 Land as a resource plays a role in the work of Nicolas Perreauxs project "From 'Weak' Kinship to Kinship as a Communicative Resource. Transformations of European Kinship in Medieval Resource Regimes" (led by Bernhard Jussen) and also in the work of Macario Lacbawans Jr. project "Political Organisations beyond the State" (led by Susanne Schröter).

voir, whose contents constantly change over time, and from which individual goals can be selected. Here, it does not matter whether the contents of this metaphorical reservoir are limitless or not: the important thing is that they change, constantly offering new possibilities which may or may not be converted into goals.

So, for instance, oil can not only be burned, but can also be used as a basic material in the chemical industry—for example, in the production of plastics. It is clear that resources can undergo a change in function. Goal definition, at historical formation level, is therefore, as a rule, broadly conceived, and can be said to represent a realm of possibilities. Resources are polyvalent. For historical formations, resources offer, first and foremost, possibilities that can be activated in practical situations—that is, possibilities that can be linked to specific goals. The crystallisation of possibilities at a practical level occurs through the agency of human actors. As a result of the identification of a goal, a substance becomes a resource, and the element is endowed with instrumental significance that draws its own specific value from this instrumentality. It is entirely possible that not all the potentials that are gathered in the reservoir of a historical formation are actually realised; instead, it is likely that only single possibilities are identified. New goals can also become visible over time. A resource is therefore a result of structured processes, and these can change from one time period to the next. Resources are discursively framed and anchored in concrete practices. The link created between a goal and a resource can, therefore, be observed through an analysis of the discourses and practices involved. Resources are generally not discussed in a vacuum, however, and it is here that resource regimes come into play (see Section II.2 below).

The second basic level for the definition of resources is the level of human actors. We may take an example of this from the late Hanseatic period. For Hanseatic trade, privileges were always extremely important. In 1603, a delegation of representatives from Lübeck and Stralsund travelled to the Russian court in Moscow. Their goal was to reinstate Hanseatic trading privileges with Russia. The representatives from Lübeck wore Russian-style clothing and drove in a sumptuously decorated carriage, whereas the representatives from Stralsund did not attempt to change their appearance. As a result, at the end of the negotiations, only the privileges of the representatives from Lübeck were reinstated.[24] Factors such as appearance,

---

[24] See Iwanow (2016), *Die Hanse im Zeichen der Krise*, 47–58.

and notions of rank and importance, are not, in themselves, a resource at historical formation level, because no goal is associated with them there. Nor do these factors offer a range of possibilities for historical formations. Instead, at this level, there is a whole set of beliefs, ideals and values—a categorical apparatus ("*Kategorialapparaturen*"), in the words of Karl Mannheim—that forms the core of a society, and was itself developed discursively. In this chapter, we call these beliefs, ideals and values, already well known in the social sciences under different names, "predetermined factors".[25] We are concerned here only with their possible pre-existing influence on resources, regimes and power, and the term used to describe them in this chapter is intended to reflect this. These factors, which are generally formed over a long period of time in historical formations, cannot, on the whole, be altered rapidly, are the result of social norms, and have the capacity to influence the future behaviour of human actors. Unlike the above example of Mao's Great Leap Forward, which rapidly imposed multiple new steel-based regimes on a single historical formation, pre-determined factors function within historical formations but across regimes. They are not codified in any formal way (and may not be codifiable at all) and are trans-individual, that is, shared among the members of the same class and often, but not always, across classes. Despite their relatively slow-changing nature, these pre-determined factors are also transferable between different historical formations and groups of actors in these formations. For example, in the early middle ages, Charlemagne deliberately adopted what he perceived to have been Ancient Roman culture. He built his palace and chapel at Aachen in a classicising style using, in part, old Roman carved masonry, and sent for Roman liturgical books in order to disseminate them across the churches of his empire. He invited scholars and musicians from Italy to teach monks Roman chants. At the Council of Frankfurt in 794 CE, he presented himself as a ruler in the late Roman imperial style. This well-documented cultural transference enabled Charlemagne to associate

---

25 Among such headings are, for example, the terms "mentality", "cognitive patterns" (Douglas), "hidden curriculum" (Dewey, among others), "habitus" (Bourdieu, Elias), "disposition" (Foucault) or simply "culture". These terms are far from synonymous. They have different connotations, function very differently in different models and point to different fields of inquiry. Nevertheless, they represent different facets of what we here call "predetermined factors". There seems to be a common ground between them: in the process of socialisation, people acquire certain behavioural and cognitive dispositions that are rooted so deeply in a given society that they appear to be ahistorical, "to have always been there"—*i. e.*, pre-determined.

himself with the legendary might of the Roman Empire, and to legitimise his rule as king through spiritual and cultural proximity to the seat of the Christian Church in Rome.[26] The transference of pre-determined factors (in this case, of Roman culture as perceived by the Carolingians) therefore carries with it a clear power dimension, which requires further study. It should also be noted, however, that the adoption of pre-determined factors by one society from another exerts its own influence upon those factors, changing them in the process of transference. What Charlemagne saw as "Roman" may not have been considered to be wholly Roman in Rome, whether ancient or contemporary. The *Hadrianum* sacramentary received in Carolingian Francia was an outdated, if recently augmented version, and did not represent a unified Roman liturgical practice. Despite these nuances, however, it is important to note that the transference of pre-determined factors does occur, and that it is one means by which one historical formation can influence another.

At the level of human actors, pre-determined factors can become resources when actors use them in specific situations for particular aims. In the above example of Hanseatic trade networks, the pre-determined factors "class-appropriate appearance" and "rank" were used as resources. Clothing and carriages were deliberately used by the Lübeck representatives in order to obtain the hoped-for privileges, and so these items became resources that were charged with pre-determined factors.

e. Some resources can substitute one another, which makes substitution a useful category of analysis for capturing resource dynamics. In the example of the Hanseatic privileges, had the nobles at the Russian court not been impressed by the appearance of the Lübeck representatives, the latter could have tried to bribe them. In other words, they might have replaced one set of resources (clothing, carriages, *etc.*) with another resource (precious metal). Gold is one of the resources that has already been identified as such at historical formation level with a range of possible goals, including payment. Although the Lübeck representatives attempted to obtain the sought–after privileges by emphasising their importance, gold remained a potential, albeit passive, resource. It played no role in this particular situation, but was nevertheless available and could have been activated by the

---

[26] Example taken from the work of Anna Dorofeeva, project "From 'Weak' Kinship to Kinship as a Communicative Resource. Transformations of European Kinship in Medieval Resource Regimes", led by Bernhard Jussen. See, also, McKitterick (2008), *Charlemagne*.

actors if they had so chosen. One or more of the possible goals associated with gold could then have been activated. In this, pre-determined identifiers play an important role, for the hypothetical example above can only work when the historical formation in which it occurs has integrated the idea of bribery.[27] Pre-determined factors can, therefore, not only be reformulated as resources, but can also influence the goal determination. This means that they can simultaneously function on different levels.

The ability to be substituted is, in this context, not an objective, natural phenomenon, but rather a means of understanding historical formations. Resources have a particular value that is expressed in their goal determination. Processes of exchange, conversion or functional equivalence are made possible based upon this value, but they are not essential. Such processes can be used as less effective resources, for example, in emergency situations. Relics or icons were able to function as substitutes for weapons in military conflicts under the Byzantine Emperor Justinian (*circa* 482–565 CE), when the empire did not have enough soldiers and weapons to protect those regions most distant from the centre. These religious resources did not, however, replace armed soldiers fully in the eyes of those living on the edges of the empire.[28] In the same way, it is possible to overcompensate. In the nineteenth century, indigo had significant economic value. Many thousand tonnes of indigo were exported from British-occupied India to Europe every year. In 1897, after years of research, the Badian Aniline and Soda Factory (BASF) learned to make synthetic indigo. Their product, which had numerous advantages such as accessibility, consistent quality and high quantity, was able to compete on the wider market. Both indigo types existed side-by-side for several decades. Because chemical production companies were able to offer their product more cheaply, Indian indigo farmers were finally forced to stop their production.[29] The syn-

---

27 See, especially, Groebner (2000), *Gefährliche Geschenke*. The archive of Wismar, for example, possesses a list of bribes given to the Danish king from 1599. He received a large silver jug, gilded both on the inside and outside, containing 200 Reichsthaler. He also received another gold-plated vessel filled with 415 Reichsthaler in various gold currencies; Jörn (2014), *Archivalien zu den Hansekontoren*, 114.
28 Example taken from the work of Christian Scheidler for the project "Sacral Objects as Military Resources in the Eastern Roman Empire from Justinian to Heraclius", led by Hartmut Leppin.
29 Example taken from the work of Carla Thiel for the project "The Use of Resources and Economic Calculation: Perception, Structures of Decisions and Practices of Adaption in the German Chemical Industry between 1860 and 1960", led by Werner Plumpe.

thetic indigo therefore had greater intrinsic value than the natural product which it replaced.

2. Regimes

Historical formations access and allocate resources through regimes, and both resources and resource regimes are therefore in an irresolvable relationship of dependency.[30] The concept of regimes is often used in political science in particular, where it is a complex cornerstone concept.[31] Stephan D. Krasner's definition is widely accepted, and defines regimes as:

"implicit or explicit principles, norms, rules, and decision-making procedures around which actors' expectations converge […]. Principles are beliefs of fact, causation, and rectitude. Norms are standards of behaviour defined in terms of rights and obligations. Rules are specific prescriptions or proscriptions for action. Decision-making procedures are prevailing practices for making and implementing collective choice."

Krasner particularly emphasises the rule-based foundation of this concept. Similarly, the CRC 1095 defines resource regimes as "norms and practices in distributing rights and opportunities to make use of resources".[32] Based upon this, it is possible to tease out the conceptual link between resources and regimes. Resource regimes can be characterised as follows:

a. New resource regimes are formed (whether they are formed spontaneously, or deliberately by actors, is still an open question) within historical formations in order to attain the specific goals for which their resources have been defined. In addition, existing resource regimes can be modified by actors, often in response to a perceived acute loss or weakness. This means that resource regimes change over time, and can originate around different resources than those with which they later become associated. Resource regimes, like resources themselves (and following Krasner's definition), are therefore goal-oriented, in that a specific aim is linked to norms and practices, which have no intrinsic purpose themselves but are deliber-

---

30 Cordes et al. (2016), *Schwächediskurse und Ressourcenregime*, 187.
31 See, with further references, Cordes et al. (2016), *Schwächediskurse und Ressourcenregime*, 185 f.
32 Leppin et al. (2017), *Discourses of Weakness and Resource Regimes*, 49. On the concept of resource regimes, see, also, Cordes et al. (2016), *Schwächediskurse und Ressourcenregime*, 177–192.

ately used by actors. The concept of resource regimes itself is a research tool that emphasises the rule-based aspect of society. Analytically, resource regimes must be distinguished from the groups of people who head various kinds of organisations or other social structures within the regimes; resource regimes cannot act, but the people in these structures can. For example, a company such as BASF, which represents a resource regime, needs organs such as a supervisory or executive board in order to act; but their actions are guided by the norms within the resource regime. This means that resource regimes themselves do not have agency, but rather guide action. To return to medieval Lübeck, we have the example of the town council, which was also the seat of the administration, the legal authority and the judicial court. Here, we see several resource regimes—that is, rule-based processes and practices of resource-handling. "Rule-based", in this context, describes a wide range of laws, regulations, customary law, prescriptions and so on. Common to all these is a set of rights and obligations applicable to concrete situations and considered to be binding, although, of course, there is also a great variety of associated complexities. As the seat of the administration, the town council regulated skilled crafts and trades through council ordinances, and, as the judicial court, it defined the law in specific cases. In the context of informing about legal rights, it even acted as the higher court for other cities in the north of the empire. The council also made decisions regarding war, peace and many other important matters. All these processes were based upon written, but, in particular, also upon unwritten prescriptions, and influenced the way in which resources were used. However, these processes rested on different legal foundations and can therefore be regarded as different resource regimes. Both the written and the unwritten laws of the council charter, coupled with long-standing practice, formed the basis for these regimes. The norms and practices of these resource regimes could not themselves, however, take any action. This occurred through the agency of the town council members. The town council, as an organ, thus "hosted" more than one resource regime.

To sum up, then, resource regimes are sets of norms and practices that are made procedurally important, whereas organs have agency. In reality, both will frequently coincide, but, analytically, they are entirely separate.

b. Different resource regimes can interact with, influence, and depend on each other through human agents. Such interaction tends to promote adaptation in situations in which there is competition, and thereby promote change. Different resource regimes can operate using the same resource(s). For example, during the so-called late Hanseatic period in the sixteenth century, both Hanseatic merchants and English merchant adventurers operated in the North Sea. Both groups of agents formed trading companies that traded in the same places with the same sets of products. These companies were competing resource regimes. Every agent constantly needed to adapt the processes and practices of using their resources and closely observed the others doing the same. This competition encouraged a "dynamic market". This example also demonstrates that resources could be selected by more than one resource regime, which could create large areas of overlap and pressure to adapt.

However, regimes may also feel the pressure to adapt even in unequal situations in which one regime heavily depends on another. For example, local non-governmental organisations (NGOs) undertaking development work in Zorgho, Burkina Faso, see themselves as being dominated by their international partners, whose requirements greatly influence the formation of norms and practices in the local NGOs which they fund. During the formation of such partnerships, Burkinabé NGOs attempt to present themselves as structurally strong and dependable partners while emphasising the needs of the local population. If they succeed in creating a partnership, they begin to adapt to the financial structures of their new funding bodies and to reproduce these within their own organisation. In other words, they take on norms and practices from outside and adapt their regime to them. However, the funding bodies are constantly dependent on local information and knowledge from their partner NGOs, which requires the development of a bilateral, rather than a unilateral, exchange.[33]

Resource regimes can not only enter into complex interdependent relationships with each other, but also nest within one another. An obvious example of this can be found in businesses with daughter companies that remain firmly tethered to their parent through profit and loss payment agreements. Various collaborative development programmes can also be considered as nesting resource regimes, as long as they demonstrate a minimum of shared, overarching norms and practices.

---

[33] This example is taken from the work of Melina Kalfelis for the project „Flexibility through poverty—Self-perception and tactics for accessing resources among local NGO-Agents in West Africa", led by Hans Peter Hahn.

c. Resource regimes are dynamic, rather than static.[34] The creation of resources through the definition of goals does not negate the fact that regimes do not by any means always attain their goals. Naturally, goals can have a strategic dimension and can, in fact, be impossible to reach. New or modified goals require concomitant changes in the resource regimes—that is, in the norms and practices that guide the ways in which resources are used. These changes may require the formation of new regimes, or simply the adaptation and modification of old regimes.[35] The resource regimes associated with development work, for example, undergo paradigmatic changes at regular intervals that lead to changes in their principal norms and processes. Since the paradigm shift of the Paris Declaration on Aid Effectiveness in 2005, and, recently, Sustainable Development Goals (2016), a process of harmonisation has led to diverse structural changes. Current funding is now primarily given to large multilateral programmes that are channelled through the governments of the targeted country.[36] This makes a multitude of political, private and development actors dependent on each other. As a consequence, political and economic interests are increasingly intertwined with social efforts.[37]

The norms and practices that constitute the regimes can, of course, be inefficient, delaying or even preventing the attainment of set goals. A resource regime can also continue existing as a "shell" of norms and processes, even when the goals have been reached or when the regime has failed to reach them entirely. In the latter case, discourses of weakness can arise which, can in turn, induce changes in the resource regime. The pursuit of specific goals can also lead to side effects (which can be desirable or undesirable), which can themselves set processes of adaptation in motion. The re-constitution or transformation of regimes in such processes is not only possible but may well occur regularly. Practices can run counter to existing norms and, if they become stable, eventually become normative themselves. It is equally possible for resource regimes to form spontaneously out of self-regulation processes. At this stage, without further investigation, it is not possible to say what critical mass of norms and practices is

---

34 Leppin et al. (2017), *Discourses of Weakness and Resource Regimes*, 49 f.
35 See Section II.2.a of this chapter.
36 This example is taken from the work of Melina Kalfelis for the project "Flexibility through poverty—Self-perception and tactics for accessing resources among local NGO-Agents in West Africa", led by Hans Peter Hahn.
37 Barefoot Collective (2011), *The Barefoot Guide*, 83.

necessary for a resource regime to form. It should be noted that there are also small constellations of processes below the level of regimes. In short, there can be manifold processes of change and adaptation, and these make it possible to study historical transformation. This question requires further empirical study.

d. Resource regimes are not equal to institutions,[38] although they may have features in common.[39] The term "institution" is often used in economic contexts. Douglass North understands institutions to be "rules of the game in a society or, more formally, the humanly devised constraints that shape human interaction."[40] As we have already discussed, regimes refer, much more narrowly, to specific resource-related processes based on norms and practices. The term "regime" does not, therefore, stand in opposition to the term "institution", but simply emphasises a different set of social processes. It permits us to examine rule-based processes more closely; law, for example, is not simply an abstract set of norms, but includes a wide range of mechanisms for regulating conflict situations in conjunction with resources.[41] These mechanisms are composed of both written and unwritten normative aggregations that shape social processes. Power, as we shall see, arises as a result of the interaction between such aggregations and human agents.

III. Power Structures in Resource Regimes

The complex analytical categories described above are an essential foundation for the study of power. Precisely because resource regimes enable us to examine rule-based processes, they enable us to investigate the function of power at the intersection of norms and human agency. Ultimately, this permits us to study historical transformation. Power is an important component of this transformation, for, as we argue, it is hardly possible to envision social relationships without a power dimension. The following section presents an initial analysis of some of the key features and functions of power within the framework of resource regimes, as described in

---

38 See North (1990), *Institutions,* 3.
39 On this aspect, see Cordes et al. (2016), *Schwächediskurse und Ressourcenregime,* 186.
40 North (1990), *Institutions,* 3.
41 See Cordes et al. (2016), *Schwächediskurse und Ressourcenregime,* 184.

Sections I and II. It should be noted at the outset that the ideas discussed below are a preliminary result of the work of the CRC 1095. As the case studies used to illustrate our understanding of power will show, the analytical framework presented here works across a range of approaches, time periods and fields of social science, and is therefore an extremely useful conceptual tool. At the same time, a great deal more research is needed to explore the full implications of these cross-disciplinary ideas.

The basic starting-point for the idea of power presented in this chapter is the relationship between resources and power. This means that resources are at the centre of the way in which the CRC 1095 thinks about change in human society. And it is here that power comes in, for both resources and the goals implicitly associated with them imply a power dimension. Conceptually, the dividing line between resources and power is a fine one. Here, Koschnick's definition is helpful:

"The main distinction between resources and power is that resources are possessed by an actor himself or herself, whereas power is only exercised by an actor in a social relationship. An actor has potential power whenever he or she possesses resources and is capable of employing them if and when desired. Power then becomes active as these resources are utilized—either to back up verbal threats or in overt actions. The main points of this 'potential-active' distinction are (1) that resources must be readily available for use before they become relevant for the creation of social power, and (2) that an actor can be seen to possess the potentiality for wielding power even though he or she never overtly uses his or her resources."[42]

Just as a resource is activated by linking it with a goal, so power is activated when a resource is used in a relationship. The advantage of this definition is that it shifts the focus from hierarchies to relationships and from teleological ideas of development or progress to processes of change. This, in turn, gives those who study human societies three advantages when observing historical change: a clearer awareness of the multiplicity of levels on which actors can enact change over time; the capacity to build more complex models of human interaction from the observable data; and a smaller bias, in that a conscious conceptual adherence to processes and relationships is, from the outset, less dependent on value judgements (including those associated with the terms "progress" and "development").

The power activated as a result of the involvement of resources in human relationships is therefore our key focus. We are not interested in rela-

---

[42] Koschnick (1993), *Resource*, 1313.

tionships in which no resources have been invoked. The reason for this is that change is driven by elements exerting pressure upon one another. We have identified these elements to be resources and human beings in relationships. By studying these, we study change in historical formations. Power is an essential component of such change, and its influence on the concepts discussed above shall be the focus of the rest of this chapter.

What, then, is power? A great deal of scholarship over the centuries has attempted to answer this question, and the results are many and varied. Max Weber identified power as the opportunity for people "to realise their own will in communal action, even against the resistance of others".[43] For Niklas Luhmann, on the other hand, power is a medium of communication and is no longer power when it becomes physical violence.[44] The thought of Michel Foucault, as expressed in many of his works but particularly in "Madness and Civilization", "The Birth of the Clinic", "Discipline and Punish: The Birth of the Prison" and "The Subject and Power", differs yet again.[45] The "bare bones of the critical consensus" on Foucault's theories of power have been aptly summarised by Jeffrey T. Nealon:

"Foucaultian power is not something *held* but something *practised*; power is not imposed from 'above' a system or socius, but consists of a series of relations within such a system or socius; there is no 'outside' of power, no place untouched by power; conversely, there is no place of liberation or absolute freedom from power; in the end, power *produces* desires, formations, objects of knowledge, and discourses, rather than primarily *repressing*, controlling, or canalizing the powers already held by preexisting subjects, knowledges, or formations. Resistance, then, doesn't primarily function 'against' power, trying to eradicate it altogether; rather, resistance attempts to harness power otherwise, in the production of different effects."[46]

Foucault's ideas on power deserve to be noted in particular because they mark:

"a radical departure from previous modes of conceiving power and cannot be easily integrated with previous ideas, as power is diffuse rather than concentrated,

---

43 "Macht bedeutet jede Chance, innerhalb einer sozialen Beziehung den eignen Willen auch gegen Widerstreben durchzusetzen, gleichviel worauf diese Chance beruht." Weber (2013), *Wirtschaft und Gesellschaft*, Chapter I, § 16, 210.
44 Luhmann (2012), *Macht*. For a systematic sociological discussion of violence, see: Popitz (1992), *Phänomene der Macht*.
45 Foucault (1972), *Histoire de la folie à l'âgeclassique*; Foucault (1963), *Naissance de la clinique*; Foucault (1975), *Surveilleretpunir*; Foucault (1982), *The Subject and Power*, 777–795.
46 Nealon (2008), *Foucault Beyond Foucault*, 24 f.

embodied and enacted rather than possessed, discursive rather than purely coercive, and constitutes agents rather than being deployed by them."[47]

However, none of these definitions is suitable for a line of thought that seeks to analyse relationships and the way in which they result in historical change. In this context, it is much more useful to view power as a result of communication. For the CRC 1095, as for Foucault, power is a societal phenomenon, dependent upon the context in which it is produced, ubiquitous in one form or another, and is changed and produces change out of its direct relationship with the discourses of the society in which it appears. The definition of power proposed in this chapter is closest to the features of power outlined by Foucault, then, but it does not depend on them, nor on the many other existing theories of power. This chapter makes no pretension to analyse or synthesise these theories, nor to reconcile the proposed modelling of power with them. The reason for this is that all such previous theories—from Machiavelli, Hobbes, Weber and Marx to Dahl, Bachrach and Baratz, Lukes, Giddens and Gaventa, to name only some of the most prominent—have depended, explicitly or implicitly, on the theoretical backgrounds of those who proposed them.[48] A reconciliation between these theories would require a much longer study, and an in-depth scrutiny of the overlap across the different fields of social science, including political theory and philosophy, which informed them. Instead, in this chapter, we take some of the fundamental concepts identified by the CRC 1095, namely, resources and regimes, as the framework within which we can study power. This framework (see Sections I and II above) enables us to adopt an explicitly empirical approach that, in turn, permits us to make a set of innovative observations about the way in which power functions in human societies.

Two preliminary observations can already be made about power from the model presented here. Firstly, power is an abstract concept that only really exists at historical formation level. At the level of human actors, it manifests as relationships of power. Such relationships are essentially the

---

[47] Gaventa (2003), *Power After Lukes*, 1.
[48] Machiavelli (1532), *Il principe*; Hobbes (1651), *Leviathan*; Weber (2013), *Wirtschaft und Gesellschaft*; Marx/Engels (1848), *Manifest der Kommunistischen Partei*; Marx (1867), *Das Kapital*, vol. 1, as well as other works: Bachrach et al. (1962), *Two Faces of Power*; Dahl (2005), *Who Governs?*; Lukes (1974), *Power. A Radical View*; Giddens (1982), *Profiles and Critiques in Social Theory* and Giddens (1984), *The Constitution of Society: Outline of the Theory of Structuration*; Gaventa (1982), *Power and Powerlessness*.

same as human relationships, but we call them relationships of power to indicate that the power aspect is our focus. We also argue that human relationships cannot exist without power. In this framework, the last person alive after an apocalypse has no power, because they cannot enter into a relationship of any kind with another person. Power, then, is an inevitable product of human communication.[49] It should be noted here that divine power, from a theist perspective, is beyond the remit of this chapter. However, the impression of divine power—for example, through a natural cataclysm—is not, in these terms, power as such, but rather a social phenomenon that can be used as a resource for one actor or group of actors to achieve their aims in relation to another actor or group.

Secondly, some relationships "produce" more power than others. It is here that the CRC 1095 diverges not only from theorists such as Weber and Luhmann, but also from Foucault. For the latter, for example, "slavery is not a power relationship when man is in chains, only when he has some possible mobility, even a chance of escape. (In this case, it is a question of a physical relationship of constraint.)".[50] However, in the model discussed here, every degree of slavery is a resource regime with a high degree of power imbalance.

A further set of features that characterise power relationships can be distilled from case studies, drawn from the projects of the researchers who have contributed to this chapter. Five of these key features are discussed below and are followed by a series of conclusions that point the way for further study.

1. Power is a Product of the (Perceived or Actual) Control of Resources

In the project of Nadine Eikelschulte on the legitimation of power in Egypt during the First Intermediate Period (Dynasties 7-11, *circa* 2170–2040 BCE) and the Middle Kingdom (Dynasties 11-13, *circa* 2040–1780 BCE), we see how the perceived control of resources leads to power:

The First Intermediate Period in Ancient Egypt was a time when there was no single ruler. The individual administrative districts (*nomes*) were ruled by nomarchs, provincial administrative officials. These districts had existed in the Old Kingdom (Dynasties 3-6, *circa* 2700-2170 BCE), where

---

[49] This point was made by Crozier et al. (1977), *L'Acteur et le système*.
[50] Foucault (1982), *The Subject and Power*, 221.

they were subordinate to the king. The nomarchs of the First Intermediate Period administrated their districts in a self-sufficient way. They presented themselves as kings, for it was essential for them to legitimise their rule, which would otherwise have run counter to the Egyptian world-view, the Ma'at,[51] that depending on the context encompassed truth, justice, law and morality (among other concepts). From the autobiographies[52] of the different officials and princes, we can see how they sought to legitimise their positions. The previously common passages in which the nomarchs referred to their legitimation through the king—as in the biography of the nomarch Weni, who listed precisely which mandates and posts he had received, and emphasised his value to the king with the words "his heart was filled with me"[53]—completely disappear. Instead, the biographies focus on famines and their prevention. The nomarch in question claims to have obtained food so as to be able to feed the district under his rule, while people in neighbouring districts suffer from hunger. Similarly, in the biography of the nomarch Mrrj, we find the following passage:

"I procured barley from Upper Egypt and barley from the north and filled the treasure-house with all things [...] in times of plenty and in times of hunger."[54]

These rulers therefore focused on legitimation through food provision and, since food was considered as an extremely important resource, succeeded in using this legitimation to remain in their positions of power.

2. The Opposite is also True—Perceived or Actual Power Determines Access to Resources

The power obtained as a result of the control of resources enables human agents to acquire further resources. This is evident in the project of Anna Dorofeeva on early medieval miscellanies as institutional resources.

The European West saw a cultural revival from *circa* 750 CE initiated and maintained by Carolingian kings. It was a fundamentally religious phenomenon that deeply influenced institutions, material production and intel-

---

51 On the concept of Ma'at, see, for example, Assmann (1990), *Ma'at*.
52 Egyptian autobiographies are essentially pseudo-autobiographical texts that were used in a funerary context. They provide an account of the deceased person's blameless life, according to Egyptian values, in order to ensure their afterlife in the next world.
53 Lichtheim (2006), *Ancient Egyptian Literature*, vol. 1, 19.
54 Schenkel (1965), *Memphis-Herakleopolis-Theben*, 38.

lectual undertakings. It encompassed all spheres of social life, from liturgy, education, art and scholarship to political authority, economic development and building programmes. Miscellanies, or manuscripts that contained a wide range of full and partial texts on a variety of topics, were a typical product of this period. They existed before the early middle ages, but became extremely common in the eighth, ninth and tenth centuries (something we do know, although there is no precise data on the numbers of these manuscripts—a question that depends on our definition of the term "miscellany"). They indicate that information was considered a very valuable resource that needed to be organised and presented in new ways to meet new needs, that institutions (monasteries) played a key role in the organisation and dissemination of this information, and that miscellanies participated in the creation of a discourse about knowledge which emphasised the importance of written, rather than memorised, learning, and aimed to promote the Christian faith. Both history and exegesis were also key to this process. Miscellanies reflect, therefore, a concerted effort by the Christian Church to promote written knowledge as a resource which it could use to consolidate its power. This consolidation could lead to the acquisition of further resources, as we can see from the example of the Abbey of Saint Gall in Switzerland. Subordinated to the bishops of Constance from the middle of the eighth century, the Abbey developed a very large scriptorium and library, with miscellanies constituting around one third of the books which it copied. The documentary output and especially the prestige earned by the abbey as a key centre of learning meant that in 818, Abbot Gozbert finally succeeded in obtaining a charter of immunity from King Louis the Pious (778–840 CE), making his monastery an independent imperial abbey (with the range of privileges that this entailed). This example not only shows that power could determine access to more resources and therefore more power, but also that certain kinds of resources, in this case knowledge, could be endowed with social prestige, thereby making them more effective.

3. Power Occurs at the Intersection of Resources and Actors

Power is relational—that is, it can only come into existence within a social context in which more than one actor is involved. The relational nature of power is clear from the project of Carla Thiel on the German chemical industry between 1860 and 1960.

In 1861, Friedrich Engelhorn, Friedrich Sonntag, Otto Dyckerhoff and Dr. Carl Clemm founded the chemical company Dyckerhoff, Clemm & Comp. in Mannheim, Germany. According to the first paragraph of the articles of partnership, the purpose of the company was to produce aniline and coal-tar dyes.[55] Due to the retirement of Otto Dyckerhoff later in the same year, the name of the factory changed to Sonntag, Engelhorn & Clemm (S. E. &. C.).[56] Unlike previous dye-making companies, the company decided to produce not only dyes, but also the important intermediate substance aniline, thereby hoping to make savings that were essential on the hotly contested dye market.[57] Although this and other measures gave the company several advantages and enabled it to reduce some of its costs, the resulting savings were not enough for the company to compete in the long term. The only remaining area in which production costs could still be optimised was the purchase of inorganic raw and auxiliary materials.[58] Among these raw materials were sodium carbonate and various acids (sulphuric, hydrochloric, nitric and arsenic), which were obtained at high cost from the Verein Chemischer Fabriken Mannheim.[59] This company, which had been founded in 1854, held a monopoly on all the important inorganic substances and could set prices at its discretion.[60] This highly profitable situation meant that the company was able to pay dividends of 35 percent between 1862 and 1864.[61] Friedrich Engelhorn opened negotiations with this powerful supplier in order to help his company make more profit. While S. E. &. C. was a small company, it was also the largest consumer of the above-mentioned raw materials. This meant that Engelhorn could exert some pressure in proposing a fusion between the two companies.[62] The suggested consortium fell apart at the eleventh hour, however, most probably because of falling prices on coal-tar dyes and the doubt felt by the

---

55 Andersen (1966), *Historische Technikfolgeabschätzung*, 242.
56 Voigtländer-Tetzner (circa 1940), *Chronik der BASF 1865–1940* (unpublished manuscript), 78.
57 Schröter (1992), *Friedrich Engelhorn*, 101.
58 Voigtländer-Tetzner (circa 1940), *Chronik der BASF 1865–1940* (unpublished manuscript), 83.
59 Glaser (1921), *Erlebnisse und Erinnerungen* (unpublished manuscript), 11.
60 Abelshauser (2002), *Die BASF*, 26.
61 Andersen (1996), *Historische Technikfolgeabschätzung*, 243.
62 Abelshauser (2002), *Die BASF*, 26 f.

Mannheim company that new kinds of dyes would be in demand in the future.[63] Since Engelhorn believed that finding his own supply of raw materials was essential for the survival of his company, he made the risky decision to produce this raw material himself.[64] He must have been aware that the cost of this production was far beyond what his co-founders were able to bear, because he turned to W.H. Ladenburg & Söhne, a bank with which he was on good terms.[65] This bank was one of the first to recognise the potential of the coal-tar dye industry, which was, at that time, still very new, and was therefore willing to support Engelhorn with the foundation of a new company.[66] This new company, called the Badian Aniline and Soda Factory (BASF), was founded on 6 April 1865.[67] Engelhorn was even able to entice the technical director Julius Giese away from the Verein Chemischer Fabriken Mannheim for the standard contractual penalty of 10,000 gulden.[68] The high investment in Giese's technical expertise quickly paid off, for the company was able to begin producing the most important inorganic raw materials as early as 1866.[69] A letter from the Mannheim company to its shareholders in 1866 shows that it was worried about the success of its new competitor, having seen the loss of its most important customers and a resulting decrease in sales. In addition, the swift start and development of BASF's production meant that it was becoming one of the company's foremost market competitors. The company therefore felt itself under pressure to come to an agreement quickly, which it eventually did.[70] BASF gave its surplus inorganic materials to the Mannheim company, which undertook their sale and shared the resulting profit. In this way, the two rivals avoided a price stand-off and BASF was able to focus on its core business—the production of coal-tar dyes.[71]

From this example, we can see how a resource regime reliant on a power imbalance can lean too heavily on this imbalance, provoking a reaction from its supposed subordinates that led to a fundamental change in the

---

63 Andersen (1996), *Historische Technikfolgeabschätzung*, 244.
64 Abelshauser (2002), *Die BASF*, 26 f.
65 Schröter (1992), *Friedrich Engelhorn*, 106 f.
66 Borscheid (1976), *Naturwissenschaft, Staat und Industrie in Baden*, 103.
67 Andersen (1996), *Historische Technikfolgeabschätzung*, 244.
68 Abelshauser (2002), *Die BASF*, 28.
69 Schröter (1992), *Friedrich Engelhorn*, 120.
70 Voigtländer-Tetzner (circa 1940), *Chronik der BASF 1865–1940* (unpublished manuscript), 91 f.
71 Abelshauser (2002), *Die BASF*, 40.

regime. The break made by S. E. &. C. with the company in Mannheim was, however, only possible thanks to the involvement of another resource regime, the Ladenburg bank, which was able to supply the missing resources—that is, the necessary money and contacts. A further resource was obtained with the employment of Julius Giese, who possessed essential technical knowledge. Most importantly, the power balance (heavily tipped in favour of the Mannheim company, thanks to its monopoly on raw materials) depended entirely on the relationships between the actors and resource regimes involved. Once these relationships changed, through the agency of Friedrich Engelhorn, who first attempted to form a consortium with the Mannheim company, and then brought in a bank to found a new company, the shift in power caused a transformation in the resource regimes themselves.

The boundaries between resource regimes in this example are not entirely clear, and it may even be necessary to allow them some degree of flexibility. As has been noted in Section II.2.a, resource regimes are processes based upon norms and practices, meaning that they not only interact with one another, but, by interacting, must, to some extent, fuse with one another. In the case study, the Ladenburg Bank and BASF were separate resource regimes before their collaboration, and, indeed, they remained financially independent of one another. However, to what extent the bank and BASF were truly separate resource regimes is debatable. Further research is required on the creation and maintenance of the boundaries between resource regimes.

One further case study, taken from the project of Lukas Jäger on the forms and functions of weak knowledge, illustrates the relational aspect of power from a different perspective.

On 5 June 1929, *Deutsche Zukunft*, a Heidelberg-based conservative and nationalist newspaper,[72] published an article with the headline: *"Der Krieg um Mannheim* [The War on Mannheim]."[73] This was not, of course, a war on the city of Mannheim, but a dispute about the German naturalisation of Karl Mannheim, a Jewish Hungarian working as a lecturer (*"Privatdozent"*)

---

72 For the original political classification of the newspaper and a short comprehensive discussion of the article's argument, see Laube (2004), *Karl Mannheim und die Krise des Historismus*, 180 and fn. 319.
73 Anonymus (1929), *Der Krieg um Mannheim*, 84. A cut-out of the original article is included in the personal file of Karl Mannheim (Universitätsarchiv Heidelberg, Personalakte 4924).

at Heidelberg Unviersity. Although no acts of physical violence were committed in this "war", the use of this term was not simply the effect of an idiosyncratic, martial style of language used by a conservative and nationalist newspaper. Rather, it demonstrates that the Prussian militaristic tradition and the nationalistic cult of "German culture"[74] retained some vigour during the Weimar Republic. For German academics, intellectuals and officials of the Weimar period, the Great War had clearly not yet ended, but had only shifted form, substituting guns and gas for legal and polemical battles.[75] Karl Mannheim, therefore, had to contend with an ideologically and power-charged resource regime between 1920 and 1929. This was made clear in the opening sentence of the *Deutsche Zukunft* article:

"The academic-political intelligence service reports that a state of war has recently been declared between the Home Offices of Württemberg and Baden, and that it was caused by the *Privatdozent* Karl Mannheim, who gives sociological lectures at the University of Heidelberg."[76]

Readers of the anonymous article were informed that the two ministries of Baden and Württemberg were currently at war with each other. Karl

---

74 At the beginning of the Great War, many German academics—especially those of the highest rank, the "Ordinarien"—and many public intellectuals were among the most war-enthusiastic German citizens. In the popular propagandistic pamphlet "Appeal to the World of Culture" ("Aufruf an die Kulturwelt") from 1914, also known as the "Manifesto of the 93" ("Manifest der 93"), ninety-three of the highest-ranked and distinguished German academics and public intellectuals literally identified German culture with the spirit of Prussian militarism. The pamphlet claimed that the German army ("Heer") and the German people ("Volk") were one, uniting all Germans regardless of education, social class and political party. Although some of these academics and intellectuals changed their minds during the war, and some publicly opposed it before the end, their names nevertheless appeared in pamphlets that affirmed their approval for the war and were widely seen by the public. On the sociogenesis of the cult of German culture in supposed contrast to a generally inferior Western civilisation, see Elias et al. (2005), *Studien über die Deutschen*; and for a recent comprehensive study on the German attempt to substitute politics with culture, see Lepenies (2006), *The Seduction of Culture in German History*.

75 The Weimar Republic's power relations can only be called non-violent in relation to the war itself. The relative instability of the Weimar Republic is historically attested, and was experienced by historical actors in economic crises, politically motivated civil violence, [Theweleit (1977/1978), *Männerphantasien*, vols. 1 and 2] and homicide [Gumbel (1922), *Vier Jahre politischer Mord*.]

76 "Der Akademisch-politische Informationsdienst informiert, daß zwischen den Innenministerien Württembergs und Badens augenblicklich ein Kriegszustand herrsche, dessen Ursache der an der Heidelberger Universität soziologische Vorlesungen haltende Privatdozent Dr. Karl Mannheim sei." English translation by Lukas Jäger.

Mannheim was, they were told right at the start, not only the object of the supposed "war", but also its direct cause. "Who is this man who has led two German ministries to fight each other?" the reader is supposed to ask. An immediate answer to this question is provided. The article tells us about Mannheim's birth in Budapest, his self-identification as Hungarian, his Jewish ancestry and faith, and, last, but not least, it tells us that he was a civilian "*während des Krieges*"—during the Great War. It paints a picture of Mannheim as a Hungarian Jew who had avoided fighting, was therefore not part of German "culture", and was now causing two respected German ministries not only to disagree with each other, but to become warring enemies.[77]

It is, furthermore, remarkable that the Ministry of Baden, which, in fact, endorsed Mannheim's naturalisation, employed the nationalistic, xenophobic and even anti-Semitic language used at that time by the wider "discursive coalition"[78]—which we can characterise as a resource regime or even as a historical formation—of which it was part:

"Although Dr Mannheim is Jewish, his case is nevertheless not that of an eastern foreigner in the usual sense, for Budapest, his birthplace, can, to a certain extent, be seen as affiliated with the German cultural sphere due to Hungary's former membership of the Austro-Hungarian Empire."[79]

---

[77] This was nothing more than speculation, probably based solely upon Mannheim not denying his Jewish ancestry for public records (Universitätsarchiv Heidelberg, Personalakte 4924). The religious authorities upon which Mannheim drew in his work were all Christian and included Meister Eckhart, Cusanus, Kierkegaard and Dostoyevsky.

[78] A "discursive coalition" designates a situation of discourse in which nominally different institutions and individuals (universities, faculties and professors; state, ministries and bureaucrats; parliament, parties and politicians; the public, salons and "Bildungsbürger") share predetermined factors: that is, they communicate not only using the same words, but attach the same meaning to them and therefore share a common ideology. The term "discursive coalition" (Diskurskoalition) was coined by Wagner (1990), *Sozialwissenschaften und Staat*. See, also, Loader (2003), *From Nationalökonomie to Kultursoziologie*, 43–69. Loader uses Antonio Gramsci's term "cultural hegemony", but "discursive coalition" is preferable as it stresses the shared codes (e.g. culture, nationhood, honour) that we have called "pre-determined factors". The discursive coalition around Karl Mannheim may be regarded as a resource regime, since the preservation of the status quo (that is, "purity of blood and soil") became a goal for a critical group of people, crossing a boundary of relevance. Here, the pre-determined factors are used discursively as a resource to achieve this goal.

[79] "Obwohl Dr. Mannheim Jude ist, so handelt es sich doch bei ihm nicht um einen Ostausländer im üblichen Sinne, da sein Geburtsort Budapest infolge der früheren Zugehörigkeit Ungarns zur österreichisch-ungarischen Monarchie in gewissen Beziehungen

There are, therefore, complex relationships at play here between actors and resources. The resource regime represented by the parties involved in the naturalisation process, which included *Deutsche Zukunft*, the abovementioned ministries and the Berlin *Reichsrat*—and which, as hierarchical structures, had internal power relationships—emphasised citizenship as a desirable resource, using a shared language that drew on notions of culture, nationhood, honour and alienation.[80] This discourse detracted from the power that Karl Mannheim was able to exert as a prominent intellectual. The power tensions in this context existed, and arose from, the relative social roles of the actors involved.

4. Power is Dependent on Social Conditions

Power is dependent on the social conditions that produce it for its presence and form, and disappears in contexts in which these social conditions are sufficiently different. The dependence of power on a particular set of conditions for both its presence and its form is illustrated by the project of Sebastian Riebold on the Chinese state at the turn of the nineteenth century.

The power of the Qing imperial court after the year 1900 underwent a profound transformation. In the wake of the events of 1898, when the so-called One Hundred Days' Reform was forcefully put down by the faction surrounding the Empress Dowager Cixi, the imperial court had lost most of its credibility, as fewer and fewer reform-minded thinkers and activists clung to the belief that the Manchu regime would be able to change from within so as to enable China to weather the challenges of modernity. Some, such as the leaders of the First Guangzhou Uprising (most notably Sun Yat-sen, the founding father of the Republic of China), had ceased to believe this as early as 1895. The shifting stance of the court *vis-à-vis* the "Boxers"—rebels whom Beijing first condemned and later supported—did

---

als zum deutschen Kulturkreis zugehörig anzusehen war." This document, as well as the remaining correspondence between the ministries of Baden, Württemberg, the Philosophische Fakultät of the University of Heidelberg, and others, concerning "The War on Mannheim", is publicly accessible in Karlsruhe (Badisches Generallandesarchiv, 235/2289). English translation by Lukas Jäger.

80 These concepts were, however, not always clearly defined.

nothing to restore faith in the imperial regime.[81] The reforms initiated by Cixi and her supporters (*i.e.*, the very people who had led the repression a few years earlier) at the beginning of the new century, were, in the eyes of many contemporaries, too little, too late. In fact, these efforts were much more ambitious and comprehensive than anything proposed in 1898, and laid the institutional groundwork for the Chinese nation-state (many of the institutions created were later taken over by the republic). But at this point, Qing authority had been corroded to such a degree that the momentousness of the New Policies (Xin Zheng) was hardly appreciated, and has been downplayed to this day.[82] In 1908, the Qing court also lost its two pivotal turn-of-the-century figures, as both Cixi and the Guangxu emperor died that year. Both die-hard conservatives and progressive loyalists lost their key figureheads. In summary, even though the Qing Dynasty, along with most of its instruments of rule, persisted until 1911, one may observe that its *power* had been severely undermined long before then.[83] This process was further encouraged by a deepening conviction among critics of the regime (inspired by newly discovered Western notions of nationalism and racial thought) that the Manchu were unfit to rule over the (Han) Chinese majority on account of their ethnicity. Political legitimacy and thus the legitimate exercise of political power was, in other words, increasingly "racialised".[84] The socio-economic and ideological changes in late imperial China—not necessarily caused, but certainly catalysed, by Western modernity—had overtaken the imperial institutions in their ability to adapt.

---

81 Esherick (1987), *The Origins of the Boxer Uprising*, 271–313. The transition "from reform to revolution" in the years in question is comprehensively summarised in Vogelsang (2012), *Geschichte Chinas*, 481–492.
82 The only English-language monograph dedicated to the topic is still Reynolds (1993), China. Arguably, the most crucial (and certainly most symbolic) move was the abolition of the infamous civil service examination in 1905.
83 The ethnicity of the ruling family also played a very important role here, but it has been omitted in this example for the sake of simplicity.
84 Early racial thinkers had only distinguished the "yellow race" as opposed to "white", "black", "brown", or "red"—the Manchu being very much included as members of the first category. The turn of the century witnessed increasing efforts to exclude the Manchu from the "Chinese nation". On the introduction of racial thinking into Chinese society, see Dikötter (1992), *The Discourse of Race in Modern China*, especially 97–125. Racism in China, as elsewhere, was not confined to intellectual debates but manifested itself brutally during the numerous local uprisings that constituted the Revolution of 1911. Nor was the violence exclusively directed against the Manchu ruling class. See Rhoads (2000), *Manchus and Han*, 173–230.

It should be noted here that the form of power in this case study is key. The social changes of the late nineteenth century robbed the Qing dynasty of most of its power, but this did not mean that power was not present in associated resource regimes or in the historical formation itself. This case study observes the disappearance of one kind of power, but the processes behind the power shifts and the directions in which power moves require further study.

5. Power is Multi-directional

Power is multi-directional (one or more kinds of power can be practiced wholly or partially by one or more actors within or across social structures, simultaneously or in turn), not fixed in location or scope, and fluid (waxing and waning). It is, therefore, an essentially contested concept. The final aspect of power identified in this chapter emphasises both its fluidity and the need for a conceptual framework in which to analyse it. The project of Melina Kalfelis on poverty and resources in a development context in West Africa highlights the contested nature of power.

NGOs in Zorgho (Burkina Faso) never speak of the power of their international partner organisations, although they consider the non-governmental development work in their region to be dominated by them.[85] They consistently describe their partners as directors who set the temporal, material and communicative norms as pre-conditions for their co-operation, and who impose their rules and standards. One of the most important challenges for local actors is to adopt and reproduce these structures within the NGOs, in order to obtain resources for their own project work and thereby legitimise their existence. Resources, in this case, are normally of a material nature (typically money). Such resources are difficult to obtain in Burkina Faso and are procured almost exclusively through development aid.

From an analytical perspective, power is an important factor in NGO work in Zorgho, even though the local actors normally do not discuss power directly. Instead, they often claim that resources are less easily available in Burkina Faso, which suggests that the Burkinabé actors are more

---

85 Bierschenk (2008), *Development Projects*; Neubert (2001), *Entwicklung unter dem Mikroskop*.

structurally dependent.[86] It further implies a structural dimension to power that permeates the normative formation of the partnerships and the rules that result from them. This makes power an invisible variable or, rather, an instance of structural determination; its existence can only rarely be observed from the inside, and can hardly be described or empirically grounded. It can only be an attribution or an interpretation, and its form will seem to change constantly to those who observe it. As Foucault noted, we see power everywhere we seek it and can always ignore it where we do not wish to see it.[87]

Authors such as Crozier and Friedberg (1977), Scott (1985), and Spittler (1981) have rightly noted that weaker actors, social groups or individuals also possess strategies that enable them to acquire power or to restrict the power of those stronger than them.[88] Just because local NGOs speak of their partners as directors this does not mean that they themselves are powerless. Simply by speaking about the dominance of their funding bodies, they express their consciousness of the power of these bodies, and communicate a certain kind of tranquillity—perhaps even complacency—about the unequal partnership. With this in mind, we are faced with the question of to what extent power can be analysed in a context that is evident "on the ground", without homogenising its relative and ambivalent aspects through theoretical analysis? In order to reflect the heterogeneity of power, one solution may be to consider the situation using different analytical levels—in this case study, the local and the global levels—which enable us to investigate the different conglomerations of power in their different forms. In this case, we might think of the structural or institutional levels of the Burkinabé actors, whose normative architecture is rooted in the modernisation theories behind development principles and (to use the words of Heinrich Popitz) represents the authoritative and instrumental power of international partner organisations.[89] The beliefs, procedures and values of these organisations permeate across physical distances and boundaries into the local rules and standards of development and cause local structures to conform with them, although this does not

---

86 Marriage (2006), *Challenging Aid in Africa*; Neubert (2001), *Entwicklung unter dem Mikroskop*; Axelby et al. (2013), *Anthropology and Development*.
87 Foucault (1976), *Histoire de la sexualité*, 122.
88 Crozier et al. (1977), *L'Acteur et le système*; Spittler (1981), *Verwaltung in einem afrikanischen Bauernstaat*; Scott (1985), *Weapons of the Weak*.
89 Popitz (1992), *Phänomene der Macht*.

preclude resistance. Another possible analytical level is the organisational level, which, to borrow from the power theory of Michel Crozier and Erhard Friedberg, contains "zones of uncertainty".[90] The interplay between the known and the unknown is extremely important in development work: knowledge is one of the most important resources, alongside money, but, unlike money, it is not exclusively possessed by the funding body.[91]

Finally, we might also consider the practical level of human actors, all of whom function "locally"—be it in Burkina Faso, Switzerland or Sweden. While some of them use normative and structural channels to reach their ideological goals, others bend their rules and regulations in order to access resources through these channels. Here, the dominance of the strong does not necessarily mean a total lack of power for the weak: both sides can pursue and succeed in attaining their aims in their respective arenas.[92]

IV. Conclusion

The power identifiers discussed above are deliberately theoretical and general. This is, in part, a result of the diffuse nature of power in human relationships, which is never the same either in comparison or over time. The constant shift of power can be examined only with reference to particular situations. The theoretical nature of the power identifiers discussed above is also an essential feature of the modelling of resource regimes presented in this chapter, a feature which underpins the approach of the CRC 1095. The modelling presents a conceptual means of identifying the complex interplay between regimes, resources and power, but does not provide a complete toolkit for the analysis of this interplay. Further work remains to be done in order to move towards a more clearly defined set of principles: on the function of power in regimes of multiple resources, on the temporality of power, on the effect of discursive processes on resource regimes and power, and on questions of typology, epistemology, agency and weakness.

---

90 Crozier et al. (1977), *L'Acteur et le système*.
91 Alber (2003), *Machttheorien*.
92 See Chapter 9 by David Rex Galindo, Melina Kalfelis, and José Luis Paz Nomey.

Literature

Abelshauser, Werner (ed.). (2003). *Die BASF. Eine Unternehmensgeschichte.* 2nd ed. Munich: C.H.Beck.

Alber, Edmute (2003). Machttheorien. In Edmute Alber, Julia Eckert, Georg Elwert (eds.). *Macht, Situation, Legitimität* (Sociologus, 53–2), 143–66.

Amelung, Iwo (2000). *Der gelbe Fluß in Shandong (1851–1911). Überschwemmungskatastrophen und ihre Bewältigung im China der späten Qing-Zeit* (Opera Sinologica, vol. 7). Wiesbaden: Harrassowitz.

Andersen, Arne (1996). *Historische Technikfolgenabschätzung am Beispiel des Metallhüttenwesens und der Chemieindustrie 1850–1933* (Zeitschrift für Unternehmensgeschichte. Beiheft, vol. 90). Stuttgart: Franz Steiner.

Angenendt, Arnold (1997). *Heilige und Reliquien. Die Geschichte ihres Kultes vom frühen Christentum bis zur Gegenwart.* 2nd ed. Munich: C.H.Beck.

Anonymus (1929). Der Krieg um Mannheim. *Deutsche Zukunft,* 10–11, 84.

Assmann, Jan (1990). *Ma'at. Gerechtigkeit und Unsterblichkeit im alten Ägypten.* Munich: C.H.Beck.

Axelby, Richard, and Emma Crewe (2013). *Anthropology and Development: Culture, Morality and Politics in a Globalised World.* Cambridge: Cambridge University Press.

Bachrach, Peter, and Morton S. Baratz (1962). Two Faces of Power. *The American Political Science Review,* 56–4, 947–52.

Bierschenk, Thomas (2008). Development Projects as Arenas of Negotiation for Strategic Groups. A Case Study from Benin. *Sociologia Ruralis,* 28, 146–60.

Borscheid, Peter (1976). *Naturwissenschaft, Staat und Industrie in Baden (1848–1914).* Stuttgart: Klett.

Corbin, Alain (1988). *Le Territoire du vide. L'Occident et le désir du rivage 1750–1840* (Collection historique). Paris: Aubier.

Cordes, Albrecht, and Philipp Höhn, Alexander Krey (2016). Schwächediskurse und Ressourcenregime. Überlegungen zu Hanse, Recht und historischem Wandel. *Hansische Geschichtsblätter,* 134, 167–203.

Crozier, Michel, and Erhard Friedberg (1977). *L'Acteur et le système. Les contraints de l'actioncollective.* Paris: Editions du Seuil.

Dahl, Robert (2005). *Who Governs? Democracy and Power in an American City.* 2nd ed. New Haven CT: Yale University Press.

Dikötter, Frank (1992). *The Discourse of Race in Modern China.* Stanford: Stanford University Press.

— (2010). *Mao's Great Famine. The History of China's Most Devastating Catastrophe, 1958–62.* London et al.: Bloomsbury.

Esherick, Joseph (1987). *The Origins of the Boxer Uprising.* Berkeley CA: University of California Press.

Elias, Norbert, and Michael Schröter (eds.). (2005). *Studien über die Deutschen. Machtkämpfe und Habitusentwicklung im 19. und 20. Jahrhundert* (Norbert Elias. Gesammelte Schriften, 11). Frankfurt/M.: Suhrkamp.

Foucault, Michel (1963). *Naissance de la clinique. Une archéologie du regard medical.* Paris.

— (1972). *Histoire de la folie à l'âge classique.* Paris: Presses universitaires de France.

— (1975). *Surveiller et punir. Naissance de la prison.* Paris: Gallimard.

— (1976). *Histoire de la sexualité.* Vol. 1. *La Volonté de savoir.* Paris: Gallimard.

— (1982). "The Subject and Power", *Critical Inquiry*, 8, 777–95.

Gaventa, John (1982). *Power and Powerlessness. Quiescence and Rebellion in an Appalachian Valley.* New edition. Urbana IL: University of Illinois Press.

— (2003). *Power After Lukes. A Review of the Literature.* Brighton: Institute of Development Studies.

Geary, Patrick (1983). Humiliation of Saints. In Stephen Wilson (ed.). *Saints and their Cults. Studies in Religious Sociology, Folklore and History.* Cambridge: Cambridge University Press, 123–40.

Giddens, Anthony (1982). *Profiles and Critiques in Social Theory.* Berkeley CA: University of California Press.

— (1984). *The Constitution of Society. Outline of the Theory of Structuration.* Cambridge: Polity Press.

Glaser, Carl (1921). *Erlebnisse und Erinnerungen nach meinem Eintritt in die Badische Anilin- und Sodafabrik im Jahre 1869.* Ludwigshafen (unpublished manuscript, BASF company archive in Ludwigshafen).

Groebner, Valentin (2000). *Gefährliche Geschenke. Ritual, Politik und die Sprache der Korruption in der Eidgenossenschaft im späten Mittelalter und am Beginn der Neuzeit* (Konflikte und Kultur—Historische Perspektiven, vol. 3). Konstanz: Universitätsverlag Konstanz.

Gumbel, Emil Julius (1922). *Vier Jahre politischer Mord.* 5th edition. Berlin: Verlag der Neuen Gesellschaft.

Hobbes, Thomas (1651). *Leviathan or the Matter, Forme and Power of a Commonwealth Ecclesiasticall and Civil.* 1st edition. London: Printed for Andrew Crooke.

Iwanow, Iwan A. (2016). *Die Hanse im Zeichen der Krise. Handlungsspielräume der politischen Kommunikation im Wandel (1550–1620)* (Quellen und Darstellungen zur hansischen Geschichte, vol. 61). Cologne et al.: Böhlau.

Jisheng, Yang (2012). *Grabstein—Mùbēi. Die große chinesische Hungerkatastrophe 1958–1962.* Aus dem Chinesischen von Hans Peter Hoffmann. Frankfurt/M.: S. Fischer

Jörn, Nils (2014). Archivalien zu den Hansekontoren im Archiv der Hansestadt Wismar—Vorstellung des Projekts eines Wendischen Inventars. *Hansische Geschichtsblätter*, 132, 105–88.

Koschnick, Wolfgang J. (1993). Resource. In Wolfgang J. Koschnik. *Standard Dictionary of the Social Sciences*, vol. 2, part 2. M–Z, 1312–1313. Munich: Saur.

Laube, Reinhard (2004). *Karl Mannheim und die Krise des Historismus. Historismus als wissenssoziologischer Perspektivismus* (Veröffentlichungen des Max-Planck-Instituts für Geschichte, vol. 196). Göttingen: Vandenhoeck & Ruprecht.

Lepenies, Wolf (2006). *The Seduction of Culture in German History.* Princeton NJ: Princeton University Press.

Leppin, Hartmut, and Christian A. Müller (2017). Discourses of Weakness and Resource Regimes: Preliminary Remarks on a New Research Design. In Anke K. Scholz, Martin Bartelheim, Roland Hardenberg, Jörn Staecker. *ResourceCultures. Sociocultural Dynamics and the Use of Resources—Theories, Methods, Perspectives* (RessourcenKulturen, vol. 5), 45–55. Tübingen: Universität Tübingen.

Lichtheim, Miriam (2006). *Ancient Egyptian literature.* vol. 1. *The Old and Middle Kingdoms.* 2nd edition. Berkeley CA: University of California Press.

Loader, Colin (2003). From ›Nationalökonomie‹ to ›Kultursoziologie‹: Structural Issues in Alfred Weber's Early Writings. In Eberhard Demm (ed.). *Soziologie, Politik und Kultur. Von Alfred Weber zur Frankfurter Schule*, 43–60. Frankfurt/M.: Peter Lang.

Luhmann, Niklas (1988). *Die Wirtschaft der Gesellschaft.* Frankfurt/M.: Suhrkamp.

— (2012). *Macht.* 4th edition. Konstanz: Universitätsverlag Konstanz.

Lukes, Steven (1974). *Power. A Radical View* (Studies in sociology). 1st edition. New York: Macmillan.

Machiavelli, Niccolò (1532). *Il principe.* 1st edition. Rome: Blado.

Marriage, Zoë (2006). *Challenging Aid in Africa. Principles, Implementation, and Impact.* New York: Macmillan.

Marx, Karl (1867). *Das Kapital. Kritik der politischen Oekonomie.* Vol. 1. Book 1: *Der Produktionsprocess des Kapitals.* Hamburg: Otto Meissner.

Marx, Karl, and Friedrich Engels (1848). *Manifest der Kommunistischen Partei.* London: Burghard.

McKitterick, Rosamond (2008). *Charlemagne. The Formation of a European Identity.* Cambridge: Cambridge University Press.

Nealon, Jeffrey T. (2008). *Foucault Beyond Foucault. Power and Its Intensifications Since 1984.* Stanford CA: Stanford University Press.

Neubert, Dieter (2001). Entwicklung unter dem Mikroskop. Der akteursorientierte Ansatz. *Entwicklung und Zusammenarbeit*, 42, 216–19.

North, Douglass C. (1990). *Institutions, Institutional Change and Economic Performance.* Cambridge: Cambridge University Press.

Palazzo, Éric (2000). *La Liturgie dans la société médiévale* (Collection historique). Paris: Beauchesne.

Popitz, Heinrich (1992). *Phänomene der Macht.* 2nd edition. Tübingen: Mohr Siebeck.

Pusey, James R. (1983). *China and Charles Darwin.* Cambridge MA: Harvard University Press.

Reynolds, Douglas (1993). *China. 1898–1912. The Xinzheng Revolution and Japan.* Cambridge MA: Harvard University Press.

Rhoads, Edward J. M. (2000). *Manchus and Han. Ethnic Relations and Political Power in Late Qing and Early Republican China, 1861–1928*. Seattle WA: University of Washington Press

Röckelein, Hedwig (2015). Mittelalterliche Sakralobjekte. Zu ihrer Bedeutung, Funktion und Rezeption. *Historische Anthropologie*, 23–3, 353–365.

Schenkel, Wolfgang (1965). *Memphis-Herakleopolis-Theben. Die epigraphische Zeugnisse der 7.–11. Dynastie Ägyptens*. Wiesbaden: Harrassowitz.

Schröter, Hans (1992). *Friedrich Engelhorn. Ein Unternehmer-Porträt des 19. Jahrhunderts*, 2nd edition. Landau: Pfälzische Verlagsanstalt.

Scott, James C. (1985). *Weapons of the Weak. Everyday Forms of Peasant Resistance*. New Haven CT: Yale University Press.

Spittler, Gerd (1981). *Verwaltung in einem afrikanischen Bauernstaat. Das koloniale Französisch-Westafrika 1919–1939* (Beiträge zur Kolonial- und Überseegeschichte, vol. 21). Freiburg i. Breisgau: Atlantis.

Tauschek, Markus, and Maria Grewe (eds.). (2015). *Knappheit, Mangel, Überfluss. Kulturwissenschaftliche Positionen zum Umgang mit begrenzten Ressourcen*. Frankfurt/M.: Campus.

The Second Barefoot Collective (2011). The Barefoot Guide 2. Learning Practices in Organisations and Social Change. URL: www.barefootguide.org/uploads/1/1/1/6/111664/barefoot_guide_2_learnin g_whole_book.pdf [2018-03-13].

Theweleit, Klaus (1977/1978). *Männerphantasien*. Vol. 1: *Frauen, Fluten, Körper, Geschichte*; Vol. 2: *Männerkörper, zur Psychoanalyse des weißen Terrors*. Basel et al.: Roter Stern.

Voigtländer-Tetzner, Walter (*circa* 1940). *Chronik der BASF 1865–1940*. Ludwigshafen (unpublished manuscript, BASF company archive in Ludwigshafen).

Vogelsang, Kai (2012). *Geschichte Chinas*. 2nd edition. Stuttgart: Reclam.

Wagner, Peter (1990). *Sozialwissenschaften und Staat. Frankreich, Italien, Deutschland 1870–1980* (Theorie und Gesellschaft, vol. 17). Frankfurt/M.: Campus.

Weber, Max (2013). *Wirtschaft und Gesellschaft* (Max Weber Gesamtausgabe, section 1: Schriften und Reden, vol. 23). Tübingen: Mohr Siebeck.

Wemheuer, Felix (2007). *Steinnudeln. Ländliche Erinnerungen und staatliche Vergangenheitsbewältigung der "Großen-Sprung"-Hungersnot in der chinesischen Provinz Henan* (Europäische Hochschulschriften, series 27: Asiatische und afrikanische Studien, vol. 100). Frankfurt/M.: Peter Lang.

Zanasi, Margherita (2006). *Saving the Nation. Economic Modernity in Republican China*. Chicago IL: University of Chicago Press.

Chapter 9
Agency and Asymmetries: Actors and their Access to Resources in Colonial and Developmental Setting

David Rex Galindo, Melina Kalfelis, and José Luis Paz Nomey

I. Introduction

How can one explain the handling of resources? The multidisciplinary Collaborative Research Center (CRC) 1095 conceptually acknowledges the regime character of a resource. The research topics are therefore not single resources, their materiality or scarcity, but the inevitable rules regarding the availability of resources: who grants access to the resource, who defines the rules regarding its appropriation, or its limitations. How does something normally recognised as an immaterial resource become accessible and practically applicable? All of these questions refer to regimes, within which the access to resources is both regulated and handled. In the long-term, such regimes will be classified by the CRC 1095 in order to focus on the overarching similarities and differences in the handling of resources.

Examining the handling of resources is especially important for situations in which the opportunities for distribution are highly unequal. For these situations, often described as asymmetrical types of regimes, it seems intuitive to show the distinctiveness of such asymmetries of the *regime* through the possibilities of actions on the part of the *actors*. Historical and ethnological empirical analysis, however, points to a more complicated picture. A look at the courses of action of local actors reveals stories that have passed unnoticed, stories which not only illustrate the structural conditions, but also the levels of action within.

The three case studies presented here were chosen because they all have one thing in common: they all—at first glance—represent asymmetrical constellations with opportunities that are distributed unequally. As a contemporary case, NGO-actors in Africa are examined, where well-organised NGOs receive European funding from the so-called Global North. The two historical cases investigate colonial constellations in sixteenth- and seventeenth-century Mexico and Peru, where indigenous actors were confronted with the imperial claim to the authority of the Spanish monarch. The three examples show how, within their respective situations, a new, albeit not completely condition-inversing, opportunity to act arose, one which is seen only inadequately from a broader macro-perspective.

To uncover such hidden phenomena, one needs a vocabulary that focuses on the actors and their contexts. In this chapter, this will be realised by using the concept of agency: linking developmental and colonial resource regimes to agency in the examined cases opens up perspectives on the levels of action which are essential in order to understand the cases in point.

Scholars have pointed out that agency is a hard concept with which to grapple. Conceptually speaking, agency can be fuzzy, particularly as agency has been approached from a variety of disciplines with varying results. We acknowledge that, when discussing agency, there are different qualitative variables associated with the nature of agency: "intentionality", "responsibility", "choice", "contingency", "desire", "resistance", "conformity", and "freedom", to cite but a few. The approach has varied. For instance, it has been commonplace in post-colonial and colonial studies to approach agency as resistance to power and domination, and thus to affirm that conformity implies a lack of agency.[1] In a legal context, though, attention has been given to the issue of how to draw the boundaries of agency around catastrophic events of the twentieth century, such as genocide and ethnic cleansing during World War II, in the former Yugoslavia, or in Rwanda.[2] In general, in a philosophical sense, agency is used to evaluate a so-called innate, natural capacity that human beings may have to respond to, to resist, to desire, or to seek, in contexts which range between the theoretical polar opposites of "free will" and "total coercion".[3]

---

[1] Frank (2006), *Agency*, 281–302. For a critique of postcolonial theory, see the specific example below on development agencies in Burkina Faso.

[2] Vetlessen (2005), *Evil and Human Agency*. In this line of thought, agency has been evoked in order to ask the question critically: "Who is responsible?"

[3] Barnes (2005), *Understanding Agency*; Passoth et al. (2012), *Agency without Actors*, 1–11. Some scholars problematised the use of agency relative to "in-born" or "natural" capacities, arguing that this over-determines the concept of agency. Thus, in some of the literature, there is a perceived tension between individual and collective power, which might also be construed as "micro" vs "macro". This debate is also frequently fused with the dialectic of "agency vs. structure". Agency proponents underscore a range of choices exerted by an individual, otherwise known as microsocial processes. Conversely, those who argue in favour of structure highlight macro level factors leading them to believe

In our case, we are interested in delineating the relationship between the actors, power relations, and the resources, through the lens of agency. Rather than having a straightforward dialectic between agency and structure, Wiilliam Sewell understands resources and rules to be forms of structure that "empower and constrain social actions and tend to be reproduced by that action". In this way, Sewell argues for a flexible quality to structure, emphasising its dynamism and porosity with respect to "processes of social interaction". He claims that actors can *both* reproduce structure *and* make transformations of the structure possible; that is to say, his concept of agency can help us to understand better which actors compete for resources, and how humans relate to resources in asymmetrical power environments. Hence, we find Sewell's definition of agency as the capacity to gain a certain amount of control over resources or perhaps the capacity to achieve certain goals (related to resources), which are applicable to our case studies.[4]

It is assumed in this chapter that all members of both historical and current formations operate within power relations, and those relations are not as obvious as one might think since it is elusive to identify where power rests or to measure the levels of the power imbalance in resource regimes. We can only implicitly assume that asymmetries in historical formations have an influence on the latter's relation to resources. Taking the fact that resources trigger power relations into account, and underscoring the role played by those who want either to control access or want to gain access to such resources, we can elucidate the inter-relational dynamics of human interaction. In this chapter, which explores three empirical examples in America and Africa in the early modern and contemporary periods, we approach agency with the explicit focus on the capacity to act, particularly as it refers to the gaining of access to resources. As mentioned above,

---

that actors are highly limited or constrained. For a further summary of this topic, see Turner and Markovsky (2007), *Micro-Macro Links*, 2997–3005.

4 Sewell (2005), *Logics of History*, 124–151. A shortcoming in conceptualising agency as the capacity to act is that it diminishes the motivations behind decision-making processes. One of the conundrums here is why some act and others do not, and what causes individuals to act in one way or another. While we acknowledge that humans exercise agency, it is more unpredictable to establish why it is exercised in such a way, or by certain actors rather than others, in similar conditions. Moreover, while Katherine Frank pinpoints that it would be erroneous to conflate agency with free will, she also encourages us to explore how people who are subjected to such pre-existing understandings and social positionings have a way of creating spaces for manoeuvre and obtain their goals. Frank (2006), *Agency*, 288, 298.

the reasons to act might stem from desires, intuitions, resistance, intentions, or the search for freedom, but, in our case, certain actors might have the capacity or ability to gain access to resources or might simply want to have such access, a point reflected by their agency. We believe that the three case studies in this chapter allow us to give empirical evidence on how agency can become an interesting conceptual tool to examine human interactions within power relations.

First, there is a case study that approaches agency in a contemporary environment through the workings of a non-governmental organisation (NGO) operating in Burkina Faso. Then, we rely on two case studies that emphasise the importance of actors in an early modern colonial context. In these two instances, we look at the early stages of Spanish colonialism in America, with a focus on religious, legal acculturation. In all of these examples, we illustrate competing discourses, motivations for acquiring resources, ways of obtaining resources, and limitations to gaining resources. We further assert that the concept of agency is very often demonstrated through the responses to a given environment, despite the prevailing power asymmetries. We hope to demonstrate that agency conceptually offers us an incisive means with which to identify actors that arise from presumed weaker positions and discourses. The following case studies showcase how the agents of our studies are entangled between the local and the resource regimes of each example through strategies, beliefs, and the economy (both material and spiritual). These actors are still able either to enact some control within resource regimes, or to exert new forms of agency that can transform or create resources in a given historical formation. It is worth noting that we also show that supposedly weak actors have resources which are needed as well. In conclusion, agents act with certain aims, sometimes even in counter-productive ways which may not be what we consider to be useful resources.

II. Development through the Lens of Agency

We wish to start with a case that stems from development studies in a contemporary context and with an anthropological view. This first case study further engages with the prolific scholarship that development studies have produced on actors and discourses. Development comprises an alliance of multilateral organisations and global players that have an impact on world events and pursue not only the interest of helping the poor, but also of preserving their own system by obtaining funds and gaining influence, or even by establishing economic relations. Understandably, therefore, various authors have correctly labelled this as an industry.[5] From a historical perspective, it cannot be dated to a definite starting-point, although President Harry Truman's inaugural address in 1949 is gladly propagated as the day that it began. But, instead, development emerged through global discourses in the twentieth century on China, British colonial power efforts in Africa, and the Cold War.[6] Paradoxically, it has both limited and infinite spatial boundaries at the same time; there is no explicit place where its unique origin can be found. If, for example, one goes to places where development is to be implemented or visits organisations such as the World Bank, one will find very different life worlds, cultures and peoples, but, at the same time, surprisingly similar practices and rules.

The existence not only of a heterogeneous cultural and institutional environment but also of homogenous language and norms lends itself to using the development industry as an empirical example for contemporary resource regimes. It comprises manifested processes of rules and procedures, which formalise the use of certain resources and are influenced by historicised and institutionalised structures.

Most of the research conducted by Melina Kalfelis took place in Zorgho, a town in Burkina Faso, from 2009 until 2017. Kalfelis worked with development actors who are active in five locally-founded non-governmental organisations (NGOs),[7] which can be labelled as *grassroots-*organisations that play a profound agentive role in the country when it comes to the managing of urgent shortages for the population. Moreover, NGOs constitute the only private sector in Burkina Faso, one which functions constantly within the French civil service system, which renders them alternative workplaces since unemployment is high. In addition, Kalfelis conducted interviews with donor[8] organisations of these Burkinabe NGOs

---

5 For an elaboration on development as an industry, see Powell et al. (1997), *NGOs and the Development Industry*, 3–10.

6 Easterly (2014), *The Tyranny of Experts*.

7 The names of actors and organisations in this research are anonymised.

8 In this chapter, the Western partners of the local NGOs in Burkina Faso are referred as *donors* to make a clear distinction for the reader and because of the limited scope of this publication. However, it should be noted that there is a discursive trend to overcome the donor-recipient vocabulary and that there are profound differences in donor structures.

in Canada and Sweden, and took part in an internship with another donor organisation in Switzerland. Thus, she exerted a multi-sited ethnography, with the main emphasis on the actors in Burkina Faso, whose perspective she has always tried to take as her empirical point of departure.

Interestingly, discourses that tackle the levels of development of the actors refer to these professionals in the target country as *local* actors, while it seems that the actors from the donor's side are referred to as *international development experts*. This is one of many examples which show how language strengthens dichotomies, such as centre and periphery, for example, which seems to be implied with these designations.[9] Consequently, the particular multi-sited perspective on development actors at different sites and their agency reveals that each of them acts locally. Moreover, it de-mystifies the alleged powerful *development experts*, who have boundaries for agency within their own environment as well. No matter how privileged one development actor in Canada, for example, might be in comparison to another in Burkina Faso, both of their actions are related not only to their own local spaces but also to distant and foreign spaces, spaces which are difficult both to grasp and to control.

At the same time, all actors within development want to acquire, organise, exchange, control and tactically act upon resources. The main difference is that they act within very different social and economic environments, and have divergent interests and starting-points when it comes to their agency. Compared to Burkina Faso, the motives of a NGO worker in Switzerland, for example, are more concerned with the satisfaction of their financial partners, to implement programmes neatly and to enable evaluation, accountability and monitoring processes to guarantee the projected outcomes: this is regardless of whether the donor is funding projects of the Burkinabe organisations itself (which happens less and less) or whether the donor implements its own programme. NGO workers in Zorgho, on the other hand, have more existential goals. While many of them struggle with their own economic insecurities, they also try to adapt to the different requirements of international donors in order to acquire resources and keep their own organisations running. The workers and their organisations in Burkina Faso mostly exist in fragile environments due to weak political structures and the harsh economic conditions in the country. As a conse-

---

9 See Chakrabarty (2000), Provincializing Europe, for a post-colonial perspective; see Lepenies (2008), Roots of Modern Concept of Development, 202–225, for an historical perspective on development concepts and rhetoric.

quence, these actors seem to take part in development from weaker positions than actors from, for example, Switzerland. This implies quite significant power asymmetries within partnerships, but, arguably, does not exclude the different actors' capacities to exert the agency and the power within their specific lifeworlds of action.

The concept of agency was the subject of radical criticism from Gayatri Spivak's post-colonial studies in the 1990s. Since then, many authors use it as a synonym for resistance and see it as being deeply entangled with subalternity.[10] As a result, one finds it hard to discover a clear definition of what agency means apart from its use in the alleged post-colonial contexts. Consequently, this chapter does not use post-colonial or subaltern agency as a general notion because it is too ideologically loaded, especially against the background of latest critiques. Nonetheless, there are some basic thoughts within the discourse which fit neatly into the position of this chapter. One is the idea of highlighting the untold stories of agency and of showing, as anthropologists managed to, that, even from weak positions, strategies exist from which to access resources, as does the capability to open up spaces of power.[11] Moreover, post-development as a branch of post-colonial theory connects the asymmetric structural and discursive grounds of development with consolidated Eurocentric narratives.[12]

In fact, the power of development discourse and the dominance of donors as well as the weak position of the Burkinabe development actors has been discussed intensively.[13] Although these facts are unquestionable, all too often they obfuscate the diverse landscapes of the different actors; in

---

10 See Spivak (1988), *Can the Subaltern Speak?*, 66–111.
11 See Comaroff and Comaroff (1991), *Of Revelation and Revolution*, Vol. 1, for forms of consciousness in South Africa during the colonial period; see Crozier and Friedberg (1993), *Zwänge des Kollektiven Handelns*, for theories of the power that spaces of manoeuvre.
12 See Escobar (1995), *Encountering Development*, and Ziai (2007), *Development Discourse*, for post-colonial thoughts on development.
13 See Amutabi (2006), *The NGO-Factor in Africa*, for perspectives on NGO work in Kenya; see Bierschenk (2008), *Development Projects*, 146–160, for examples from Nothern Benin. see Michael (2004), *Undermining Development*, for three case studies on NGOs in Africa; Escobar (1995), *Encountering Development*, for post-development perspectives as well as Ziai (2007), *Development Discourse*; see Lewis (2016), *Abandoned Pasts*, 61–83, for NGO work within global development regulatory frameworks.

particular, the capabilities of actors in African contexts are often neglected.[14]

Consequently, this chapter tries to provide a distinct perspective: it aims to emphasise the capacities and boundaries of agency, and its relation to power. Hereby, we want to contribute to our general inquiry of understanding agency in relation to resources and resource regimes as well as how, when, and where power appears and becomes tangible. As a first step, it is necessary to ask which specific resources play a role within the resource regime of development. This is certainly not easy to answer, since our understanding of resources is quite dynamic and large. This is why it is important to narrow the analysis to the question of which resources are exchanged and negotiated within the partnership.

1. Resources in the Regime of Development

During Kalfelis' research, it became clear that, as soon as the aim of establishing an NGO is realised, it is indispensable to adapt it to the resource regime of development aid in order to acquire resources. In this process, there are two important aspects that Burkinabe NGO workers strive for: money, and control over people. Both empower the grassroots organisations to enter the resource processes within the regime.[15] Humans are important in two ways: for the organisation itself, as well as for projects and programmes which form the legitimating core of the NGO's existence. Without humans and their capacity to act, it is impossible to achieve the appointed goals within the development projects. Therefore, within development, humans are crucial to manage the administrative apparatuses that result from the projects and keep accountability procedures functioning. Moreover, money is crucial because it is scarce for NGOs in Burkina Faso. Its only sources are potential donors outside the country or sometimes national funds. As soon as the aim of finding an external co-operation partner is attained, a pool of new resources opens up, which are also appealing for the NGO workers themselves. Donors offer education and knowledge (workshops, training, qualifications, certificates, *etc.*), which is mostly due to general professionalisation processes in non-governmental

---

14 See De Bruijn et al. (2007), *Trajectories of Agency in Africa*, 9–20, and Chabal (2009), *Africa*, 7–16.
15 Hart (2000), *Ausbreitung zur Warenwirtschaft*, 67–97.

development aid. Many young people in Burkina Faso do not have the privilege of finishing cost-intensive schooling, which makes education most valuable. Last, but not least, international donors offer technical and other material equipment to the NGOs, and, in the end, this can be connected to the lack of money as well.

But it would be a one-sided idea to conclude that, because Burkinabe actors have no money, they are powerless and simply dependent. On the contrary, within the regime, they, too, have something to offer which turns into a resource. First of all, most of the international development organisations are highly dependent on the development discourse. In this respect, because of the paradigm of ownership and sustainability, the demand for the strengthening of civil society and the growing doubts about security in West Africa, they increasingly tend to implement their projects through organisations and actors from the target country. This means that international donors rely heavily on the information drawn by these actors in the field, which makes them important knowledge carriers. In addition, these actors have the capacity to find reliable recipients, which are important to legitimise the resources that donors channel into projects. As noted above, accountability and outcomes are the most important keys to prove project success. Consequently, even though the Burkinabe NGO actors may not have many of the so-called material resources to offer, they nonetheless have the capacity to implement projects. Through this, they become human resources themselves, and are thereby able to offer time, knowledge, mobility, flexibility, and information, as well as reports and photographic images (which are most important for accountability efforts). Thus, it seems that different kinds of resources are offered and possessed by both sides within development, which indicates that agency can arise from both directions.[16]

Nevertheless, this does not imply that the relationship between the donors and the Burkinabe NGOs is symmetrical and not historically burdened.[17] My disgression on resources cannot neglect other inevitable observations: The Burkinabe NGO actors usually try to do everything they can to fulfil the, often short-noticed, requests of their partners. If necessary, they change their profile, focal points and even sack long-time NGO workers to demonstrate that they are suitable organisations.[18] Moreover,

---

16 Sewell (2005), *The Logics of History*, 143–144.
17 Büschel et al. (2009), *Einleitung*, 7–29.
18 Rottenburg (1994), *We Have to Do Business as Business is Done!*, 165–186.

there seems to be a continuous lack of information and explanation from the donors' side. For example, procedures are not sufficiently explained, communication often has a top-down tendency, and donors impose a lot of rules without clear reasoning.

2. The Limitations and Capacities of Agency

Thus, it becomes clear how deeply established asymmetries are on the structural level of development, which lies at the core of our research. Many proponents of dependency theory in the disciplinary field of sociology tackle the historical reproduction of these post-developmental and post-colonial structures.[19] They claim that the "development industry" consists of normative presumptions and "imaginative geographies", as Edward Said proclaimed in his famous work on Orientalism.[20] What used to be a territorial occupation of space has transformed into the race of spreading Western values.[21] Hence, development can be viewed as a mobilising ideology that constructs the universal meaning of "a good life", with hierarchies of knowledge, and applies homogeneous concepts, irrespective of the region and its history.[22]

The latest critiques on post-colonial theory state that it has become an implicit political left-wing, neo-marxist project that can result in strong polarisations and perpetuate old binaries.[23] Other current debates show that one has to be careful not to fall into the trap of "reviving a well-established Orientalist notion", as Vivek Chibber assumes for the work of Partha Chatterjees (1993) and Ranajit Guha (1999) on peasants in Colonial

---

19 For an overview see Abubakar (1989), *Africa and the Challenge of Development*, and Ziai (2007), *Development Discourse*, 3–17; for a research study within postcolonial contexts, see Randeria (2007), *Global Designs*, 12–30.
20 See Said (1994), *Orientalism*, and as a more recent reflection of practical thoughts as a result of these discourses, see Husseini de Araújo et al. (2012), *Welche Praxis nach der postkolonialen Kritik?*, 139–145.
21 See Escobar (2007), *Post-development* as concept and social practice; on the history of post-development, see Ziai (2012), *Post-Development*.
22 On knowledge production of development discourses, see Kees (2004), *Unpacking and Re-Packing Knowledge*; for a discussion on the ideology of development, see Ziai (2007), *Development Discourse*, 7–8.
23 See Hardt et al. (2004), *Multitude*, and Ziai (2012), *Post-Development*, 136.

India.[24] Moreover, authors such as Gregor McLennan have shown the contradictions by criticising Western universalism, since sociology, as a discipline, stems from Western institutions itself and has an objectifying approach.[25]

When speaking about the agency of actors in Africa, it is important to not fall into the trap of adopting too pessimistic or idealistic tones:[26] There is suffering, poverty, dependency and adaptation, but there is also resistance and transformative power: the capability to choose action or to choose not to choose. Resource regimes only function with actors who, on the one hand, have not only to agree with certain procedures, albeit to some extent, but also perpetuate them (since, otherwise, they would not be able to engage with them) and, on the other, have the capacity to negotiate, resist or appropriate resources and processes. As mentioned above, all development actors want to interact with resources, and multi-sited research reveals their ability to achieve such goals. Albeit from very different starting-points and conditions, actors show complicity, manoeuvre and negotiate.

As a result, the Burkinabe NGO workers may be weaker in terms of their economic background and their professional environment, but they are not incapable of acting: if a NGO worker is employed by an international donor, who expects his or her employee to work full time, he or she still manages to keep one or more alternative strategies in place. The donor knows how fragile partnerships are and thus maintains several security nets, irrespective of contractual obligations. The workers also have tactics or strategies in order to meet demands: for example, the Canadian NGOs asked the local workers to make advanced payments for material costs. But because their salary was too low, they bought the printing paper and other materials at the shop of a friend who allowed them to purchase on credit. But when the Canadian actors found out, they prohibited this behaviour. The reason for this was that the continuous purchase at one shop gives the

---

[24] See Chibber (2013), *Postcolonial Theory*, 158. The approach of these postcolonial theorists was to show that universal Western theory cannot be applied to the consciousness of Indian peasants since their collectively motivated way of thinking stands in contrast to an individual interest and rationality, which is one of the exact clichés Western discourses used to attribute to "the other".

[25] See McLennan (2013), *Postcolonial Critique*. As a response to this criticism, see Sinha et al. (2017), *Marxism and Postcolonial Theory*.

[26] See Kaag (2004), *Ways Forward in Livelihood Research*.

impression of favouritism. In the end, the Burkinabe workers negotiated and their donors conceded.

In general, one can say that the NGO workers show astonishing flexibility in their ability to react constantly to the requirements of extra tasks, such as sudden requests to join a meeting or harsh deadlines. If there is a second or third partnership, they adapt to each one in a different manner if necessary. They quickly learn new rules, appropriate paradigms and filter priorities. It is not uncommon for donors to terminate contracts when there is no new partnership in sight. NGO workers may go for months without receiving their salary but nonetheless continue to stick to their organisation in the hope of a new donor. In fact, the Burkinabe NGOs and their actors continue to exist with these continuous ups and downs, and are very resilient in mastering this challenge. Falling back into poverty is a common experience for many men and women in Burkina Faso, and they have their own strategies to withstand such phases through a combination of help from relatives, spontaneous economic opportunities, or simply by holding out. Meanwhile, it is the responsibility of the NGO founder to find a new financial donor; otherwise, the NGO will collapse—at least for a certain period.

The capability to act from an unprivileged position is an interesting example of the limits of agency in strong positions. Indeed, the international donors of the Burkinabe NGOs also suffer from a lack of knowledge about procedures in Zorgho. Besides the donor actors lack of knowledge of the cultural, political and social peculiarities of Burkino Faso, which was somehow to be expected, it is surprising how uninformed they are about their "on-site" partners, local conflicts, and ongoing projects. Thus, it should be stated that, independently of whether they are in Switzerland, Canada or Burkina Faso, all development actors are locally intertwined and face limitations to information and action.

In the Swiss NGO, for example, most decisions have to be aligned with the NGOs own guidelines, the financial partner that funds the programme and the actors in the targeted country. Often, the Swiss development actors face a challenge in satisfying the different content-related directives, rule-bound processes and practical needs for implementation. Hence, the need to realise that certain tasks can entail profound limitations and compromises. Moreover, the need for specific tasks can only be transmitted to the Burkinabe partners through several stages[27] of (tele-) communications, which makes the process of creating action quite complicated. The distance and the intermediate levels between communicating about an action and initiating the action in the targeted field thus occur in an unsynchronised manner and are very often altered. Consequently, the capability of the Swiss actors to act is—apart from evaluation trips—confined to its office space.

It is a comparable case to that of information, although information for the donor has to move in the opposite direction—from the targeted country to that of the donor. What is even more problematical is that information mostly comes in the form of written text with "'objective representations'"[28] of what happened in reality. As a consequence, the Swiss actors receive a lot of information but can never know how credible it is. Interestingly, this obstacle is a daily limitation to their work and sometimes seems tolerated, despite the risks it poses. To conclude more generally, the information that arrives from the targeted country frequently raises (or ignores) the question of trust and mistrust, and truth and falsehood.

3. Power

Development actors make decisions and act initially within the boundaries of their local space, however boundless and global development may be. Within these local environments very distinctive life worlds exist, social and cultural structures, as well as institutions and rationalities.[29] It is from here that development actors obtain agency to use, exchange and negotiate the resources available, with the objective of controlling and acquiring the desired resources in turn. They face both the possibilities as well as the limitations to their actions in these different environments, and the same, arguably, is true for power, which also reaches its limits on the action levels of development work in Burkina Faso.

As mentioned above, critical development theory usually puts an emphasis on the structural, practical and normative power of Western devel-

---

27 In many cases, the donors' Headquarters communicates with the Country Office in the capital of the targeted country, which passes the information to the local partner organisations, which then have to inform the recipients (e.g., farmers).
28 Rottenburg (2002), *Weit hergeholte Fakten*, 217–221.
29 Chabal (2012), *The End of Conceit*.

opment institutions and organisations. Although this is true, an examination of Burkinabe NGO workers as actors with particular tactical and dynamic capacities opens a perspective from which it can be pointed out that power does not solely exist, as is often alleged, at the so-called top of the resource regime of development. Rather, it implies that power, as a fluid concept, emerges everywhere actors have resources and the capability to act.[30]

Meanwhile, power seems to be a capacity that can arise at every level within heterogeneous environments. The term "weakness" thereby loses its strength as a descriptive category, but marks an important analytical starting-point for further research on power. Ultimately, power is always at work when it comes to structures and the people who act within them.[31] Hence, agency is surely embedded within power structures which are, we would argue, not as clearly aligned as it may seem to be at first sight.[32]

The Burkinabe NGO actors showed their agency by shaping, using and reproducing resources, such as knowledge, which are entangled both within their own life worlds and in their social and cultural environment. Although they are acting within an economic environment which is constantly fragile, they are nonetheless able to negotiate and gain access to resources. Moreover, the NGO workers are fully aware of their disadvantaged position and the dominant character of their donors. The highlighting of their consciousness is the last important step in stressing their advantage, as it determines another strength to their agency.

However, it is not just in contemporary anthropological research contexts that one can find signs of complex, horizontal connections between resource regimes, power and actors. Similar patters can also be found within the colonial regimes that European monarchies imposed throughout the early modern period as we will see.

---

30 Sewell (2005), *Logics of History*, 132.
31 Sewell (2005), *Logics of History*, 145.
32 On the heterogeneity of power relations in Africa and agency, see Chabal (2009), *Africa*; for perspectives on power of the weak, see Scott (1985), *Weapons of the Weak*. For historical perspectives on power in relation to postcolonial contexts, see Wolf (1982), *Europe and the People without History*.

III. Native Agency and Religious Normative Knowledge in Sixteenth-Century Mexico

Analysing cultural encounters from the perspective of agency allows us to describe empirical evidence of the power relations emerging from asymmetrical contexts in the early modern period. *A priori*, the colonial nature of the establishment of European regimes in the Americas implies that power relations between the coloniser and the colonised emerge as a presupposed principle that needs no qualification. For example, in colonial Mexico, one could point out that the Spanish conquistadors held power over their Mexican subjects—the colonised—despite the fact that few Spaniards would exercise this abstract "power" over vast territories and the inhabitants, who outnumbered them. In recent decades, scholars have shown that domination among different bodies is never total and that power is never unlimited. As the title of a collection of essays on indigenous agency in colonial Mexico points out, in colonial regimes, there is always a space for negotiation within colonial domination.[33]

Because the emphasis here is on the colonised, rather than the coloniser, it is easier to identify less noticeable actors through the use of agency as a tool, rather than power as a relational factor. By assuming that resources played an essential role in the conformation of colonial regimes, we can further unveil how various actors create, negotiate, resist, and conform to an emerging context of hegemony and domination. This seems obvious if we just take into account the search for material resources behind the growth of global European empires from the late fifteenth to twentieth centuries. Following William Sewell, who builds upon the work of the sociologists Anthony Giddens and Pierre Bourdieu, we can trace how local actors (both colonised and colonising in this case) exercised certain capacities to adapt and extend resources in new contexts, *i.e.*, colonial regimes. Agency can stem from a desire to attain certain goals, but it must also entail that actors have certain capacities. Since knowledge, particularly normative knowledge, took an important dimension in the conformation of colonial domination in Spanish America, knowledge turned into a desired resource in the Spanish colonial regime. Thus, this section looks at those actors who might have had certain abilities and possibilities in order to gain

---

[33] See Owensby (2010), *Foreword*, and Kellogg (2010), *Introduction*.

access to the normative knowledge that eventually frames the legal, colonial regime.

American native peoples played a pivotal role in the creation and application of legal and political cultures in Spanish America. The encounter between the European and American worlds brought together different approaches to justice and conflict regulation on American soil. Scholars have pointed out that, through negotiation, resistance, and conformity, indigenous peoples contributed to the processes that shaped the colonial regime. In fact, they have shown that the establishment of the Spanish legal system permitted colonised peoples to voice their complaints to the Spanish authorities, thus appeasing tumultuous intentions and preventing rebellions.[34] However, the processes of creating, translating, and consolidating colonial juridical tools in the early post-conquest period still remains enigmatic.

A good starting-point is to explore the cultural processes of Christian evangelisation, and, more specifically, as Yanna Yannakakis points out in her review article of recent books on law and colonial societies, to focus on cultural translation and those who took part on it. This is even more true if we want to comprehend better the formation of a colonial normative regime that inherited local legal practices from the translation of European legal systems and effervescent new contingent local normativities. In the case of Spanish America, evangelisation played a pivotal role in the epistemological debates after conquest; it was through Christian missionaries and local native scholars that European ideas of normative orders were translated to indigenous communities. Rather than a one-way process, acculturation was thus multidirectional and owes much to the participation of indigenous scholars who acted as cultural brokers in defining and redefining normative orders that stemmed not just from traditional legal orders but also from normativities with a deep religious significance.[35] As was the case of colonial Mexico, indigenous agents played a particular role in framing the colonial normative fabric that eventually regulated the daily lives of most colonial subjects.

---

34 Kellogg (1995), *Transformation of Aztec Culture*. Scholars such as Kellogg have pointed out that, in studying resistance to the colonial order, for instance, communal violent resistance should not be taken for granted as most individuals would rather explore all possibilities—particularly through formal, legal appeals and informal complaints to authorities.

35 For a review of the state of the art, see Yannakakis (2008), *The Art of Being In-Between*. See, also, Kellogg (2010), *Introduction*.

The study of indigenous agency is not new to Latin American studies. Building on the work from post-colonial and subaltern studies, earlier works pinpointed resistance and rebellion against Spanish colonialism as the ultimate expression of indigenous agency. They focused on the motivation and intentionality of local peoples to resist colonialism, illustrating the driving forces which enhanced community, kinship, and individual empowerment and survival within the new colonial regimes. Scholars have also emphasised other roles that native peoples played in forming the post-conquest world in the Americas. For instance, we know that some native leaders maintained their authority soon after the arrival of Spaniards, while other indigenous peoples found the opportunity to ascend the social ladder after the demographic and violent disruption of their local communities. This could not be otherwise, as most indigenous communities could uphold a certain autonomy of governance within the Spanish colonial system. In central Mexico, indigenous parishes maintained similar internal, hierarchical organisation to those in place before the conquest, and, in many cases, local rulers continued to control tribute collections.[36] Throughout Spanish America, as in other colonial situations, many indigenous people became "cross-cultural brokers" or mediators between both the colonisers and the colonised, contributing not only to the resulting cultural intermingle but also to the development of a colonial regime. These indigenous brokers assimilated new worldviews into their own and facilitated the cultural transitions of their own communities as well as those of the invaders. Franciscan missionaries and indigenous men and women are characteristic examples of the cross-cultural experience in the Americas.[37]

In colonial Mexico, where indigenous peoples and religious missionaries worked closely, the process of religious conversion offered opportunities for people to gain access to resources, be they resources with material or immaterial qualities: the normative knowledge of the supernatural world that guides the Christian oecumene and forms the basis of the Spanish

---

[36] Lockhart (1992), *The Nahuas After the Conquest*, points out that the *encomiendas* or Indians who paid tribute to *conquistadores* were under the power of *tlatoani* (plural of *tlatoque*) or local rulers (local caciques). See, also the essays in Ruiz Medrano et al. (2010), *Negotiation Within Domination*; and Ramos et al. (2014), *Indigenous Intellectuals*.

[37] I have borrowed the idea of "strangers" and "cross-cultural brokers" from Curtin (1998), *Cross-Cultural Trade*, especially the "Preface" and 1–5. The book deals with the importance of trade as an aspect of cross-cultural encounters. Curtin defines traders as typical cross-cultural brokers. For a study of indigenous cultural brokers in colonial Mexico, see Yannakakis (2008), *The Art of Being In-Between*.

early modern juridical regime, and the texts that frame such knowledge. Sewell points out that agency is inherent to the knowledge of procedures—broadly conceived—that characterise all minimally competent members of society. In other words, all human beings maintain some degree of agency because of their minimal accessibility to resources in their lives despite their position on the social and hierarchical ladder. As pointed out above, colonial domination is limited, as the dominated can interplay in the interstices of power and thereby create their space for negotiation within domination. Applied to the case study of a colonial regime, agency exists on both sides of the colonial processes, *i.e.*, that of the coloniser as well as that of the colonised. However, not everyone has the same capacity to act or to gain access to resources, as there are asymmetries of power and divisions of interests within societies. Accordingly, the cultural and institutional context is relevant to assess the capacities of human beings to transpose and advance their agendas.[38]

Broadly speaking, this section focuses on Catholic evangelism in the first century after the conquest of Mexico City (1519/21) to focus on processes of cultural translation that bear important moral and institutional compounds. In the case of early modern Mexico, it should be noted that indoctrination and religious conversion imply the implementation of normative structures that stem from moral theology. Moral theology provided the normative arena and the norms that directed customs; thus, it is considered a fundamental instrument of guidance to ideal Catholic behaviour. According to the Catholic Encyclopaedia, moral theology includes "the rule, or norm, of the moral order, human actions as such, their harmony or disharmony with the laws of the moral order, their consequences, the Divine aids for their right performance". So, "as jurisprudence must enable the future judge and lawyer to administer justice in individual cases, so must moral theology enable the spiritual director or confessor to decide matters of conscience in varied cases of everyday life".[39] In our context,

---

38 Sewell (2005), *The Logics of History*, 128–141. His starting-points are Anthony Giddens' approach to agency within structures and Pierre Bourdieu's concept of habitus.

39 This research is part of a broader project at the Max Planck Institut for European Legal History entitled "Knowledge of the pragmatici: Presence and significance of pragmatic normative literature in Ibero-Americain the late 16th and early 17th centuries", which studies the use of moral theology and canon law as normativities within an early modern colonial context. My research centres on the creation and application of religious norms as practical standards that regulate frontier lives in the immediate aftermath of conquest.

the application of codes of conduct and modes of behavioural control at community level stemmed from the ecclesiastical authorities but required high levels of local involvement. In this sense, there is a good amount of pioneering works by other scholars who study moral theology as a juridical science. These scholars demonstrate that moral theology was a pillar of the colonial legal system in Spanish America and, as such, we can observe processes of legal implementation which emphasised the role played by indigenous scholars in the creation and diffusion of Catholic normative knowledge to the American peoples.[40]

Instead of approaching indoctrination as a unidirectional process, a focus on Catholic evangelism becomes a give and take process with a bidirectional flux. The process of Catholic indoctrination implies an active role on the part of the converted as much as of the missionary. Moreover, translating Catholic moral concepts into American languages became paramount to the process of conversion. Indigenous interpreters and intellectuals played a key role in transforming the message for wide American audiences and thus were crucial in indoctrinating the American populations. In this case, agency thus lies on multiple agents in the process of Catholic conversion.

European religious men and indigenous intellectuals produced practical texts (what we call pragmatic literature), with less theoretical concepts and abstractions which contained a moral theological ground, and were used for the catechetical and pastoral work among American indigenous communities. These texts circulated in printed and manuscript formats throughout the Americas. This literature, with a strong moral component, served as the basis for the conversion of Spanish America. Given that mendicants, mostly Franciscans, dominated the early evangelical landscape in the Americas, and that some archival material has been preserved, Franciscan missionary activities in sixteenth-century Mexico become the lens through which to address cultural processes. As pillars of the empire, Franciscan convents mushroomed throughout the sixteenth and seventeenth centuries to become the largest religious order in terms of manpower and extension in the Hispanic world. In Mexico, the Franciscan evangel-

---

See Rex Galindo (forthcoming), *The Creation of a Legal State*. For moral theology, see Lehmkuhl (1912), *Moral Theology*.
40 Decock (2012), *Theologians and Contract Law*; Duve (2010), *Catequesis y Derecho Canónico entre el viejo y el nuevo mundo*; and Moutin (2016), *Legislar en la América hispánica en la temprana edad moderna*.

ical programme quickly spread among native communities in the aftermath of conquest through the erection of convents and churches, and their establishment in Indian parishes. Hence, the focus on the Franciscan missionary agenda and their partnership with indigenous peoples.[41]

Since conversion was the goal, there can be no doubt that the vast majority of the texts that circulated were religious. In a major co-operation scheme, Catholic missionaries and native peoples wrote extensively in local Indian languages, predominantly Nahuatl, the *lingua franca* in central Mexico, but also in Purépecha and Matlazinga, the languages of Michoacán, Chontal Maya, and Otomi, to cite a few. In terms of their functionality, we can distinguish between texts written to train other specialists, particularly the confession manuals, and others written to entice a non-erudite audience, particularly catechisms, sermons, and speeches. In our CRC project at the Max Planck Institute for European Legal History in Frankfurt, and, in our case, for Mexico, we want to show how these pragmatic texts with a pastoral and catechetical aim were produced, circulated, and saved.[42]

For most of the colonial period, most native peoples communicated both with each other and with the colonial authorities in their local languages. Thus, bilingual pastoral pragmatic literature was relevant in the conversion of indigenous peoples. The production of Indian language texts was the result of joint-research projects between the friars and the local leaders. The most well-known example is the co-operation between the

---

41 For the use of pragmatic literature in early modern Spanish America see Duve et al. (forthcoming), *Knowledge of the Pragmatici*. For the evangelisation of Mexico, see, for instance the classic Robert Ricard (2014), *La conquista espiritual*; and Duverger (1993), *La Conversión de los Indios de Nueva España*, 24, 30–31. Capuchins and discalced Franciscans were also present in America, but their numbers paled compared to those of the observant Franciscan branch. For the dates of foundation of the North American, and South American provinces, see Habig (1945), *Franciscan Provinces of Spanish North America*; and Habig (1945), *The Franciscan Provinces of South America*.

42 In his study of religious texts written in Maya and Nahua languages, historian Mark Christensen distinguishes 3 categories depending on the format and authorship of these texts. Most surviving works were produced through the cooperation of clerics and Indians and printed. But manuscripts also circulated amply. Many were also the result of interethnic cooperation that never saw the printed press. Others, Christensen claims, were the sole production of native peoples, with perhaps little clerical guidance. Of course, there are other religious texts written in Spanish and to a lesser degree in Latin. Christensen (2013), *Nahua and Maya Catholicisms*, Chapter 2. For Nahuatl as the *lingua franca* of central Mexico, see the articles in Schwaller (2012), *Ethnohistory*. For a bibliographical study of catechisms published in America in the 16th century, see Resines Llorente (1992), *Catecismos americanos del siglo XVI*.

Franciscan Fray Bernardino de Sahagún and his indigenous collaborators. Sahagún had arrived in Mexico in 1530, where he pursued a long missionary career until his death in 1590. For years, he trained, in the Franciscan College of Tlatelolco (then outside Mexico City), Mexican scholars such as the famous Antonio Valeriano as well as Alonso Begerano, Martín Jacobita, and Andrés Leonardo, who collaborated with the Spanish friars to compose their pastoral literature. Through teamwork, friars and indigenous advisers produced Christian catechisms and other pastoral texts that contained basic Christian doctrinal prayers. These texts list a series of mandatory religious rituals to be performed regularly. Catechisms usually include an explanation of the sign of the cross and the Lord's Prayer, the prayer taught by Christ to his disciples, beginning "Our Father", the Hail Mary prayer, the creed, the *Salve Regina* prayer, the Ten Commandments, the five commandments of the church, the seven sacraments, the 14 articles of the Catholic faith (seven regarding the blessed divinity of God and seven regarding the holy humanity of Jesus—the Christian deity), 14 corporal and spiritual works of mercy,[43] general confession, the Eucharist, and the act of contrition. Other catechisms added mortal sins and the theological and cardinal virtues to the basic Catholic knowledge.[44]

Unsurprisingly, most missionaries never mentioned their tandem work with local scholars. However, a late sixteenth-century Franciscan friar not only credited his collaboration, but also unveiled that other friars also relied on local knowledge to write their pastoral works. In the prologue to his book of sermons in Nahuatl published in 1606, Franciscan missionary Fray Juan Bautista Viseo acknowledged the help of Mexican assistants, mostly local native peoples educated in a local Franciscan college from their childhood, who reached prominence through less well-known scholarly careers. In his Prologue to his sermons, Bautista Viseo further highlights the contributions of indigenous people to other texts written by other Franciscan missionaries. Interestingly enough, Bautista lists his Mexican collaborators before his intellectual debt to his fellow Franciscan

---

43 Delany (1911), *Works of Mercy*. The traditional enumeration of the corporal works of mercy is as follows: To feed the hungry; To give drink to the thirsty; To clothe the naked; To harbour the harbourless; To visit the sick; To ransom the captive; To bury the dead. The spiritual works of mercy are: To instruct the ignorant; To counsel the doubtful; To admonish sinners; To bear wrongs patiently; To forgive offences willingly; To comfort the afflicted; To pray for the living and the dead.
44 For a list of basic Christian doctrine and the Mexican Council of 1555, see Franco Mendoza (2015), *Eráxamakua*, 112–113.

brethren. These contributors had also been educated at the Franciscan College of Tlatelolco in Mexico City. It seems that the Mexican Hernando de Ribas, a linguist in Nahuatl, Latin and Spanish, and an instructor of Nahuatl, who helped various Franciscan missionaries such as Fray Alonso de Molina and Fray Joan de Gaona to compose their bilingual works, contributed especially to the texts of Fray Juan Bautista Viseo. Bautista further praised the support of other indigenous collaborators such as Joan Berardo, Diego Adriano, Francisco Bautista de Contreras, Esteban Bravo, the aforementioned Don Antonio Valeriano, and Agustín de la Fuente.[45]

These indigenous intellectuals, working together with Franciscan missionaries, shared their knowledge in order to bring innovative changes to the indigenous communities. As indoctrinators, the thoughts, motives, and intentions of native scholars owed much to the context in which they lived: this included not only their own cultures and institutions, but also those of the new regime that the Spaniards—including the Franciscan missionaries—aimed at implementing. In line with Sewell's understanding of the spaces wherein actors operate, native scholars could, and, in many cases, were forced to, innovate the rules that governed their lives. Or to apply Sewell's own words to our approach, native scholars in colonial Mexico were "capable of putting their structurally formed capacities to work in creative or innovative ways". Following other studies that highlight native political pre-eminence within their own communities under European colonial rule, a similar assertion could be pointed out for the relevance of indigenous legal and theological scholarship in the implementation of a colonial normative order. Certainly, power asymmetries appear, particularly at the macro level of Spanish colonialism in the Americas. But the daily life that involves a deeper knowledge of the internal structures of each community might reveal the way in which a few Catholic missionaries had to deal with communities of dozens, if not hundreds, of Indians. Not only were native scholars "knowledgeable", they were also "enabled". If knowledge, culture, and the capacity to access the former defines human agency, then, clearly, indigenous scholars exercised it in the midst of colonial asymmetries.[46]

---

45 Bautista Viseo (1606), *A Iesu Christo S.N. ofrece este Sermonario en lengua Mexicana*, Prólogo.
46 Sewell (2005), *Logics of History*, 127. For native political preeminence in a colonial setting, see, for instance, Hackel (1997), *The Staff of Leadership*.

IV. The Brotherhood of the Souls in Purgatory at the Cathedral of Lima. Colonial Lima, Catholic Agency and the Holy See (Sixteenth–Seventeenth Century)

In the case of early Peru, too, most important studies on agency concentrate on the analysis of resistance movements against the Spanish invasion and the processes or cultural conquests, such as the insurrection of Tupac Amaru I,[47] the millenarian and messianic movement of the *Taki Onqoy*,[48] or the evangelisation of the indigenous people.[49] An insight into Peruvian brotherhoods within the context of Catholic reform in the sixteenth century allows for a deeper understanding of the scope of action involved in a colonial setting during the early modern period. This investigation thus examines the "Brotherhood of the Souls in Purgatory" at the Cathedral of Lima in the Viceroyalty of Peru, its devotion to the souls in purgatory, and the strategies used by the local ecclesial community in adapting Catholic doctrine among the members of the fraternity. To achieve this goal, we ask the following questions: What was the Tridentine discourse about the "souls of purgatory"? How was this discourse transmitted to the Peruvian church? And what strategies did the brotherhood at the Cathedral of Lima use to introduce this discourse into the society?

Some clarifications and definitions are in order. The doctrine of "Purgatory" constituted one of the most important elements of conflicts of the Catholic Church in the sixteenth and seventeenth centuries, prompting the Protestant Reformation, along with a re-evaluation of the Bible as a "sacred text" of the dogmas of faith and of the forms of evangelisation inherited from the Middle Ages. The belief in purgatory was a recourse used by Martin Luther (1483–1546) in his *Disputatio pro declaratione virtutis indulgentiarum* (1517),[50] better known as the *95 Theses*, to criticise the sale of indulgences in the diocese of Mainz by the Dominican Johann Tetzel. According to Protestant theology, there is no specific reference to purgatory as a space between Heaven and Hell, in which a soul can be purified. The absence of this concept in the Bible was perceived as a weakness by the same Catholic Church until the early sixteenth century, when it was

---

[47] Vargas Ugarte (1951), *Historia del Perú*, 258.
[48] Quechua word: "drunkenness singing". Millones (1990), *El retorno de las huacas*.
[49] Estenssoro Fuchs (1998), *Del Paganismo a la Santidad*.
[50] Martin Luther's ideas mainly questioned the efficacy of indulgences; these were nailed to the door of the Wittenberg Palace church on 17 October 1517.

remedied in the Council of Trent (1545–1563). According to Catholic theology, Purgatory[51] is not a physical space, but a religious concept, describing a period after death during which dead souls without mortal sin can be purified and reach eternal life. This transition period can be shortened by believers by various actions: for example, by praying for the dear departed (the deceased) and by the practice of communion and confession.

At the beginning of the sixteenth century, the Catholic Church faced an institutional and, in particular, doctrinal crisis due to the rise of Lutheran ideas. In this sense, the Council of Trent constituted a powerful response to Protestantism, since it confirmed Catholic doctrine regarding the dogmas of faith, such as the Trinity, the ten commandments, the Creed, the sacraments, the Virgin Mary, the doctrine of justification, Purgatory, and many others. The Council of Trent was soon ratified by Philip II, the King of Spain, throughout his kingdom and in all the dominion of Spain.[52] In relation to Purgatory, the Tridentine norms re-affirmed the existence of this concept, and commissioned the bishops to ensure obedience to the "sane doctrine of Purgatory received from the Holy Fathers".[53] Thus, the doctrine was to be taught everywhere in order to ensure the conversion of all non-believers to Christianity. Likewise, the Tridentine prescriptions recommended that delicate or difficult subjects should not be taught in vernacular language to nominal Catholics and non-Christians in the colonies because these topics did not contribute to their edification, or promote piety. To implement this policy, the Tridentine Council recommended certain practices relating to death and life after death: the celebration of Masses, prayers, charity, and other works of piety, usually done for the dear

---

51 According to Jacques Le Goff Purgatory is a Christian invention born of Indian and Egyptian religious beliefs, as well as in Greek and Roman philosophy (especially Plato and his ideas on the immortality of the soul). These ideas were developed by the fathers of the Catholic Church Saint Augustin and Gregory Magnus and were valid throughout almost the entire middle ages until the twelfth century, in which it was consolidated thanks to Dante Alighieri's *Divine Comedy*. Le Goff (1989), *El nacimiento del purgatorio*; in the Council of Florence (1439–1445), the diffusion of the doctrine of Purgatory was determined through prayers, examples of charity, and the creation of fraternities for suffrages to the souls in Purgatory. These ideas were later confirmed by the Council of Trent, see: Denzinger (1963), *El Magisterio de la Iglesia*, 331, 554.

52 "Cédula de Felipe Segundo en que manda la observancia del Concilio, que es la Ley 43 Tit. 4 Lib. 4 Novisima Recop.", in: López de Ayala (Translator) (1847), *El sacrosanto y ecuménico Concilio de Trento*, 435–436.

53 López de Ayala (Translator) (1847), *El sacrosanto y ecuménico Concilio de Trento*, 327–328.

departed, practices which were to be done according to the established norms of the Catholic Church in a pious and devout manner.[54]

In 1532, while Europe discussed Luther's theses, Francisco Pizarro invaded Peru. Starting in Cajamarca, he captured Atawalpa and initiated the Spanish invasion of the Inca Empire, which he consolidated in 1534 with the sacking to the city of Cuzco, and ultimately with the murder of the Inca sovereign. The Viceroyalty of Peru (*Virreinato del Perú*), created in 1542, was an administrative institution implemented by the Spanish Crown in the New World, which had its capital in Lima and covered from its inception the former governments of New Castile and New Toledo, *i.e.*, it was formed based upon what had, in the pre-Hispanic period, been the territory of the Inca Empire, that is to say, almost all the Andean territory of the present South America, except for part of Brazil.[55]

It was in this historical context that the Tridentine doctrine was translated into the New World. In relation to brotherhoods, it was the Second Provincial Council of Lima (1567–1568)[56] which adopted the discourse of confraternity for Peru, although it was the Third Provincial Council of Lima (1582–1583) which regulated the creation and functioning of the brotherhoods in two ways: it established regular inspections of all brotherhoods (*visitas ordinarias de confradias*), independently of what kind, and it prohibited the creation of new confraternities and ensured their oversight by "having thus some priests present who guide them and direct the things that are to the service of God and good for their souls".[57]

Brotherhoods or *Cofradias* were Christian associations that originated in Europe and peaked in the late Middle Ages, whose practices were regulated by a "rule of life" and "constitutions". They were mostly secular, but there were also clerical or mixed brotherhoods at times.[58] Their main objective was to intensify the piety of their members and to contribute to the solemnity of the cult.[59] However, they also acquired social functions, turning into systems of mutual and social assistance among the brothers, such as the

---

54 López de Ayala (Translator) (1847), *El sacrosanto y ecuménico Concilio de Trento*, 328.
55 Inca empire or Tawantinsuyu was organized in four "Suyus" or region: Chinchasuyu (North), Collasuyu (South), Antisuyu (East) and Contisuyu (West). Early et al. (1998), *The History Atlas of South America*, 28–29.
56 Vargas Ugarte (1951), *Concilios limenses*, 140.
57 "teniendo entonces algún sacerdote presente que los coja y encamine las cosas que tan al servicio de Dios y bien de sus ánimas", see Vargas Ugarte (1951), *Concilios limenses*, 299.
58 Barnadas (2002), *Cofradías*, 553–554.
59 Celestino et al. (1981), *Las cofradías en el Perú*, 147–157.

assistance offered to sick and elderly members in the "hour of death" through the devotion to the "holy souls of Purgatory". Throughout the sixteenth century, Lima and its hinterlands witnessed the foundation of sixteen confraternities of the "Holy Souls in Purgatory", which was the most frequently and widely represented brotherhood.[60]

The Brotherhood of the Souls in Purgatory of the Cathedral Basilica of Lima was created in 1553 by Jerónimo de Loayza, the first Bishop of Lima. Its foundation was based upon the need to attend to "the obligation and reason that we, the living Christian faithful, have to pray to God and to do well for the souls of the dear departed".[61] According to Church practice from the beginning of Christianity to the present, the beginning of a devotion to images or sacred objects (Jesus Christ, the Virgin Mary, the saints and their relics) must be previously approved by the Holy See, because religious practices must conform to the teachings of the sacred scriptures and the magisterium of the Church. In order to spread the devotion according to the Catholic doctrine and to solve any issues related to it, the confraternity developed some agency processes in the sixteenth and seventeenth century. Catholic Agency was to be found in the ability of the Brotherhood to act through mediation between the Holy See and the laymen in Peru. In this sense, the Brotherhood becomes an intermediary between the laity and the confrères who seek the solution to their conflicts before the Holy See and *vice versa*. Contrary to the "individual" kind, the agency of the confraternity was "collective", *i.e.*, the group decided to establish contact with the Holy See in order to achieve certain rights. In this sense, we can see how collective efforts through confraternities offered their members a framework to co-ordinate actions, to gain a sense of community amidst adversities, and ultimately, to mobilise resources for the benefit of the group.[62]

One can first look at the supplications that the brotherhoods sent to Rome, such as a request to the Pope for the approval of an altar dedicated

---

[60] Campos y Fernández de Sevilla (2014), *Catálogo de cofradías del archivo del Arzobispado de Lima*, 32.

[61] "Atendiendo a la obligación y razón que los fieles cristianos vivos tenemos de rogar a Dios y hacer bien por las ánimas de los fieles difuntos", Campos y Fernández de Sevilla (2014), *Religiosidad popular*, 1116.

[62] This goes in line with Sewell, who argues that "agency entails an ability to coordinate one's actions with others and against others, to form collective projects, to persuade, to coerce, and to monitor the simultaneous effect of one's own and others' activities." Sewell (2005), *Logics of History*, 145.

to the Souls of Purgatory which was to be built in the Cathedral Basilica of Lima.[63] This petition was answered by Pope Clement VIII (1502–1605) with the pontifical Brief *Cum sicut accepimus*,[64] dated 1 July 1598. It was accorded freely, *i.e.*, without cost, and approved the mentioned privileged altar "*ad perpetuam*", in return for prayers and Masses dedicated to the dear departed. In another supplication, the same confraternity requested concessions to celebrate two Masses a day, instead of one, "one at the rising of the sun and [the] other after meridian",[65] because some members of the Brotherhood were merchants, craftsmen, farmers, native people, slaves and others, who could not participate in the Holy Mass at dawn.[66] This request was answered by Clement VIII with the Brief *Exponi nobis nuper fecistis*[67] 15 February 1603, which authorised a Mass at dawn and late in the afternoon as long as it was still day (light), "*so long as morning*".[68] During the pontificate of Paul V (1605–1621) the Brief *Urbis vitalis mius*[69] granted to this confraternity a full indulgence for the remission of the sins to those brothers who "in the moment of death call the name of Jesus Christ".[70] This indulgence was also addressed to the brothers who "visit the chapel on All Souls' Day"[71] (2 November), and the days of "Conception, Nativity, Annunciation [and the] Assumption of [the] Holy Virgin Mary".[72] Finally, by pontifical Brief of 20 March 1628, Innocent X granted a full indulgence to the Brotherhood for the celebration of the days of Saint Jerome, All Souls' Day, and the Triumph, Inventions and Exaltation of the Cross.[73]

While the content of Papal Briefs is crucial to understanding the relationship between Rome and Colonial Lima, it is equally crucial to understand the transformations that occurred in the confraternity as a result of

---

63 ASV, Sec. Brev., Indulg. Perpetuae 20, fol. 101v.
64 ASV, Sec. Brev., Indulg. Perpetuae 20, fol. 101v.
65 "un hora solis ortum et una post meridium", see: ASV, Sec. Brev., Indulg. Perpetuae 20, fol. 101v.
66 ASV, Sec. Brev., Reg. 330, fol. 210.
67 ASV, Sec. Brev., Reg. 330, fol. 209.
68 "dummodo illucescat dies", see: ASV, Sec. Brev., Reg. 330, fol. 209.
69 ASV, Cam. Ap., Sec. Cam. 107, fol. 634.
70 "in mortis articulo nomen Jesucristi invocant", see: ASV, Cam. Ap., Sec. Cam. 107, fol. 634.
71 "vell capellam in die commemorationis virum defunctum visitaverint", see: ASV, Cam. Ap., Sec. Cam. 107, fol. 634.
72 "in conceptionis et nativitatis necnon annuntiationis et assumptionis beatae mariae virginis visitantibus", see: ASV, Cam. Ap., Sec. Cam. 107, fol. 634.
73 Campos (2014), *Religiosidad popular*, 1118.

them. We argue that this complex process of translation,[74] appropriation, reproduction, regulation and re-elaboration of the norms granted by the papacy can be seen in the "Constitutions" of 1553 and 1659,[75] which regulated the internal functioning of the confraternity. In fact, the founding constitutions of 1553 did not contain any indulgences by the Pope. However, both constitutions agree on the income requirements for new brothers: the confraternity is open to all types of persons, both ecclesiastical and secular.

For all the payments made to the Brotherhood, the Spaniards and Creoles had to pay the total amount (namely, 1 *peso* and 1 pound of wax), while natives only paid half. The main Masses were on All Saints' Day, and the "patron's day" of the brotherhood. However, Masses were given every day for the souls of all deceased brothers, including the children of the brothers. The Constitutions of 1659 begin by listing the indulgences granted by Innocent X mentioned above. There were twenty chanted and prayed Masses on the day of the funeral of a brother. In addition, two Masses were held every normal day. In this scenario, in just one year, more than five thousand masses were held for the benefit of the Souls in Purgatory. Finally, brothers or sisters who were six months late in paying their fees were expelled.

In summary, the agency of the Brotherhood served to obtain the power to solve problems: in this sense, we can find the extension, translation and appropriation of (European) practices and traditions of the Roman Church in the Peruvian space. The confraternity depends on the Roman jurisdiction to have a religious status and to obtain privileges in church matters. An example of this can be found in its constitution and in the indulgences obtained by popes. This provided not only spiritual but also social and material support for its members and spiritual support for dead members (according to the beliefs of its members). The social context created a collective entity with a specific shared identity that gave them a sense of belonging and recognition on the part of the Church (and the state). With its own agency, it maintained and reframed the integration of the social hierarchies of the natives and slaves in the Catholic, *i.e.*, "universal", Church, thereby establishing social equality despite maintaining the socio-economic differences. The agency of the Brotherhood binds its members, and creates a social fabric, a network which can be useful for all of them,

---

74 Duve (2014), *European Legal History-Concepts*.
75 Campos (2014), *Religiosidad popular*, 1116–1119.

which gives them more power than they would have as individuals. Finally, the material support was concretised in resource pooling, thanks to a differentiated fee structure which allowed for the provision of services for the sick and the dead members, *i.e.*, health care and the funeral itself, which, of course, created a market for wax and fabric merchants, for example.

V. Conclusion

Our goal in this chapter was to centre on local actors as an important part of processes of change within historical formations. Beyond the commonplace definition of agency as resistance to power, we wanted to uncover local actors in the context of asymmetrical relations by identifying their role in the creation and use of resources, and likewise we sought to trace their actions within the processes of resource generation. By underscoring the triangular relations between agency, power and resources, we hope to have pinpointed how certain actors that might be dismissed because of their perceived subordinated positions are pivotal to the formation and transformation of the norms and practices that allocate resources, even if these actors find themselves in the midst of entrenched power relations. Since human beings are not completely alienated from their own history, we have approached agency as a prism to reflect on the various means that the less acknowledged actors have to create, access, and control what they might consider to be valuable items. Overall, scrutinising agency helps to illuminate how power asymmetries can create new forms of agency and new pathways for accessing resources within a given historical context. We identify different resources and actors in varying settings and historical epochs. In this sense, by focusing on agency as a capacity to gain access to resources (in the broad definition of this volume), the dichotomies of the centre and the periphery blur, the local gains relevance within the global, and humans relate to each other with certain aims, desires, beliefs, and intentions that might contradict their own existence within a certain power system.

A: In the lifeworld of the development-actors of Burkina Faso, this ranged from the reproduction and shaping of knowledge to the mobility and flexibility of human resources. Despite the asymmetries, which mean that international donors impose rigid rules often without clear comprehension of the cultural environment in the target country, Burkinabe NGO actors were found to exercise agency through, for example, adapting or negotiating processes, reflecting possible spaces for manoeuvre, and, where necessary, circumventing specific rules. Above all, these organisations proved highly resilient to the turbulence and short-term cycles of donor contracts because the actors kept the structures of their NGOs flexible. In many ways, their fragile economic situation served to heighten the NGO actors' consciousness of vulnerability, and reinforced their ability to be pliable within the resource regime of development.

B: Also from a historical perspective, as the case from sixteenth-century Mexico shows, native peoples kept some levels of epistemological entitlement in the application of normative orders under the Spanish colonial regime. Because religious men were at the forefront of Spanish-Mexican relations in the early stages of colonisation, the dialogue that resulted had a strong religious component. As contributors to the Franciscan evangelical programme, indigenous intellectuals maintained certain manoeuvrability to act and eventually to gain the upper hand in the creation of normative knowledge. Because native leaders—political, spiritual, and intellectual—construed the knowledge and culture of their communities, Spanish civil and religious authorities were dependent on them to adapt Catholic theological features to the local realities. Knowledge turns into a resource within regime structures, which, in our case study, is religious normative knowledge, and the texts that materialised these norms became a contested space to which both Spanish friars and native scholars contributed.

C: In Peru, we can track the results of the actions of various agents through the local Catholic confraternities. The emergence of new regulations on brotherhoods, as the result of local Councils, limited access to resources. When they were restricted in their power to make decisions, the Brotherhood initiated the Catholic agency to the Holy See in order to obtain certain rights that granted them access to the resources that the local regulations denied them. This led to the establishment of a more direct information regime between the community of lay people in the Peruvian periphery and the Church in Rome, which granted more autonomy and decision-making power to the Brotherhood against the local ecclesiastical and civil authorities. Thanks to the emission of several pontifical briefs by the Pope, the Brotherhood was able to decide in relation to resources such as devotions, liturgical celebrations, burials, membership fees and the granting of indulgences, principally.

Abbreviations

ASV	Archivio Segreto Vaticano
Cam. Ap.	Camera Apostolica
Reg.	Registra
Sec. Brev.	Secretaria Brevium
Sec. Cam.	Secretaria Camerae
Indulg. Perpetuae	Indulgentiae Perpetuae

Literature

Abubakar, Ahmad (1989). *Africa and the Challenge of Development. Acquiecence and Dependency versus Freedom and Development.* New York: Praeger.

Amutabi, Maurice N. (2006). *The NGO Factor in Africa: The Case of Arrested Development in Kenya.* New York: Routledge.

Barnadas, Josep María (2002). *Diccionario Histórico de Bolivia.* Sucre: Grupo de Estudios Históricos.

Barnes, Barry (2000). *Understanding Agency: Social Theory and Responsible Action.* London: Sage Publications.

Bautista Viseo, Fray Juan (1606). *A Iesu Christo S.N. ofrece este Sermonario en lengua Mexicana.* Mexico City: En casa de Diego Lopez Daualos.

Bierschenk, Thomas (2008). Development Projects as Arenas of Negotiation for Strategic Groups: A Case Study from Benin. *Sociologia Ruralis,* 28 (2–3), 146–160.

Büschel, Hubertus, and Daniel Speich (2009). "Einleitung – Konjukturen, Probleme und Perspektiven der Globalgeschichte von Entwicklungszusammenarbeit". In Hubertus Büschel, Daniel Speich (eds.). *Entwicklungswelten. Globalgeschichte der Entwicklungszusammenarbeit,* 7–29. Frankfurt/M.: Campus.

Campos y Fernández de Sevilla, Javier (2014). *Catálogo de cofradías del archivo del Arzobispado de Lima.* Madrid: Estudios superiores del Escorial.

— (2014). Religiosidad popular en las Reglas y constituciones de Cofradías de Ánimas del Mundo Hispánico. In Campos y Fernández de Sevilla, Javier (ed). *El mundo de los difuntos: culto, cofradías y tradiciones.* San Lorenzo de El Escorial: Estudios Superiores del Escorial.

Celestino, Olinda, and Albert Meyers (1981). *Las cofradías en el Perú: región central.* Frankfurt/M.: Vervuert.

Chabal, Patrick (2009). *Africa. The Politics of Suffering and Smiling.* London: Zed Books.

— (2012). *The End of Conceit: Western Rationality after Postcolonialism.* London: Zed Books.

Chakrabarty, Dipesh (2000). *Provincializing Europe: Postcolonial Thought and Historical Difference*. Princeton: Princeton University Press.
Chibber, Vivek (2013). *Postcolonial Theory and the Specter of Capital*. London: Verso.
Christensen, Mark Z. (2013). *Nahua and Maya Catholicisms: Texts and Religion in Colonial Central Mexico and Yucatan*. Stanford: Stanford University Press.
Comaroff, John, and Jean Comaroff (1991). *Of Revelation and Revolution Vol. 1*. Chicago: University of Chicago Press.
Crozier, Michel, and Erhard Friedberg. (1993). *Die Zwänge des Kollektiven Handelns. Über Macht und Organisation*. Weinheim: Beltz Athenäum.
Curtin, Philip D. (1998). *Cross-Cultural Trade in World History*. Cambridge: Cambridge University Press.
De Bruijn, Mirjam, and Rijk van Dijk, Jan Bart Gewald (2007). Social and Historical Trajectories of Agency in Africa. In Leo De Haan, Ulf Engel, Patrick Chabal (eds.). *African Alternatives* (African Dynamics 6, 9–20). Leiden: Brill.
Delany, Joseph (1911). "Corporal and Spiritual Works of Mercy." *The Catholic Encyclopedia*. Vol. 10. New York: Robert Appleton Company. URL: http://www.newadvent.org/cathen/10198d.htm [2018-02-17].
Denzinger, Enrique (1963). *El Magisterio de la Iglesia*. Barcelona: Herder.
Duve, Thomas (2014). European legal History-Concepts, Methods, Challenges. In Thomas Duve (ed.). *Global perspectives on Legal History*. Frankfurt/M.: Max Planck Institute for European Legal History.
Duve, Thomas, and Otto Danwerth (eds.). (forthcoming). *Knowledge of the pragmatici: Presence and Significance of Pragmatic Normative Literature in Ibero-America in the late 16th and early 17th Centuries*.
Duverger, Christian (1993). *La Conversión de los Indios de Nueva España: Con el Texto de los Coloquios de los Doce de Bernardino de Sahagún (1564)*. Trans. by María Dolores de la Peña. Mexico City: Fondo de Cultura Económica.
Early, Edwin, and Elizabeth Baquedano, Rebecca Earle, Caroline Williams, Anthony McFarlane, Joseph Smith (1998). *The History Atlas of South America*. New York: Macmillan.
Escobar, Arturo (1995). *Encountering Development. The Making and Unmaking of the Third World*. Princeton NJ: Princeton University Press.
— (2007). "Post-development" as Concept and Social Practice. In A. Ziai (ed.). *Exploring Post-development. Theory and Practice, Problems and Perspectives*, 18–31. New York: Routledge.
Estenssoro Fuchs, Juan Carlos (1998). *Del Paganismo a la Santidad. La incorporación de los indios del Perú al catolicismo. 1532–1750*. Lima: l´Institut Français d´Études Andines.
Easterly, William (2014). *The Tyranny of Experts: Economists, Dictators, and the Forgotten Rights of the Poor*. New York: Basic Books.
Franco Mendoza, Moisés (2015). *Eráxamakua: La utopía de Maturino Gilberti*. Zamora: El Colegio de Michoacán.
Frank, Katherine (2006). Agency. *Anthropological Theory*, 6, 3, 281–302.

Habig, Marion A. (1945). The Franciscan Provinces of Spanish North America. *The Americas 1*, (3), 330–344.
— (1945). The Franciscan Provinces of South America. *The Americas 2*, (2), 189–210.
Hackel, Steven W. (1997). The Staff of Leadership: Indian Authority in the Missions of Alta California. *The William and Mary Quarterly*, 54, (2), 347–376.
Hardt, Michael, and Antonio Negri (2004). *Multitude. War and Democracy in the Age of Empire*. London: Hamish/Penguin.
Hart, Keith (2000). Ausbreitung der Warenwirtschaft und Lebensstandard. In Amartya Sen (ed.). *Der Lebensstandard*, 67–97. Hamburg: Rotbuch.
Husseini de Araújo, Shaida, and Philippe Kersting (2012). Welche Praxis nach der postkolonialen Kritik? Human- und physisch-geographische Feldforschung aus übersetzungstheoretischer Perspektive. *Geographica Helvetica*, 67, 139–145.
Kaag, Mayke (2004). Ways Forward in Livelihood Research. In Don P. Kalb, Wil G. Pansters, Hans Siebers (eds.). *Globalization and Development. Themes and Concepts in Current Research*, 47–74. Dordrecht: Kluwer.
Kees, Jansen (2004). Unpacking and Re-Packing Knowledge in Development. In Don P. Kalb, Wil G. Pansters, Hans Siebers (eds.). *Globalization and Development. Themes and Concepts in Current Research*, 163–190. Dordrecht: Kluwer Academic.
Kellogg, Susan (2010). Introduction: Back to the Future. Law, Politics, and Culture in Colonial Mexican Ethnohistorical Studies. In Ethelia Ruiz Medrano, Susan Kellogg (eds.). *Negotiation Within Domination: New Spain's Indian Pueblos Confront the Spanish State*, 1–17. Boulder: University of Colorado Press.
Kellogg, Susan (1995). *Law and the Transformation of Aztec Culture, 1500–1700*. Norman OK: University of Oklahoma Press.
Le Goff, Jacques (1989). *El nacimiento del purgatorio*. Madrid: Taurus.
Lehmkuhl, Augustinus (1912). Moral Theology. *The Catholic Encyclopedia*. Vol. 14. New York: Robert Appleton Company. 17 Feb. 2018 URL: http://www.newadvent.org/cathen/14601a.htm
Lepenies, Philipp H. (2008). An Inquiry into the Roots of the Modern Concept of Development. *Contributions to the History of Concepts*, 4, 202–25.
Lewis, David (2016). Abandoned Pasts, Disappearing Futures: Further Reflections on Multiple Temporalities in Studying Non-Governmental Organisation Worlds. *Critique of Anthropology*, 36 (1), 61–83.
Lockhart, James (1992). *The Nahuas After the Conquest: A Social and Cultural History of the Indians of Central Mexico, Sixteenth Through Eighteenth Centuries*. Stanford: Stanford University Press.
López de Ayala, Ignacio (Translator) (1847 [1564]). *El sacrosanto y ecuménico Concilio de Trento*. Barcelona: Imprenta de Ramón Martin Indár.
McLennan, Gregor (2013). Postcolonial Critique. The Necessitiy of Sociology. *Political Power & Social Theory*, 24, 119–44.
Michael, Sarah (2004). *Undermining Development. The Absence of Power among local NGOs in Africa*. Oxford: Currey.

Millones, Luis (1990). *El retorno de las huacas. Estudios y documentos sobre el Taki Onqoy (siglo XVI)*. Lima: Instituto de Estudios Peruanos.
Owensby, Brian (2010). Foreword. In Ethelia Ruiz Medrano and Susan Kellogg (eds.) *Negotiation Within Domination: New Spain"s Indian Pueblos Confront the Spanish State*, xi-xv. Boulder: University of Colorado Press.
Passoth, Jan-Hendrik, and Birgit Peuker, Michael Schillmeier (2012). Introduction. In Jan-Hendrick Passoth, Birgit Peuker, Michael Schillmeier (eds). *Agency without Actors? New Approaches to Collective Action*, 1–11. London/New York: Routledge.
Powell, Mike, and David Seddon (1997). NGOs and the Development Industry. Review of African Political Economy, 24, 71, 3–10.
Ramos, Gabriela, and Yanna Yannakakis (eds.). (2014). *Indigenous Intellectuals: Knowledge, Power, and Colonial Culture in Mexico and the Andes*. Durham NC: Duke University Press.
Randeria, Shalini (2007). Global Designs and Local Lifeworlds. Colonial Legacies of Conservation, Disenfranchisment and Environmental Governance in Postcolonial India. *Interventions*, 9 (1), 12–30.
Resines Llorente, Luis (1992). *Catecismos americanos del siglo XVI*. 2 vols. Valladolid: Junta de Castilla y León, Consejería de Cultura y Turismo.
Rex Galindo, David (forthcoming). The Creation of a Legal State: Franciscan Missionaries and Ecclesiastical Normativities in New Spain's Frontiers, 1524–1630. In Thomas Duve, Otto Danwerth (eds.). *Knowledge of the pragmatici: Presence and Significance of Pragmatic Normative Literature in Ibero-America in the late 16th and early 17th Centuries*.
Ricard, Robert (2014). *La conquista espiritual de México 1933*. Mexico City: Fondo de Cultura Económica.
Ruiz Medrano, Ethelia, and Susan Kellogg (eds.). (2010). *Negotiation Within Domination: New Spain"s Indian Pueblos Confront the Spanish State*. Boulder CO: University of Colorado Press.
Rottenburg, Richard (2002). *Weit hergeholte Fakten. Eine Parabel der Entwicklungshilfe*. Stuttgart: Lucius&Lucius.
— (1994). "We Have to Do Business as Business is Done!". Zur Aneignung formaler Organisation in einem westafrikanischen Unternehmen. *Historische Anthropologie*, 2, 165–186.
Sewell, William H. (2005). *Logics of History, Social Theory and Social Transformation*. Chicago IL: University of Chicago Press.
Said, Edward W. (1994). *Orientalism: Western Conceptions of the Orient*. New York: Vintage Books.
Scott, James C. (1985). *Weapons of the Weak. Everyday Forms of Peasant Resistance*. New Haven CT: Yale University Press.
Sinha, Subir, and Rashimi Varnas (2017). Marxism and Postcolonial Theory: Whats Left of the Debate. *Critical Sociology*, 43, Issue 4-5, 1–14.

Spivak, Gayatri (1988). Can the Subaltern Speak? In Cary G. Nelson, Lawrence Grossberg (eds.). *Marxism and the Interpretation of Culture*, 66–111. Chicago IL: University of Illinois Press.
Turner, Jonathan, and Barry Markovsky (2007). Micro-Macro Links. In George I. Ritzer (ed.). *The Blackwell Encyclopaedia of Sociology*, 2997–3005. Malden/Oxford: Blackwell Publishing.
Vargas Ugarte, Rubén (1951). *Concilios limenses (1551–1772)*. Lima: Carolus Gomes Martinho.
— (1949). *Historia del Perú, Virreinato (1551–1600)*. Lima: Carlos Mila Bartes.
Vetlessen, Arne Johan (2005). *Evil and Human Agency: Understanding Collective Evildoing*. Cambridge: Cambridge University Press.
Wolf, Eric R. (1982). *Europe and the People Without History*. Berkeley CA: University of California Press.
Yannakakis, Yanna (2008). *The Art of Being In-Between: Native Intermediaries, Indian Identity, and Local Rule in Colonial Oaxaca*. Durham NC: Duke University Press.
Ziai, Aram (2007). Development Discourse and its Critics. An Introduction to post-development. In Aram Ziai (ed.). *Exploring Post-development. Theory and Practice, Problems and Perspectives*, 3–17. New York: Routledge.
— (2012). Post-Development: Fundamentalkritik der "Entwicklung". *Geographica Helvetica*, 67, 133–138.

Authors

Iwo Amelung is the speaker of CRC 1095 *Resource Regimes and Discourses of Weakness* and a professor of Chinese Studies at the Goethe University, Frankfurt/Main. His research focuses on late Imperial and Republican Chinese history with a special focus on Sino-Western interactions and history of science.

Otto Danwerth is a post-doctoral research fellow at the Max-Planck-Institute for Legal History. His research focuses on the legal and cultural history of early modern Ibero-America.

Teresa Dittmer is a research fellow at the CRC 1095 *Resource Regimes and Discourses of Weakness* at the Goethe University, Frankfurt/Main. Her research focuses on Assyriology and Mesopotamian history of science.

Anna Dorofeeva is a post-doctoral research fellow at the CRC 1095 *Resource Regimes and Discourses of Weakness* at the Goethe University, Frankfurt/Main. She is currently an IRC post-doctoral fellow at University College Dublin. She is a cultural and intellectual historian whose research centres on the Western book in the early Middle Ages.

Nadine Eikelschulte is a research fellow at the CRC 1095 *Resource Regimes and Discourses of Weakness* at the Goethe University, Frankfurt/Main. Her research focuses on the history of science and the relation between knowledge and power in the ancient near east.

Seto Hardjana is a post-doctoral research fellow at the CRC 1095 *Resource Regimes and Discourses of Weakness* at the Goethe University, Frankfurt/Main. His research focuses on citizenship, activism, and online community transformation in Indonesia.

Daniel Hausmann is a post-doctoral research fellow at the CRC 1095 *Resource Regimes and Discourses of Weakness* at the Goethe University, Frankfurt/Main. His research focuses on modern Chinese history.

Philipp Höhn is a research fellow at the CRC 1095 *Resource Regimes and Discourses of Weakness* at the Goethe University, Frankfurt/Main. His research focuses on Northern European merchant conflicts in the late medieval period, the history of research concerning the Hanse in the 20th century and the development of concepts of maritime deviance in the North Sea and Baltic region (1400-1600).

Lukas Jäger is a research fellow at the CRC 1095 *Resource Regimes and Discourses of Weakness* at the Goethe University, Frankfurt/Main. His research focuses on the pre-disciplinary phase of early twentieth century continental sociology and history of science.

Melina C. Kalfelis is a research fellow at the CRC 1095 *Resource Regimes and Discourses of Weakness* at the Goethe University, Frankfurt/Main. Her research focuses on development and NGO-work, organisation research and action theory, while also placing an emphasis on audiovisual anthropology.

Kathrin Knodel is a post-doctoral research fellow at CRC 1095 *Resource Regimes and Discourses of Weakness* at the Goethe University, Frankfurt/Main. Her research focuses on NGO-actors in Burkina Faso, their working- and life-worlds, as well as their role as brokers between local groups and international donors.

Alexander Krey is a post-doctoral research fellow at the CRC 1095 *Resource Regimes and Discourses of Weakness* at the Goethe University, Frankfurt/Main. His research focuses on the legal history of the Middle Ages and the early-modern period.

Hartmut Leppin is the former speaker and current board member of the CRC 1095 *Resource Regimes and Discourses of Weakness* and a professor of ancient history at the Goethe University, Frankfurt/Main. His research focuses on late antiquity, early Christianity and the history of political thought in Ancient Greece.

Christian A. Müller is the research coordinator of the CRC 1095 *Resource Regimes and Discourses of Weakness* at the Goethe University, Frankfurt/Main. His research focuses on business history and media history.

José Luis Paz Nomey is research fellow at the Max-Planck-Institute for Legal History. His research focuses on the Holy See and the colonial Latin American Catholic Church, as well as the legal and indigenous history in Colonial Latin America (sixteenth to eighteenth century).

Nicolas Perreaux is a post-doctoral research fellow at CRC 1095 *Resource Regimes and Discourses of Weakness* at the Goethe University, Frankfurt/Main. His research focuses on space, literacy and kinship during the Early and High Middle Ages, but also on Digital Humanities.

David Rex Galindo is a former post-doctoral research fellow at the Max-Planck-Institute for Legal History. He is now a professor of history at the Universidad Adolfo Ibáñez in Santiago, Chile. His research focuses on colonial Latin America, borderlands history, and the Franciscan missionary programme in the early-modern Hispanic world.

Linda Richter is a research fellow at the CRC 1095 *Resource Regimes and Discourses of Weakness* at the Goethe University, Frankfurt/Main. Her research focuses on the history of science and other ways of knowing during the eighteenth and nineteenth century.

Sebastian Riebold is a research fellow at CRC 1095 *Resource Regimes and Discourses of Weakness* at the Goethe University, Frankfurt/Main. His research focuses on the history of modern China and the Chinese reception of western knowledge.

Christian Scheidler is a research fellow at the CRC 1095 *Resource Regimes and Discourses of Weakness* at the Goethe University, Frankfurt/Main. His research focuses on the Byzantine Empire in the sixth and seven century, as well as Ancient and Medieval military history.

Klaus Seidl is a former a post-doctoral research fellow at the CRC 1095 *Resource Regimes and Discourses of Weakness* at the Goethe University, Frankfurt/Main. Recently, he has joined the Research Services of the German Bundestag in Berlin. His research focuses on Modern European history, the history of revolutions (especially 1848), exile and emigration after 1933, and the history of historiography.

Anselm Spindler is a post-doctoral research fellow at the CRC 1095 *Resource Regimes and Discourses of Weakness* at the Goethe University, Frankfurt/Main. His research focuses on the role of collective agency in the political philosophy of the Middle Ages and today.

Frederic Steinfeld is a research fellow at the CRC 1095 *Resource Regimes and Discourses of Weakness* at the Goethe University, Frankfurt/Main. His research focuses on business history and the history of economic thought.

Carla Thiel is a research fellow at the CRC 1095 *Resource Regimes and Discourses of Weakness* at the Goethe University, Frankfurt/Main. Her research focuses on economic and business history of the nineteenth and twentieth century.

Marco Toste is a research fellow at CRC 1095 *Resource Regimes and Discourses of Weakness* at the Goethe University, Frankfurt/Main. His research focuses on Medieval and Early Modern Political Thought as well as Medieval Philosophy.

David Weidgenannt is a former research fellow at CRC 1095 *Resource Regimes and Discourses of Weakness* at the Goethe University, Frankfurt/Main. He is currently a research fellow at the German-French research project "Koinon: Common Currencies and Shared Identities". His research focuses on Greek epigraphy and Numismatics.